Shakespeare's
Unorthodox Biography

Recent Titles in
Contributions in Drama and Theatre Studies

SHAKESPEARE'S UNORTHODOX BIOGRAPHY

New Evidence of an Authorship Problem

Diana Price

Contributions in Drama and Theatre Studies
Number 94

GREENWOOD PRESS
Westport, Connecticut • London

Library of Congress Cataloging-in-Publication Data

Price, Diana, 1949–
    Shakespeare's unorthodox biography : new evidence of an authorship problem /
Diana Price.
        p.   cm.—(Contributions in drama and theatre studies, ISSN 0163–3821 ; no. 94)
    Includes bibliographical references and index.
    ISBN 0–313–31202–8 (alk. paper)
    1. Shakespeare, William, 1564–1616—Authorship.   2. Dramatists, English—
Biography—History and criticism.   3. Drama—Authorship.   I. Title.   II. Series.
PR2937.P75   2001
822.3'3—dc21   00–022333

British Library Cataloguing in Publication Data is available.

Library of Congress Catalog Card Number: 00–022333
ISBN: 0–313–31202–8
ISSN: 0163–3821

First published in 2001

Greenwood Press, 88 Post Road West, Westport, CT 06881
An imprint of Greenwood Publishing Group, Inc.
www.greenwood.com

Printed in the United States of America

The paper used in this book complies with the
Permanent Paper Standard issued by the National
Information Standards Organization (Z39.48–1984).

10 9 8 7 6 5 4 3 2

Copyright Acknowledgments

The author and publisher gratefully acknowledge permission for the use of the following material:

Diana Price, "Reconsidering Shakespeare's Monument," *Review of English Studies* vol. 48, no. 190 (May 1997): 168–182. Reprinted by permission of Oxford University Press.

Diana Price, "What's in a Name," *The Elizabethan Review* vol. 4, no. 1 (spring 1996): 3–13. Reprinted by permission of *The Elizabethan Review*.

Cover art: Drawing (ca. 1634) of Shakspere's Stratford monument by Sir William Dugdale, photograph by Gerald E. Downs, by permission of Sir William Dugdale; inscription from Shakspere's monument; detail from the frontispiece to the 1640 anthology of Shakespeare's *Poems*, courtesy of the Ohio State University Libraries, Rare Books and Manuscripts; signature of William Shakespeare from page three of his will, 1616, courtesy of The Cleveland Public Library.

For Pat
with love

Contents

Part Three: Misleading and Missing Evidence

Part Four: Overwhelming Evidence

Illustrations

Acknowledgments

Anyone who undertakes to write another book questioning William Shakespeare's authorship is indebted to past scholars, and much in this book builds on the ground-breaking research of Alden Brooks (who argued for Sir Edward Dyer), J. Thomas Looney (who argued for the earl of Oxford), and Sir George Greenwood (who argued for no particular candidate). During my odyssey into Shakespeare, I have incurred many other debts. I did most of my research at the Cleveland Public Library, and I thank the staff for endless courtesies and assistance. For comments, encouragement, and helpful feedback on various drafts, I thank Patricia Adler-Ingram, Elaine D'Arcy, Judith E. Daykin, Michael Dwyer, Fran Gendlin, Peggy Gifford, Gary B. Goldstein, Carole Sue Lipman, Michael McConnell, Sharon Richardson, Mary Rodenboh, Barbara Shore, Dr. Johanna Krout Tabin, Jim Wood, my uncle Robert "Jim" Price, my brother John, and especially my late mother Connie. One cannot choose one's own parents, but I am grateful to both of mine for surrounding me with theatre and cultural adventures. I came to write this book because of my father, Johnny Price, whose lifelong passion for Shakespeare evidently rubbed off on me. He always said that the only stupid question is the one you don't ask, and I am grateful that back in 1990, he finally persuaded me, after years of resisting, to have a look at the authorship question. Since then, I have been the lucky recipient of his unflagging enthusiastic support.

A number of scholars were exceedingly generous with their time and specialized knowledge. I was rescued from numerous blunders and gained valuable perspectives from Verily Anderson, Andy Hannas, Warren Hope, Peter R. Moore, Roger Nyle Parisious, and C. Wayne Shore. To Mr. Hannas I also owe thanks for several translations from Latin. This book quotes liberally from *Shakespeare's Impact on His Contemporaries* with the kind permission of its author, E.A.J. Honigmann, despite his strong disagreement with the anti-Stratfordian case. I am also grateful to A. Kent Hieatt, who went out of his way to extend professional courtesies to me.

One of the most delightful obligations I have incurred is to David A. Richardson, Professor of English and Director of Liberal Studies at Cleveland State University, who invited me into his classroom on numerous occasions to share my research with his students. I am grateful to him for his gentle guidance and good offices. I am particularly indebted to my dear friend Vicky Holder at San Francisco State University for extensive editorial advice. My final and most effusive expression of thanks is to my friend and colleague, Gerald E. Downs. Without the benefit of his thoughtful criticism, encouragement, and generosity, this book would not have developed as it did. Any errors or lapses in judgment in the book are, of course, my sole responsibility.

Introduction

Some people don't believe that William Shakespeare wrote the works of William Shakespeare. They believe that someone else wrote the works that have come down to us under that name, and that the man from Stratford-upon-Avon was not the poet and playwright we all thought he was. Over 400 years after the plays were written, the Shakespeare authorship question remains unresolved, at least for some.

Like most Shakespeare aficionados, I had always discounted the authorship question as an eccentric theory with little basis in fact. Some years ago I picked up a book about the authorship solely to keep up my end of an anticipated conversation with a so-called "anti-Stratfordian." Certainly, I had no intention of reading any more than a chapter or two, or just enough to ask one or two intelligent questions. But the first few chapters intrigued me, and I began to wonder about the validity of the Shakespeare authorship question.

The anti-Stratfordian challenge to the traditional authorship struck me as logical, yet I found it hard to believe that any standard biography of Shakespeare could be vulnerable. So I read Samuel Schoenbaum's *William Shakespeare: A Compact Documentary Life*, and it changed my mind. I was surprised to find nothing in it to prove that Shakespeare had written any plays. What emerged from both books—one orthodox and one unorthodox—was the weight of probability that the man from Stratford did not write the works attributed to him. Ironically, it was a traditional biography that convinced me that the Stratford man was no writer, and I found myself joining the ranks of the skeptics and doubters.

Fact after fact stopped me in my tracks. No biography could account for Shakespeare's education. His own children grew up functionally illiterate. Shakespeare retired to an illiterate household at the height of his presumed literary powers. He wrote nothing during the last several years of his life. He left behind dozens of biographical records, but unlike those surviving for other writers of the day, not one of them suggests literary activity.

Other problems in the biography were more complex. How did Shakespeare, born and bred in a provincial market town, learn to write plays from an aristocratic perspective? Walt Whitman thought that the plays were written "for the divertisement only of the élite of the castle, and from its point of view" (2:408). Indeed, Shakespeare's language reveals an intimate familiarity with sports and pastimes of the aristocracy, Continental geography, and all manner of courtly culture. When Juliet sighs for her Romeo, "O for a falconer's voice / To lure this tassel-gentle back again," she is using technical terms for the imagery, drawn from the privileged sport of falconry. The "tassel-gentle" is the male peregrine, a falcon favored by the Elizabethan aristocracy, and "to lure" it is to recall the hawk after it has struck or missed its target. Shakespeare's poetic imagery is full of such specialized terminology, and it is unlikely that the dramatist thumbed through manuals on falconry just to create metaphors. Those lines from *Romeo and Juliet*, and too many others like them, came from someone to whom the terminology was second nature, pulled out of the mental stockpile accumulated from the writer's own experience. Yet the standard biography left Shakespeare's early and extensive exposure to the sport of falconry both unaccounted for and unlikely.

The few known facts about Shakespeare's formative years do not equip him for his supposed life's work. Even legends don't bestow on Shakespeare any schooling beyond about age thirteen. If it is true that "no other writer has ever had anything like Shakespeare's resources of language" (Bloom, 47), then it is hard to believe that he developed those resources on the strength of an incomplete grammar school education.

Shakespeare's biography is deficient in many other critical areas. Far from following the fragmentary literary trails in his personal life, the orthodox biography fails to find *any* personal literary fragments. The documents that literary biographies are based on—academic records, letters, manuscripts, diaries, and remnants of the personal library—simply do not exist for Shakespeare.

This book raises questions about Shakespeare's biography. It delves into the historical documents and restores some of the vital evidence that most biographers omit. The fuller reading of contemporary references will reveal, not a writer, but a sharp businessman who would certainly have been willing to turn a profit by brokering plays or taking credit for their authorship.

This book also explores the hypothesis that "William Shakespeare" was the pen name of a courtier. The theory that Shakespeare was a *nom de plume* may sound far-fetched at first. Yet over the centuries, people have adopted pen names for a wide range of reasons. Eric Blair, an English upper-class socialist, chose to write under the pseudonym George Orwell because it was a "convenient way to resolve his ambivalence toward literary success" (Shelden, 154). Marian Evans published under the name of George Eliot because female writers found it tough to be taken seriously in the male-dominated literary world of nineteenth-century England. During the 1950s, the Joseph McCarthy inquisitions so intimidated Hollywood that most major studios would not openly hire anyone on the blacklist. So many screenwriters, such as Dalton Trumbo, wrote under assumed names.

The motive behind most pen names in Shakespeare's day was a social custom as entrenched as the prejudice against female writers in more recent British history. In Elizabethan England, a gentleman of rank could not publish under his own name lest he be suspected of having a profession. He could circulate poems privately among his friends, but to write as a professional—especially for the stage—was unthinkable. So this book hypothesizes that the plays and poems of an unnamed gentleman were published over the name "William Shakespeare." This book further hypothesizes that the man from Stratford exploited the similarity between his name and the published pen name.

If you want to know whether there is anything of substance to the Shakespeare authorship question, then the following pages may help you make up your own mind. This review of Shakespeare's life story may convince you that not all anti-Stratfordians are lunatics or victims of misinformation.

DEFINING TERMS

Since this book attempts to show that William Shakespeare of Stratford-upon-Avon was *not* the author of the works that have come down to us under that name, I will use the following spellings to distinguish him from the author, whoever he was:

WILLIAM SHAKSPERE (1564–1616): A man born in Stratford-upon-Avon who is credited with the literary work of "William Shakespeare."

WILLIAM SHAKESPEARE: The *nom de plume* used to identify the author of the Shakespeare canon.

I enclose the name in quotation marks to signify the spelling in an original document and have retained the spelling chosen by the authority being cited. Otherwise, for convenience, I use "Shakespeare" when talking about the writer whose literary works have come down to us under that name, and "Shakspere" when referring to the man from Stratford.

NOTE

Most quotations are taken from orthodox (Stratfordian) sources. Unorthodox (anti-Stratfordian) sources are introduced as such. Most of the archaic spelling and punctuation from original sources has been modernized, except when retained by others being quoted or if pertinent to the discussion. Unless otherwise noted, this book uses the texts and play chronology as set forth in *The Arden Shakespeare* (2nd series, 38 vols.; London and New York: Methuen, Routledge, and University Paperbacks, 1946–91) and in C. H. Herford and Percy Simpson's *Ben Jonson* (11 vols.; Oxford: Clarendon Press, 1925–52).

PART ONE

BIOGRAPHICAL EVIDENCE

Chapter One

What's the Question?

Biography today, then, may be defined as the accurate presentation of the life history from birth to death of an individual, along with an effort to interpret the life so as to offer a unified impression of the subject.

—William Harmon and C. Hugh Holman,
A Handbook to Literature (59)

Nobody questions whether a man named William Shakspere was born in Stratford-upon-Avon in 1564 and died there in 1616. We know he did because surviving records prove his existence. These records do not answer the larger question: Did the man from Stratford write the works that have come down to us under the name of William Shakespeare? If the answer to that deceptively simple question were a clear-cut yes, there would be no need for this book.

Shakespearean biographers presumably have tested the links in the biographical chain and have pronounced them to be sound, so anti-Stratfordians should have a hard time finding a weak link. But most skeptics claim that no links connecting Shakspere of Stratford to the works of Shakespeare have ever been found. Readers are often surprised to discover that there are no manuscripts or surviving letters in his hand. Gerald Eades Bentley acknowledged that "letters to or from or about William Shakespeare have all disappeared except for a few referring to business transactions; diaries or accounts of his friends are gone. In the absence of personal material of this sort which provides the foundation of most biographies, the temptation to amplify, to embroider, in fact to create an appealing and interesting figure, has been too strong for many of Shakespeare's admirers" (*Handbook*, 4–5). Bentley has thus diagnosed a major symptom of the problem: Biographers rely too much on conjecture and fanciful guesswork. For example, standard biographies leave the reader with the impression that Shakspere attended the Stratford grammar school, that he established a personal relationship with the earl of Southampton, that he was a drinking buddy of playwright Ben Jonson, and that he made money from writing plays. No reliable records exist to support any of those statements. As Shakspere went about the business of his life, he left behind documentation that biographers have uncovered. These documents account for his activities as an actor, a theatre shareholder, a businessman, a moneylender, a property holder, a litigant, and a man with a family, but they do not account for his presumed life as a professional writer.

Indeed, Shakspere's contemporaneous records reveal nothing of his alleged literary vocation. As we will see, he has been credited with literary activity solely on the basis of posthumous evidence. It is highly unusual, if not unique, to find only posthumous literary evidence remaining for an individual who supposedly lived by his pen.

SHAKESPEARE WHO?

Imagine you're sitting at home, and someone slides an envelope under your door. You open it and take out a manuscript entitled *Hamlet—A Play by William Shakespeare*. You now know that somebody writing under the name of William Shakespeare has written a play called *Hamlet*, but you do not know from the title page whether William Shakespeare is a real or fictitious name.

You know nothing more about the identity of the author after reading a review of *Hamlet*, the new Shakespeare play. You consult the telephone directory and find numerous William Shakespeares. Neither the reviews nor the directory tell you which William Shakespeare, if any, is to be conferred with the authorship honors. Not until you read an interview in the paper, or see him on camera accepting his award for Best Play, thanking his wife Anne and his friend Ben Jonson, will you know which William Shakespeare is the author.

Now suppose that everyone has died of the plague. You, the literary archaeologist, are trying to reconstruct Shakespeare's life, and all you can uncover are some scripts and reviews. Those will not be enough to identify your man. You are going to have to find those videotapes, interviews, or other *personal* references in order to confirm which William Shakespeare was the author.

That's the problem with the standard Shakespearean biography. Historians have found lots of literary references to "William Shakespeare," but they are references to his published works, attributions of authorship, or reviews. No one has yet found any personal records left by Shakspere or by anybody else during his lifetime that would link him to the occupation of writing.

Literary critics regularly review work by people whom they do not know personally. Back then, John Weever and Francis Meres, both Elizabethan writers, praised "Honey-tongued Shakespeare" and "Shakespeare's fine filed phrase" in what we might call Elizabethan book reviews. Those reviews prove that Weever and Meres thought that the poems or plays written under the name of William Shakespeare were excellent. The reviews do not prove that Weever or Meres personally recognized the man from Stratford as the author.

Nevertheless, biographers assume that Shakspere of Stratford was the dramatist, and they support that assumption with posthumous evidence, hearsay, and legend. Finally, they accept all the impersonal literary references to "Shakespeare" as personal evidence of William Shakspere's literary life. Yet biographers present no evidence—hard evidence left behind during Shakspere's own lifetime—that proves he was the writer. Moreover, they produce no evidence to show that Shakspere was capable of writing literature.

Despite the unusual absence of literary records, that is, evidence linking the Stratford man directly to the works, a standard Shakespearean biography reads plausibly enough on the surface. However, skeptical readers, or those adept at spotting logical fallacies or contradictions, are likely to find a startling number of conflicts between the known life of the man from Stratford and the literary evidence for William Shakespeare.

WHY BOTHER?

There are those who say it doesn't matter who wrote the Shakespeare plays. Like other great works of art, the plays stand on their own, no matter who created them. But like other works of art, the plays take on new dimensions when we know something about their historical context and who wrote them. That is one reason why literary biographies continue to be written and read.

Consider Arthur Miller's play *After the Fall*. It is a painful, intense play on its own terms, but theatregoers who know that Miller was married to Marilyn Monroe probably find the play more fascinating than those who view it in the abstract. Those who know that Miller suffered through the Joseph McCarthy Communist witch-hunts of the 1950s will see more in *The Crucible* than those who see the play strictly as a historical drama about witchcraft in Puritan New England.

Hamlet is usually considered the most autobiographical of the Shakespeare plays. But so far, about all that biographers can find in common between *Hamlet* and the man from Stratford is a passing mention of "sheepskin" in the fifth act and the possibility that Shakspere was apprenticed to his father in the leather trade. A Shakespearean biography based on the life of someone else might reveal events and relationships that tell us far more about *Hamlet* than does Shakspere's proximity to the glover's workbench.

The life of Shakespeare must matter to many people. Hundreds of biographies have been written, and millions of copies of them have been bought and read. When John Updike mulled over the reasons why people bother with literary biography, he decided that "perhaps the most worthy is the desire to prolong and extend our intimacy with the author—to partake again, from another angle, of the joys we have experienced within the author's *oeuvre*" (3).

In addition, if documentary evidence is ever found that upsets the traditional biography, it will be front-page news. Why? Not just because the discovery would satisfy anti-Stratfordians who are convinced that the wrong man has been getting all the credit. Not just because stage directors, actors, and audiences would suddenly find new meaning in all the plays. Such a discovery would surely have a momentous impact on school curricula, literary criticism, and future research.

DOUBTS AND THEORIES

Too often, those defending the orthodox position categorize *all* anti-Stratfordian arguments, regardless of merit, as illegitimate. Typically, they make little or no distinction between, say, the solid research in Sir George Greenwood's *The Shakespeare Problem Re-*

stated, and cryptographic or paranormal revelations, such as those transmitted through Dr. Orville Owen's mystically inspired cipher wheel. In the late 1950s, Frank W. Wadsworth (*The Poacher from Stratford*) and R. C. Churchill (*Shakespeare and His Betters*) rebutted the anti-Stratfordians, and interestingly, a reviewer for the *Shakespeare Quarterly* criticized both orthodox defenders for their lack of discrimination: "One impressed by the learning and dialectic of a Sir George Greenwood may well feel perhaps that [Wadsworth and Churchill], eager to write amusingly, have generally chosen to discuss the more patently absurd claims and to disregard arguments less easily ridiculed" (Maxwell, 437).

People who persist in asking questions about Shakespeare's authorship have often been dismissed as fantasizers interested in grotesque fiction or crackpots hooked on conspiracy theories. Walt Whitman was skeptical, and most literary professionals would not consider him a crackpot. Whitman himself was well aware of the stigma that might attach to anyone with the audacity to question Shakespeare's authorship. In his words, "beneath a few foundations of proved facts are certainly engulf'd far more dim and elusive ones, of deepest importance—tantalizing and half-suspected—suggesting explanations that one dare not put in plain statement" (2:404). Nevertheless, Whitman questioned the traditional authorship because he perceived an unbridgeable gap between the aristocratic perspective in the plays and the nonaristocratic perspective emanating from Shakspere's documented life. According to film star Charlie Chaplin, writing along the same lines, "it is easy to imagine a farmer's boy emigrating to London and becoming a successful actor and theatre owner; but for him to have become the great poet and dramatist, and to have had such knowledge of foreign courts, cardinals and kings, is inconceivable to me. . . . I can hardly think it was the Stratford boy. Whoever wrote them had an aristocratic attitude" (364). Chaplin went on a guided tour of Stratford and added that after "hearing the scant bits of local information concerning his desultory boyhood, his indifferent school record, his poaching and his country-bumpkin point of view, I cannot believe he went through such a mental metamorphosis as to become the greatest of all poets. In the work of the greatest of geniuses humble beginnings will reveal themselves somewhere—but one cannot trace the slightest sign of them in Shakespeare" (364).

Such doubts about Shakespeare's authorship are not new. Questions emerged almost as soon as Shakespeare's work appeared in print (see Chapter 12). It was not until the 1800s, however, that the inquiry gained momentum when Delia Bacon advanced the theory that Francis Bacon (no relation) and several others had written the works collectively. Francis Bacon seems to have stuck in many people's minds as the major contender for Shakespeare's laurels, even though the claim for Bacon foundered shortly after it was first proposed. One orthodox critic went so far as to say that "the Baconian opinion is an extravagant hallucination" (Robertson, 6). That "hallucination" was Ignatius Donnelly's theory that the plays were encoded with a cipher that supposedly revealed Bacon as the playwright. Donnelly's theory, published in 1888 as *The Great Cryptogram*, was outrageous enough to give the authorship question a bad name (see Hope and Holston, 39–56), but that was not what disqualified Bacon. Today, many doubters consider the substance, style, and dates of Bacon's acknowledged writings insurmountable obstacles to his candidacy, despite strong points in his favor.

Over the years, anti-Stratfordians have proposed theories around the earl of Derby, Sir Edward Dyer, Queen Elizabeth, Christopher Marlowe, the earl of Oxford, and the earl of Rutland, among at least fifty others. Some consider the plethora of candidates something of a joke. At first glance, it might seem that almost anyone who was close to the Elizabethan literary scene has been shoved forward as a candidate. Yet the testing of many candidates is indicative of a logical process. Doubters have identified a gap, and they are trying to fill that gap.

If, for some reason, you were convinced that the man from Stratford did not write Shakespeare's plays and poetry, you would be led to the next question: *Who did?* Then you would start casting through the Elizabethan landscape in search of a candidate. After you identified one, you would probably investigate the documentary records, and you would disqualify a candidate whose known activities were incompatible with the literary output. If you found a candidate who passed your preliminary tests, you would intensify your investigation to look for a historical document that confirmed authorship.

That scenario describes precisely what has been happening. Doubters have been testing their candidates, and those who believe that they have identified a viable candidate are looking for a "smoking gun." Regardless of which candidate they have investigated, all skeptics have first rejected the man from Stratford. That is why most

books about the authorship summarize the contradictions in the traditional biography before introducing a contender for the laurels.
This book, however, is not concerned with evaluating any particular
candidate. It is concerned with those who would never look at *any*
candidate as long as their confidence in the official biography of William Shakspere remains unshaken. And it intends to shake that confidence.

SACRED TRADITION

Despite orthodoxy's claims to the contrary, numerous professors
have raised questions about Shakespeare's authorship, but their names
(e.g., Abel Lefranc or Pierre S. Porohovshikov) are unknown outside
their respective academic communities. However, the general public
does recognize the names of Charlie Chaplin, Daphne DuMaurier,
Sir John Gielgud, Sir Derek Jacobi, Henry James, the Hon. John
Paul Stevens, Mark Twain, and Walt Whitman—all of them anti-
Stratfordian.

Nevertheless, the skeptics who question Shakespeare's authorship
are relatively few in number, and they do not speak for the majority
of academic and literary professionals. Considering academia's continued acceptance of the traditional biography, the question of authorship is understandably looked at with cynicism by the public at
large. After all, these literary experts can't all be wrong. And they are
not out there organizing panel discussions on the subject. Apparently,
they have not considered the questions raised by anti-Stratfordians to
be serious or worthy of attention.

Still, the evidence was sufficiently compelling for PBS to dedicate
a 1989 *Frontline* documentary to an examination of both William
Shakspere and the front-running candidate, the seventeenth earl of
Oxford. The episode was rebroadcast in 1997. In October 1991, the
Atlantic published a cover story debate between an orthodox scholar
and an Oxfordian. William F. Buckley Jr. moderated a televised discussion for GTE in September 1992, which convened opposing views
and took questions from a nationwide audience. Buckley confronted
the issue again on *Firing Line* in 1994. Some of the publicity surrounding the film *Shakespeare In Love* touched on the authorship
question; for instance, a story in *Time* magazine (15 February 1999)
and a cover story debate in *Harper's* (April 1999). Several books, such
as Jonathan Bate's *The Genius of Shakespeare*, have devoted some

space to defending the traditional authorship. However, despite the broadcasts, magazine articles, and a number of books over the years, there has been nothing resembling a vigorous public or academic debate on the subject.

Generally speaking, persistent questions and investigative efforts have come from those outside the fortresses of academia and literary criticism. Laypersons who ask penetrating questions about Shakespeare's authorship frequently end up talking to each other more than to the academic community. For whatever reason, most academic and literary professionals have been reluctant to reconsider Shakespeare's authorship, and that has left it largely to outsiders, that is, nonacademics, to investigate the case.

The purpose of the investigation is simply to answer the question: Was William Shakspere of Stratford-upon-Avon the poet and playwright, or is the literary biography constructed around him a fiction? Whitman's and Chaplin's confidence in the traditional biography was shaken for one reason or another. Perhaps whatever shook their confidence justifies another look at the issues. This book re-examines the Shakespeare authorship question by analyzing the evidence from a skeptical perspective, freed from the constraints of preconceived notions. When unencumbered by prior assumptions about the playwright, one can follow the evidence wherever it leads, even if it leads to a surprisingly different Shakspere.

Chapter Two

Shakspere's Footprints

> We know more about the life of Shakespeare, both in terms of
> facts and of rational conclusions that they suggest, than of any
> other Elizabethan dramatist. . . . Documents relating to Shake-
> speare's activities, including letters to him and material relating
> to his family, are extant in quantity in the Shakespeare Centre
> records office at Stratford upon Avon. Few could reasonably re-
> main sceptical if they examined these.
>
> —Gareth Evans and Barbara Lloyd Evans,
> *Companion to Shakespeare* (17)

Biographies are constructed around documentary evidence. The authors quoted above assure their readers that there are plenty of Shakespearean documents for the biographer to work with, among them
many extant "letters" to him—"letters" plural, "in quantity." In fact,
only one letter addressed to William Shakspere survives. It is about
borrowing £30, and it was never delivered.

A WELL-DOCUMENTED BLANK

Is Shakspere's life otherwise as well-documented as the Evanses
claim? The authorities cannot agree among themselves. One writes

that his life "is unusually well documented, for a commoner's of his period," while another refers to "the scanty biographical *data*" (Levin, *Riverside*, 3; Chambers, *Facts*, 1:vii).

Even if the biographical *data* are scanty, Shakespearean bibliography is not. There are hundreds of thousands of titles published on Shakespeare, and the subject usually commands its own section in a bookstore or library. No other writer in the English language has been the object of such interest—or such intense scrutiny. Scholars have ransacked the archives looking for the dramatist's documentary remains. They have plowed through millions of civic records, legal records, birth registers, death registers, marriage registers, corporation records, correspondence, regulatory documents, state papers, school records, tax rolls, church records, financial records, commonplace books, personal diaries, theatrical diaries, antiquarian books, personal manuscripts, and the like for over two centuries.

All this research has uncovered about seventy undisputed biographical records for the man. Yet the typical Shakespearean biography is over 300 pages long. How can such a meager collection of facts produce such large biographies? The answer is simple. Most of the pages in a Shakespearean biography are filled with descriptions of Elizabethan England, analyses of plays and characters, discussions of theatre conditions, other writers, and so on. In addition, conjecture, legend, hearsay, and opinion are frequently commingled with the facts. Richard Dutton acknowledged that "later ages have filled in the picture with guesswork, legend and sentiment" (*Life*, 2). Mark Twain's skeptical comments were more droll, but he said essentially the same thing: "Shall I set down the rest of the Conjectures which constitute the giant Biography of William Shakespeare? It would strain the Unabridged Dictionary to hold them. He is a Brontosaur: nine bones and six hundred barrels of plaster of paris" (49).

If you took a highlighter to any standard Shakespearean biography and inked through only those sections quoting biographical source material, most pages would remain unmarked. On the other hand, if you took the highlighter and inked through passages containing either ancillary information or conjecture surrounded by phrases such as "might have," "we have no doubt that," "could have," "it is likely that," "doubtless" this and "doubtless" that, most pages would be thoroughly marked up. Stripped of conjecture and ancillary information, any biography of Shakspere can be reduced to a few pages of actual "facts"—a presentation of the source material.

BEGINNING DOUBTS

In 1909, Twain wrote *Is Shakespeare Dead?* He had decided that the man from Stratford could not have written the plays because they contained jargon from fields in which Shakspere had no documented experience. Using his own Mississippi riverboat slang as an illustration, Twain made the point that any experienced practitioner can tell a pro from a layman by the use, or misuse, of technical terms. As many critics have observed, Shakespeare's command of legal jargon suggests that the author had legal training, but no records have ever been found to support that hypothesis. So Twain was dubious.

Twain was struck by another inexplicable phenomenon: Shakspere's neighbors in Stratford-upon-Avon were oblivious to the supposedly famous poet in their midst. Twain's own literary fame came on top of a small-town childhood followed by years of manual labor and years on the Mississippi. Yet late in his life, he found that those who knew him way-back-when as Samuel Clemens still talked about him as the local boy who made good writing under the name of Mark Twain. In contrast, not one of Shakspere's neighbors, relatives, or even second-generation descendants ever suggested that he or she recognized Shakspere as a writer. For some years, the good folks of Stratford kept pushing stories about his apprenticeship to a glover or butcher; his "natural wit"; his having composed doggerel epitaphs for his neighbor John Combe, Ben Jonson, or himself; and his career as an actor. Stratford legends about his career as a playwright did not surface until around 1661, when a vicar named John Ward wrote that Shakspere "was a natural wit, without any art at all; he frequented the plays all his younger time . . . and supplied the stage with 2 plays every year" (Chambers, *Facts*, 2:249). Ward's report is too little, too late, and too vague. As Twain concluded, "it all seems to mean that he never had any literary celebrity, there or elsewhere" (63).

In a chapter entitled "Facts," Twain assembled what is known about Shakspere into a dry narrative. The next section is devoted to the same task: Introducing the documentation that Shakspere left behind. (Disputed literary records, which are "regulation issue" with the standard biography, will be considered in subsequent chapters.) Suspend for a few pages the popular images of the poet who found a patron in the earl of Southampton, who was the boon companion of Ben Jonson, and who became the literary toast of the Elizabethan and Jacobean courts, while we pick up Shakspere's trail.

A CONCISE DOCUMENTARY LIFE

The Scene: The town of Stratford-upon-Avon, in the county of Warwickshire, in the Diocese of Worcester, about ninety miles north-west of London, Tudor England.* The story begins with William's parents, John and Mary Shakspere. John owned property; held public office; worked as a glover or saddler; traded in wool; was fined for illegal wool-trading; was fined for having a dunghill in front of his house; borrowed money; was accused twice of usury; sued and was sued for debts; was avoiding creditors by 1592; and was granted a coat of arms.

Both parents were illiterate. John Shakspere had been raised in a rural area that had no school, and he signed with his mark. Over the years, he served as alderman, constable, ale-taster, and, for one term, bailiff (equivalent to mayor) for Stratford-upon-Avon. However, literacy was not a prerequisite for holding public office. In the year that John was elected alderman (1565), only seven out of nineteen aldermen and burgesses could write their names (Knight, 15–17).

1564	On 26 April, "Gulielmus [Latin for William] Shakspere" is baptized.
1565–81	We know nothing of William's childhood, upbringing, or possible schooling. Records for the Stratford grammar school do not survive.
1582–83	In November, a marriage license is issued to eighteen-year-old "William Shaxpere" and Anne Whateley of Temple Grafton. The following day, a marriage bond is posted for "William Shagspere" and a different bride, Anne Hathaway of Shottery, who is already three months pregnant. (Some biographers have decided that some fool of a clerk bungled the entry in the registry. In any event, there is no further explanation of the betrothal on one day to Miss Whateley and the bond posted on the next to Miss Hathaway. But one might speculate that the Hathaways got wind of the Shagspere-Whateley license, and Anne Hathaway's father escorted Mr. Shagspere by pitchfork to the altar.) No record of

*Principal documentation for this account is found in Chambers (*Facts*), Lewis, Thomas and Cox, and articles by Wallace.

the marriage ceremony survives, but six months later, the newlyweds christen their firstborn, Susanna.

1585   The "Shaksperes" welcome a set of twins and name them Hamnet and Judith, after their neighbors, the Sadlers.

1585–91   William "Shackespere" is named in legal action involving his mother's property. A complaint states that on 26 September 1587, John, Mary, and son William, now twenty-three years old, met with the defendant in Stratford to discuss a settlement. John files suit in 1588, and William is named as an interested party. Otherwise, these six years, Shakspere's professionally formative years, are a complete blank.

1592   London. "Willelmus Shackspere," who turns twenty-eight in April, loans £7 to John Clayton. A pamphlet, *Groatsworth of Wit*, warns three playwrights of an "upstart" actor called "Shake-scene."

1593–94   No records.

1595   A payment of £20 is recorded in March to "William Kempe, William Shakespeare, and Richard Burbage, servants to the Lord Chamberlain" for performances at court during the previous December.

1596   Stratford-upon-Avon. In August, Shakspere's eleven-year-old son Hamnet is buried.
                London. In October, an application is made to obtain a coat of arms for John Shakspere. Then a second application is made. Evidently the applications are not approved immediately, as John is described in a 1597 document as a yeoman, not yet a gentleman.
                A writ of attachment is issued against "William Shakspare" for surety of the peace. In other words, the plaintiff feared that Shakspere might inflict bodily injury on him and sought protection. Also cited in the writ are two women and Francis Langley, proprietor of the Swan theatre in Southwark, on the south bank of the Thames.

1597   London. "William Shackspere" is listed as owing taxes for the 1593 subsidy in Bishopsgate, north of the Thames near Shoreditch, but he has apparently already moved out of the neighborhood. (The eighteenth-century scholar Edmond Malone found a document that showed that Shakspere "appears to have lived in Southwark, near the Bear Garden in 1596." The document has since disappeared.)

Stratford-upon-Avon. "Willielmim Shakespeare," now thirty-three years old, purchases New Place, a big house, for at least £60.

1598   London. "William Shakespeare" is listed as owing taxes again in Bishopsgate.

Stratford-upon-Avon. "William Shackspeare" is cited for hoarding grain during a famine. Warwickshire neighbors Abraham Sturley and Richard Quiney exchange a series of letters, hoping to borrow money from "Mr. Shakspere." Quiney writes the only surviving letter written to Shakspere, but it was never delivered. It was discovered in 1793 among Quiney's papers.

"Mr. Shaxspere" receives ten pence for selling a load of stone.

London. "Willelmus Shakespeare" is cited again as a tax defaulter.

1599   Stratford-upon-Avon. John Shakspere's coat of arms has evidently been granted, because a third application is made to incorporate the Shakspere arms with those of the Ardens. Such an "exemplification" application could be lodged only if the Shakspere arms had already been granted. There is no evidence that this third application was approved.

London. "Willelmum Shakespeare" becomes a founding shareholder in the new home to the Lord Chamberlain's Men, the Globe theatre, and a legal document names "Willielmi Shakespeare" as one of the theatre's occupants. "Willelmus Shakspeare" is listed as still owing taxes in Bishopsgate, but a marginal notation indicates that he had moved to the Bankside, near the Globe.

1600   London. "Willelmus Shackspere" takes action to recover his 1592 loan to John Clayton. "Willelmus Shakspeare" turns up on the tax rolls for the last time, again as delinquent.

1601   Stratford-upon-Avon. Shakspere's father dies. Thomas Whittington, formerly a shepherd in the Hathaway household, also dies. His will instructs the executors to recover an outstanding loan of forty shillings that he had made to "Wyllyam Shaxpere's" wife.

London. "Our fellow Shakespeare" is lampooned in a Cambridge University play. Two legal documents name "Richard Burbadge and William Shackspeare gent" as occupying the Globe.

1602   Stratford-upon-Avon. Shakspere purchases 107 acres of real estate from the Combe family for £320. He also buys a cottage in Chapel Lane.

Meanwhile, a heraldry official lodges a complaint concerning coats of arms granted to commoners who don't deserve them. The grant made to John Shakspere is one of twenty-three cited. (William Dethick is the venal and unruly official who gets called on the carpet. He successfully defends himself against these particular accusations but is ultimately discharged.)

1603   London. "William Shakespeare" is listed in the Letters Patent creating the King's Men, the royal acting company, shortly after the accession of James I. The document appoints the actors as servants to the King and effectively changes the name of the Lord Chamberlain's Men to the King's Men.

1604   London. Shakspere rents lodgings from the Mountjoy family in Cripplegate, north of the Thames, for an unspecified period of time. "William Shakespeare" heads the list of "Players" who are issued red cloth for ceremonial livery on the occasion of King James's procession through London.

Stratford-upon-Avon. In March, April, and May, Shakspere sells malt to Phillip Rogers. In June, he lends Rogers two shillings. "Shexpere" then sues Rogers to recover the amount owing plus damages, a total of £1 15s. Meanwhile, Shakspere's growing real estate empire is recorded in a neighborhood survey.

1605   Stratford-upon-Avon. "Shakespear" invests £440 in tithes. These tithes yield corn, grain, hay, wool, and so on. As a tithes owner, Shakspere automatically becomes a lay rector, entitled to burial in the parish church chancel.

London. Actor Augustine Phillipps dies, bequeathing "to my fellow William Shakespeare a [30-shilling] piece in gold."

1606   No records.

1607   Stratford-upon-Avon. Daughter Susanna "Shaxspere" marries physician John Hall.

1608   Stratford-upon-Avon. Ralph Hubaud, the man from whom Shakspere bought the tithes, passes away, and his will makes provision for the collection of £20 owed by "Mr. Shakespre." "Shackspeare" sues a man named John Addenbroke for a debt of £6 plus damages. Addenbroke skips town, so "Shackspeare" takes legal action against the man who served as Addenbroke's security against default.

London. A legal document names Burbage and "William Shakespeare" as tenants of the Globe. According to a deposition filed in 1615, "William Shakespeare" became a partner in the Blackfriars theatre on 9 August 1608.

1609   Shakspere's litigation against Addenbroke continues.

1610   Stratford-upon-Avon. There is a property transfer to "Shakespere" from William and John Combe.

1611   Stratford-upon-Avon. The tithes that "Shakespear" had bought in 1605 are now netting 10% annually on a 14% gross return, and an inventory shows that "Shaxper" has leased a barn to a man named Robert Johnson. "William Shackspeare of Stratford-upon-Avon" and two others file a complaint to protect their real estate interests against default by other lessees. Some of the citizens of Stratford contribute to a fund to improve the roads, and the name "William Shackspere" appears in the margin next to the list of donors.

1612   London. "Shakespeare of Stratford" testifies in a domestic dispute that dates back to 1604, when he was a lodger in the Mountjoy household in Cripplegate. The first of his six extant signatures appears on his deposition.

1613   London. "William Shakespeare of Stratford-upon-Avon" invests £140 in a gate-house located near the Blackfriars theatre, and he mortgages the property the next day for £60. The documents are subscribed with the second and third of his six signatures.

The earl of Rutland pays "Mr. Shakspeare" to make an *impresa*, an accessory for a tournament. Actor and artist Richard Burbage is paid for painting the *impresa*.

1614	"Mr. Shakspeare" is listed as a landowner in Stratford, and his name appears in a series of documents concerning the proposed pasture enclosures in nearby Welcombe. In one memo, Thomas Greene, the town clerk, refers to two letters he had written to "Shakspeare" about the enclosures, but the letters do not survive.
1615	London. A bill of complaint is lodged in London concerning the legal title to the gate-house that Shakspere bought in 1613. A deposition is filed naming "William Shakespeare" as one of the original shareholders in the Globe and Blackfriars theatres; Shakspere is not a party to the suit. In Stratford, a wealthy moneylender, John Combe, dies and leaves £5 to "mr. William Shackspere."
1616	Stratford-upon-Avon. Lawyer Francis Collins draws up and witnesses Shakspere's last will, which makes detailed provisions for the distribution of real estate, clothes, silver, and other assets. Shakspere's wife is left "the second best bed." Fellow actor-shareholders John Heminges, Richard Burbage, and Henry Condell are left money with which to buy mourning rings. Shakspere signed all three pages of the will, and all three pages survive. On 25 April, the Stratford register records the death of "Will. Shakspere, gent.," and he is buried in Holy Trinity Church.

And that concludes the historical trail left by William Shakspere during his life.

SHAKSPERES GALORE

You have just read through records left by someone named William Shakspere, and yet some scholars initially decided that a few of those records belonged in the biography of some other man of that name.* Sidney Lee concluded that Anne Whateley became engaged to another of the "numerous William Shakespeares who abounded in the diocese of Worcester" (*Life*, 24). In two articles entitled "Other William Shakespeares," Charles William Wallace reassigned the 1604 malt sales to one of those other Shakespeares.

---

*Material in this section and in the next chapter, previously published as "What's in a Name? Shakespeare, Shake-scene and the Clayton Loan" in *The Elizabethan Review* 4 (spring 1996), appears here by permission of the editor, Gary B. Goldstein.

While the number of namesakes has been overestimated (Ingram, *Business*, 23 n), Wallace's and Lee's decisions illustrate a problem. If they believed that there were so many Shakroperes running around, how did they assign a particular record to *this* "William Shakspere" as opposed to *that* "William Shakspere"?

This problem of identification is not exclusive to Shakspere. Biographers of Christopher Marlowe reject one set of university records previously accepted by literary sleuth Leslie Hotson, because it turns out that "there were two, not one, Christopher Morleys or Marlowes at Trinity, Cambridge, in the later years of Elizabeth's reign" (Boas, *Marlowe*, 23). According to Frederick S. Boas, "there were five other Christopher Morleys living in London in 1592," raising another question of identity for the "Christopherus Marle" penalized to keep the peace in Shoreditch (236). Dramatist Thomas Middleton presented a similar problem for A. H. Bullen, who concluded that "there is no evidence to show whether he received an academic training. A Thomas Middleton was admitted member of Gray's Inn in 1593, and another in 1596; the earlier entry *probably* refers to the dramatist" (Middleton, 1:xii, emphasis added). Here were records of a "Thomas Middleton"—complete with a first name—in a place where a biographer might reasonably have expected to find one, and Bullen still could not be sure that either entry identified the same Thomas Middleton, because there was no corroborating information. In fact, neither entry refers to the dramatist Middleton.* The standard of corroborating proof required in the previous example is sometimes suspended by Shakespearean biographers and replaced with something that looks suspiciously like bias. Why are some name-only records accepted into Shakspere's biography while others are rejected?

Look back at the 1592 and 1600 references to a £7 loan to John Clayton in London. The loan was made in Cheapside, not far from Bishopsgate, Shakspere's first known London domicile. Lee initially accepted this transaction as one of several prompted by Shakspere's "love of litigation" (*Life*, 213), but E. K. Chambers rejected it because the plaintiff's place of domicile was not specified (*Facts*, 2:52). The borrower's place of domicile was Willington in Bedfordshire, and

---

*Later researchers found evidence of Middleton's matriculation at Oxford, including his signature on a university record. In a 1601 deed, Middleton referred to money "disbursed for my advancement . . . in the University of Oxford where I am now a student," confirming his education not at Gray's Inn, but at Oxford (Eccles, "Middleton's," 436–37; Christian, 90).

Leslie Hotson discovered yet another William Shakespeare, a farmer, who resided eight miles south of Willington. Hotson concluded that this Shakespeare was Clayton's moneylender. However, Hotson did not cite any evidence to show that this Bedfordshire Shakespeare ever loaned any other money (as did Shakspere of Stratford) or was ever in London (as was Shakspere of Stratford). Nor did Hotson postulate why the loan would have been transacted in London rather than in Bedfordshire. However, after establishing the mere existence of the Bedfordshire Shakespeare, Hotson viewed the "question as settled" (*Sonnets*, 229–30). On the other hand, Richard Savage, who transcribed the *Minutes and Accounts of the Corporation of Stratford-upon-Avon*, accepted the Clayton loan as one of Shakspere's business transactions (4:151–52).

The record of the Clayton loan names "Willelmus Shackspere" but contains no age, occupation, or signature to identify the claimant further. Therefore, the record has no more identifying information than the 1596 writ of attachment, which most biographers *do* accept, or even than the London tax records of 1597–99, which are just lists of names. Moreover, the Clayton loan is entirely consistent with undisputed records that reveal Shakspere as a businessman making loans, being approached as a source of financing, and suing to recover moneys owed. And as we will see in Chapter 4, Shakspere was called a usurer in another record dated in the same year.

Chambers could just as easily have decided to accept the record. However, if the £7 Clayton loan is accepted, it casts Shakspere in the role of moneylender for his London debut, and that is not a very glamorous entrance for an aspiring poet. Maybe that is why Chambers tossed the record out of his biography. Most biographers following Chambers do not mention the Clayton loan.

Yet they usually accept other records with less to recommend them, for example, the 1613 *impresa* payment.* This payment to "Mr. Shakspeare" does not specify in what capacity "Shakspeare" was paid, nor does it even provide a first name. The payment in question was for the earl of Rutland's equestrian regalia for a tournament in 1613. A competitor's *impresa* was a sort of logo, consisting of a picture and an allegorical or enigmatic motto. An *impresa* shield was usually pre-

---

*Recent biographers who accept the *impresa* record and reject or omit the Clayton loan are Bentley, Chambers, Chute, Halliday, Honan, Kay, Levi, Schoenbaum, Thomson, and I. Wilson. Honigmann and Quennell accept both records. Bradbrook omits both records.

sented to the monarch, and additional images of the *impresa* might be painted or embroidered on, or otherwise affixed to the competitor's costume and the horse's caparison. Shakspere is supposed to have come out of retirement to write the slogan or motto. Richard Burbage, the actor and artist, is supposed to have painted the designs. (The tournament took place at court in March; in that month, Shakspere was in London buying and mortgaging the Blackfriars gatehouse.)

The original *impresa* record reads

Paid To Mr. Shakspeare *in gold*, about my Lord's impresa, [44 shillings]; To Richard Burbage for painting and making it, *in gold* [44 shillings]

Mrs. C. C. Stopes first proposed that Shakspere might have been paid in the capacity of agent for someone else (Ingleby, *Allusion*, 234; Stopes, "Impreso," 604). However, she ultimately decided that the above-named "Mr. Shakspeare" was *not* the man from Stratford, because "there was in court at the time another of the name, who was in the habit of preparing decorations for tournaments, Mr. John Shakespeare, the Prince's, afterwards the King's bitmaker." Stopes concluded that "Mr. John Shakespeare" was the subject of this record (*Burbage*, 109). Samuel Schoenbaum rejected that suggestion on the grounds that Burbage and Shakspere were both named in the same entry. Having nothing else to go on, Schoenbaum put all the weight on the juxtaposition of the names "Shakspeare" and Burbage to justify accepting the record. In addition, Schoenbaum introduced the *impresa* payment with a comment about Shakspere's egalitarian attitude; despite his supposed status as the preeminent dramatist for London's premiere company, Shakspere "did not disdain to try his hand at trifling assignments" (*Documentary*, 220).

The 1613 *impresa* record is generally accepted, while the £7 Clayton loan of 1592 is generally tossed out, and it is the absence of objective criteria that is significant. The moneylending record is entirely consistent with Shakspere's other documented mercenary activities, but it is early in his career. If accepted, then Shakspere's first explicit recorded activity in London is moneylending. By contrast, Shakspere's alleged assignment to write an *impresa* motto in 1613 interrupts his financially independent retirement but has a certain appeal. Shakspere is associated with Burbage, and his no-job-too-small work ethic is attractive. In both instances, the decision to identify or reject William Shakspere as the man named in a historical record has been based on subjective attitudes, not objective criteria.

The problem of identification is further complicated by the fact that many contemporaneous allusions to "Shakespeare" refer only to the written works, not to the man who wrote them. If "William Shakespeare" was a pseudonym used by someone in the Elizabethan theatrical milieu, then some of the literary records accepted into the traditional biography might belong in somebody else's life story.

Chapter Three

The Theatrical Scrapbook

> About Shakespeare's histrionic gifts we know unfortunately very little, except that he frequently acted both in his own and in other dramatists' plays.
>
> —Peter Quennell, *Shakespeare: The Poet and His Background* (148)

Elizabethan actors were topics of conversation, and the subjects of poems, pamphlets, and prose commentary. They are mentioned in account books, stage directions, and occasionally stage dialogue. We know from such records that Richard Tarlton and Will Kempe were comedians. Theatre accounts show outlays for Kempe's costumes. Kempe also turns up in stage directions, as do John Sincklo and Robert Gough (e.g., "Enter Mr. Gough"). Others, such as Nathan Field, turn up in stage dialogue. According to Peter Quennell, quoted above, Shakspere was a busy actor, so he ought to have a few theatrical clippings.

SHAKSPERE'S FIRST CLIPPING

The first theatrical allusion to Shakspere is found in a 1592 pamphlet, *Groatsworth of Wit*, attributed on its title page to dramatist

Robert Greene. In the pamphlet, the author warns three playwrights of an actor derogatorily referred to as "Shake-scene":

> *To those Gentlemen his Quondam [sundry] acquaintance,*
> *that spend their wits in making plays . . .*

thou famous gracer of Tragedians . . . young Juvenal . . . and thou no less deserving than the other two. . . . Base-minded men all three of you, if by my misery you be not warned: for unto none of you (like me) sought those burrs to cleave: those Puppets (I mean) that spake from our mouths, those Anticks garnished in our colors. . . . Yes trust them not: for there is an upstart Crow, beautified with our feathers, that with his *Tiger's heart wrapped in a Player's hide*, supposes he is as well able to bombast out a blank verse as the best of you: and being an absolute *Johannes fac totum*, is in his own conceit the only Shake-scene in a country.

Biographers assume that the name Shakespeare, however spelled, was sufficiently familiar to make "Shake-scene" a comprehensible epithet to at least some Elizabethan readers. The epithet itself conjures up the image of a ham actor disrupting a scene. Later records corroborate Shakspere's activities as a shareholding actor, so the "Shake-scene" reference gets pasted onto page one of his scrapbook. Biographers proceed from the Shake-scene passage to a much-quoted response, Henry Chettle's apology.

A BORROWED APOLOGY

Groatsworth of Wit was published shortly after its reputed author, Robert Greene, had died. A printer, editor, and writer named Henry Chettle found Greene's manuscript, so the story goes, and took it upon himself to see the work printed. As soon as *Groatsworth* was published, two of the three playwrights to whom the open letter was addressed registered their displeasure with its contents. Biographers generally identify those three addressees as Christopher Marlowe ("famous gracer of Tragedians"), Thomas Nashe ("young Juvenal"), and George Peele ("thou no less deserving . . . by sweet S. George"). One of these playwrights had been accused of Machiavellian atheism, and another of being unworthy of better luck. Any one of the three might have resented the insults aimed at both their profession and their association with the immoral players. Or they might have resented being called "base-minded" should they not heed the advice given.

A few months later, Chettle published his own pamphlet, *Kind-Harts Dreame*, in which he responded expressly to the two disgruntled playwrights. Unfortunately, Chettle did not name names, so we do not know to which of the three addressees (Marlowe, Nashe, or Peele) he directed his remarks:

About three months since died M. Robert Greene, leaving many papers in sundry booksellers' hands, among other[s] his Groats-worth of wit, in which a letter written to divers play-makers [i.e., Marlowe, Nashe, Peele], is offensively by one or two of them taken, and because on the dead they cannot be avenged, they willfully forge in their conceits a living Author: and after tossing it to and fro, no remedy, but it must light on me. . . . With neither of them that take offence was I acquainted, and with one of them I care not if I never be: The other, whom at that time I did not so much spare, as since I wish I had . . . I am as sorry, as if the original fault had been my fault, because myself have seen his demeanor no less civil than he excellent in the quality he professes: Besides, diverse of worship have reported, his uprightness of dealing, which argues his honesty, and his facetious grace in writing, that approves his Art.

Chettle's apology is explicitly directed to two of the three addressees referred to in *Groatsworth*, that is, Marlowe, Nashe, and Peele. However, traditional biographers claim that Chettle had apologized instead to Shakspere. In making that claim, biographers magically transform Shake-scene from being the *subject* of the open letter into one of its three *addressees*, and therefore into one of "those gentlemen" who spends his wits "making plays":

Chettle's apology . . . is valuable for what it tells us, or at least what it implies, about Shakespeare at this obscure point of his career. We even get a fleeting sense of *what he was like as a man. . . .* Chettle concedes the *good opinion held of Shakespeare by "divers of worship."* . . . The earlier attack on a swindling skinflint, a selfish hoarder, a derivative usurer, has clearly caused influential men to rally round and praise Shakespeare's "uprightness of dealing" and "honesty" (*in writing* and in business, presumably) as well as his *"facetious grace" and "art"* in composition. (Kay, 166–67, emphasis added)

The redirection of Chettle's apology to Shakspere is a sleight-of-hand resulting in what one recent critic described as "mythography at its best," and one that has "far-reaching implications" (Erne, 434).

This misappropriated apology gives traditional biographers a personal testimonial to work with, and they begin to build Shakspere's character profile around his "uprightness of dealing," "honesty," and highly placed acquaintances. Those credentials rightly belong instead to Marlowe, Nashe, or Peele. Notice also that by redirecting the apology to Shakspere, biographers create the impression that Shake-scene had been referred to specifically as a dramatist.

So, the apology from *Kind-Harts Dreame* gets pasted into somebody else's scrapbook. And there is more to it than that.

AUTHORSHIP FRAUD

Groatsworth was published shortly after Greene's death. Greene's authorship was immediately challenged, and both Thomas Nashe and Henry Chettle were suspected of being the real author. Nashe disavowed responsibility, branding *Groatsworth* a "scald, trivial, lying pamphlet," a disclaimer suggesting that Nashe himself may have viewed the pamphlet as a forgery. Chettle ducked for cover in *Kind-Harts Dreame*:

I had only in the copy this share, it was ill written, as sometimes Greene's hand was none of the best, licensed it must be, ere it could be printed which could never be if it might not be read. To be brief I writ it over, and as near as I could, followed the copy, only in that letter I put something out, but in the whole book not a word in, for I protest it was all Greene's, not mine nor Master Nashe's, as some unjustly have affirmed.

Notice that Chettle admitted that the printer had typeset the pamphlet from Chettle's handwritten manuscript.

Authorship doubts about *Groatsworth* have persisted ever since. Chauncey Elwood Sanders, the author of *An Introduction to Research in English Literary History*, considered it "unlikely that Robert Greene wrote three—or even two—moderately long pamphlets during the last days or weeks of his life, especially since during some part of that time he must have been too ill to write" (156). Sanders first expressed his doubts about Greene's authorship of *Groatsworth* in 1933, years before the advent of the computer.

Then, in 1969, Warren B. Austin subjected 43,190 words written by Chettle and 104,596 words written by Greene to a computer analysis. Austin developed tests to measure lexical and linguistic preferences peculiar to each writer, even if that writer had made a deliberate attempt to mimic someone else's style. His analysis caught Chettle red-handed as the author of *Groatsworth*, intentionally imitating Greene's writing style. Austin not only found "overwhelming cumulative evidence denying Greene's authorship" of *Groatsworth* and confirming Chettle's, he retested the letter containing the "Upstart Crow" passage and found that it, too, was covered with Chettle's linguistic fingerprints (*Stylistic*, 74–75).

Austin compared each author's habitual choice of prefixes, suffixes, Latin tags, phrase inversions, reflexive pronouns, interspersed poetry, and so on, and found that "the total rates for all discriminant categories are 1.34 in Greene, 4.75 in Chettle, and 4.38 in the *Groatsworth*" (*Stylistic*, x). Austin's conclusions are slowly gaining acceptance.

D. Allen Carroll, who published a critical edition of *Greene's Groatsworth of Wit* in 1994, agreed that while "Greene *may* have had something to do with the writing of *Groatsworth*, Chettle *certainly* did" (x). John Jowett, one of the editors of the *Oxford Shakespeare*, accepted Austin's results as "a hard core of impressive evidence for Chettle's authorship of the *Groatsworth*. The best of it, in aggregate, still provides ample evidence of Chettle's hand and leaves little scope for Greene's. Chettle's contribution cannot be confined to scribal sophistication, or even editorial overlay. . . . Nor can Chettle's presence be confined to certain sections of the pamphlet; it is ubiquitous. The letter to the playwrights is of special interest here. . . . Though the passage is short, it contains an unexpected hoard of features that point to Chettle's authorship" ("Notes," 387).

Jowett was critical of those in academia who have resisted Austin's conclusions, concluding that "scholars are not justified in passing by Austin's findings with a footnoted shrug, nor in persisting to attribute the pamphlet to Greene" ("Johannes," 476). Jowett could have had any number of scholars in mind. For example, Samuel Schoenbaum could not bring himself to accept the conclusion that Chettle forged *Groatsworth*. Instead, he clouded the issue:

This does not mean that the hypothesis is invalid, only that Austin has not proved his case. It is unlikely that such a case can be proved. In the absence of conclusive proof to the contrary, Greene must continue to bear responsibility for his mean death-bed diatribe. (*Documentary*, 118)

In other words, since Austin did not *disprove* Greene's authorship ("in the absence of conclusive proof to the contrary"), Schoenbaum still accepted Greene as the author. But Austin's research identified Chettle as the author, and one cannot prove a negative.

The *Groatsworth* authorship episode raises an interesting question. Why would Chettle have written a pamphlet and palmed it off as the recently deceased Greene's? Greene's name on a pamphlet guaranteed a quick sale, and since Chettle was perpetually in debt, he may simply have been cashing in on Greene's reputation. But was anything else on his agenda? Chettle himself suggested a motive: "because on the dead they cannot be avenged."

The very fact that Chettle attributed his piece to Greene suggests that the risk associated with publishing *Groatsworth* was high. *Groatsworth* was registered for publication with an unusual caveat, that is, "upon the peril of Henry Chettle." Most commentators believe that *Groatsworth* contains topical satire and caricatures of real persons, Greene and Shakspere being the two most obvious. Carroll supposed that an "admission [of authorship] might also jeopardize [Chettle's] position as writer for the players attacked . . . or, perhaps, his chances of getting work" (4). If Chettle felt it was safer to frame a dead man as the author, then he could very well have been concerned about his own future employment.

Whatever Chettle's motive, this episode tells us that confusion over authorship could and did occur. And 400 years later, scholars are beginning to figure it out. Yet many have remained reluctant to confront the *Groatsworth* authorship question, and Jowett acknowledged a probable reason:

Admittedly, the reattribution [of *Groatsworth*] detracts from the certainties of literary history and from our knowledge of Greene in particular, and if it adds to the Chettle canon it does so on terms that are most unfavourable to him. Those relying on [Harold Jenkins's] relatively benign portrayal of Chettle will justifiably doubt whether such a well-willing figure would be guilty of such a gross deception. ("Johannes," 476)

By simply extending Jowett's logic, one might argue that the reattribution of Shakespeare's works would also detract from the certainties of literary history and would require substantial revision to the orthodox and relatively benign portrayal of Shakspere.

SHAKSPERE'S SCRAPBOOK, CONTINUED

In 1595, the Elizabethan court paid "William Kempe, William Shakespeare, and Richard Burbage, servants to the Lord Chamberlain . . . for two several Comedies or interludes showed by them before her Majesty." This payment, the first on record to the newly reorganized Lord Chamberlain's Men, is traditionally cited as evidence of Shakspere's meteoric rise to prominence in that company. Muriel C. Bradbrook, for example, used the payment to conclude that "Shakespeare was among the leading sharers of the new company, *ranking with its chief comic and tragic actors. He had arrived*" (*Poet*, 92, emphasis added).

Yet this payment marks the first—and the last—time "Shakespeare" appears in *any* payment to the Lord Chamberlain's Men or any other company. By contrast, Burbage and Kempe both show up elsewhere as payees. If Shakspere's name as payee is indicative of his new status as a leading actor in the Lord Chamberlain's Men, then either that status did not last very long or he was named as a payee for some other reason.

In fact, this record does not tell us precisely in what capacity "Shakespeare" was paid. A designated payee was invariably a shareholder (or sharer) but not necessarily a leading actor. Over the years, payees included George Bryan, Richard Cowley, Augustine Phillipps, and most frequently, John Heminges, none of whom are considered leading actors. Historians have concluded that Heminges regularly accepted payments in his capacity as business manager. Similarly, a 1576 warrant to pay Leicester's Men named James "Burbage and his company," but according to historian William Ingram, "it is not clear whether [Burbage] was still a stage player in March 1576. . . . *This phrasing is inconclusive*. He may well have been traveling with the company, *whether playing or not*" (*Business*, 187, emphasis added).

It is merely an assumption that Shakspere was paid in 1595 *for acting* in the holiday performances. Payment could have been made to "Shakespeare" as a shareholder, business manager or agent, banker, or some combination thereof. Shakspere had not necessarily "arrived" as a performer. If anything, he had arrived as a shareholder. As we will see, it is highly unlikely that Shakspere was ever a leading, or even a steadily working, actor.

SHAKSPERE AWOL

Close scrutiny of the historical records reveals some schedule conflicts in Shakspere's biography, and these conflicts raise questions about the nature of his theatrical commitments. Certainly, he was not always where he was supposed to be. A case in point concerns performances given by the Lord Chamberlain's Men in 1597–98. In that holiday season, the company performed at court on 26 December, 1 and 6 January, and 26 February.

In *William Shakespeare: A Documentary Life*, Schoenbaum described some of Shakspere's activities for 1597–98 in a chapter entitled "A Gentleman of Means":

Shakespeare moved into New Place before the year was out or, at the latest, early in the new year. We know because, in a survey of corn and malt made on 4 February 1598, he is listed as a resident. (178)

Schoenbaum pictured Shakspere moving into his new Stratford residence and hoarding grain at the same time that the Lord Chamberlain's Men were fulfilling holiday commitments at court. Performances at court were the company's most important and prestigious assignments, and Schoenbaum considered Shakspere one of the company's leading members. Yet he cited a document to support his statement that Shakspere was in Stratford for at least part of the 1597–98 holiday season. Many biographers also suppose that Shakspere was remodeling or making repairs at New Place over the 1598–99 holiday season, when the Lord Chamberlain's Men were again performing at court.

It would be risky to speculate that Shakspere commuted during holiday seasons, since a round trip between London and Stratford involved an average of six travel days, three each way. It would be almost as risky to speculate that he commuted during nonholiday periods. *Any* contemplated commuting would need to be reconciled both with court commitments and ongoing public performances.

The major acting companies performed continuously except during Lent, times of plague, or legal injunction, or on certain holy days. In the nonplague seasons between 1594 and 1600, the rival company played "six days a week and, on average, 236 days, or forty weeks, a year" (Berry, "Aspects," 41; see also Knutson, *Company*, 27–29, and Gurr, *Companies*, 100, 238), and nobody supposes that the Lord

Chamberlain's Men were any less busy than their principal competitor.

In 1597–98, the acting companies were either performing continuously in London or touring during the closure of the theatres from August to October 1597. Dennis Kay assured his readers that we "can be certain of [Shakspere's] *continued active daily involvement* in his company, and of this participation in its business ventures as well as its theatrical productions. And the years 1597–8 were exciting times for the Lord Chamberlain's Man" (230, emphasis added). So *any* commuting to Stratford that Shakspere may have done during these periods would represent a conflict with his ongoing professional commitments in London or on the road.

Yet the purchase of New Place (spring 1597), the grain-hoarding record (February 1598), and the Quiney-Sturley correspondence tell us that Shakspere was doing just that—commuting between London and Stratford in 1597 and 1598. On 24 January 1598, Abraham Sturley sent a letter to Richard Quiney, who was in London on business. The local news from Stratford was that Shakspere was well-disposed toward investing in some real estate and tithes. Sturley assumed that Quiney would know where to find Shakspere in London to follow up on the possibility. However, the source of the news about Shakspere was Quiney's father Adrian, who was in Stratford, not London. Sturley wrote to Quiney *fils* that

This is one special remembrance from your father's motion. It seemeth by him that our countryman, Mr. Shaksper, is willing to disburse some money upon some odd yardland or other at Shottery or near about us; he thinketh it a very fit pattern to move him to deal in the matter of our tithes.

Shakspere evidently had been in Stratford recently scouting out investment opportunities. It is during this same period that, according to Schoenbaum, Shakspere was moving into New Place and stockpiling grain. The Sturley letter corroborates Schoenbaum's statement, but that means that Shakspere was absent from London during a busy performance season.

Another schedule conflict occurs in 1604. In that year, "William Shakespeare" heads the roster of actors who were issued red cloth for the occasion of King James's procession through London on 15 March. On 27 March, not quite two weeks later, Shakspere was back in Stratford selling malt to Phillip Rogers. He continued to sell malt throughout April and May, and in June, he loaned Rogers 2*s.* In July, a lawyer filed Shakspere's suit against Rogers to recover the amount due plus damages. The lawsuit states that Rogers had repeatedly bought malt from "the same William" Shakspere, and that Shakspere had, on several occasions, requested Rogers to pay. The sales transactions, dated 27 March, 10 and 24 April, 3, 16 and 30 May, and 25 June, establish Shakspere's physical presence in Stratford, so he could not have been in London continuously during those months.

Meanwhile, back in London, the injunction against public performances was lifted on 9 April, allowing the King's Men to resume operations at the Globe. E. K. Chambers speculated that they had resumed before the ban was lifted (*Stage*, 4:350). One would therefore expect Shakspere to be in London with the company from February when the company performed at court, through 15 March when they received red cloth, through the resumption of public performances, and right on through other documented activities in the second half of 1604. Biographers leave you with the impression that he was.

Schoenbaum cited the 15 March document dispensing red cloth to Shakspere and his fellows, then segued straight to August when the King's Men waited upon a visiting dignitary. Schoenbaum assumed that Shakspere, as a ranking member of the acting company, was present for both activities, but did not report that Shakspere had been in Stratford during the intervening months. Few of his readers would notice that the 1604 malt sales in Stratford, mentioned in the previous chapter, conflicted with ongoing responsibilities of the King's Men in London (*Documentary*, 196, 184).

Schoenbaum suggested elsewhere that some of the less glamorous transactions in Stratford, such as the 1604 malt sales and the load of stone sold at New Place in 1598, might have been handled by someone else in Shakspere's household.* Perhaps the stone sale was; the record names only "mr. Shaxpere." Another biographer suggested that Shakspere's wife or brother Gilbert might have transacted the malt sales (Brown, 287). But when Gilbert acted as proxy for one of Shakspere's business transactions (i.e., a real estate purchase in 1602),

---

*Compare *A Documentary Life* (184) and *A Compact Documentary Life* (240–41). In the latter, Schoenbaum added the qualifier that perhaps "someone else in his household" sold the malt. In *Records and Images*, he stated that "usually the womenfolk in Jacobean households attended to the brewing, so Rogers may have dealt with Anne" (57).

the relevant document said so. The Rogers lawsuit makes no mention of a proxy. It explicitly and repeatedly names the seller as "the same William."

Nevertheless, in 1915, Charles William Wallace attempted to prove that the malt sales were transacted by some other William Shakspere, a divestiture of unsavory documentation that appealed to Wallace because it "unfetters the life and ideals of the poet from the sordid business of the brewery and the still" ("Other," 6). One of Wallace's principal arguments was that Shakspere could not have been in both London and Stratford at the same time (11). Since Wallace assumed that Shakspere had ongoing theatre commitments in London, he ruled out the possibility that Shakspere might actually have been in Stratford for the period in question.

On the other hand, B. Roland Lewis argued that the volume of malt sold was of sufficient quantity to constitute commercial commodity trading, and that "there was no other William Shakespeare in Stratford who was rich enough to be able to sell to a local apothecary a quantity of malt such as was sold to Philip Rogers" (2:371). Actually, there was no other William Shakspere in Stratford, period.* No matter how much the traditional biographer would like to get around the problem, the commercial malt sales conflict with Shakspere's supposed theatrical commitments in 1604.

LONDON LODGINGS

Records of Shakspere's London domiciles raise more questions and issues. Shakspere was listed in the Bishopsgate tax records for 1597, 1598, and 1599, and biographers generally conclude that Shakspere chose to live there because it was convenient to the Shoreditch theatres, which were then home to the Lord Chamberlain's Men. An annotation in the 1599 tax roll indicates that Shakspere had moved to the Liberty of the Clink, in Southwark, and that record is cited as evidence that he moved to be near the Globe, which was built in 1598–99.

At first glance, the inference seems reasonable. Other shareholders listed in default are presumed to have moved for similar reasons. For

---

*The 1997 International Genealogical Index lists no other William Shakspere in Stratford in the sixteenth or early seventeenth centuries. Namesakes are listed in Rowington (Warwickshire) and in Staffordshire.

example, Mary Edmond proposed that Cuthbert Burbage's tax delinquency in 1599 in the Blackfriars precinct and his brother Richard's delinquency in 1600 in Shoreditch together suggested that the brothers had relocated, at least temporarily, to be near the Globe in Southwark (40). In Shakspere's case, however, the inference is contradicted by other evidence.

According to the Public Record Office, "by the time the commissioners came to look for him in 1597 [in Bishopsgate], he had moved away." The evidence for that statement is the first tax record in which Shakspere's name appears. It is dated November 1597 and relates to the taxable period 1593–97, specifically the assessment made in October 1596 that was payable by February 1597 (Thomas and Cox, 8, 6; Chambers, *Facts*, 2:89). Shakspere was listed as one of the parishioners who were "either dead, departed, and gone out of the said ward," or gone into hiding. He could have moved away by October 1596, when the assessment was made.

Another record supports Shakspere's move to Southwark in 1596. In November of that year, a justice of the peace for the bishop of Winchester took out a writ of attachment, that is, a court order for the arrest of Shakspere, Francis Langley, and two women to protect the complainant from injury. The writ was issued to the sheriff of Surrey, who had jurisdiction in Southwark. Since no other sheriff was informed, all parties named are assumed to have been residents of Surrey (Thomas and Cox, 8). According to Langley's biographer, if Shakspere "neither lived nor worked in Surrey, such an assumption about him would be hard to explain" (Ingram, *Langley*, 145). Finally, Edmond Malone inspected a document, now missing, that would also corroborate Shakspere's move to Southwark in 1596:

From a paper now before me, which formerly belonged to Edward Alleyn, the player, our poet appears to have lived in Southwark near the Bear-Garden, in 1596. (Chambers, *Facts*, 2:88)

All the evidence, then, supports the conclusion that by 1596, Shakspere was living in Southwark, not Shoreditch.

Schoenbaum considered all this documentation on various occasions. By comparing each treatment, we see how biographers can downplay or deflect attention from troublesome evidence. In his essay "The Life of Shakespeare," Schoenbaum followed up on the construction of the Globe in 1598–99 with this account:

Shakespeare lived near where he worked. From tax assessments we know that
before October 1596 he dwelt in St Helen's, Bishopsgate, a short distance
from the Theatre, and that later (by October 1599) he had moved across
the river to the Liberty of the Clink on the Bankside, where, in Southwark,
the Globe stood. He may have been living on the Bankside as early as Mich-
aelmas Term [autumn], 1596, when one William Wayte swore the peace
against William Shakspere, Francis Langley, and two unknown women. . . .
    Some time before 1604 he was lodging—for how long is not certain—
with the family of a French Huguenot . . . in Silver Street, near St. Olave's
church in north-west London. (7–8, emphasis added)

If Shakspere was living in Southwark several years *before* the Globe
was built, and in northwest London (Cripplegate) five years later,
then he did *not* choose lodgings based on their proximity to the Lord
Chamberlain's Men's resident theatres, that is, "near where he
worked." (In *Records and Images*, Schoenbaum traced the half-hour
journey from Cripplegate to the Globe [22].)
    Schoenbaum's 1975 and 1977 accounts are similar to the one
above, and like Chambers before him (*Facts*, 2:90), Schoenbaum informed his readers that Shakspere had moved to Southwark *possibly*
by 1596–97, but in any case no later than 1599. In his 1975 biography, he concluded that Shakspere had moved to Southwark "no
later than 1598." Such statements show a reluctance to admit that
Shakspere moved to the Bankside well before the Globe was built.
In both accounts, Schoenbaum stated that Shakspere "ordered his
life according to his professional needs, with first the Theatre and
afterwards the Globe *as the fixed foot of his compass*," concluding that
"Shakespeare crossed the river when his company did" (*Documentary*,
164, emphasis added; see also *Compact*, 223). Yet elsewhere in *A
Documentary Life*, Schoenbaum asserted that Shakspere lived in
Southwark in 1596, when the alleged assault with Langley took place
(147).
    Schoenbaum's reports are inherently contradictory. All the evi-
dence supports the conclusion that Shakspere crossed the river at least
two years *before* his company did. By emphasizing Shakspere's move
to Southwark *by 1599 at the latest*, Schoenbaum deflected attention
from Shakspere's premature move *in 1596*. Such a point may seem
trivial, but misleading statements can pile up on each other and create
entirely erroneous impressions. These particular statements neatly
corroborate the assumption that Shakspere was the guiding genius

who propelled the Lord Chamberlain's/King's Men to prominence, and that he was dedicated exclusively to their repertory and business. Or, as Stanley Wells put it, "by the time Shakespeare was thirty he was established as a leading member of the company with which he was to be exclusively associated for the rest of his life" (25).

By assuming that Shakspere's logistical moves followed those of the acting company, Schoenbaum need not pursue some awkward questions. Was Leslie Hotson correct when he proposed that the Lord Chamberlain's Men performed briefly at Langley's theatre in 1596 (*Shallow*, 11–13)? Schoenbaum did not think so. But if not, why was Shakspere living or working in Southwark? What business did he have there? Why is he named in a writ of attachment, siding in an altercation with a competing theatre landlord? Did he have the interests of the Lord Chamberlain's Men in mind? Or could his relationship with Langley be indicative of divided loyalties?

Not all biographers mention the 1596 writ of attachment, but most of those who do mention it follow Hotson, and speculate on Shakspere's possible dealings with Langley concerning the Lord Chamberlain's Men's use of the Swan (e.g., Bentley, *Handbook*, 75; Chute, 135; Honan, 260, 266; see also Ingram, "Closing," 114). On the other hand, Schoenbaum apologized for the 1596 writ, relegating Shakspere to the possible status of innocent bystander (*Documentary*, 146–47). Despite what is known about some of the antagonists, there is no more reason to suppose that Shakspere was an innocent bystander than to suppose he was one of the troublemakers. But by choosing the least objectionable option, a biographer can more easily sustain the portrait of the legendary gentle playwright, assume Shakspere's exclusive allegiance to his theatre company, and avoid asking too many questions about the altercation.

Schoenbaum's position on Shakspere's London whereabouts remained inconsistent. In *Shakespeare's Lives*, he stated categorically that the 1596 writ of attachment "indicates that by then the playwright had migrated across the Thames" to Southwark (18). Even so, he was skeptical of Hotson's theory that all the Lord Chamberlain's Men migrated at that same time to perform at Langley's theatre, the Swan, and questioned whether Shakspere would have "felt obliged to live so close to his place of employment." He then suggested that Shakspere was "a visiting bystander rather than a resident" of Southwark in 1596 (542 n). These statements again are inherently contradictory.

Despite evidence to the contrary, the theory that Shakspere organized his lodgings around the Shoreditch and Southwark theatre districts continues to hold the field. Kay's 1992 biography (173) makes the same point about Shakspere's chosen proximity to his workplace, and Park Honan's 1998 biography (321) does nothing to clarify the matter.

Of course, it is possible that Shakspere chose lodgings less convenient to his presumed principal place of business. Or perhaps he maintained more than one London residence, as did some of his fellow shareholders. Heminges and Henry Condell both owned or leased homes in Aldermanbury, near Silver Street, but Condell also owned property on the Bankside and in Blackfriars. Heminges built a house adjacent to the Globe, and his burial in Aldermanbury listed him as a "stranger," that is, not a resident. Historians know less of Shakspere's London domiciles during most of his professional life, but another note left by Malone—and since lost—suggests that Shakspere did maintain multiple London residences:

Another curious document in my possession, which will be produced in the History of his Life, affords the strongest presumptive evidence that he continued to reside in Southwark to the year 1608. (Chambers, *Facts*, 2:88)

If Shakspere resided in Southwark from 1596 to 1608, then his lodgings at the Mountjoy household in Cripplegate in 1604 may have been a pied-à-terre, perhaps one of several. (By 1599, "Willielmi Shakespeare" was "in occupation" of the Globe theatre as a tenant, but biographers do not suppose he was living there.)

Interestingly, Shakspere seems never to have thought of London as home base but evidently fancied himself a country squire with important business in London. Later legal documents describe him as "of Stratford-upon-Avon," never "of London." He rented his city lodgings but purchased his house in Stratford, and invested most of his profits in Warwickshire real estate. Not until 1613, at age forty-eight, did he buy the Blackfriars gate-house in London as a commercial investment; the 1613 deed refers to the gate-house's "profits," "rents," and "commodities." If he rented or owned other city residences, records of them have not yet been found.

The records that do tell us something about Shakspere's whereabouts conflict with his presumed theatrical and literary activities in London. His lodgings were not always convenient to the Lord Chamberlain's Men's places of business. He seems to have been able to come and go from London at his pleasure. Since he remained a company shareholder throughout these years, his periodic and extended absences suggest that any services requiring his physical presence were not needed on a daily basis. Indeed, as we will see, Shakspere's most important contributions to the acting company were probably monetary and entrepreneurial.

MORE THEATRICAL SOUVENIRS

While a law student at the Middle Temple in 1602, John Manningham recorded a naughty backstage anecdote:

Upon a time when Burbage played Richard III, there was a citizen grew so far in liking with him, that before she went from the play she appointed to him to come that night unto her by the name of Richard the Third. Shakespeare overhearing their conclusion went before, was entertained, and at his game ere Burbage came. Then message being brought that Richard the Third was at the door, Shakespeare caused return to be made that William the Conqueror was before Richard the Third. Shakespeare's name William. (39)

The last three words in Manningham's entry suggest that as late as 1602, the actor "William Shakespeare" was *not* well-known, at least not to this student. Otherwise why would Manningham have needed to make note of Shakspere's first name in order to explain the punch line? Nor did Manningham take it for granted that the first name of this "Shakespeare" was the same as that of the published author Shakespeare.

In a diary entry dated about six weeks earlier, Manningham had described a performance of *Twelfth Night* but made no mention of the author there (18). So either he did not know that "Shakespeare" wrote *Twelfth Night*, or he was unaware that the "Shakespeare" in his anecdote was also the playwright. Yet Manningham's familiarity with prominent writers is evident elsewhere in his diary, since he mentioned Ben Jonson, Edmund Spenser, and John Marston—all specifically as poets.

Some critics are reluctant to accept the excerpt from Manningham's diary at all, because it was examined in 1831 by John Payne Collier, a notorious forger. But if the entry is genuine, Manningham made no connection—as late as 1602—between Burbage's rival "Shake-speare" and a published writer with the same name.

In 1605, Augustine Phillipps, an actor and shareholder, left thirty shillings to his "fellow William Shakespeare" in his will, evidence that Phillipps recognized Shakspere as a professional colleague. A 1615 lawsuit confirms that "William Shakespeare" was a founding share-holder in the Globe and Blackfriars theatres. In 1616, Shakspere left money in his will to "fellows John Heminges, Richard Burbage & Henry Condell," confirming his professional relationship with those three shareholders.

In Ben Jonson's collected *Works*, originally published in 1616, "Will. Shakespeare" heads the cast that performed in the 1598 pre-miere of *Every Man In His Humour*. "Will. Shake-Speare" is listed in the cast for the 1603 premiere of *Sejanus*.

In 1623, seven years after Shakspere died, thirty-six Shakespeare plays were published in the collection known today as the *First Folio*. "William Shakespeare" heads the roster of "The Names of the Prin-cipal Actors in all these Plays." The *First Folio* cast list is, in fact, the *only* evidence that can be used to support Quennell's statement in the epigraph to this chapter that Shakspere frequently performed in his own plays, and this evidence is posthumous. Not one contem-poraneous record survives to show that Shakspere performed in *any* of the plays he supposedly wrote. Biographers are forced to rely on posthumous hearsay to cast him in two small parts, the Ghost in *Hamlet* and Adam in *As You Like It*. The only support for Quennell's statement that Shakspere acted in "other dramatists' plays" are the two cast lists published in Jonson's *Works* of 1616.

Andrew Gurr concluded that "some sharers seem never to have taken major parts. Shakespeare was never noted for his playing" (*Stage*, 106). Shakspere is, in fact, one of the least recited names in the extant cast lists and one of the least noticed in allusions as a performer.

SHAKSPERE'S RÉSUMÉ

Biographers infer from the 1595 court payment that Shakspere had achieved leading status with the Lord Chamberlain's Men, and that the years 1594 through 1604 represent the height of his theatrical career. However, the attempts in this chapter to reconcile known activities of the Lord Chamberlain's/King's Men with Shakspere's

documented activities and whereabouts have revealed serious schedule conflicts. Shakspere's absences during critical periods, including
holiday performances at court, certainly cast doubts on his supposed
role as the creative leading light in "his" company.

Shakspere's absences from London strongly suggest that his *primary* role with the acting company was one for which his continuous
presence was not necessary. From the evidence cited so far, Shakspere
was probably a minor rather than a leading actor, and one who performed infrequently. But was his primary role with the company really
that of resident dramatist? The next few chapters take a closer look
at some of the preceding theatrical clippings, and by restoring material that biographies generally omit, bring Shakspere's professional
career into sharper focus.

PART TWO

~∞~

INADMISSIBLE AND CONTROVERSIAL EVIDENCE

Chapter Four

Johannes Factotum

> In a survey of the evidence for an "ungentle" Shakespeare, we
> must also look at his record as a businessman.
> —E.A.J. Honigmann, *Shakespeare's Impact on*
> *His Contemporaries* (11)

Most biographers devote a full chapter to the "Upstart Crow" letter
in *Groatsworth of Wit*, and they use the reference to "Shake-scene"
as evidence of Shakspere's *literary* debut. They point out that the
description of Shake-scene, "with his tiger's heart wrapped in a
player's hide," paraphrases a line from *3 Henry VI*. They conclude
that the *Groatsworth* passage establishes Shakspere's presence in London theatre, that *3 Henry VI* had been written by Shakspere, and that
his early literary success was sufficient to warrant envy from fellow
dramatists. Not all of these conclusions are justified.

Jonathan Bate is one of many scholars who have quoted *Groats-*
worth as evidence that by 1592, Shakspere had arrived *as a dramatist:*
"Shakespeare's is a double offence: as an actor, he gains credit for
mouthing fine lines which really belong to the university wits, and as
an upstart writer he is now imitating their style, even borrowing their
phrases, in his own plays" (*Genius,* 16). Likewise, according to Harry
Levin, writing in *The Riverside Shakespeare,* the *Groatsworth* attack

"makes it quite explicit that Shakespeare had meanwhile become a player and was already emerging as a playwright" (4).

However, in his critical edition of *Groatsworth*, D. Allen Carroll was wary of drawing any hard-and-fast conclusion from the "Shake-scene" allusion: "Something ambiguous hovers at the center of its expression just at the point where we might hope, in this first certain allusion to Shakespeare in London, for a clue to his early practice as a dramatist. . . . It was the sapling, [according] to W. W. Greg in 1942, from which 'sprang a whole jungle of critical and biographical error' " (132, 133). In other words, the Shake-scene passage is ambiguous and various interpretations are possible.

For one thing, the passage itself gives no clue as to the authorship of the original line about the "tiger's heart." Furthermore, the play was first published in 1595 in a corrupt and anonymous version, so in 1592, general readers would have had no reason to associate the "tiger's heart" lines with anyone named Shakespeare. In addition, most biographers present the "Upstart Crow" letter in isolation, without taking into account the common themes and threads that tie it to other episodes in the pamphlet.

ROBERTO AND SHAKE-SCENE

Groatsworth is divided into tales about a character named Roberto, a contrite deathbed repentance, the open letter to the playwrights, and a fable about the Ant and the Grasshopper. Each of these sections sheds light on the Shake-scene allusion. According to Muriel C. Bradbrook, the "passage on Shakespeare, the highest point of [the author's] invective, is not detachable from the rest of the pamphlet, in which the poet tells his life-story as the tale of the prodigal Roberto" ("Beasts," 65). All these tales introduce themes that recur throughout *Groatsworth*, that is, hatred of profiteers and poverty, and remorse over profligate spending.

At the beginning of the story, we learn that Roberto is a scholar and his father a moneylender. Roberto has come to resent usurers and the fortunes they make, but his younger brother is following in his father's footsteps, much to his father's delight. The brother eventually inherits their father's tainted fortune, while Roberto inherits only a groat, a worthless coin. After several episodes, Roberto is feeling sorry for himself when a stranger interrupts his brooding.

The stranger had begun in poverty when "the world once went

hard with [him], when [he] was fain to carry [his] playing Fardle a footback," that is, to travel on foot like a hobo. For seven years he was a puppet master and "a country Author," but now that his morality plays and "almanac" are outdated, he makes his living from scholars whom he hires to write plays. Now he is a "Gentleman" and a "player." The "gentleman player" is evidently successful because he dresses well and owns clothing worth £200. He refers to the apparel as his "share," as though he were a theatrical shareholder who owns costumes. Although he does not have the voice of a professional performer, he nevertheless brags that he has played Delphrigus and King of the Fairies to great acclaim. He embellishes his speech with a Latin phrase but is not sure what it means, extemporizes some doggerel of which he has an overblown opinion, and ends up recruiting the destitute Roberto to write plays for him.

The poet Roberto represents Greene ("break I off Roberto's speech; whose life in most parts agreeing with mine. . . . Hereafter suppose me the said Roberto"), while the "gentleman player" shares several characteristics with Shake-scene. Both are actors with a predilection for extemporizing. Both are braggarts. Both hire needy playwrights. A few critics have accepted the "gentleman player" in "Roberto's Tale" as a caricature of Shakspere (see Carroll, 116; Simpson, *School*, 2:12).

"Roberto's Tale" is followed by a repentance and the open letter containing the "Upstart Crow" diatribe, but that diatribe is usually edited by biographers. When missing pieces from this letter are reinstated, the salvo leveled at Shake-scene turns out to be an attack against an untrustworthy actor who is also a moneylender and, like the "gentleman player," a paymaster of playwrights.

This passage alternates between the singular and the plural, a technique often used to blur satiric material. As Ben Jonson wrote in *Timber, or Discoveries*, "where censure is general, there is no injury to individuals" (Walker, 48). Here again is the "Upstart Crow" section of the open letter, with the reinstated sentences:

And thou [Peele] no less deserving than the other two [Marlowe and Nashe], in some things rarer, in nothing inferior; driven (as myself) to extreme shifts, a little have I to say to thee: and were it not an idolatrous oath, I would swear by sweet St. George, thou art unworthy better hap, since thou dependest on so mean a stay. Base-minded men all three of you, if by my misery you be not warned: for unto none of you (like me) sought those burrs to cleave: those Puppets (I mean) that spake from our mouths, those Anticks garnished in our colors. Is it not strange, that I, to whom they all have been beholden: is it not like that you, to whom they all have been beholden, shall (were ye in that case as I am now) be both at once of them forsaken? Yes trust them not: for there is an upstart Crow, beautified with our feathers, that with his *Tiger's heart wrapped in a Player's hide*, supposes he is as well able to bombast out a blank verse as the best of you: and being an absolute *Johannes fac totum*, is in his own conceit the only Shake-scene in a country. O that I might entreat your rare wits to be employed in more profitable courses: and let those Apes imitate your past excellence, and never more acquaint them with your admired inventions. I know the best husband of you all will never prove an Usurer, and the kindest of them all will never prove a kind nurse: yet whilst you may, seek you better Masters; for it is pity men of such rare wits, should be subject to the pleasure of such rude grooms.

Anticks. According to Bradbrook, "antics" were "among the lowest and most scurrilous type of actor." This type of player "had begun as a tattered, gaudily dressed stroller, with the slipperiness, the capacity for betrayal, of all wandering tribes—gipsies, fiddlers, minstrels, tinkers" ("Beasts," 64).

Crow. Æsop's crow was a proud strutter who borrowed the feathers of others, Horace's crow was a plagiarist, and Pliny's raven was an overrated bird on a privileged perch. There is no consensus on which bird was intended, and some have seen the "Upstart Crow" as a conflation. Thomas Nashe, in his 1592 pamphlet *Pierce Pennilesse*, was outraged that "the Cobbler's crow for crying but *Ave Caesar*, [would] be more esteemed than rarer birds that have warbled sweeter notes unrewarded" (2:34). Years before, in his 1579 *Defense of Poetry*, Thomas Lodge wrote that "Aesop's crafty crow be never so deftly decked, yet is his double dealing easily deciphered: & though men never so perfectly polish their writings with others' sentences, yet the simple truth will discover the shadow of their follies: and bestowing every feather in the body of the right M[aster] turn out the naked dissembler into his own coat, as a spectacle of folly" (G. G. Smith, 1:63–64).

Tiger's heart. Leslie Hotson hunted the tiger in Elizabethan literature and found that it was typically associated with cruelty, double-dealing, and hypocrisy (*Hilliard*, 142–47). The line paraphrased from Shakespeare's *3 Henry VI* ("O tiger's heart wrapt in a woman's hide!"), is part of a scathing speech (I.iv.111–49) vilifying the queen as a "stern, obdurate, flinty, rough, remorseless" she-wolf "whose tongue more poisons than the adder's tooth," and who feeds off others' misfortune.

Supposes. One definition of "suppose" (*OED*, def. 12), now obsolete but in use at that time, was "to feign, pretend; occasionally to forge."

Factotum. A "factotum" is "a would-be universal genius," or "person of boundless conceit, who thinks himself able to do anything, however much beyond the reach of real abilities" (*OED*; Carroll, 134). (The meaning as Jack-of-all-trades is not recorded until 1618.) A "fac-totum" was also a printer's term, specifically an "ornamental surround that will take any capital letter in its middle. . . . The factotum is impressively ornamental and very versatile, but empty within and incapable of textual signification" (Jowett, "Johannes," 482–83). Incidentally, Henry Chettle was also a professional typesetter.

Usurer. In Shakespeare's day, "usury" meant moneylending at interest, regardless of the amount charged. The Act Against Usury of 1571 had the effect of "sanctioning lending at interest" of 10% or less, but moneylenders did not enjoy an improved reputation as a result. By the early seventeenth century, "usury was coming to mean extortionate rates of interest . . . and was increasingly identified as a crime of the social-climbing *nouveaux riches*" (Jones, 145, 146).

The following is a skeptic's paraphrase of the "Upstart Crow" diatribe:

George Peele, you are no less talented than Marlowe or Nashe. You have been impoverished as I have, but you don't deserve any better luck than I if you rely on such a despicable prop to support you.

Contemptible fellows, all three of you [Marlowe, Nashe, and Peele], if you don't learn from my misfortune. The actors are only as good as our words make them, and they owe me. They owe you too, but since I have been deserted by them (by one in particular) in my time of need, beware. Beware of one untrustworthy actor, the "Upstart Crow." We make him look good in the roles we write, but this player is callous, duplicitous, and arrogant; he fancies himself able to extemporize lines in blank verse that are as good as any of yours. He even passes off some of your material as his own. And this know-it-all thinks he's the most important actor around.

I beg all three of you to redirect your skills in a more profitable direction, and away from this unscrupulous actor. Let him recite, plagiarize, or vulgarize your past plays. Don't give him any new ones. I know that the most financially prudent ["best husband"] of you would not stoop to usury (i.e., as did Shake-scene), and the most compassionate usurer is not charitable at all to someone driven to desperation, on his deathbed and needing care. So while you still have a chance to escape my fate, find some paymasters with more compassion and integrity. Stay away from actor-paymasters and usurers (like *Johannes Factotum*), because you three are too talented to be exploited by such contemptible knaves.

The reinstated passage completes one unbroken paragraph, and it provides uncomplimentary fodder for Shakspere's character profile. This Shake-scene is untrustworthy, arrogant, a "rude groom," a "Usurer," Greene's erstwhile paymaster, and now a "mean stay" for whom the other playwrights work.

The open letter was intended to be read following "Roberto's Tale," and when it is, the common elements become obvious. In the overall organization of *Groatsworth*, the tale about Roberto serves as the prequel to the *Johannes Factotum* passage, explaining how Roberto became dependent on the Upstart Crow. This actor hired the destitute Roberto to write plays but then left him to die in poverty. The brutal allusion to Shake-scene's "tiger's heart," paraphrased from *3 Henry VI*, carries charges of unnatural cruelty and deceit, further suggesting that Shake-scene, like the "gentleman player," has no compassion for a dying man.

"Shake-scene" is resented, not as a promising dramatist who threatens the *status quo*, but as a paymaster, callous usurer, and actor who *thinks* himself capable of extemporizing blank verse. He is arrogant enough to presume that his ad-libbing can compete with or improve upon lines written by professional dramatists, the very same writers whom he exploits. Moreover, he thinks he can pass off their words as his own. (Compare the language to that in the 1589 preface to *Menaphon*, in which Nashe derided "idiot art-masters, that intrude themselves to our ears as the alchemists of eloquence, who (mounted on the stage of arrogance) think to outbrave better pens with the swelling bombast of a bragging blank verse" [G. G. Smith, 1:308].)

The open letter urges the three playwrights to stop writing for this disreputable actor and to find another "Master": "thou dependest on so mean a stay . . . if by my misery you be not warned . . . trust them not . . . there is an upstart Crow . . . never more acquaint them [him] with your admired inventions . . . the best husband of you will never prove an Usurer . . . seek you better Masters." Chettle's warning was about a particular actor who exploits the playwrights, not a rival dramatist who could write better than they. He was attacking the "Puppets," or rather, one Puppet in particular. The passage is telling the three addresses to write for a "better" master than the one with a "tiger's heart."

The diatribe further suggests that Shakspere was appropriating lines from *3 Henry VI* in an underhand fashion. Chettle first accuses Shake-scene of dishonesty ("trust them not"), of making himself look good in the words of the playwrights ("beautified with our feathers"), and then of *supposing* or pretending that he can "bombast out a blank verse." Many critics have inferred that Shake-scene is being accused of plagiarism, or literary theft. An inferior and unauthorized version of *3 Henry VI* had been performed onstage, so Chettle's accusation may imply that Shakspere was involved with the performance and publishing history of that play. If so, the advice to the three unnamed playwrights to stop supplying Shake-scene with new plays ("never more acquaint them [him] with your admired inventions") would be quite justified. In any event, Shake-scene returns in another incarnation in the closing fable.

THE GRASSHOPPER AND SHAKE-SCENE

The allegory following the "Upstart Crow" passage in *Groatsworth* is a fable about a squandering Grasshopper and an acquisitive Ant. The profligate Grasshopper accuses the Ant of being a greedy miser whose "thrift is theft." Then the Grasshopper falls on hard times, the frugal Ant refuses to help him, and the Grasshopper, like Greene, dies an impoverished death. And the Ant, like Shake-scene, forsakes an associate in time of need.

The Ant, a heartless "bourgeois, antlike, thrifty husbandman," is another incarnation of Shakspere (Kay, 164; see also Honan, 160). E.A.J. Honigmann also proposed that the author of *Groatsworth* intended the Ant, "a waspish little worm," as another satire of Shake-scene:

Is Aesop's ant a greedy miser, whose thrift is *theft*? Is it said to *work others woe*? These surprising charges pick up the very accusations levelled against "Shake-scene." (*Impact*, 5)

The tiger-hearted Ant is another Scrooge, resented for his business acumen, miserly habits, and profiteering.

These recurring satires suggest that Shakspere was already sufficiently prominent as a money-man in theatrical circles to warrant such notice. The years 1590–94 were transitional ones for the acting companies, and out of the shifting conditions came new business ventures and companies with restructured personnel. Philip Henslowe was one of several "theatrical bankers or paymasters" who emerged at this time. In addition to being the landlord of the Rose theatre, Henslowe was also the banker for its resident acting company, the Lord Admiral's Men. Honigmann proposed that another financier emerged at about the same time in a comparable role with the Lord Chamberlain's Men, that financier being William Shakspere (*Impact*, 7–8). Honigmann further proposed that like Henslowe, Shakspere loaned money at interest as a sideline, the earliest such transaction on record being the £7 John Clayton loan of 1592 (*Impact*, 12).

The Clayton loan fits quite comfortably alongside Shakspere's other documented loans and lawsuits for recovery of debt, and Shakspere was elsewhere associated with moneylenders. One was Francis Langley, the theatre landlord cited with Shakspere for assault in 1596. Shakspere was not keeping good company on that occasion. Langley's biography is a litany of unscrupulous activities, greed, and extortion. Another friend was John Combe, a rich moneylender from Stratford. He and Shakspere were close friends, because Combe remembered Shakspere with a £5 bequest in his will, and Shakspere bequeathed his sword to Combe's nephew, Thomas. The biographer can trace few personal relationships in the life of Shakspere, but that with John Combe is one of them.

Shakspere's known associations with these two usurers lend some weight to the charges in *Groatsworth* that he was already recognized as a paymaster and moneylender himself. Dennis Kay supposed that the satires skewering "Shake-scene" and the Ant suggested that Shakspere "was—largely through thrift and usury—comfortably off, and already dealing with writers as other proprietors and entrepreneurs did" (169). Kay did not, however, sustain that line of discussion for long. He left the "swindling skinflint" behind by shifting the focus to Shakspere, the "writer, to whose defense . . . his friends rush," that defense being the misappropriated Chettle apology (169).

All three caricatures in *Groatsworth*—Shake-scene, the "gentleman player," and the miserly Ant—are entirely consistent with Shakspere's extant business records. He is an investor in the theatrical community. In 1598, he is hoarding commercial quantities of grain during a famine. The 1598 Quiney correspondence details Richard Quiney and Abraham Sturley's hopes of securing a loan from Shakspere and attests to Shakspere's skills at the bargaining table. In 1604 Shakspere sues Phillip Rogers for £1 5s 10d plus damages; part of the amount due was for a cash loan. In 1608, Shakspere sues John Addenbroke for a debt of £6 plus damages, and when Addenbroke leaves town,

Shakspere proceeds against the man who served as security against default. In 1611, Shakspere and two others file a complaint to guarantee a return on their real estate investment in the event of default by other lessees and sublessees. In 1614, Shakspere is scheming to safeguard his own interests when most Stratford citizens are resisting the pasture enclosures at Welcombe. These records reflect a consistent pattern of behavior and character. They show that Shakspere was a tightfisted businessman with a selfish streak, and that he was viewed by others as a source of loans or financing—both portraits to keep in mind when considering the 1592 charges of duplicity and usury. In *Groatsworth*, then, the greedy Ant is the third character to conjure up the image of a paymaster and moneylender, and the third character to resonate with the Shakspere of historical record.

SHAKSPERE REARRANGED

The Ant completes the *Groatsworth* trio of Shakspere lampoons, and the similarities among Shake-scene, the "gentleman player," and the Ant are obvious. Both players hire writers and exploit them, fancy themselves able to bombast out verse extempore, and are *factotums* who think they excel at more than one craft. Both Shake-scene and the Ant leave a needy associate to die in poverty. The reader is repeatedly advised to stay away from profiteers and their ill-gotten gains. These recurring characters and themes serve to unify the sections of *Groatsworth* into a cohesive whole.

At this point, the jigsaw puzzle pieces begin to fit together, but most traditional biographers rearrange or leave out many of the unflattering but essential pieces. They ignore the £7 loan to Clayton and omit the reference to usury in the "Upstart Crow" letter, even though the two records reinforce each other.* They omit the part of the "Upstart Crow" passage that describes, not a budding literary

---

*Among the biographers who omit the reference to usury in *Groatsworth* are Bentley, Bradbrook, Brown, Chute, Dutton, Levi, Quennell, and I. Wilson. In *A Documentary Life* (115–16), Schoenbaum reproduced the uncut passage in black-letter facsimile. In *A Compact Documentary Life*, he omitted the usury reference in his transcription (151). Kay included the usury reference and considered its significance. So did Honan, who suggested that the passage contained a "hint that Shakespeare had viciously refused to lend money" (160). Thomson duly noted Honigmann's argument "that Shake-scene's real offence is not authorship but moneylending," and further supposed that Shakespeare "went in for [usury] on a small scale" (17, 35).

genius, but a moneylending actor. The fables about Roberto and the miserly Ant are rarely mentioned. Those who do find parallels among Shake-scene, the "gentleman player," or the Ant assume that Shakspere quickly transcended such ungentle episodes. To make absolutely sure the reader goes down the right path, Chettle's subsequent apology to somebody else is filched to build a dignified character profile of an emerging playwright, so that the duplicitous paymaster is lost in the shuffle.

The traditional interpretation of *Groatsworth* is both distorted and selective, but we could perhaps be more confident of the unorthodox interpretation if there were any way of knowing what Elizabethans made of the pamphlet. As it happens, an Elizabethan "take" on parts of *Groatsworth* does survive. It has been ignored by biographers, and it is at odds with their interpretations of *Groatsworth*.

AN ELIZABETHAN INTERPRETATION OF *GROATSWORTH*

Vertues Common-wealth, by the obscure Henry Crosse, was published in 1603.* When tracing Shakspere's financial and social ambitions, B. Roland Lewis considered Crosse's allusion to

these copper-lace gentlemen [who] grow rich, purchase lands by adulterous plays, and not [a] few of them usurers and extortioners which they exhaust out of the purses of their haunters so they are puffed up in such pride as self-love as they envy their equals and scorn their inferiors. (2:335)

("Copper-lace" conveys a meaning of "spurious, pretentious, worthless," following the *OED* definition of "copper" as "a base metal.")

Chambers reprinted more of Crosse's passage, not in his biography of Shakspere, but in *The Elizabethan Stage*:

it were further to be wished, that those admired wits of this age, Tragedians, and Comedians,† that garnish Theaters with their inventions, would spend their wits in more profitable studies, and leave off to maintain those Anticks, and Puppets, that speak out of their mouths: for it is pity such noble gifts,

*Henry Crosse has never been successfully identified; the name Crosse (X?) may be a pseudonym.
†The terms are used here to signify "wits," or writers of comedies and tragedies. See *OED* "tragedian" (def. 1) and "comedian" (def. 2).

should be so basely employed, as to prostitute their ingenious labors to enrich such buckram gentlemen. (4:247)

Compare this passage to the "Upstart Crow" letter in *Groatsworth*. Crosse was obviously plagiarizing that letter, and the previous two passages show that he picked up on the connection between usurers and puppets.

In fact, Crosse picked up on far more than that. He picked up specifically on the bombastic braggart:

He that can but bombast out a blank verse, and make both the ends jump together in a rhyme, is forthwith a poet laureate, challenging the garland of bays, and in one slavering discourse or other, hang out the badge of his folly. Oh how weak and shallow much of their poetry is, for having no sooner laid the subject and ground of their matter, and in the Exordium moved attention, but over a verse or two run upon rocks and shelves, carrying their readers into a maze, now up, then down, one verse shorter than another by a foot, like an unskillful Pilot, never comes nigh the intended harbor: in so much that oftentimes they stick so fast in mud, they lose their wits ere they can get out, either like Chirrillus, writing verse not worth the reading, or Battillus, arrogating to themselves, the well deserving labors of other ingenious spirits. Far from the decorum of Chaucer, Gower, Lydgate, etc., or our honorable modern Poets, who are no whit to be touched with this, but reverently esteemed, and liberally rewarded. (109)

This passage shows that the one who bombasted out blank verse and fancied himself a "poet laureate" commanded no respect whatsoever, was hardly the subject of any professional envy, and indeed was not to be classified with the likes of Geoffrey Chaucer or John Gower. The bombaster was an incompetent hack and broker who took credit for someone else's literary effort, a "Battillus," or a "Chirrillus."

Chirrillus of Iasus was, according to *The Oxford Classical Dictionary*, "a bad poet." A "Battillus" was an agent for writers who did not wish to see their own names in print. In his 1584 dedication to *The Mirror of Modesty*, Greene wrote of "Aesop's Crow, which decked herself with others' feathers, or like the proud Poet Battillus, which subscribed his name to Virgil's verses" (3:7). In *Farewell to Folly* (1591), Greene wrote about poets who "for their calling and gravity, being loath to have any profane pamphlets pass under their hand, get some other Battillus to set his name to their verses. Thus is the ass made proud by this underhand brokery" (9:232–33). Crosse's bombaster of blank verse was an underhanded broker.

Both Chambers and Lewis cited passages from *Vertues Common-wealth*, but neither mentioned the line about "he that can bombast out a blank verse," much less connected it to the subsequent "synopsis" of the "Upstart Crow" letter (see Carroll, 80n). Nor did they mention that several pages later, Crosse cribbed a version of the fable about the Ant and the Grasshopper from *Groatsworth*. In short, Chambers and Lewis made no connection at all between these critical passages and Shake-scene. Yet in his introduction to *Vertues Common-wealth*, Alexander B. Grosart acknowledged that Crosse's pamphlet contained "*hits* at Shakespeare" (vi).

Crosse's use of *Groatsworth*, complete with its swipes at the bombaster of blank verse and the miserly Ant, shows that the traditional biographers' interpretations of *Groatsworth* are at variance with those of an Elizabethan. Crosse did not detect resentment toward a budding playwright whose work challenged the established playwrights. He detected resentment toward a braggart who passed off somebody else's writing as his own, or whose own improvised verse was hardly worth the paper it was written on. Crosse also repeated the charges of usury, brokering, and profiteering.

KEEPING WILL LIKABLE

The unexpurgated *Groatsworth of Wit* passages confirm Shakspere's presence in London's theatrical world, but not in the role usually assigned to him. Instead of the emerging playwright of legend, we find a rather obnoxious actor and usurer who pays playwrights to write for him. Shake-scene, the theatrical paymaster, could conceivably be reconciled to Shakspere, the legendary actor/playwright, but the "gentleman player" recruited scholars to write for him. Any Shakespearean biographer who accepted all of *Groatsworth* would be faced with the embarrassing problem of having to explain why an emerging literary genius would hire "scholars" to write for him just as he is supposedly struggling to make his own debut.

In Chapter 2, we found traditional biographers sacrificing their objectivity in order to accept or reject certain records. Now we have found that biographers have edited out unsavory information and embezzled a compliment to somebody else to create a gentle playwright. They have transformed the tiger-hearted *Johannes Factotum* and "greedy miser" of *Groatsworth* into a budding playwright who was attracting the attention of "diverse of worship."

Anthony Burgess flatly admitted his philosophy: "Let us try to keep Will likable" (259), and his approach is not unique. As we will see, most biographers would sooner dismiss some allusions as cryptic rather than admit that they point to a pseudonymous Shakespeare— or to a less likable Shakspere.

Chapter Five

Shake-speare in Sport

> Any resemblance in the plays of Jonson to persons either living
> or dead, contrary to the old libel-proofing demur, was probably
> intended (if he thought of it).
> —William W. E. Slights, *Ben Jonson and
> the Art of Secrecy* (147)

Some of the richest sources of information on Shakspere are also
among the most complex pieces of evidence. This chapter takes a
close look at some of the more cryptic or unflattering allusions to
Shakspere. In these allusions we will find more characters similar to
the Shakspere we uncovered in *Groatsworth of Wit*. We will examine
each allusion for content, context, and in two cases, potentially significant punctuation.

THE INTERMITTENT HYPHEN

One of the controversial elements in a discussion of Shakespeare's
authorship is the intermittent presence of the hyphen in his name.
The hyphen appeared in 45% (fifteen out of thirty-three) of the plays
published before the *First Folio* in 1623; in two editions of poetry
(the *Sonnets* and the appended *A Lover's Complaint*, and *Love's Mar-*

tyr); in one cast list; and in six literary allusions.* It is worth noting that the first time the author's name was ever alluded to, in a poem prefixed to *Willobie His Avisa* (1594), it was spelled with the hyphen.

No other Elizabethan or Jacobean author appeared in hyphenated form with comparable frequency. The hyphen in Shake-speare is an unprecedented aberration, occurring frequently, but inconsistently. Anti-Stratfordians hypothesize that the hyphen signified a made-up name, a pseudonym. Traditional biographers consider that theory utter nonsense.

In Shakespeare's day, a hyphen was likely to be occasional or arbitrary but not frequent. Now and then, a hyphen was inserted into a name for no apparent reason. One orthodox scholar, Irvin Leigh Matus, discovered an Elizabethan printer, Robert Walde-grave, who made a deliberate choice in midcareer to hyphenate his own name (29), but Walde-grave therefore makes for a poor comparison to the idiosyncratic hyphens in Shakespeare's name. In his personal business, Shakspere of Stratford never once chose to hyphenate his own name. Furthermore, those who credit Shakspere with writing plays agree that he had nothing to do with publishing them. The hyphen was inserted by typesetters (i.e., compositors), publishers, or commentators, but not by the author. Clearly, it was not Shakspere himself who chose the hyphen, as did Walde-grave. In addition, after 1582, Walde-grave apparently used the hyphen all the time, whereas the hyphen in Shake-speare is frequent but intermittent.

Matus also explained that most of the hyphens could be attributed to "a common practice in the printing trade for title-page information to be repeated from one edition to the next" (28). However, the relevant title pages reveal too many arbitrary variations in wording, typeface, layout, spelling, and punctuation to support Matus's conclusion. Contrary to his theory, the hyphenated name appeared, for example, on the 1598 and 1605 quartos of *Richard III*, but *not* on the intervening 1602 quarto.

Another hypothesis postulates that compositors deliberately inserted the hyphen to prevent the long tails present in the *K* and *S* italic type fonts from bumping into each other and breaking. The *K*

---

*The six allusions are found in *Willobie His Avisa* (1594); Anthony Scoloker's epistle to *Daiphantus* (1604); John Davies's epigram (1610); John Webster's epistle to *The White Devil* (1612); and I. M.'s and Leonard Digges's poems in the *First Folio* (1623). The hyphen in W. C.'s *Polimanteia* (1595) is ambiguous, because it occurs at a line break.

and *S* in roman fonts had no long tails, were not at risk, and consequently would not account for hyphenation. However, anti-
Stratfordian Peter R. Moore's investigations showed that nearly all of
the hyphenated "Shake-speares" (e.g., on the title page of the *Sonnets*,
the 1603 edition of *Hamlet*, the *Sejanus* cast list, Digges's poem of
1623, etc.), were set in roman rather than italic type, and any compositor had several options available to prevent type-font collisions
("Shake-hyphen-speare," 58–60).

There remain two more possibilities. Either the name inexplicably attracted hyphen-mongers, or "Shake-speare" was regarded as a
made-up name. Nobody has postulated hyphen-mongering. Regarding the second possibility, hyphens were often used in made-up names.
Martin Mar-prelate, for example, was the notorious pen name cloaking
the author(s) of inflammatory pamphlets critical of the Anglican
Church in the late 1580s. Like "Shake-speare," the name "Mar-
prelate" and its satirical variants (e.g., "Mar-Martins," "Mar-ton and
Mar-tother," and so on) were hyphenated often but inconsistently.
"Master Shoe-tie," referred to in *Measure for Measure*, and Sir Luck-
less Woo-all, a Jonsonian character, are other examples of made-up
names. Notice that in these examples, the combined syllables denote
action. The hyphenated "Shake-speare" denotes action, and Ben Jonson suggested its significance when he wrote that Shakespeare "seems
to shake a Lance / As brandish'd at the eyes of Ignorance."

The name "Shake-speare" could have been chosen to represent the
Elizabethan ideal of a soldier-scholar, a chivalrous man of letters, often celebrated in the Greek goddess Pallas Athena. In a dedication,
Thomas Lodge flattered a potential patron, Lord Hunsdon, as a "patron of all martial men, and a Maecenas of such as apply themselves
to study; wearing with Pallas both the lance and the bay" (Lodge,
Rosylynde, 1:4). In his dedication to *Perimedes* (1588), Robert Greene
wrote that Pallas Athena, known for "her spear, and her pen; [was]
counted as well the patroness of scholars, as of soldiers" (*Works*, 7:
5). In *Never Too Late* (1590), Greene wrote that "when the Trojans
sought to pacify the wrath of *Pallas*, the people's presents were books
and lances, to signify her deity, as well defended by letters as arms"
(8:5). The theory that Pallas Athena was the spear-shaking inspiration
for a pen name is enhanced by the presence of the hyphen and by
Jonson's illustration of the name's significance. Jonson was one of
several contemporaries, whether writers or printers, who inserted the
hyphen into Shakespeare's name. The hyphenated name does con-

note action, Jonson commented on that action, and collectively, those factors constitute another anomaly in the Shakespearean biography.

Traditional biographers dismiss the hyphens as signifying nothing. If there were only one or two hyphens, the anti-Stratfordians would probably ignore them also. However, the frequency of the hyphen in Shakespeare's name remains a phenomenon for which there is no comparable example found in a real name. Consequently, many anti-Stratfordians consider the hyphen a red flag signifying that Shakespeare was a made-up name, a *nom de plume* used to represent an unnamed gentleman.

A CRYPTIC ALLUSION

In class-conscious Tudor England, being a published writer, particularly of plays or verse, was not a sign of good breeding. While commoners published openly for gain, the gentleman circulated his work privately in manuscript among friends, a practice consistent with the aristocrat's image of the accomplished dilettante. Gentlemen-amateurs were particularly careful to distance themselves from the profession of dramatist "lest anyone might think that they would demean themselves to provide plays regularly for the commercial theatres" (Bentley, *Dramatist*, 14). While such double standards and conflicting values are alien to twentieth-century readers, they reflect the prevailing social codes in Shakespeare's England.

Cryptic or satiric allusions to Shakespeare are therefore of particular interest to the anti-Stratfordian who suspects that an aristocrat's works were published under a pen name. If most allusions to Shakespeare were encoded or ambiguous, they would lend weight to the theory that "William Shakespeare" was the pen name of a gentleman of rank.

John Davies of Hereford, a poet and writing master, wrote a verse about Shake-speare, spelled with a hyphen. The epigram was published in *The Scourge of Folly* in 1610–11, although its date of composition is not known.

To our English Terence Mr. Will: Shake-speare.

SOME say good *Will* (which I, in sport, do sing)
    Had'st thou not played some Kingly parts in sport,
Thou hadst been a companion* for a *King*,
And, been a King among the meaner sort.
Some others rail; but rail as they think fit,
Thou hast no railing†, but, a reigning‡ Wit:
    And honesty *thou sow'st, which they do reap*,
    So, to increase their Stock *which they do keep.*
                    (Davies, 2:26)

Anti-Stratfordians theorize that the hyphenated Shake-speare signifies a pseudonym, and in this instance the sobriquet, "our English
Terence," reinforces this theory. Terence was known in ancient Rome
as a comic dramatist, but he was also accused of taking credit for the
plays of aristocratic authors Scipio and Lælius.

    Terence's reputation was well-known to the Elizabethans. In Roger
Ascham's *The Scholemaster* (1570), we read that "it is well known by
good record of learning, and that by Cicero's own witness, that some
Comedies bearing Terence['s] name were written by worthy Scipio
and wise Laelius" (G. G. Smith, 1:28). *The Scholemaster* was reprinted
in 1579 and 1589. In his *Essays*, published in French in the 1580s
and translated into English by John Florio in 1603, Michel de Montaigne made reference to Terence's reputation:

And if the perfection of well-speaking might bring any glory suitable unto
a great personage, *Scipio* and *Lelius* would never have resigned the honor
of their Comedies, and the elegancies, and smooth-sportfull conceits of the
Latin tongue, unto an African servant: For, to prove this labor to be theirs,
the exquisite eloquence and excellent invention thereof doth sufficiently de-
clare it: and *Terence* himself doth avouch it: And I could hardly be removed
from this opinion. It is a kind of mockery and injury, to raise a man to

---

*Companion. A colleague or partner. After the Fortune theatre burned down in
1621, John Chamberlain wrote that "those poor companions are quite undone."
Some of Chamberlain's other letters reveal a "half-hostile, half-tolerant" attitude toward the theatre, and "to the players themselves he applies the somewhat contemptuous terms 'fellows' and 'companions' " (see J. Q. Adams, 284; Chamberlain, 1:
21).

†*Rail.* To utter abusive language; to brag or boast.

‡*Reigning.* Ruling, in the sense of exercising authority, but also used in the pejorative
sense to describe disease or trouble (e.g., "reigned a great pestilence").

worth, by qualities mis-seeming his place, and unfitting his calling, although for some other respects praise-worthy; and also by qualities that ought not to be his principal object. (199)

Terence was recognized, therefore, as both a writer of comedies and as a Battillus or agent who took credit for the plays of "great personages." So Davies's title could be read as a reference either to a comic playwright or to a Battillus. However, the epigram itself contains no explicit *literary* praise.

In fact, biographers find Davies's poem almost incomprehensible. According to Stanley Wells, the sobriquet *Terence* "seems to imply that Davies thinks of [Shake-speare] primarily as a comic playwright, but goes on to speak of him in cryptic terms as an actor." After quoting the first four lines, Wells concluded that the verse is "too vague to be helpful" (26). Most biographers find the epigram similarly vague and enigmatic and there is no agreement on any one interpretation. Peter Thomson thought that the epigram "could as well allude to a shared memory of participation in mock-king ceremonies" (62). Anti-Stratfordian Alden Brooks compared the line about "kingly parts in sport" with the anecdote in Manningham's diary about William "the Conqueror" seducing one of Burbage's conquests (339).

Davies's "cryptic" and "vague" epigram is therefore unlike one that he addressed "To acute Mr. John Marston," in which he explicitly mentions that Marston's play, "Thy *Mal-content*, or Malcontentedness, / Hath made thee change thy Muse" (2:33), or one to satirist Joseph Hall, who

> made them groan between thy Satire's fangs,
> As if (for sin) of hell they felt the pangs.
> For that and for the wit, the grace, the art,
> Thou show'st in all that from thy pen doth part. (2:33)

or this to John Donne: "(I know) thy pen hath rightly done, / Which doing right makes bright the name of Donne" (2:18). Unlike these verses, Davies's epigram to Shake-speare is not straightforward, and it does not explicitly praise literary achievement. Nothing in the text of the epigram suggests that "Terence" was intended to identify Shake-speare as a playwright. Therefore, the title is just as likely intended to signify a pseudonym.

Equally importantly, this epigram does not confirm that Davies knew "Shake-speare" personally. First of all, the verse reads like hearsay ("Some say . . ."). Secondly, the epigram is no. 159 in a series, and it is instructive to examine the title in its original setting. Compare it with the titles that precede and follow it:

155. To my worthily-disposed friend Mr. Sam. Daniel.

156. To my well-accomplish'd friend Mr. Ben. Johnson.

157. To my much esteemed Mr. Inego Jones, our English Zeuxis and Vitruvius.

158. To my worthy kind friend Mr. Isacke Simonds.

159. To our English Terence Mr. Will: Shake-speare.

160. To his most constant, though most unknown friend; No-body.

161. To my near-dear well-known friend; Some-body.

162. To my much-regarded and approved good friend Thomas Marbery, Esquire [followed by others to his dear pupil, his beloved friend, and so on].

Davies addressed epigrams to people he obviously recognized as personal friends ("my worthily-disposed friend") until he got to "our English Terence." Even in no. 157, before he addresses Jones as "our English Zeuxis and Vitruvius," he personally addresses him as "my much esteemed Mr. Inego Jones." Why did Davies suddenly switch gears and shift to the editorial "our," dropping any personal salutation to introduce an epigram that is supposed to be complimentary?

Or is the epigram *un*complimentary? If Davies intended his verse to be complimentary, why did he write cryptic copy? Was Davies keeping his distance because he was writing topical satire? What are we to make of the fact that Davies placed the Shake-speare epigram next to enigmatic verses to "No-body" and "Some-body"? In contrast to his straightforward and personal poems, Davies's epigram to "our" Shake-speare comes across as deliberately cryptic and impersonal.*

Davies's other poems suggest that he was in the thick of literary and dramatic London, and his epigrams, including this one, have all

*Davies wrote other epigrams about players, including two in which the initials "W.S.R.B." appear in the margin. Most commentators assume that those initials stand for William Shakspere and Richard Burbage. Both epigrams are riddles that have defied attempts at deciphering.

the earmarks of contemporary gossip. Davies's reference to "kingly parts" may describe some episode involving Shakspere in his capacity as one of the King's Men. Shakspere's last recorded onstage appearance was in *Sejanus* in 1603, and the last King's Men document in which his name appears is the red cloth record of 1604. Of his shareholding in the Globe, the Blackfriars, and the King's Men, only his shareholding in the Globe is documented after 1608. His name is conspicuously missing from a 1610 lawsuit against the principal partners in the Blackfriars.*

Davies's epigram, published in 1610–11, may suggest that Shakspere's separation from the King's Men and the Blackfriars partnership was not an entirely amicable parting of the ways. Here is an unorthodox paraphrase:

To our own Battillus, Master Will: Shake-speare

Scuttlebutt has it, my good man Will (which I, just for fun, put in verse), that had you not behaved arrogantly, as though you were the king of the troupe, you would still be a member of the King's Men, and a king among those lowly actors and shareholders.

Some of the King's Men criticize you, as they believe you crossed them. But you don't get abusive. You keep your condescending sense of humor. And you have inspired the King's Men to value honesty, because now they take more care to hold on to their "Stock" of playbooks ("which they do keep"). They do not want them sold out from under them by someone dishonest like you. So now they will guard their assets ("increase their stock"), and it will be more difficult for you to get your hands on them, since you are no longer a partner in the operation.

This interpretation is just another guess, but it has one advantage: It allows for a coherent reading of the entire epigram, not just three or four lines. It is also one of several allusions that can be seen to point to Shakspere as an under-handed play broker.

The very ambiguity that renders Davies's "Shake-speare" epigram almost incomprehensible to today's readers suggests uncomplimentary satire. Furthermore, Davies put a distance between himself and "our" Shake-speare, whether he knew Shakspere personally or not. In any case, Davies joins the roster of literary men who wrote cryptically about Shakspere when the dramatist was supposedly at the

---

*In 1910, Wallace discovered the 1610 Keysar suit that names the principal Blackfriars shareholders, but Shakspere's name is missing.

height of his literary fame. His choice to hyphenate the name suggests that he regarded Shake-speare, like Terence, as a pseudonym or someone who took credit for the plays of aristocratic playwrights.

JONSON'S CAST LISTS

When Jonson published several plays in his collected *Works* (1616), each play was accompanied by a list of actors who had appeared in the premiere performances many years before. In the list for the 1598 premiere of *Every Man In His Humour*, "Will Shakespeare" heads the first column of actors. In this list, Jonson spelled Shakespeare the way we usually see it today. In the list for the tragedy *Sejanus*, first performed in 1603, "Will. Shake-Speare" heads the second column of names. Here, the name is spelled not only with the hyphen, but also with a capitalized second syllable, thereby suggesting more emphatically a made-up name denoting action. Recall that Jonson was the first to suggest that Shakespeare's name denoted action, that it seemed "to shake a Lance / As brandish'd at the eyes of Ignorance." Even so, Jonson's spelling of "Shake-Speare" is ambiguous. It could signify the pseudonymous playwright or the actor-agent who took credit for them. But throughout his works, Jonson was usually deliberate in his spelling, his punctuation, and his treatment of names.

According to a recent Jonsonian biographer, David Riggs, Jonson's education and cultural outlook included the notion that " 'the reason of the name' frequently contained additional layers of meaning that held the clue to a person's true identity" (16). Jonson paid particular attention to the spelling of his own name:

A keen observer of visual signs might have noticed that [Jonson] had changed the spelling of his own last name by dropping the medial "h" in the first syllable of "Johnson." The new spelling was not a casual aberration: Jonson would employ it in his printed works and private correspondence for the rest of his life. Names meant a great deal to Jonson. Like his master Camden, he was a keen student of etymologies and family nomenclature, and often ruminated on the relationship between names and persons. (Riggs, 114)

Historians regard Jonson as a meticulous editor, particularly with respect to his *Works*, and it cannot be a mere accident that he spelled "Shake-Speare" as he did. Variations in his spellings of other actors' names are less extreme, for example, Sly and Slye, or Tooley and Tooly.

There is additional cause for suspicion. These two lists mark Jonson's first mentionings of Shakespeare. Although Jonson's *Works* had been in production for some time, it was not published until 1616, the year that Shakspere died. In other words, during Shakspere's lifetime, Jonson wrote *nothing* about Shakespeare—or Shakspere—by name, a surprising omission for an author who wrote explicitly about most of his literary colleagues. Moreover, when Jonson wrote down the name in the *Sejanus* cast list, he spelled it "Shake-Speare." It is a unique spelling.

SOGLIARDO

Even during the years when he remained silent on "Shakespeare," Jonson satirized Shakspere. The first parody turns up in his 1599 play *Every Man Out of His Humour*, in which he lampooned Shakspere as a social climber with a new coat of arms.

Recall that in 1596, the first of two applications for John Shakspere's coat of arms was rejected. Neither application appears to have been executed. By 1599, however, the application had evidently been resubmitted to the College of Arms and approved, because in that year a third application was lodged, this time to combine the Shakspere and Arden arms. An initial grant of arms was a prerequisite to the 1599 application. Most biographers assume that it was William who initiated, bankrolled, and lodged the applications. William was first referred to as a "gentleman" in 1601.*

However, a number of statements made in the applications were not accurate, and the author of *The Heraldry of Shakespeare* inferred that John himself had little or nothing to do with the applications:

---

*John Shakspere had been entitled to use the honorific title of "Mr." ever since his election as high bailiff, but by 1601 he was entitled to burial as a "gent." However, the Stratford register lists the burial of "Mr. Johannes Shakspeare." So either John was less interested in the coat of arms and social rank of "gent." that went with them than was his son, or, less charitably, he may have been unaware that he was entitled to use the arms. One might speculate that to the unsophisticated, William might try to pass *himself* off as newly armigerous, although technically, he would have been entitled to style himself an armigerous gentleman only after his father had died (see Lewis, 1:212). John Shakspere was buried 8 September 1601. William Shakspere was styled "gent." in a deed for the Globe theatre property dated 7 October 1601.

"What is strange about all this is that by 1580 John Shakespeare was involved in debt, and in 1586 had ceased to be an Alderman. It, therefore, appears that we have to deal here with the ambitions of William, who, though still an actor, was buying property in his native town, and preparing to settle down as a landed proprietor" (Rothery, 13). In other words, William Shakspere exaggerated or misrepresented some of his father's qualifications on the application in order to further his own social ambitions.

In *Every Man Out of His Humour*, the character Sogliardo purchases a coat of arms with the motto "Not Without Mustard," which is viewed as a parody of the Shakspere "motto" "Not Without Right." Despite his misgivings, Chambers included the Sogliardo scene as one of the "Contemporary Allusions" to Shakspere.

PUNTARVOLO: What? has he [Sogliardo] purchased arms, then?

CARLO: Ay, and rare ones too: of as many colors, as e'er you saw any fool's coat in your life . . .

. . . .

SOGLIARDO: . . . By this parchment, gentlemen, I have been so toil'd among the Heralds yonder, you will not believe, they do speak in the strangest language, and give a man the hardest terms for his money, that ever you knew.

. . . .

I can write myself gentleman now, here's my patent, it cost me thirty pound, by this breath. . . . how like you the crest, sir?

PUNTARVOLO: I understand it not well, what is 't?

SOGLIARDO: Marry, sir, it is your Bore without a head *Rampant*.

PUNTARVOLO: A Boor without a head, that's very rare!

CARLO: Ay, and rampant, too: troth, I commend the *Herald's* wit, he has deciphered him well: A swine without a head, without brain, wit, anything indeed, ramping to gentility.

. . . .

CARLO: . . . it's a hog's cheek, and puddings in a pewter field, this.

SOGLIARDO: How like you them, signior?

PUNTARVOLO: Let the word [motto] be, *Not without mustard*; your crest is very rare, sir. (III.ii.27–30; III.iv.46–87)

The words "Non sanz droit" appeared on Shakspere's first two applications for a coat of arms (figs. 1 and 2). "Non sanz droit"

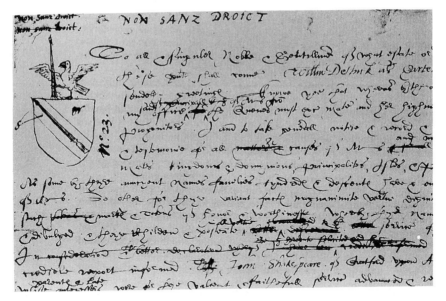

Figure 1. The first application (1596) for John Shakspere's coat of arms. The comma in "Non, sanz droict" in the upper left corner suggests that the herald wrote "no, without right" to signify rejection of the application. Perhaps the herald was instructed by an outraged applicant to put the words back in as a fine-sounding "motto," comma removed, over the main part of the application before resubmitting. *Courtesy of The Cleveland Public Library.*

translates as "Not without right," which, we are told, was Shakspere's motto, but one that was never used. The "motto" does not appear with the coat of arms carved on Shakspere's funerary monument, nor does it appear on the third application of 1599 (fig. 3).

Note that the phrase "Non sanz droit" in figure 1 was crossed out and then written again. Also note the comma after the word "Non" on the first application. Why was this comma inserted? It disrupts the meaning.

The College of Heralds initially rejected Shakspere's application, and "Non, sanz droit," comma *included*, translates literally as "No, without right"—words of rejection. Jonson was probably ridiculing someone who mistook the herald's rejection as his new fine-sounding motto.

"Not without mustard" stands as a joke on its own (Nashe had

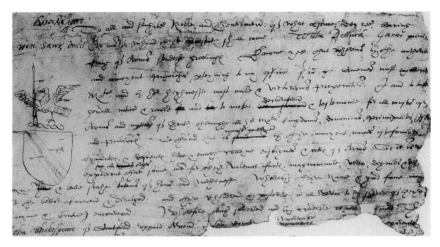

Figure 2. The second application (1596) for John Shakspere's coat of arms. The words "Non sanz droit" appear here without the comma, suggesting perhaps that the applicant had prevailed in his wish to adopt the phrase as a "motto." However, the "motto" does not appear subsequently where one would reasonably expect to see it, that is, on the third application (fig. 3) or with the coat of arms on the Stratford monument (fig. 16). The fact that it was never used, not even on the third application, strongly suggests that the phrase was no motto after all. *Courtesy of The Cleveland Public Library.*

used the phrase several years earlier in *Pierce Pennilesse*), but Jonson seems to have been extending a joke. The "boar" in Sogliardo's coat of arms puns on the word "boor," in the sense of an ill-bred fellow. In his 1598 *A Worlde of Wordes*, Florio defined a boor as synonymous with "a clown" or a "rude fellow" (see the entry for "grossolano"). Boor's or Peasant's Mustard had been identified by 1548 and was included in John Gerard's *Herbal* encyclopedia, along with Clown's or Knave's Mustard (described as "too bad for honest men"). Jonson may also have been thinking of the line "his wit's as thick as Tewksbury Mustard" from *2 Henry IV*.

Sogliardo announces that he "will be a gentleman, whatsoever it cost," and goes on to complain about his negotiations with the heralds ("they do . . . give a man the hardest terms for his money" [I.ii.3; III.iv.50]). Jonson was probably satirizing someone who bribed the heraldry office. Bribes were "customarily offered in lieu of . . . proof" of lineage or other qualifications (Riggs, 116), and Shakspere's ap-

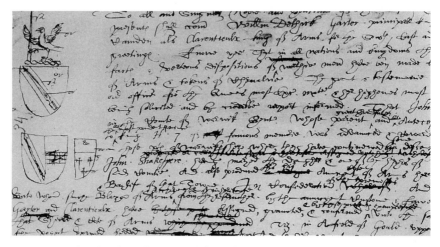

Figure 3. The third application (1599) for the Shakspere coat of arms. Permission was requested to combine an Arden coat of arms with Shakspere's, but no such "exemplification" is known to have been approved. *Courtesy of The Cleveland Public Library.*

plication trumped up several principal qualifications. The claim that John Shakspere had married an Arden "heir" was technically true, inasmuch as anyone who inherits anything is an "heir." But Mary Arden's father was not a "gent." or "esquire," as one of the applications claimed. He "was described during his lifetime as husbandman," at best, one of the "principal farmers" from Wilmcote (Eccles, *Warwickshire*, 85; Poole, 315). Shakspere then tried to lay claim to the arms of the illustrious Ardens of Park Hall, to whom no familial connection has been found. In fact, erasures on the third application show that the heralds were "search[ing] for a suitable coat-of-arms already in existence to represent Mary Arden" (De Groot, 62; see also Eccles, *Warwickshire*, 85–86), which is to say casting around for a design they thought they could get away with. The claim that John was descended from a worthy warrior who had defended Henry VII was another fabrication, as was the claim that he was worth £500. Documents show that John Shakspere's financial decline began in the mid-1580s and continued through the 1590s. He sold off his wife's small inheritance, was exempted from certain taxes, was sued many times for debt, and in 1592 stayed away from church "for fear of process for debt." Nor did his tenure as bailiff of Stratford in 1568–69 correspond with the term of office specified in the application.

Clearly, the applications were filled with errors, exaggerated claims, and misrepresentations.

In a formal complaint of 1602, the York Herald accused the heraldry office of granting arms to undeserving base persons (see fig. 4), John Shakspere being one of twenty-three such persons. Irregularities in these cases included the misappropriation of somebody else's design, combining arms when no original arms existed in the first place, and inventing one's lineage. The official response to the complaint concerning Shakspere defended only those claims in the application that were true—that John Shakspere had been a bailiff, did marry someone named Arden with a small inheritance, and had proposed a design that did not encroach on those of other families. The herald avoided mentioning that John Shakspere's valiant ancestor was an invention, that he had married a farmer's daughter rather than an Arden heiress of Park Hall, and that he was not worth £500. Nothing further came of the complaint, but the complaint and the misrepresentations in the application itself lend weight to the suggestion that a bribe compensated for any deficiencies.

Nevertheless, most biographers brush aside the fraudulent claims and put an almost gallant spin on the affair. For example, Jonathan Bate defended the College of Heralds' decision, since John Shakspere qualified as a "magistrate . . . who had married a daughter and heir of the highly respectable Arden family" and was a man of substance (*Genius*, 70). Other actors, notably Augustine Phillipps and Thomas Pope, were also accused of making fraudulent claims in their applications to the heraldry office. Ironically, nobody has tried to make excuses for them.

MORE ABOUT SOGLIARDO

When he wrote the Sogliardo satire, Jonson supposedly knew full well he was ridiculing the poet and playwright who was at that time riding the crest of popularity for *Venus and Adonis, Love's Labour's Lost,* and other works. Several passages in *Every Man Out* demonstrate Jonson's familiarity with *Henry IV*. Yet the parody did not so much as hint that Jonson recognized Shakspere as a fellow playwright or poet. It suggested instead that Jonson was contemptuous of Shakspere's pretensions.

In *The Shakespeare Claimants*, H. N. Gibson wrote that "there can be little doubt that Shakspere was one of [Jonson's] victims in *Every*

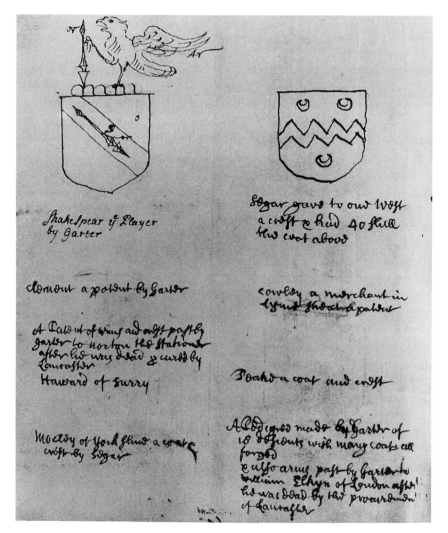

Figure 4. "Shakespeare ye Player by Garter." When discussing Shakspere's coat of arms, many biographers reproduce this document, supposedly in the hand of the York Herald, Ralph Brooke. Around 1602, Brooke complained about certain coats of arms, Shakspere's included, granted to undeserving recipients. However, Lewis (2:342–43) and, more recently, Matus (79–81) have shown this document to be a transcript from the early eighteenth century, rather than Brooke's original. Matus maintained confidence in the integrity of the transcript, but part of it may be an eighteenth-century fabrication. Notice that the handwriting under the Shakspere arms differs from that on the rest of the page. In addition, the grant application, the complaint, and the subsequent defense all related to John's qualifications, not William's, so a more plausible subscription, if the York Herald really wrote it, would have read "Shakspere ye glover by Garter." *Courtesy of The Cleveland Public Library.*

Man Out of His Humour. The play was produced soon after he had been granted his coat-of-arms, and Sir Puntarvolo's words 'Not without mustard' are an obvious parody on Shakspere's actual motto 'Non sanz Droict'. Moreover there are various suggestions in what we know of him that Shakspere did aspire to gentility" (44; see also Honan, 228). Critics such as Gibson who accept this satire of Shakspere's social ambitions stop short of examining Sogliardo as an extended caricature, probably because of Sogliardo's intellectual and social shortcomings. For example, one character in the play comments that the coat of arms fits Sogliardo perfectly, because the design shows "a swine without head, without brain, wit, anything indeed, ramping to gentility," but Gibson did not comment on that description. Yet any biographer who acknowledges Sogliardo as a direct hit at Shakspere is stuck with the entire scene, indeed, with the rest of the play.

In fact, Sogliardo is such a laughingstock that some biographers have introduced the satire only to dismiss it. Schoenbaum rejected it because the design of the arms was different and Sogliardo was not parodied as an actor per se. But Sogliardo boasts of having performed the role of the horse in a morris dance and is later set up as a pseudo scholar who excels at imitation. His supposed "specialty" is imitating clowns, specifically one who can "so peerlessly imitate any manner of person for gesture, action, passion, or whatever . . . especially a rustic, or a clown . . . that it is not possible for the sharpest-sighted wit (in the world) to discern any sparks of the gentleman in him, when he does it" (V.ii.41–46). Sogliardo is so impressed with himself that he never catches on that he *is* a clown.

Sogliardo reveals his ignorance of heraldry when he says that the heralds "speak in the strangest language." By the time this satire was written, the author of *Venus and Adonis, The Rape of Lucrece*, and *Merry Wives* had already displayed a sophisticated knowledge of heraldry. And in another scene, Sogliardo is ridiculed for his untrained "natural" intellect:

CARLO BUFFONE: Faith, gallants, I am persuading this gentleman [Sogliardo] to turn courtier. He is a man of fair revenue, and his estate will bear the charge well. Besides, for his other gifts of the mind, or so, why, they are as nature lent him 'em, pure, simple, without any artificial drug or mixture of these two threadbare beggarly qualities, learning and knowledge. (IV.viii.8–14)

Sogliardo accepts this insulting speech as a compliment and remains oblivious to the plotting going on right in front of him. Buffone and his cohorts set him up as the butt of a practical joke, persuading Sogliardo to woo a lady at court. When they brief the lady, they describe Sogliardo's nephew, Fungoso, as "kinsman to justice Silence." Silence is the justice of the peace who gets drunk, bursts into song, and is eventually carried off to bed in *2 Henry IV*.

Gullible, conceited, and unaware that the lady is expecting to be entertained by a gentleman *pretending* to be a boor, Sogliardo tries to charm her in his pidgin Italian, Latin, and Spanish, pitching the following dubious woo: "*Bona roba, quæso, que novelles? que novelles?*" (V.ii.70–71). Sogliardo thinks he is saying "Fine lady, I beg you, what is the news?" But "bona robas" translates colloquially into "fine showy wantons," "smarter whores," or, "as we say, good stuff" (Shakespeare, *Arden, 2 Henry IV*, 96 n). The lady herself is taken in by Sogliardo's pretensions, buys into the ruse, and sees through the setup only when Sogliardo's rough-hewn hands prove him to be no gentleman after all.

Think back to the "gentleman player" in *Groatsworth of Wit*. He and Sogliardo are arrogant, moneyed, and well-dressed, but the opposite of genteel. Both are would-be gentlemen who misuse foreign phrases, can't pronounce them, and don't know exactly what they mean. The "gentleman player" had done a hitch as a puppet master. One character thinks of Sogliardo as "Captain Pod," who was a puppet master (see *Bartholomew Fair*, V.i). Sogliardo owns property in the country and lodges at an inn when in London. By 1599, Shakspere had purchased New Place in Stratford.

Just as a trio of characters in *Groatsworth* satirizes Shakspere, so *Every Man Out of His Humour* introduces a trio of similar characters. Like Shake-scene, Sogliardo is a pretentious upstart. Like the miserly Ant, Sogliardo's brother Sordido hoards grain, an activity viewed as a "branch" of usury (C. T. Wright, 195). Recall also that Shakspere was cited for hoarding grain during the famine of 1598, the year before the play was produced. Sordido's son, Fungoso, is obsessed with turning up in the latest courtier's fashions; the player in *Groatsworth* dresses so impressively as to be taken for a man of "great living" and boasts of his £200 wardrobe.

In his introduction to Jonson's plays, Felix E. Schelling described the *Humour* plays as containing "two kinds of attack, the critical or generally satiric, levelled at abuses and corruptions in the abstract;

and the personal, in which specific application is made of all this in
the lampooning of poets and others, Jonson's contemporaries" (Jonson, 1:xiii). Some commentators see Sogliardo and others as stock
characters with no particular targets in mind. Some anti-Stratfordians
view the Sogliardo-Sordido-Fungoso triumvirate as three faces of
Shakspere.

Chapter Six

Monstrous Theft

The implication of plagiarism begins in Shakespeare's own life-time and is carried forth into the succeeding century as tradition. . . .
. . . Each discrete example is capable of being explained away by orthodox scholarship, but individually and cumulatively they pose a serious problem.

—Richmond Crinkley, "New Perspectives on the
Authorship Question" (519)

Contemporary allusions to Shakespeare and his works were written in an age of regulation and strict social codes. All forms of communication were subject to censorship. Even personal papers were not immune from scrutiny. In 1595, one correspondent testified in a letter that "to write of these Things are dangerous in so perilous a Time" (E. H. Miller, 175). While professional writers learned to encrypt potentially sensitive material in allegory or ambiguous language, they were nevertheless constantly at risk. Ben Jonson and Samuel Daniel were summoned to explain themselves before the Privy Council when their plays (*Sejanus* and *Philotas*) were perceived as political commentary on certain members of the nobility. The authorities threw Jonson in prison for his part in writing *The Isle of Dogs*, and again for *Eastward Ho!* During the latter imprisonment, Jonson feared his nose and ears would be slit or cut. In 1610, an ambassador reported that a cousin to King James "complain[ed] that in a certain comedy the play-wright introduced an allusion to her person. . . . The play [Jonson's *Epicene*] was suppressed" (Clare, 169). In 1606, a correspondent wrote that there "was much speech of a play in the Blackfriars, where, in [playwright John Day's] *The Isle of Gulls,* from the highest to the lowest, all men's parts were acted of two diverse nations: as I understand sundry were committed to Bridewell [prison]" (Hillebrand, "Child," 194 n). Hillebrand attributed the ill fortunes of those involved to "the dangerous business of satirizing public personages and events" (194). In 1603, George Chapman defended himself in Star Chamber against accusations that a play he had written libeled real individuals (Sisson, *Lost*, 60). In 1599, the Archbishop of Canterbury ordered that several books of topical satire be destroyed; in the same injunction, satirist Thomas Nashe was prohibited from publishing again.

In such conditions, Elizabethan writers routinely used cloaking devices to obscure their meaning, and there are abundant acknowledgments of that practice. John Marston wrote "whilst my satiric vein / Shall muzzled be," and Thomas Freeman wrote "Why am I not an epigrammatist? / I write in covert, and conceal their names / Whose lives I burden with some bitter jest" (Marston, *Works* 3:325; *Tudor Poetry*, 531). In *The Arte of English Poesie* (1589), we read that traditionally, a satirical epigram "had no certain author that would avouch them, some for fear of blame, if they were over saucy or sharp" (G. G. Smith, 2:57).

In addition to obscuring their satirical targets, writers took care to avoid offending highly placed personages. The prologue to *The Hector of Germany* announced:

> What pen dares be so bold in this strict age
> To bring him while he lives upon the stage?
> And though he would, Authority's stern brow
> Such a presumptuous deed will not allow.
> (Bentley, *Dramatist*, 176)

In 1601, the Privy Council ordered an injunction against the players at the Curtain Theatre who "represent upon the stage . . . the persons of some gentlemen of good desert and quality that are yet alive under obscure manner" (Chambers, *Stage*, 4:332). In this case, an indiscretion provoked an official response.

However, there were fewer constraints on writers who satirized mere commoners, as long as the content was politically innocuous. Similarly, panegyrics, even to the élite, were written with less restraint. It is therefore striking to discover that so many contemporary allusions to Shakespeare are impersonal or obscure.

GULLIO AND SHAKESPEARE

The *Parnassus* plays were performed at Cambridge University between 1598 and 1602.* These satires contain explicit allusions to Shakespeare as well as some indirect hits. However, the allusions to Shakespeare, the poet, are sufficiently unlike those to the actor as to suggest two different individuals. In addition, the authors lampooned another pretentious paymaster, and this one is fond of quoting Shakespeare's poetry.

One editor summarized the second part of the trilogy:

we are entertained with another adventure of Ingenioso's with a new patron-gull, named Gullio. This personage . . . is convinced that he possesses all the talents to which man can be heir, but does not care to weary himself by exercising them too frequently. Accordingly he invites Ingenioso to supply him with verses to palm off as his own, "written in two or three divers veins—Chaucer's, Gower's, and Mr. Shakespeare's." . . . But Gullio becomes an intolerable nuisance with his overweening conceit, and Ingenioso after quarrelling with him . . . betakes himself to London. (Smeaton, xvii–xviii)

Gullio "is convinced that he possesses all the talents to which man can be heir," which is to say that he is the very model of a *Johannes Factotum*. Like Sogliardo, he is conceited and uncultured but well-dressed in a satin suit, and his apparel is worth, by his own reckoning, £200. Recall that the "gentleman player" in *Groatsworth* owns a wardrobe that would "not be sold for two hundred pounds." Gullio keeps quarters in Shoreditch, the theatre district. According to posthumous gossip, Shakspere had lived in Shoreditch. Like Shake-scene,

---

Parnassus 1 is *The Pilgrimage to Parnassus* (1598–99), *Parnassus 2* is *The First Part of the Return from Parnassus* (1599–1600), and *Parnassus 3* is *The Second Part of the Return from Parnassus* (1601–2).

Gullio is a conceited paymaster of scholars and is associated with lines improvised from Shakespeare.

Gullio appropriates literary scraps for his own use, and Ingenioso dismisses Gullio as a blowhard who "never spoke [a] witty thing but out of a play." Gullio hires Ingenioso to write for him in the style of other poets and then "corrects" his work. Like the "gentleman player," Gullio is another arrogant paymaster who makes a fool of himself by thinking himself a scholar. Like Shake-scene, he fancies himself able to bombast out verse ("it was but a sudden flash of my Invention"), improvising speeches patched together from contemporary pamphlets, *Venus and Adonis, Romeo and Juliet*, and textbook Latin ("thus extempore into English"). He mangles foreign phrases and quotations but thinks he has a command of scholarly works. He is condescending to those who trained at the university, brazen enough to palm off someone else's poetry as his own, and ignorant enough to dismiss Edmund Spenser and Geoffrey Chaucer while rhapsodizing indiscriminately over Shakespeare's poetry:

GULLIO: Let this duncified world esteem of Spencer and Chaucer, I'll worship sweet Mr. Shakspeare, and to honour him will lay his *Venus and Adonis* under my pillow, as we read of one (I do not well remember his name, but I am sure he was a king) slept with Homer under his bed's head. (IV.i.1200–1205)

Gullio boasts that he is "very lately registered in the rolls of fame, in an Epigram made by . . . Weever." At first glance, it would seem that Gullio could not have read John Weever's epigrams very carefully. Weever's disreputable "fat Gullio" was hanged at Tyburn and left "freely to worms for their meat." So it might seem that the *Parnassus* authors were ridiculing Gullio as an egotist ignorantly basking in fat Gullio's infamy. But Gullio goes on to say, "I merit his praise." Weever had no praise for fat Gullio. However, in the same collection, Weever wrote a sonnet in praise of "honey-tongued" "Gulielmum Shakespeare." The name "Gullio" is derivative of "gull"—a gullible dupe or fool, but "Gullio" is also derivative of the Latin for William, "Gulielmum." Gullio was shamelessly accepting Weever's tribute to "Gulielmum Shakespeare."

The *Parnassus* authors also made fun of Gullio's social pretensions when they have him say, "as I am a gentleman and a scholar," which was one of many "meaningless oaths" made by disreputable types who would swear on various expendable grounds (Shakespeare, *Arden, 2 Henry IV*, 45 n). Similarly, when Sogliardo states his intention to "be a gentleman whatsoever it cost," Carlo Buffone advises him to "affirm, upon your credit, as you are a true gentleman" (I.ii.3, 49).

Finally, a scene between Gullio and Ingenioso has led some orthodox critics back to *Groatsworth*. Ingenioso's parting words to Gullio are delivered when he is safely out of earshot: "Farewell base carle [churl] clothed in a satin suit." J. B. Leishman, editor of the *Parnassus* trilogy, wondered whether these lines are "a reminiscence of . . . the 'upstart Crow.' " He also pointed out that Gullio, like Sogliardo, is a "countryman who is ambitious to become a courtier." Sogliardo had been advised to " 'pretend alliance with Courtiers and great persons,' " and Gullio likewise exaggerates his court connections (205, 188). Ingenioso also bids farewell to Gullio's "base brokers post." Gullio is a broker, and Leishman supposed that he deals in secondhand clothes, or frippery.*

A GRAVER SUBJECT

The *Parnassus* plays contain scenes that deliver conflicting impressions of Shakespeare, and they suggest that the authors were careful not to associate the poet Shakespeare with writing plays. In the final installment, Ingenioso and Judicio poke fun at poets, playwrights, and pamphleteers. Christopher Marlowe and Ben Jonson are censured as play-makers. Then it's Shakespeare's turn:

INGENIOSO: *William Shakespeare.*

JUDICIO: Who loves not *Adon's* love, or *Lucrece's* rape,
His sweeter verse contains heart-robbing lines,
Could but a graver subject him content,
Without love's foolish lazy languishment. (I.i.300–304)

The authors of this speech expected their audience to be familiar with the dedication prefixed to *Venus and Adonis,* which promised a future "graver labor." Most biographers identify *The Rape of Lucrece* as that "graver labor," but apparently it was not grave enough for Judicio, whose speech raises a significant issue.

Judicio lampooned Shakespeare in the company of playwrights

---

*Cast-offs or leftovers, often used to describe secondhand or out-of-date clothes.

Marlowe and Jonson, so why did he associate Shakespeare only with narrative poetry? Reading the lines about Adonis and Lucrece, you would never guess that at least twenty Shakespeare plays had been written by 1601. The omission is indicative of a mystery detected by E.A.J. Honingmann, who found that prior to 1598, nearly all the allusions to Shakespeare were confined to commentary on his poetry, not his plays (*Impact*, 28). By 1601, not only *Hamlet*, but also most of the history plays had been written. Surely the history plays were of some "graver" merit; they certainly were not about "love's foolish lazy languishment."

Samuel Schoenbaum's explanation for the omission was that "evidently word of *Julius Caesar* and *Henry V* had not yet found its way to cloistered Cambridge. Or, being plays, perhaps they did not count" (*Documentary*, 133). Neither explanation is credible.

The savvy Cambridge crowd had to know that the poet of *Venus and Adonis* had also written serious plays. The *Parnassus* plays themselves quote some of them, including the famous opening line from *Richard III*. By 1601, *Richard III* was one of nine plays in print with Shakespeare's name on them. *Palladis Tamia*, a book that named twelve plays by "William Shakespeare" had been in print since 1598, so Shakespeare should have been fair game as a playwright as well as a poet. Yet when the *Parnassus* authors spoofed Shakespeare, the writer, they spoofed him only as a poet, not as a playwright.

Elsewhere in *Parnassus 2*, the playwrights spoofed Shakespeare's poetry and plays but stopped short of identifying Shakespeare as the dramatist. In fact, when Gullio mangles a line from *Romeo and Juliet*, Samuel Daniel gets the authorship credit:

GULLIO: Pardon, fair lady, though sick-thoughted Gullio makes amaine [exceedingly] unto thee, and like a bold-faced suitor 'gins to woo thee.

INGENIOSO: We shall have nothing but pure Shakespeare, and shreds of poetry that he hath gathered at the theatres.

GULLIO: Pardon me my mistress, as I am a gentleman, the moon in comparison of thy bright hue a mere slut, Anthony's Cleopatra a black browed milkmaid, Helen a dowdy.

INGENIOSO: Mark, Romeo and Juliet: o monstrous theft. I think he will run through a whole book of Samuel Daniel's.

GULLIO: Thrice fairer than myself, thus I began. (I.i.983–95)

In this scene, Gullio first appropriates some lines from *Venus and Adonis*, which Ingenioso attributes to Shakespeare, even though Gullio later tries to pass them off as his own ("thus I began"). Then Gullio recites some shredded lines from *Romeo and Juliet*, which Ingenioso attributes to Daniel. In 1597, a corrupt edition of *Romeo and Juliet* was published without author attribution, but in 1598, Francis Meres attributed the play not to Daniel, but to Shakespeare. In 1599, the year of *Parnassus 2*, a corrected edition of *Romeo and Juliet* was published, but again without author attribution. However, in a sonnet published in that same year, Weever attributed *Romeo* to Shakespeare.

In his sarcastic asides, Ingenioso tells the audience that Gullio is plagiarizing Shakespearean poetry and play lines. Then he associates the "book" of *Romeo and Juliet* with Daniel. Is his misattribution deliberate? Or is Ingenioso trying to guess the identity of the dramatist? Whatever the answer, the *Parnassus* authors are pointing to confusion over the authorship of *Romeo and Juliet*, while making fun of a conceited plagiarist.

"OUR FELLOW SHAKESPEARE"

In *Parnassus 3*, two actors impersonating tragedian Richard Burbage and comedian Will Kempe address the student audience, handing out advice on how to succeed as playwrights. It is this scene from the *Parnassus* trilogy, more than any other, that magnifies the disparity between the Shakspere/Shakespeare *personas*:

BURBAGE: A little teaching will mend these faults, and it may be besides they will be able to pen a part.

KEMPE: Few of the university pen plays well, they smell too much of that writer *Ovid*, and that writer *Metamorphoses*, and talk too much of *Proserpina and Jupiter*. Why here's our fellow *Shakespeare* puts them all down—ay, and *Ben Jonson* too. O that *Ben Jonson* is a pestilent fellow, he brought up *Horace*, giving the Poets a pill, but our fellow *Shakespeare* hath given him a purge that made him bewray [betray, defile, or malign] his credit.

BURBAGE: It's a shrewd fellow indeed. (IV.iii.1764–74)

Most biographers quote this passage, scratch their heads about the "purge" that Shakspere gave to Jonson, and move on. There was a "theatre war" going on in 1600–1602, with Jonson, John Marston, and Thomas Dekker taking potshots at each other in a series of plays. In Jonson's *Poetaster*, for example, the Marston character was administered a "pill" to make him regurgitate his pompous-sounding vocabulary. Biographers speculate that Shakspere got tangled up in the crossfire, but are unable to agree on what his "purge" was. Yet there is much more information provided by this short scene.

Kempe's speech tells us that some of the university wits had written for the stage. Biographers acknowledge that Shakspere had no university training, so Kempe's opening lines about writers "of the university" cannot be directed at Shakspere. But Kempe further describes those university writers as smelling "too much of that writer *Ovid*, and that writer *Metamorphoses*," comically unaware that *Metamorphoses* was one of Ovid's poems. According to anti-Stratfordian Sir George Greenwood,

The whole scene is evidently a burlesque in which the poor players are held up to ridicule for their ignorance generally, and for their distorted notions as to "Shakespeare" and Jonson in particular. Moreover, the fact that Kempe urges as objections to "the University pen" those very things which might particularly be urged as objections to Shakespeare, viz. his Ovidian thoughts and utterances, and his uncalled for classical allusions, seems to show that Master Kempe, as conceived by the [*Parnassus* playwright], had no very clear idea of what he was talking about. (*Restated*, 328–29)

Leishman suggested that the *Parnassus* authors intended Kempe's praise of Shakespeare as a playwright to possess "precisely the same significance as Gullio's admiration for Shakespeare" (337), in other words, worthless praise from a fool.

Kempe delivers an error-ridden and mixed message about Shakespeare. He describes dramatists whose works are saturated with Ovid, and Shakespeare would be the first to qualify. He also describes those dramatists as university educated, so Shakspere of Stratford would be immediately *dis*qualified. Since it is Shakespeare himself who is most saturated with Ovid, Kempe's speech makes no sense unless Shakspere and Shakespeare were two different individuals.

Kempe makes fun of "Shakespeare," who puts down, that is, is condescending or insulting to, the university-trained playwrights. Recall Shake-scene's arrogance thinking himself able to extemporize lines as good as those by the professional writers. Sogliardo looks down his nose at scholars ("I scorn to live by my wits" and "[if] he be a scholar, you know I cannot abide him"). Recall Gullio's ignorant dismissal of poets ("Let this duncified world esteem of Spenser and Chaucer") and his condescension toward his hired scholar, Ingenioso. Kempe's "fellow Shakespeare" in *Parnassus 3* is consistent with the recurring Shakspere *persona*, the egotistical "master" who puts down the very scholars whom he exploits.

The character of Burbage then dubs Shakespeare "shrewd," a term associated more with business dealings than with playwriting. In Shakespeare's day, the word had the more pejorative connotation of "a malignant, malicious fellow . . . given to railing" (Leishman, 338; *OED*, def. 13a). The language used to describe "our fellow Shakespeare" resonates with that in the "Upstart Crow" diatribe.

The *Parnassus* plays are filled with plenty of deliberate and specific satires, but when it comes to identifying "Shakespeare," they convey two distinctly separate images. Scenes and dialogue that deliver Shakspere, Kempe's arrogant theatrical colleague, are distinct from those that deliver Shakespeare, the admired poet. And the admired poet is safely distanced from the profession of playwriting.

A few years before the *Parnassus* plays were written, a book called *Polimanteia* was published over the initials "W. C." One section of the book is titled "A letter from England to her three daughters, Cambridge, Oxford, [and] Inns of Court" in which "W. C." critiques the "children" or students trained by these institutions. In a discussion of university writers appear the marginal notes, "All praise / worthy. / Lucrecia / Sweet Shak- / speare / Eloquent / Gaveston. / Wanton / Adonis." The notes are adjacent to a tribute to the poetry of, not Shakespeare, but Daniel. In addition, C. M. Ingleby suggested that this marginal reference had led one scholar to "the rather hazardous conclusion that Shakespeare was a member of 'one (or perhaps more) of the English Universities' " (*Allusion*, 23). The *Parnassus* authors led their audience to the same hazardous conclusion.

MORE FARDELS AND GROOMS

One passage from *Parnassus 3* brings us full circle to the rude groom of *Groatsworth* and the "fardle on footback" phraseology. Some of the lines are particularly reminiscent of *Groatsworth*:

STUDIOSO: But is't not strange these mimic apes should prize
    Unhappy Scholars at a hireling rate?
    Vile world, that lifts them up to high degree,
    And treads us down in groveling misery.
    England affords those glorious vagabonds,
    That carried erst their fardels on their backs,
    Coursers to ride on through the gazing streets,
    [Sweeping] it in their glaring Satin suits,
    And Pages to attend their masterships:
    With mouthing words that better wits have framed
    They purchase lands, and now Esquires are named.
PHILOMUSUS: What e'er they seem being even at the best,
    They are but sporting fortune's scornful jest.
STUDIOSO: So merry fortune's wont from rags to take
    Some ragged groom, and him a gallant make. (I.ii.1918–32)

These aspiring playwrights are as unhappy in their poverty as they are resentful of "mimic apes" who hire them. These mimic apes make more as their paymasters than they do, wear expensive clothes, and have become landowners. Edward Alleyn and Shakspere were the two most successful "apes" at that time who could therefore fit the description. Ian Wilson, a vigorous defender of traditional biographies, accepted the speech as a lampoon that illustrates "the sheer spite felt in certain quarters about Shakespeare and his fellows in their heyday, and also represents one of the best arguments against those who cannot accept that Shakespeare could have been a mere low-born player who achieved dramatic success through his and his fellows' own efforts" (271). Wilson used the scene to validate Shakspere's "dramatic success," but notice again that this scene does nothing to validate the mimic ape *as a writer*. It validates him as a ragged groom who hires scholars, who—like the "gentleman player"—used to carry his fardle on footback, and who has made enough money to style himself a gallant.

WHO IS LESBIA?

Back to Gullio. In *Parnassus 2*, Gullio hires Ingenioso to write Shakespearean-sounding verses with which to woo his lady at court. The lady's name is Lesbia, and she turns up again alongside another allusion to a Shakespeare play.

Marston's satire, *The Scourge of Villainy*, was published in 1598, about a year before *Parnassus 2*. Marston seems to have had the same Lesbia-wooer in mind:

> I set thy lips abroach, from whence doth flow
> Naught but pure *Juliet* and *Romeo*.
> Say, who acts best? *Drusus*, or *Roscio*?
> Now I have him, that ne'er of aught did speak
> But when of plays or Players he did treat.
> [He] hath made a commonplace book out of plays,
> And speaks in print, at least what e'er he says
> Is warranted by Curtain *plaudities*.
> If e'er you heard him courting Lesbia's eyes;
> Say, (Courteous Sir) speaks he not movingly
> From out some new pathetic Tragedy?
> He writes, he rails, he jests, he courts, what not,
> And all from out his huge long scraped stock
> Of well penned plays. (3:372–73)

Marston could be describing Gullio, who "never spoke [a] witty thing but out of a play" and misquoted *Romeo and Juliet*. When Marston's play-scavenger speaks, he likewise lifts lines out of *Romeo and Juliet*. He serenades Lesbia with speeches lifted from some new tragedy. He borrows lines when he writes, criticizes, recites, jokes, or woos—for whatever purpose—lines all borrowed from his stockpile of plays by other writers.

Marston's satirical book took aim at people, city life, and current events, and was among those banned by the archbishop of Canterbury in 1599. Apparently, Marston had stepped over the line.

Regulations and custom prompted writers of topical satire to be ambiguous and to avoid explicit commentary about "public personages." Consequently, those who brought Shakspere or Shakespeare onto the printed page stayed within certain bounds. Contemporary portrayals of Shakspere or Shakespeare—whether the pretentious paymaster and entrepreneur, or the respected poet—are ambiguous.

Chapter Seven

The "Poet-Ape"

> The image of the crow and the accusation "beautified with our feathers" suggest that Shakespeare may even have been filching with his pen.
>
> —Jonathan Bate, *The Genius of Shakespeare* (15)

Writers satirized Shakspere in print, not as a budding playwright and not as "gentle Shakespeare," but as a braggart, opportunist, paymaster, or pretentious gentleman by purchase. Several allusions pointed to a paymaster or broker who traded in plays and costumes, including secondhand clothes or frippery. Some allusions further suggested shady dealings or callous conduct.

SO BOLD A THIEF

As we have seen, authors generally wrote their satires in code to avoid undesired consequences. Like other writers, Ben Jonson wrote his satires using allegory, riddles, epithets, conflated or fragmented images, and the plural instead of the singular—anything but plain English. In his play *Poetaster* (1601), Jonson ridiculed pretentious actors who have acquired coats of arms:

They forget they are i' the *statute* [most actors were legally classified as vagabonds], the rascals; they are *blazon'd* there, there they are trick'd, they and their pedigrees; they need no other *heralds*. (I.ii.53–54)

Shakspere was one of several shareholders who had adopted (or appropriated) coats of arms, and biographers assume he was included in the barb, if not singled out by name.

Another of Jonson's nasty digs at actors was in language similar to that in *Groatsworth*:

> Are there no players here? no poet-apes,
> That come with basilisk's eyes, whose forked tongues
> Are steeped in venom, as their hearts in gall? (Ind. 35–37)

Jonson used the term "poet-ape" as a derogatory epithet for untrustworthy, callous actors.

However, one particular "poet-ape" rated an entire epigram. In the following poem (Epigram 56), dated sometime between 1595 and 1612, Jonson cast himself as the victim of a dishonest play broker. A few traditional commentators have identified this scoundrel as William Shakspere.

On Poet-Ape

> Poor POET-APE, that would be thought our chief,
>   Whose works are e'en the frippery of wit,
> From brokage is become so bold a thief,
>   As we, the robbed, leave rage, and pity it.
> At first he made low shifts, would pick and glean,
>   Buy the reversion of old plays; now grown
> To a little wealth, and credit in the scene,
>   He takes up all, makes each man's wit his own.
> And, told of this, he slights it. Tut, such crimes
>   The sluggish gaping auditor devours;
> He marks not whose 'twas first: and after-times
>   May judge it to be his, as well as ours.
> Fool, as if half eyes will not know a fleece
>   From locks of wool, or shreds from the whole piece?
>   (8:44–45)

Note that this "Poet-Ape" assumed that most readers or playgoers were too indiscriminate to care much about authorship attribution.

But how would any of Jonson's more discriminating readers have known *whom* he was satirizing?

Jonson gave his readers a surprising amount of information with which to make an identification. This "Poet-Ape" is an actor and play broker who began by procuring plays with lapsed copyrights ("the reversion of old plays"). He then became "so bold a thief," which could mean that he passed off someone else's work as his own; sold plays that were not his to sell; or adapted or vulgarized someone's work for popular consumption. The "Poet-Ape" is well-known enough to "be thought our chief," probably because he is a prominent actor-shareholder and paymaster. He has established some "credit in the scene," which seems to refer to his financial resources. He has certainly made money ("grown / To a little wealth") and is brazen and arrogant. The list of successful actor-brokers who could fit this description would be quite short.

Edward Alleyn was an actor and an entrepreneur, made a great deal of money, and might therefore be considered a contender. Henslowe's papers show that Alleyn procured plays for resale, but those records suggest above-board transactions (Foakes and Rickert, 204, 205, 273–74). In addition, Jonson's derogatory opinion of this "Poet-Ape" conflicts with his opinion of Alleyn, to whom he wrote a laudatory epigram, deeming it only fitting and "just, that who did give so many Poets life, by one should live." Alleyn has not been nominated as the "Poet-Ape."

After Alleyn, Shakspere was the wealthiest actor-shareholder of his day, and an early critic, George Chalmers, identified Shakspere as the "Poet-Ape." His proposal utterly outraged the Jonsonian editor, William Gifford:

Mr. Chalmers will *take it on his death* that the person here meant is Shakspeare! Who can doubt it? For my part, I am persuaded, that Groom Idiot in the next epigram is also Shakspeare; and, indeed, generally, that he is typified by the words "fool and knave," so exquisitely descriptive of him, wherever they occur in Jonson. (Jonson, 8:173)

Gifford's sarcasm may have been misplaced.

According to A. C. Partridge, "it has been suggested that Shakespeare may be the victim, because of the words 'would be thought our chief' in the first line" (64). H. N. Gibson tentatively conceded that Jonson "may have had Shakspere in mind when he wrote" (45).

Richmond Crinkley, formerly director of programs at the Folger Shakespeare Library, was more specific: "William Shakespeare is being accused of passing off the writing of others as his own. . . . Among contemporaries who referred to him, there is a shared view that William Shakespeare appropriated the work of others" (519). Crinkley then identified Shakspere as the epigrammatic *"Poet-Ape."*

"On Poet-Ape" is one of several uncomplimentary epigrams in a cluster, and some of Jonson's other epithetic characters read like clones of Shake-scene, Sogliardo, Gullio, and others. "Groom Idiot" is so inept at reading verse that he "laughs in the wrong place." "Person Guilty" shows no artistic judgment, appears to have appropriated some of Jonson's verse, and Jonson threatens to reveal his identity. "Play-wright" has coarse manners and steals Jonson's material. Certainly, somebody with no scruples and no taste was pirating Jonson's works.

"Don Surly" is pretentious, puts down Jonson's verses, and "aspire[s to] the glorious name / Of a great man, and to be thought the same." "Don Surly" hopes to be mistaken for someone far above his station, to be recognized *by name* as somebody else. Surly's ambition has something in common with Sogliardo's preoccupation with the sound of his name:

SOGLIARDO: but, for my name, Signior, how think you? will it not serve for a gentleman's name, when the Signior is put to it? Ha?

CARLO: Let me hear: how is't?

SOGLIARDO: *Signior Insulso Sogliardo*: methinks it sounds well.

CARLO: O excellent! tut, an[d] all fitted to your name, you might very well stand for a gentleman. (I.ii.6–12)

John Florio's Italian-English dictionary, *A Worlde of Wordes*, was published in 1598, the year before *Every Man Out of His Humour*, and Florio defined "Sogliardo" as "a mocker, a scoffer, a quipper . . . a jester. Also slovenly, sluttish, or hoggish. Also . . . a gull, a fool, a flatterer." He defined "Insulso" as "unsavory, foolish, without . . . wisdom." Yet Sogliardo thinks his name "sounds well."

Sogliardo, as well as "On Poet-Ape" and other epigrams were scathing satires, so Jonson played it safe and left out the names of his targets. But he left one other clue with which to identify the "Poet-

Ape." Jonson wrote only three poems in the form of a Shakespearean sonnet. "On Poet-Ape" is one of them.*

A CONJECTURAL NARRATIVE

Scholars who have identified Shakspere in the satirical portraits have done so tentatively or piecemeal. As Richard Dutton put it, biographers "are bedevilled by the need always to show Shakespeare in the best possible light" (*Life*, 3), and no biographer can confront the composite of documentary evidence *and* satirical allusions† without discrediting their gentle Shakspere. The caricatures, most of which have been identified by orthodox commentators as probable parodies of Shakspere, are convincing only to the extent that they are consistent with the documentary evidence. The characters of Shake-scene, the "gentleman player," the miserly Ant, Gullio, Sogliardo, and now the "Poet-Ape" are consistent. They reinforce one another, and taken together, they corroborate the Shakspere of factual record.

Biographers have faced the seemingly insurmountable problem of constructing a "unified impression" of Shakspere's life based on the documentary evidence. Stanley Wells admitted that "new documentary evidence still occasionally turns up, and new theories are constantly devised in the effort to construct a coherent narrative on the basis of what is known" (5). There would seem to be scope, then, for attempting a narrative of Shakspere's life based on the unexpurgated evidence. If one integrates the historical documents with the satirical allusions, a more plausible history of Shakspere's professional career begins to take shape. What follows is largely conjectural, but the character profile and narrative sketch are better supported by the evidence than is the traditional story.

By the mid-1580s, Shakspere has put his "natural wit" to work and debuted as an Elizabethan busker, reciting extempore in the village

---

*The other two are for Nicholas Breton's *Melancholic Humors* (1600) and "An Epigram, to the house-hold" (1630) pleading for his allotment of wine from court.
†R. Simpson thought that the character Post-hast in the play *Histrio-Mastix* (ca. 1593–99) also represented Shakspere (2:89). Helgerson tentatively suggested the same identification (*Forms*, 203), while anti-Stratfordian A. Brooks was sure of it, describing Post-hast as "a would-be poet" who "wishes to pass as a gentleman," who "furnishes plays, plays of others," "haggles over prices," "can only rhyme extempore doggerel, . . . misuses words, shows business acumen, and controls the disposal of the company's playing apparel" (69, 71).

squares of Warwickshire and neighboring counties. As he tours the provinces, fardle on footback, he expands his repertoire and styles himself a "country author passing at a moral," improvising or patching together old morality plays. He finds that puppet shows are suited to his carnival-barker style, and the minimal investment quickly pays dividends.

Late in 1587, at age twenty-three, Shakspere leaves Stratford for London, a city rich with opportunities. He takes lodgings in Bishopsgate, strategically located near the Shoreditch theatres and the Cross Keys, another performing venue. He freelances in and around the theatre districts or at fairs, producing more puppet shows and recycling his old morality plays. He converts his daily receipts into more money by making high-interest loans, just as his own father had. In 1592, he makes a £7 loan in Cheapside to John Clayton.

As a confident huckster for his own entertainments, he attracts the attention of local actors and is hired to perform bit parts in the public theatres. He parlays the temporary onstage work into additional backstage assignments, instinctively gravitating to potentially money-making projects. He vends refreshments or tends the gate as cashier (gatherer). Shakspere thrives on juggling one assignment after another, playing each angle, using each project as an opportunity to find a better one. He invests in theatrical paraphernalia and costumes (his "share in playing apparel"). He turns a profit by renting them out to various companies and starts to wear some of the more elegant satin clothes himself.*

Shakspere bargains for old playbooks with derelict or nonexistent copyrights. He also sees a potential for profit in commissioning plays and brokering them to performing companies or publishers, sometimes both. He has no scruples about hiring needy scholars and paying them a mere pittance. He knows he can buy cheap and sell at a higher price. He has a head for negotiating, and he is solvent, so he can afford the time it takes to drive a harder bargain.

At this point Shakspere has done nothing more literary than cobble together morality stories, improvise street theatre, and put scholars on his payroll, but he starts to think of himself as a sophisticated

---

*A 1614 document shows that the Lady Elizabeth's company penalized shareholders who wore their stage costumes outside the theatre, and a year later Henslowe was accused of appropriating some of their costumes (Chambers, *Stage*, 2:256–57, 250). Compare to MacIntyre and Epp: "Alleyn and Christopher Beeston bought, sold, and perhaps rented out costumes, as did [two others in the 1570s]" (278).

dandy. He can afford to dress better than most writers or actors, and since he can quote—or misquote—lines from plays, he easily impresses the less discriminating. Shakspere begins to think that he is a better judge of plays than the dramatists whom he hires, and his arrogance starts showing up in his performances.

Shakspere's London career as a stage performer is already handicapped by his Warwickshire accent and his lack of cultural sophistication. While his memory is good, his ear for dialogue is not. Consequently he never learns his parts exactly as written but takes pride that his ad-libs are better than the original lines. Shakspere's penchant for extemporaneous speechifying irritates both the actors and the playwrights, especially since he thinks that he can improve upon the text ("supposes he is as well able to bombast out a blank verse"). He is arrogant enough to think that his hamming and ad-libbing make him "the only Shake-scene in a country," so his fellow actors are faced with a dilemma. Shakspere is a liability onstage, but he is too valuable to the company as a source of financing and as the agent for some of the more prolific playwrights, such as Robert Greene. Their solution is to make few demands on him as a thespian, an arrangement that suits everybody.

Shakspere's minimal production assignments give him the flexibility to juggle other freelance projects or travel to Stratford, even during peak performance periods. In that sense, his professional conduct was not unlike Alleyn's, who "was a good deal occupied with other business, and was occasionally away from town without any interruption in the activities of the [acting] company" (Greg, "Alleyn," 11).

A CONJECTURAL NARRATIVE: SHAKSPERE THE SHAREHOLDER

In 1594, Richard Burbage and several others organize the Lord Chamberlain's Men. A share in the Lord Chamberlain's Men "in 1596 was probably the same as the Admiral's, at £50" (Gurr, *Companies*, 94), so the original share price was likely about the same. Shakspere provides a portion of the investment capital and probably finances some of the other investors' shares at interest, as Henslowe occasionally did at the Rose. Shakspere views his theatrical shareholding as a strictly commercial investment, and one which now gives him some prestige through his status as servant to a nobleman. His acting "skills" are, in this case, virtually irrelevant.* In the 1594–95 court payment to the Lord Chamberlain's Men, Shakspere is named in his capacity as financier.

Shakspere is as valuable to his company as Henslowe is to the Admiral's Men. Like Henslowe, he provides both working capital and tangible assets. His theatrical wardrobe is essential to the Chamberlain's Men and, on the side, Shakspere trades in frippery, brokering some of the secondhand clothes. His playbooks are equally valuable to the company as it starts to build its repertory.†

Always on the lookout for a likely deal, Shakspere continues to commission scripts and scavenge old plays to build up his "stock of well-penn'd plays," which he brokers to acting companies. Perhaps like the obscure Rowland Broughton a few decades earlier (Benbow, 5–6), he formally contracts to supply plays over a period of time. Perhaps like Robert Keysar, a shareholder in the Blackfriars theatre, he loans money to playwrights who agree to provide him with plays. (Keysar sued playwright Thomas Middleton for defaulting on a loan, and one historian supposed that Keysar was acting in that instance "not as a money broker but as a theatrical manager, and that the debt [Middleton] incurred was in earnest of a play" [Hillebrand, "Brood," 35–36].) In any event, he eventually concludes that he can get away with outright piracy. Shakspere progresses from brokering to "become so bold a thief," occasionally filching a play and selling it to a publisher or rival acting company, sometimes both. Having worked backstage, Shakspere knows when and where to intercept a playbook.

Shakspere's underhanded play-brokering can be detected in the publication circumstances of *Locrine*. An annotation scribbled on its title page by Sir George Buck, the Master of the Revels, tells us that in 1595, "some fellow" made off with an old court play (cf. the

*According to Bentley, "the contribution of capital as well as histrionic ability was a requirement for the sharers [shareholders] in those dramatic companies. . . . In at least one known instance, and one suspects in others, the money was more important than the acting ability" (*Player*, 32).

†Dutton suggested that "Shakespeare contrived somehow to hold on to [the early Shakespeare playbooks]" that were produced by other companies prior to the formation of the Lord Chamberlain's Men, adding that "such a collection of plays would have been ideal collateral for a founding shareholder" (*Life*, 49). Likewise, Gurr supposed that "the transfer of [Shakespeare's] entire early corpus of plays to the new Chamberlain's suggests that he had been in the habit of keeping ownership of the plays in his own hands" ("Patrons," 169). Of course, Dutton and Gurr both assumed that Shakspere also wrote these plays.

"Poet-Ape," who began with "the reversion of old plays") and published it as "Locrine . . . Newly set forth, overseen, and corrected By W. S."* Chambers supposed it "not inconceivable that Shakespeare or some other W. S. may have been asked to 'oversee' the printing" (*Facts*, 1:537), even though nobody thinks that Shakespeare ever took the trouble to oversee the printing of his own plays.

Other published plays suggest that Shakspere took credit for producing them. *Locrine* was only the first of several plays published between 1595 and 1616, subscribed with the initials "W. S." (as were *Thomas Lord Cromwell* and *The Puritan*) or falsely attributed to "William Shakespeare" (as were *The London Prodigal* and *A Yorkshire Tragedy*). When acquaintances confuse Shakspere with the published author of *Venus and Adonis* or later, *Love's Labour's Lost* or *Richard III*, Shakspere brazenly accepts the compliments.

A CONJECTURAL NARRATIVE: SHOREDITCH TO SOUTHWARK

In 1596, James Burbage is exploring alternative performing venues for the Chamberlain's Men, because the lease for the Theatre is due to expire. The company falls behind in its rent. Shakspere capitalizes on the landlord problems by investigating alternative performance venues, both with Burbage and independently.

Shakspere hedges his bets by splitting his time between the Shoreditch and Southwark theatre districts. He takes lodgings in Southwark and begins to negotiate with Francis Langley, who has built the Swan theatre. In November a writ is issued for the arrest of Shakspere and Langley, who are ordered to post bond to keep the peace. Four months later, Langley signs up Pembroke's Men to perform at the Swan, following a brief playing season there by an unnamed company which may have been, as Hotson and others have suggested, the Chamberlain's Men. In February 1597, James Burbage dies, leaving the problem of a future permanent performance venue unresolved.

However, Shakspere's various business ventures are going well. In the spring of 1597, he travels to Stratford to complete his purchase

---

*According to this annotation, Charles Tilney had written a tragedy on the subject of Locrine some years previously. Buck thought that *Locrine* was the same play and that "some fellow hath published it." Tannenbaum judged Buck's annotation a forgery, but others including Greg, Eccles, Bald, and more recently, Nelson, have accepted it as genuine.

of New Place and then returns to London. In early May, he obtains an elaborate exemplification of his purchase in the court of Westminster. By this time the Chamberlain's Men are performing back at the Curtain in Shoreditch, but conditions are far from stable. To make matters worse, all the theatres close in late July and are not reopened until October. Most of the company leave to tour the provinces in August. During the company's absence Shakspere brokers some plays to publishers, among them *Richard II* and *Romeo and Juliet*. As the company's play-purchasing agent, he is well-placed to wheel and deal with publishers.

Shakspere then returns to Stratford to finish setting up his household at New Place. He invests in grain, which he stockpiles as famine conditions force up the price.* He also scouts for other real estate investments, and some Stratford neighbors try to secure financing from him to alleviate their own cash flow problems.

Early in 1598, he is back in London. The plan for an indoor theatre at Blackfriars has derailed, and attempts to negotiate a new lease with the Theatre landlord have failed. By the end of 1598, the company tears down the Theatre, hauls it in pieces across the river, and uses the timbers to build the Globe in Southwark.

Shakspere invests in the enterprise, probably assisting in the financing arrangements for Cuthbert and Richard Burbage, whose fortunes suffered a reversal when their father died. In 1597, their "inherited capital was locked up in their father's abortive attempt to create the new hall," that is, the Blackfriars (Gurr, *Companies*, 107). According to historian Irwin Smith, "to his son Richard . . . [James Burbage] left his costly and profitless investment in the Blackfriars; to his son Cuthbert he left the Theater, now tottering under a load of lawsuits and debts" (173). The timbers of the Theatre had belonged to the Burbages, so perhaps that was considered a significant part of their initial investment in the Globe. Otherwise, the Burbages would not seem to have been in a position to finance 50% of the Globe themselves, but they get the money from somewhere, "at interest" (I. Smith, 558). Shakspere is a likely source.

In early 1599, the Globe partnership papers are drawn up. The circumstances at this juncture resonate with the scenario advanced by historian Andrew Gurr (although not quite as he intended):

*Shakspere was one of a number of Stratford residents hoarding grain at this time, and Fox cited the records as evidence of "the importance of Stratford as a market for malt" (*Accounts*, 5:xxiii).

For two years [the Lord Chamberlain's Men] had paid rent for the Curtain, and had lacked a banker or landlord-impresario like Henslowe who could make them loans for new costumes and playbooks while taking his repayments from the daily takings. Now they still lacked finance, but they would be their own landlords. They could, in fact, become their own financiers. (*Companies*, 293)

Shakspere was a company financier, just like Henslowe and Langley.

A CONJECTURAL PROFILE: SHAKSPERE THE ENTREPRENEUR

Shakspere is an entrepreneur who exploits anyone and everyone, including writers. He brokers plays and clothes, cuts all kinds of business deals, and arranges loans at interest. He patches together plays, produces corrupt or vulgarized texts, and pilfers others. Shakspere is also a Battillus to a few courtier writers who sell their written works to him, provided they remain anonymous. Despite some of his shady dealings, he is able to operate successfully for many years because it suits those who need his services, whether as a Battillus, paymaster, broker, or moneylender.

Shakspere comes across as a city slicker on first acquaintance, but his coarse manners and provincial accent soon betray his lack of sophistication. Like Sogliardo, he is prone to exaggerate his court "connections." However, he is so impressed with himself that he remains oblivious to his social and intellectual shortcomings. His ignorance of polished manners and foreign phrases makes him an easy target among those who are initially impressed with him but quickly figure him out.

Shakspere's social gullibility notwithstanding, writers take care not to antagonize him overtly. He is in a good position to negotiate deals with impoverished playwrights, either as their paymaster or as a moneylender, and he can be a callous employer or litigant. Too blatant an attack could prove foolhardy. Henry Chettle passes off his attack on Shake-scene under a dead man's name to avoid retaliation, and others write about Shakspere in ambiguous or vague language.

A CONJECTURAL PROFILE: SHAKSPERE AND
HIS MONEY

Shakspere's professional profile is remarkably similar to that of Philip Henslowe, landlord and impresario of the Rose theatre, whose voluminous papers left Bentley with no doubt about his range of activities. Bentley had concluded there were others like Henslowe operating on rival turfs:

Often, perhaps usually, there were middle men who facilitated the dealings between a company of actors and their writers. The intermediary best known to us now—because his records are the only ones which have been preserved—is Philip Henslowe. His function as play-purchasing agent for the company has often been misinterpreted by modern critics, who are incensed by his commercial attitude toward art and confused by accounting practices which inadequately distinguished his actions as financial agent for Worcester's men or the Lord Admiral's men from his related but independent transactions as pawnbroker, theatre owner, and personal loan agent. (*Dramatist*, 63)

Bentley noted that historians have found some of Henslowe's mercenary dealings unpalatable and his arbitrary commingling of financial activities frustrating. Many of the records that survive for Shakspere are likewise unpalatable and suggest similarly diverse financial activity.

As early as 1592, writers begin to think of Shakspere when they need money. Shakspere is always ready to make a loan and even readier to collect. However, he has no time for deadbeats, and he leaves playwright Robert Greene to die in poverty. By 1598 Stratford residents are also thinking of Shakspere when they need money. Abraham Sturley and Richard Quiney exchange letters on how best to negotiate with him. Quiney wrote the only surviving letter to Shakspere, and it was to obtain financing:

You shall friend me much in helping me out of all the debts I owe in London . . . and if we bargain further you shall be the paymaster yourself.

Quiney is willing to defer to Shakspere as the "paymaster" if he'll arrange financing for £30. The wording suggests that in addition to making loans himself, Shakspere also brokers loans. When Sturley hears that Shakspere will arrange for the hoped-for capital, he writes the equivalent of "I'll believe it when I see it" ("which I will like of as I shall hear when, and where, and how"). In Stratford or in London, Shakspere is viewed as a shrewd operator and a financier.

Shakspere was financially successful. By contrast, most actors and writers lived close to or below the poverty line. According to Bentley, perhaps twenty out of about one thousand actors are "known to have accumulated respectable estates" and those were shareholders who invested well (*Player*, 5–6). A few inherited estates or married well. With the one exception of stage star and impresario Edward Alleyn, who made most of his fortune as a landlord and brothel owner, no actor or dramatist is known to have made as much money as William Shakspere. (Alleyn's wealth far outstripped any others in the profession; he invested over £12,000 in real estate alone.) In one day in 1605, Shakspere invested £440. His will specified over £350 in cash and over £1,000 in real estate and other assets. The only record of income to survive from any theatrical work is the 1595 payment of £20 to the Lord Chamberlain's Men as a whole for performing "Comedies or Interludes."

While it is safe to conclude that Shakspere made money from theatrical investments, even his shareholding does not fully explain his financial history. He bought New Place in Stratford in 1597, three years after he became a shareholder in the Lord Chamberlain's Men, but two years *before* he became a shareholder in the Globe theatre. Obviously, Shakspere had other sources—major sources—of income.

If Shakspere had sold all thirty-seven known Shakespeare plays, he would have earned somewhere between £185 and £350 during his lifetime (the going rate for plays increased from roughly £5 to £10 after James I came to the throne). There is not one record to verify a penny of that alleged income. In the absence of any evidence to show that Shakspere was paid as a writer, one can only speculate on what money he may have made from selling plays, regardless of whether he wrote, vulgarized, or otherwise brokered or "supplied" them. In fact, in the first local report of Shakspere's association with plays, John Ward, vicar of Stratford, wrote (ca. 1661) that "I have heard that Mr. Shakespeare . . . *supplied* the stage with 2 plays every year" (Chambers, *Facts*, 2:249, emphasis added).

Even in the absence of payment records, a few biographers have concluded that Shakspere wrote plays mainly to make money. According to Jonathan Bate, it was "the economic urge which drove Shakespeare to write" (*Genius*, 49). If an Elizabethan were determined to get rich, why would he invest his time in a financially insecure and time-consuming profession when his sidelines were more lucrative? If Shakspere really wanted to make money from writing, why did he do nothing to stop the unauthorized sales of his, or his company's, plays to publishers? He was not otherwise so careless where his vested interests were concerned.

Traditional scholars assume Shakspere made money by writing plays, but they have no records to prove it. Some have supposed that he supplemented his business income by brokering other men's plays. *Locrine* is probably one of those plays. Most biographers, however, attribute the bulk of Shakspere's income to his Globe and Blackfriars theatre shares, commodity deals, tithes, and other real estate investments. Shakspere did not have to write a single word to make any of that money.

EVIDENCE OF HIS GUIDING GENIUS

Shakspere's name figures prominently in documentation concerning the Globe and Blackfriars theatres as well as the Lord Chamberlain's/King's Men. Various Shakespearean authorities have commented on the "honor" of his being singled out for mention, or being listed first in so many of these documents. These authorities generally consider the prominence afforded to Shakspere indicative of his presumed value to the company as principal playwright and guiding genius. For example, a 1599 legal document named "Willielmi Shakespeare *et aliorum*" as being in occupation of the Globe, and Charles William Wallace wrote:

Of peculiar interest is the mention of "William Shakespeare and others," which may fairly be taken as an incidental recognition of Shakespeare's eminence among official residents of the immediate neighborhood. The Commissioners . . . knew the [Globe] theatre and the genius that presided in it. They were men of standing, who, apparently, knew Shakespeare so well for his plays that his name obscured the names of his associates. It was to them, indeed, Shakespeare's theatre. Their source of information was not simply the deeds, none of which thus single out Shakespeare. It is as if they said, "We, the undersigned, personally know William Shakespeare, the dramatist, as the most eminent man among the company who have recently built the Globe Playhouse in our midst." ("Light," 4)

This is one of the more extreme statements, but others, for example, Bentley, have interpreted the evidence along similar lines,

The [1594–95 court payment] record suggests that Shakespeare was one of the leaders in this organization, for when the new company performed before the court in the Christmas season of 1594–1595, payment was made to Richard Burbage, *the principal actor,* Will Kemp, *the principal comedian,* and William Shakespeare. How did the great possibilities offered by this new troupe, destined to become the most famous and most successful in the history of the English theatre, initially affect the writing of *its chief dramatist?* (*Theatre,* 66–67, emphasis added)

Park Honan commented on the 1599 document in which Shakspere et al. were listed as "being in occupation" at the Globe:

Significantly, this implies that in May 1599 Shakespeare was thought to be the most prominent Globe tenant,

while a 1601 deed

lists eighteen tenants including "Richard Burbage and William Shackspeare, gent."—and here *the troupe's leading actor and its regular dramatist* are the Globe's chief tenants. (268–69, emphasis added)

Taken in context, these authorities correlate Shakspere's prominence in theatrical documents with his supposed preeminence as the company's chief dramatist.

In the catalogue of logical fallacies, these interpretations fall under "confusion of correlation and causation." There is, in fact, no reason to conclude that Shakspere was named first because he was the company's playwright. Numerous theatrical documents survive from the time period, so it is possible to analyze them to determine who was listed first or prominently, and why.

Primacy of position generally had nothing to do with a shareholder's artistic contributions, whether as dramatist or performer. Primacy of position was directly related to working capital and business dealings. An early example is found in a 1583 document of complaint concerning Worcester's Men, which stated that the "aforesaid [George] Haysell is now the chief player." Chambers was faced with the problem that while Haysell was "chief player," he was not named in the warrant authorizing Worcester's Men. Chambers reasoned that "there are other cases in which the constitution of a company in the eyes of its lord was not quite the same as its constitution from the point of view of business relations, and I should suppose that *Haysell, who was evidently not himself acting at the time, was the financier of the enterprise*" (*Stage*, 2:222, 223–24, emphasis added).

An earlier theatrical record names James Burbage as one of six fellows petitioning the earl of Leicester. According to William Ingram, "the letter makes it clear that Burbage was already one of the earl's players, and the prominence of his name in the letter—he was the first of the six signatories—has suggested to some scholars that he must have been the leader of the troupe" (*Business*, 111–12).

A lawsuit of 1609 concerning the Children of the King's Revels recites the contractual terms between a principal partner, actor Martin Slater, and his colleagues. One clause expressly concerns the wording on the company patent:

When their patent for playing shall be renewed, the *said Martin Slater his name, with the said Michael Drayton shall be joined therein*, in respect that if any restraint of their playing shall happen by reason of the plague or otherwise, it shall be for more credit of the whole Company that the said Martin shall travel with the Children, and *acquaint the Magistrates with their business*. (Hillebrand, "Child," 223, emphasis added)

Primacy of position in these theatrical documents had to do with finance and management.

Leaders of acting troupes headed up complex operations. These operations included purchasing plays; purchasing and maintaining costumes and props; hiring actors, musicians, seamstresses, and craftsmen; casting; scheduling rehearsals and performances; handling receipts, disbursements, and keeping accounts; representing the company to court officials; obtaining permits and licenses; negotiating contracts; promoting performances; and renting the theatre. Further, when shareholders owned the theatre, one might add to that list what we now call front-of-house management, such as collecting admissions, vending refreshments, and maintaining the building.

Among the shareholders who served in various managerial capacities for their respective companies were Heminges (King's Men), Alleyn (Admiral's Men), Thomas Greene (Queen Anne's Men), and Greene's successor, Christopher Beeston (Queen Anne's and Lady Elizabeth's Men).

Beeston's administrative activities are especially well documented, in part because he ended up being sued for appropriating company assets. In one of the lawsuits, we read about some of Beeston's responsibilities and qualifications:

for that the provision of the furniture [props] & apparel [costumes] was a place of greatest charge and trust and must of necessity fall upon *a thriving man* & one that was *of ability and means.* (Wallace, "Three London," 321, emphasis added)

Liquid assets were a major factor in the assignment of certain responsibilities, and Beeston brought his own working capital to the party. Not surprisingly, his name figures prominently, or first, in relevant theatrical documents as company agent or payee.

Bentley considered the implication of being named first in theatrical documents when examining the administrative career of Beeston's predecessor with the Queen's Men, Thomas Greene. Bentley found that "*there is evidence that Greene was the manager*, at least for the last eight or ten years before his death. His name *heads the list* of sharers in the draft patent for the company probably in 1603 or 1604. He is also *named first* in the company's patent dated 15 April 1609 in the Patent Rolls" (*Player*, 164–65, emphasis added). After Greene died, Beeston assumed his responsibilities.

Shakspere is likewise named first or prominently in company documentation, not because of any presumed creative roles, but *because he had working capital and entrepreneurial skills.* After he retired from the King's Men, it is *not* stage luminary Richard Burbage who replaced Shakspere as first named in company documents. It is business manager John Heminges who heads the lists until his death in 1630, even though he is never considered one of the company's important actors. In fact, historians conclude that Heminges retired from the stage around 1611, and later evidence shows him to have been involved in the landlord operations. In 1634, his son-in-law described him as having been "a principal agent employed in and about the oversight of the building of the said Playhouse [the second Globe of 1614]." The son-in-law had assisted Heminges's negotiations with carpenters (Berry, *Playhouses*, 192).

Heminges, not Shakspere, was the usual payee, either singly or jointly, for the Chamberlain's/King's Men during the years in which Shakspere was active with the company. Heminges's business responsibilities are amply documented in historical records. Richard Burbage also had a head for business, and he and his brother Cuthbert were frequent partners in real estate dealings. According to Gurr, Cuthbert was a nonacting "manager of sorts and investor" who tended to handle the company's real estate or "property management" rather than performance-related activities (*Companies*, 115, 299 n). Still, essential questions remain concerning the structure and delegation of responsibilities for the Chamberlain's/King's Men. By comparing their records to those for the Admiral's Men, one can isolate some critical areas that remain unaccounted for in the Chamberlain's Men's dossier.

In *A New History of Early English Drama*, W. R. Streitberger described the theatrical conditions and transitions that led to the building of the permanent theatres:

Essential to permanent settlement in London was the financial backing to expand the companies' repertories, hire additional actors, commission new scripts, obtain and store costumes, and undertake a host of other expenditures that traveling companies had not encountered. Companies that could not afford to rent a theater or buy costumes, properties, or scripts turned to a financier like James Burbage, or Francis Langley, or—the most famous of them—Philip Henslowe. . . . The company [at Henslowe's Rose theatre] had to pay for scripts, properties, garments, and licensing fees to the Master of the Revels. From 1597 Henslowe regularly met these payments and debited the sums advanced to a running account with the company. He had good relations with the poets and actors, who were frequently in debt to him for small loans, and on occasion he lent the money needed to buy a share in a company and accepted installment payments on it. (344–45)

And like Shakspere, Henslowe "died a wealthy man in 1616" (345).

Henslowe's role as financier for the Admiral's Men and the Rose is well documented,* but comparable financial details for the Chamberlain's Men and the Globe do not survive. Evidence concerning the Theatre in Shoreditch shows that James Burbage was good at using other people's money, especially for the up-front investment. When he died in 1597, he left his sons a legacy of debt, and the Chamberlain's Men's residency at the Curtain would have done little to stabilize their finances. Gurr described their tenancy at the Curtain as "financially a hard time" (*Companies*, 284). So the Burbages were

---

*It is worth noting that both Foakes and Rickert, editors of *Henslowe's Diary* (xxxix n. 4), and Cerasano (248) speculated that Henslowe may have held a share in the Admiral's Men, even though no one supposes that Henslowe ever performed onstage.

unlikely sources of major investment capital in 1598–99. However, Shakspere is known to have had plenty of investment capital at that time.

Heminges's or the Burbages' known business activities during the early history of the Lord Chamberlain's Men do not correspond to those handled by Henslowe. In particular, arrangements for purchasing plays, costumes, and props remain unaccounted for. The company's licensing activities also remain unaccounted for until 1623, when Heminges sought permission to perform *Winter's Tale*. Shakspere's prominence in theatrical documentation and his general financial history, corroborated by the satirical characterizations in *Groatsworth*, *Parnassus*, and "On Poet-Ape," strongly suggest he assumed these roles of financier and purchasing agent for the Chamberlain's Men.

Bentley commented that "a Beeston's Diary would probably offer many parallels to Henslowe's Diary" (*Stage*, 2:364). So might a Shakspere's Diary. Like Beeston, Shakspere had liquid assets and a head for business. Like Henslowe, he was a paymaster of playwrights, a moneylender, and a source of financing. And if the charges in *Groatsworth* and "On Poet-Ape" are anything to go by, Shakspere, like Beeston, developed a reputation for shady dealings.

PLAY POACHER OR PLAYWRIGHT

Thus far, we have examined most of Shakspere's theatrical documentary evidence, as well as some of the more complex allusions. These records reveal an unscrupulous actor-*factotum*, a shareholder, a broker, a braggart with social pretensions, and a moneylender, but not a writer. None of the records examined thus far offers evidence of Shakspere's supposed career as a playwright. Yet to be examined are the literary allusions to Shakespeare.

Chapter Eight

Literary Paper Trails

Most of the professional dramatists of the time are in exactly the same position as . . . Shakspere. There are no records to connect them with authorship, not even a letter to show that they had anything to do with books and writing.
—H. N. Gibson, *The Shakespeare Claimants* (261)

Biographers construct their narratives around documentary evidence. Some types of documentation are of a general character, such as christening, marriage, or tax records. Such records tell us that someone was born or paid taxes, but they do not necessarily tell us about the person's profession. Other types of evidence, however, are specific to a vocation or make incidental reference to an occupation.

Shakspere's biography is presumably about a writer. The documentary evidence left by a writer is different from that left by a doctor, for example, because some personal records are peculiar to the respective professions. Evidence for a doctor might include payments for medical supplies, handwritten prescriptions, records of medical training, or, as in the case of the physician John Hall (Shakspere's son-in-law), medical journals or casebooks found in his house. In other words, some of Hall's personal records reveal what he did for a living. Such records are *personal* in character, because they can be directly linked to Hall himself, and *professional* in character, because they shed light on his vocation. Similarly, a man of letters may be expected to leave behind personal records that reveal his chosen vocation.

Stephen Greenblatt assured his readers that "Shakespeare was quite well-known in his own time as the author of the plays that bear his name" (Shakespeare, *Norton*, 46). However, a reference to Shakespeare, the writer, is not necessarily a reference to Shakspere, the man from Stratford. This chapter examines the Shakespearean literary records to determine which ones, if any, also qualify as Shakspere's personal records and can therefore be admitted into his biography.

PERSONAL PAPER TRAILS

Literary allusions can be personal (reflecting personal acquaintance with the author), impersonal (showing familiarity only with the author's written work or reputation), or ambiguous. Giles E. Dawson touched on the problem of distinguishing between personal and impersonal allusions: "Yet men did talk about Shakespeare and held opinions about him and his writings, and some fifty or sixty persons commented on him or alluded to him in print during the poet's lifetime. Most of these printed allusions, however, are concerned with one or another of Shakespeare's plays or poems; *few speak of the poet himself*; none furnish details about his private life" (Wright and LaMar, 25, emphasis added).

Testing evidence for that personal link is critical but not always easy. If one considered the following tribute to Sir Philip Sidney, what might one safely conclude about the identity of the speaker? Was the eulogy given by a member of his family, a friend, a writer who benefited from Sidney's patronage, or a complete stranger?

Gentle *Sir Phillip Sidney*, thou knewst what belonged to a Scholar, thou knewst what pains, what toil . . . conduct to perfection: well couldst thou give every Vertue his encouragement, every Art his due, every writer his desert: cause none more virtuous witty, or learned than thy self.

But thou art dead in thy grave, and hast left too few successors of thy glory, too few to cherish the Sons of the Muses . . . which thy bounty erst planted.

The writer of these lines was Thomas Nashe (2:12), who was still in residence at Cambridge University when Sidney died in the Lowlands in 1586. Nashe wrote the tribute six years later in *Pierce Pennilesse* without ever having personally met Sidney. He was repeating hearsay, expressing "the common opinion" (D. N. Smith, 2:194). Yet the eulogy could easily be mistaken at first glance as evidence that Nashe had been acquainted with Sidney or had even benefited from his patronage. However, since Nashe's comments show familiarity only with Sidney's writings and reputation, they do not qualify as *personal* evidence. Neither do most book reviews and literary allusions.

In contrast, *personal* literary paper trails provide a direct link to the man holding the pen and could include:

- Records of matriculation or degree, presence during an academic term, or reference to or from a teacher
- Extant books from a personal library, including those with annotations and marginalia; references to books read, borrowed, bought, given, or bequeathed; records of payments for books
- Autograph manuscripts, drafts, presentation copies, and so on
- Surviving letters, inscriptions, notes, and so on, related to the occupation of writing
- Records of payments for writing, or commissions to write
- References in letters, notebooks, lawsuits, and so on, recognizing the profession of the writer
- Prefatory poems to or from other writers, testifying to personal acquaintance, and miscellaneous records associating a writer with other writers as friends or colleagues
- Letters, personal references, or dedications that show a direct and personal link between author and patron
- Personal tributes, eulogies, or memorials at death testifying to the literary profession

If such evidence is extant for other writers of Shakespeare's day, then it will be possible to compare the types of documentation supporting their literary biographies with that for Shakspere's.

ENTER: SHAKESPEARE'S CONTEMPORARIES

Ben Jonson is by far the best-documented writer of his day, so he provides a standard against which to measure other men of letters.* Among the many personal literary paper trails that Jonson left behind are handwritten manuscripts, among them his 1609 *The Masque of Queenes* (fig. 5); personal correspondence; an epigram acknowledging his indebtedness to his mentor, William Camden, who had taught at Westminster School,

> Camden, most reverend head, to whom I owe
> All that I am in arts, all that I know,
> ....
> What weight, and what authority in thy speech!
> Man scarce can make that doubt, but thou canst teach.

and his dedication of *Every Man In His Humour* to Camden "the instructor" for "the benefits confer'd upon my youth"; Henslowe's Diary, showing at least ten payments to Jonson by name, expressly for writing; court records of payments to Jonson "the Poet" for writing masques and plays; a 1630 royal patent to increase his pension for "those services of his wit and pen"; imprisonment for writing *The Isle of Dogs* and *Eastward Ho!*; over 100 books, written in English, Latin, Greek, French, and Hebrew, still extant from his personal library, despite the fact that his first collection was destroyed in a fire; John Selden's 1614 preface to *Titles of Honour* ("I went for this purpose, to see [a book] in the well-furnished Library of my beloved friend that singular Poet Mr. Ben Jonson, whose special Worth in Literature, accurate Judgment . . ."); handwritten marginalia and inscriptions in gift copies of his own works (fig. 6); and burial in Westminster Abbey, followed by a eulogy within three months, and a published collection of commemorative poems six months later.

The preceding represents only a fraction of the documentation surviving for Jonson. Far less survives for his colleagues, but some of their literary activities are documented. A pamphlet, written around 1585 and published in 1606, describes a friendly gathering at which

---

*See the Chart of Literary Paper Trails and notes in the Appendix for documentation of evidence presented in this chapter for Jonson and his fellow writers.

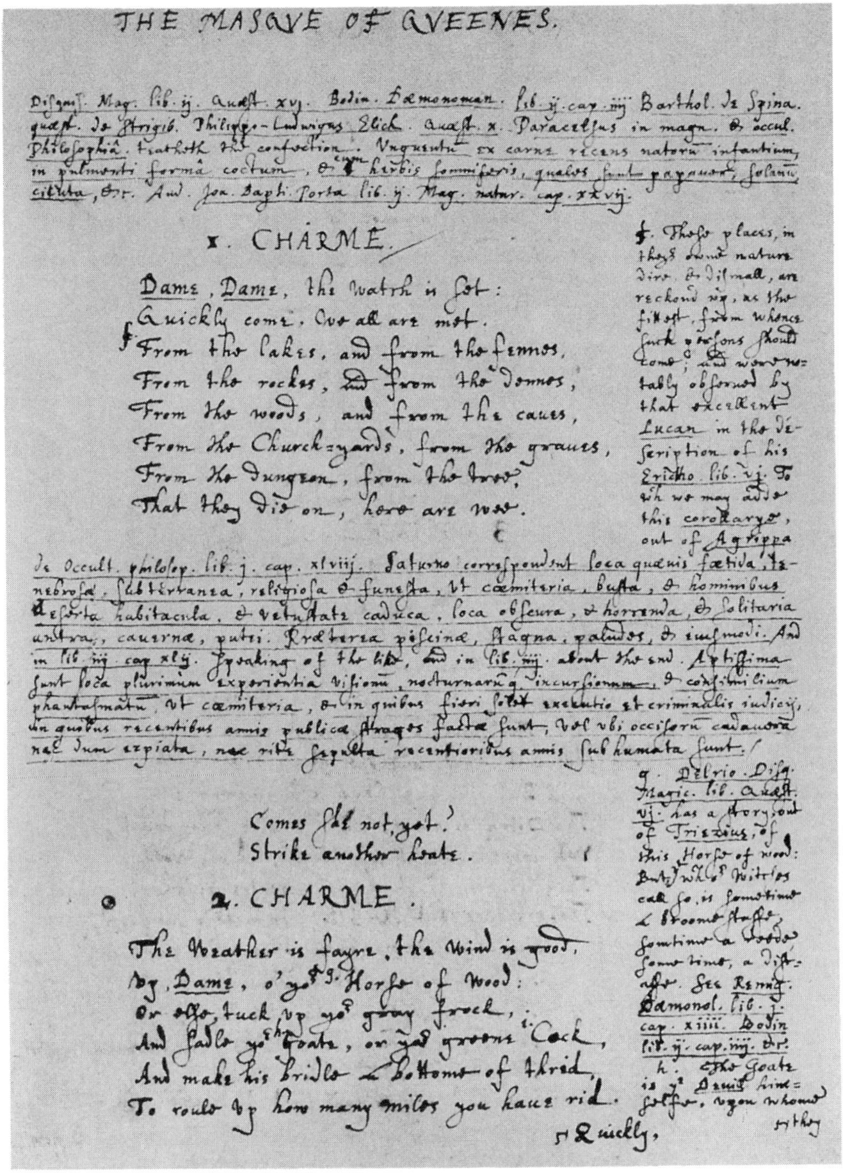

Figure 5. Ben Jonson's handwritten presentation copy of *The Masque of Queenes. Courtesy of The Cleveland Public Library.*

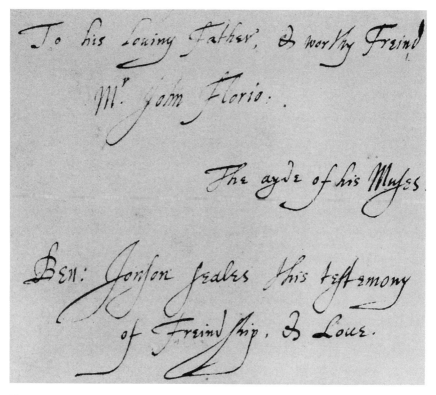

Figure 6. Ben Jonson's handwritten inscription on a copy of *Volpone* to his "worthy Freind Mr. John Florio: The ayde of his Muses." *Courtesy of The Cleveland Public Library.*

Edmund Spenser spoke of his "*heroical verse,* under the title of a *Faerie Queen,*" then a work in progress. Spenser's elementary education at the Merchant Taylors' School is a matter of record, as is his matriculation and graduation at Cambridge. A few days after he died in 1599, a correspondent wrote that "Spenser, our principal poet, coming lately out of Ireland, died at Westminster on Saturday last." Spenser was buried in Westminster Abbey near Geoffrey Chaucer.

Gabriel Harvey left behind over 150 books written in five languages, many filled with handwritten marginalia. Spenser gave him several books and dedicated a sonnet to "my singular good friend, M. Gabriel Harvey." There are records of Harvey's education at Cambridge.

Pamphleteer and satirist Thomas Nashe left behind a handwritten

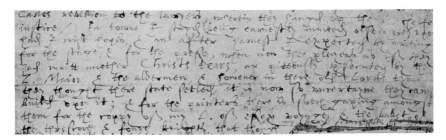

Figure 7. Part of Thomas Nashe's 1596 letter to Will Cotton, servant to Sir George Carey, later Lord Chamberlain. Toward the top, Nashe refers explicitly to his professional activities: "an after harvest I expected by writing for the stage, & for the presse, when now the players as if they had writt[en] another Christs tears, ar piteously persecuted by the L[ord] Maior." Nashe had dedicated *Christ's Tears Over Jerusalem* to Sir George's wife in 1593. *Courtesy of The Cleveland Public Library.*

verse in Latin, composed during his university days. His letter to William Cotton (fig. 7), servant to Sir George Carey, refers to his frustrations "writing for the stage and for the press." A 1593 letter by Carey reports that "Nashe hath dedicated a book unto you [Carey's wife] with promise of a better. Will Cotton will disburse . . . your reward to him." Carey also refers to Nashe's imprisonment for "writing against the Londoners."

Robert Greene contributed an epistle on "behalf of my absent friend, Mr. Thomas Lodge" for *Euphues Shadow*, and Lodge wrote a prefatory poem for Greene, his *"doux ami."* The 1585 accounts of the earl of Leicester show a payment to "Robert Greene that presented a book to your lordship." Greene's death in 1592 was the talk of the literary town, and there is a record of Greene's education at Cambridge.

A testator in a 1617 lawsuit stated that George Chapman "hath made diverse plays and written other books." Chapman contributed a commendatory poem to his "loving friend" John Fletcher for *The Faithful Shepherdess* and received one from Michael Drayton (his "worthy friend Mr. George Chapman").

Drayton was treated by physician John Hall, and described in Hall's casebook as an "excellent poet." Drayton inscribed a presentation copy of *The Battle of Agincourt* (1627) to his "much honored friend the worthy Sir Henry Willoughby" (fig. 8). Drayton was buried in Westminster Abbey.

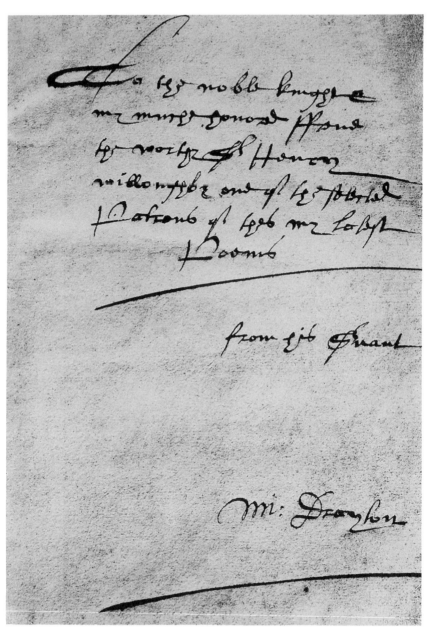

Figure 8. Michael Drayton's handwritten inscription to his "honored friend," Sir Henry Willoughby, on a copy of his 1627 poem *The Battle of Agincourt. Courtesy of The Cleveland Public Library.*

Figure 9. Part of the manuscript of *Sir Thomas More* in Anthony Mundy's handwriting. *Courtesy of The Cleveland Public Library.*

Anthony Mundy was paid for numerous plays by Henslowe and wrote "shows and speeches" for the Lord Mayor's pageant. Manuscript pages of the play *Sir Thomas More* survive in his handwriting (fig. 9), and he was commemorated posthumously as a "servant to the City, With his Pen."

Drayton, Chapman, Henry Chettle, and John Webster, among many others, were paid by Henslowe to write plays (e.g., figs. 10 and 11). Thomas Dekker's name appears in the Henslowe Diary, usually as a payee, over fifty times, and receipts in his handwriting survive (fig. 11). So does a letter he wrote to Edward Alleyn (fig. 12), in which he enclosed his testimonial to Alleyn for the founding of Dulwich College.

Thomas Heywood, Samuel Rowley, William Rowley, and Nathan Field were actor-dramatists, and therefore comparable to the professional Shakspere of traditional biography. Heywood and Samuel Rowley were paid by Henslowe for writing plays, and Rowley bequeathed books to his brother (Somerset, 294). William Rowley contributed a commendatory verse "To his friend, Mr. John Webster" for *The Duchess of Malfi*. Nathan Field was paid by Henslowe for writing plays (Greg, *Papers*, 65–67), and Jonson told Drummond that Field "was his scholar, and he had read to him the Satires of Horace, and some Epigrams of Martial" (Nungezer, 136). Chapman wrote a commendatory verse "To his loved son, Nat. Field" for a 1612 comedy.

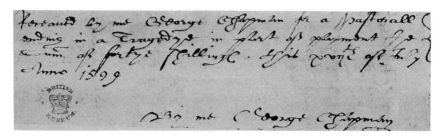

Figure 10. Signature of George Chapman acknowledging partial payment of "fortye shilling*e*" for "a Pastorall ending in a Tragedye." *Courtesy of The Cleveland Public Library.*

Playwright John Marston's father bequeathed law books to him. The dedication to *The Malcontent* reads (translated from Latin) "John Marston, disciple of the muses, gives and dedicates this his harsh comedy to his frank and heartfelt friend, Benjamin Jonson, the weightiest and most finely discerning of poets." Marston was a student at the Middle Temple at the Inns of Court, and there is a record of his education at Oxford.

Francis Beaumont wrote a prefatory verse for his collaborator and "Friend Mr. John Fletcher." There are records of Beaumont's education at Oxford University and the Inner Temple. Beaumont was buried next to Chaucer in Westminster Abbey. Fletcher wrote a verse for "his worthy friend Mr. Ben Jonson," and Fletcher's father left him books in his will.

William Drummond recorded his conversations with Jonson, and the two men discussed many subjects, including poetry. (Jonson mentioned Shakespeare twice. Neither comment was personal; both are considered in Chapter 11.) Drummond and Drayton exchanged letters discussing poetry, including Drayton's *Polyolbion*. Many of Drummond's books survive, some with handwritten marginalia, as do numerous papers and a commonplace book.

Poet and dramatist Samuel Daniel left behind a few manuscript pages of *Hymen's Triumph*, as well as numerous letters (fig. 13). In one letter, he explained that necessity had reduced him to "making the stage the speaker of my lines," and went on to apologize for whatever offense was given by his tragedy *Philotas*. In his 1603 *Defense of Rhyme*, Daniel acknowledged his early educational training, "having been first encouraged and framed thereunto by your most worthy and honourable mother [the countess of Pembroke], and re-

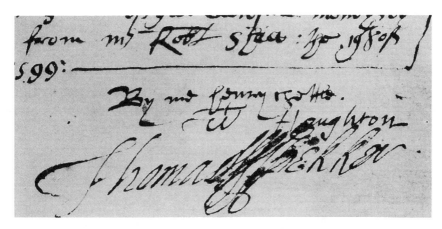

Figure 11. Signatures of Henry Chettle, William Haughton, and Thomas Dekker, acknowledging partial payment from Phillip Henslowe's agent Robert Shaw for writing *Patient Grissel*. *Courtesy of The Cleveland Public Library.*

ceived the first notion for the formal ordering of these compositions, at Wilton, which I must ever acknowledge to have been my best school."

A poem written by George Peele for a 1595 tournament survives in his handwriting, and the earl of Northumberland paid him for a poem in 1593. His letter to Lord Burghley (fig. 14) begging for patronage also survives. There is a record of Peele's education at Oxford.

Several letters survive in the hand of playwright John Lyly. In one of them, he sought favor from Sir Robert Cecil concerning the post of Master of the Revels. He wrote an epistle to Thomas Watson, "the Author his Friend." There are records of Lyly's education at Oxford and Cambridge.

Christopher Marlowe and Watson were arrested and jailed together after a street fracas. Shortly after Marlowe's death, Thomas Kyd wrote in a letter that he had shared a room with Marlowe for writing, and that Marlowe had been "writing for his [Lordship's] players." Within a month of Marlowe's death, Peele paid tribute to "Marley, the Muses' darling, for thy verse." There are records of Marlowe's education at Cambridge.

Although each of the preceding writers left behind fewer records than Jonson, some personal records survive to prove that their vo-

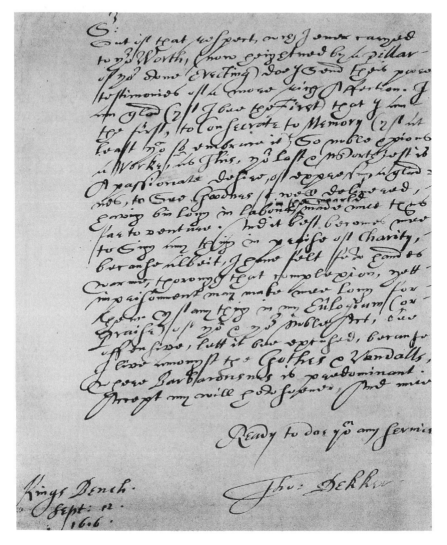

Figure 12. Thomas Dekker's letter (1616) from King's Bench prison to Edward Alleyn, referring to his "Eulogium (or Praise)" for the dedication of Alleyn's Dulwich College Chapel. *Courtesy of The Cleveland Public Library.*

cation was writing. Even in the cases of Marlowe, Watson, or Webster, three of the least documented writers, a few personal *literary* records survive, such as personal tributes or payments for writing.

Nevertheless, the critic quoted in the epigraph to this chapter

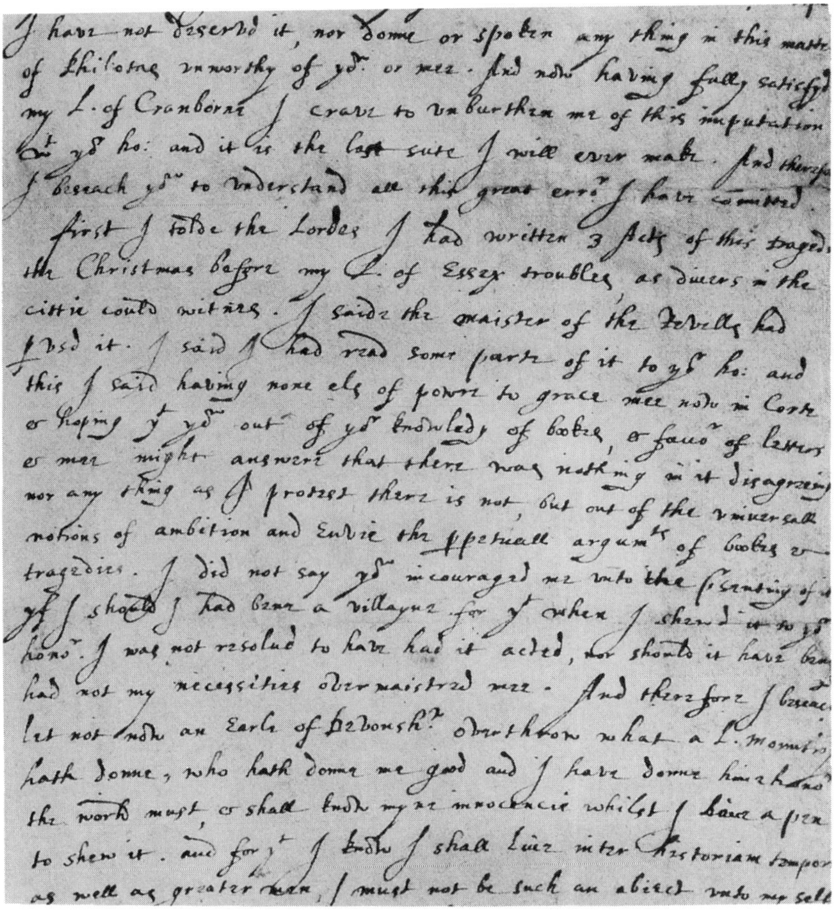

I have not deserved it, nor donne or spoken any thing in this matter
of Philotas unworthy of yor or mee. And now having fully satisfyd
my L. of Cranborne I crave to unburthen me of this imputation
wt yr ho: and it is the last suite I will ever make. And therefore
I beseach yow to understand all this great error I have committed.
first I tolde the Lordes I had written 3 Acts of this tragedie
the Christmas before my L. of Essex troubles, as divers in the
cittie could witnes. I saide the maister of the Revells had
pervsed it. I said I had read some parte of it to yr ho: and
this I said having none els of powre to grace mee now in Corte
& hoping yt yow out of yr knowledg of bookes, or favor of letters
& mee might answere that there was nothing in it disagreeing
nor any thing as I protest there is not, but out of the universall
notions of ambition and Envie the perpetuall argumts of bookes or
tragedies. I did not say yow incouraged me unto the presenting of it
yf I should I had been a villayne for yt when I shewd it to yr
honor I was not resolud to have had it acted, nor should it have bene
had not my necessities overmaistred mee. And therefore I beseach
let not now an Earle of Devonshr overthrow what a L. Mountioy
hath donne, who hath donne me good and I have donne him honor
the world must, or shall know myne innocencie whilst I have a pen
to shew it. and for yt I know I shall live inter historiam tempor
as well as greater men, I must not be such an abiect unto my self

Figure 13. Samuel Daniel's letter around 1604 to the earl of Devonshire. At the top, Daniel writes that his letter concerns "this matter of Philotas" and four lines further down, that he first "tolde the Lordes I had written 3 Acts of this tragedie the Christmas before my L[ord] of Essex troubles." *Courtesy of The Cleveland Public Library.*

claimed that most of Shakespeare's contemporaries left behind no evidence of their literary careers. Other authorities have claimed that we know more about the life of Shakespeare than of any other Elizabethan dramatist. While Shakspere probably left more documentary records in his wake than any of his contemporaries except Jonson, the claim that more is known about his life "than of any other Elizabethan dramatist" implies that Shakspere left behind more personal

Salue Parens Patriæ, tibj plebs, tibj curia nomen
hoc dedit, hoc dedimus nos tibj nomen æ ques.

In these tearmes (r. honorable) am I bolde
to salute yo'. Lordeship whose highe desertes in &
Englandes greate designes haue earned Large praises
euen from Indies mouthes. Pardon greate Patrone of
Learninge & Vertue, this rude enconnter, in that I
presume, A Scholler of so meane merit to present yo'.
wisdome with this finall manuell by this simple Messenger
my eldest Daughter of necessities seruent. Longe
sicknes harminge so enfeebled me maketh bashfullnes
allmost become impudency. Sed quad Esitaco nam Rogra
Expediui / Magister artis ingeny Largitor Venter.
The subiect wherewth I presume to greete yo' honor
is the history of Troy in 500 verses set downe &
memorable accidents thereof. Receiue it noble Senator of
Englandes Comcell-house) as A schollers duties signification
& Liue Longe in honor & prosperitie as happie as
Queene Elizabeths gracious comtenance can make yo'.

Ecce tibj nihilum magno pro munere mitto /
Else botest aliquid (te capiete) nihil.

yo' honors most
bomden George
Peele

literary paper trails than any of his contemporaries except Jonson. In other words, the claim implies that Shakspere is well documented *as a writer*. We now turn to the Shakespearean literary records to determine whether any of them also qualify as personal records for Shakspere.

HANDWRITING AND CORRESPONDENCE

According to Chambers, "every man, not completely illiterate, commits himself during his lifetime to the writing of letters or other documents, sometimes of a legal character" (*Sources*, 8). Fortunately for us, writers tend to leave behind written records for posterity. One can inspect dozens of specimens, most of them related to literary activity, by Chapman, Chettle, Daniel, John Davies of Hereford, Dekker, Drayton, Drummond, Harvey, Jonson, Kyd, Lyly, Marston, Philip Massinger, Mundy, Nashe, Peele, and Spenser, all collected in *English Literary Autographs* (see Greg et al.). However, the man from Stratford left behind only six signatures (fig. 15), all fixed to legal documents that date from the last four years of his life, when he supposedly had stopped writing professionally.

Shakspere's six signatures are spelled differently, one is incomplete, and two are blotted. Even allowing for the abbreviations employed in the Elizabethan "secretary hands," it is surprising that Shakspere failed to complete his full name when cosignatories completed theirs. He had such difficulty finishing his own name that some biographers account for the scrawls by postulating ill health. Scholars also disagree on the spellings of some of the signatures. In pretypewriter England, illegible penmanship would have been no asset to a writer whose original manuscripts were the only source for printers, playhouse transcripts, or private copies.

According to Jane Cox, writing in *Shakespeare in the Public Records*, "literate men in the sixteenth and seventeenth centuries developed personalized signatures much as people do today and it is unthinkable that Shakespeare did not" (Thomas and Cox, 33). But as far as his extant signatures show, Shakspere never developed his own consistent signature. Cox also postulated that some of the signatures could have been written by scribes. If biographers accepted Cox's analysis, the evidence for Shakspere would be reduced by up to four signatures.

Shakspere's shaky handwriting compares unfavorably with speci-

Figure 15. Shakspere's six signatures. The signatures appear on (from the top): the 1612 deposition in the Mountjoy lawsuit; the 1613 deed for the Blackfriars gate-house; the 1613 mortgage for the Blackfriars gate-house; page one of his will, 1616; page two of his will, 1616; page three of his will, 1616. *Courtesy of The Cleveland Public Library.*

mens left by his contemporaries (figs. 5–14). Even their messier or harder-to-read handwriting reveals some facility with the pen, whereas Shakspere's signatures suggest discomfort. Posthumous scuttlebutt by John Aubrey dating from about 1681 tells us that when Shakspere was asked to write, he begged off with a sore hand:

> the more to be admired [because] he was not a company keeper lived in Shoreditch, would not be debauched, & if invited to writ ; he was in pain. (*Malone Society Collections* [Pts. 4 and 5, 1911], 342, 347)

Some biographers have altered the punctuation in this snippet of gossip and thereby altered its meaning. By inserting a comma after the words "& if invited to," some have claimed that Shakspere responded indignantly in writing when invited to be debauched. For example, Park Honan quoted the passage to show that "when actors invite him to carouse, he writes that he is 'in paine' (with toothache or worse) to avoid being debauched in a famous red-light area" (122). James G. McManaway agreed that "Shakespeare did not care for drunken riots and, if invited, pleaded a headache" (181). One can only speculate on the wording of Shakspere's RSVP's to these rowdy parties.

Aubrey's tattle is hardly reliable evidence that Shakspere declined any opportunities to demonstrate his penmanship, but the six extant signatures suggest that there may have been a grain of truth in the story. At the least, shaky penmanship is an odd characteristic to find in a professional writer, but it could be expected of someone with perhaps six years of schooling. If, as seems probable, Shakspere attended grammar school for five or six years, his reading and oral skills would have exceeded his writing skills, as handwriting was not included in most curricula.

The poor quality of Shakspere's penmanship is as suspicious as is the paucity of extant handwriting for a man who supposedly lived by his pen, and scholars continue to search for more specimens. Some have pored over manuscript pages of the play *Sir Thomas More*, hoping to find Shakspere's handwriting in it. Yet there remain only six inconsistent, blotchy signatures against which to make any comparisons. At best, the six signatures support the conclusion that Shakspere could sign or at least scrawl his name, but they do not support the conclusion that he was a professional writer. Moreover, unlike most of the handwriting specimens left by Jonson, Drayton, and others,

Shakspere's signatures appear *only* in nonliterary legal instruments. His signatures are *not* evidence of a literary career.

Lest this disqualification appear arbitrary, let us ask whether signatures by themselves qualify as literary evidence. Marlowe left behind only one signature, on a legal document, but one could not use that signature in isolation to prove that Marlowe was a writer. In fact, the vast majority of surviving signatures belong to people whose vocations were *not* writing. Langley, the landlord of the Swan theatre, signed numerous documents, but one could hardly use his signatures to claim that he was a professional writer. His signatures, like those for Shakspere and Marlowe, have nothing to do with the vocation of writing. Such signatures compare poorly with other types of handwritten evidence. Chapman's signature in Henslowe's papers (fig. 10), for example, is good evidence that Chapman was paid to write a play. Drayton's signed inscription on a book of his poetry (fig. 8) is good evidence that he was the poet. But Langley's signatures are hardly evidence that he, too, wrote poetry. Even Spenser's handwriting, extant in letters he wrote as secretary to Lord Grey, fail to qualify as evidence of his vocation as a poet. Likewise Shakspere's isolated signatures—and Marlowe's—are by themselves not evidence of a career in writing.

Nearly every Shakespeare play mentions letters, so we know the dramatist considered correspondence part of everyday life, yet not one letter written by William Shakspere survives. Documents prove that Shakspere divided his time between London and Stratford, a situation particularly conducive to letter-writing, so this gap in his records is doubly suspicious.

SHAKSPERE'S LIBRARY

Where are Shakspere's books? The dramatist's reading list had to have amounted to many hundreds, if not thousands of books. Why have none of them ever been located? If he owned any, why didn't he mention them in his detailed will? Did he borrow every single one he ever read? There was no such thing as an Elizabethan public library, so some biographers speculate that Shakspere borrowed regularly from printer Richard Field, a Stratford man who relocated in London. There is no evidence to support that theory, nor does Field's inventory of books begin to account for Shakespeare's reading list (see Chapter 13).

While historians have to guess how the dramatist got hold of his books, they don't have to guess about some other writers' access to books. They *know* that Jonson borrowed books, and many volumes from his personal library have survived to the present day. So have over 150 volumes once owned by Harvey. Both men had less money than Shakspere, yet they bought books. Spenser gave books as gifts. Marlowe, Greene, Nashe, and other "university wits" had access to academic collections. Fletcher and Marston were left books by their fathers. Shakspere's bookless trail stands in striking contrast to the trails of many of his lesser contemporaries.

TITLE PAGE ATTRIBUTIONS

According to Chambers, "the canon of Shakespeare's plays rests primarily on the authority of title-pages" (*Facts*, 1:205). Over fifty editions of Shakespeare's plays, many of them reprints and some of them anonymous (e.g., three editions of *Romeo and Juliet*) were published between 1594 and 1622.

However, title page attributions are not *personal* records. In fact, they are not even reliable as evidence of authorship. *The London Prodigal* of 1605 and *A Yorkshire Tragedy* of 1608 were not written by Shakespeare, yet they were originally published over his name. In addition, the reader who picks up a copy of *Hamlet* cannot tell from the title page whether "William Shakespeare" is a real or fictitious name. Indeed, the title page of *Hamlet* tells us no more about the identity of the author than does the title page of *Huckleberry Finn*. The reader knows only that *Hamlet* has been attributed to someone writing under the name of William Shakespeare. Title page attributions count as literary allusions, but not as *personal* literary paper trails. In other words, Shakespearean title pages are not necessarily personal records belonging to Shakspere, unless corroborating evidence is found to confirm them as such.

"STOLNE AND SURREPTITIOUS COPIES"

Shakespeare's plays were pirated, that is, published without authorization in corrupt versions, with unprecedented frequency for a living writer. Inferior texts printed during Shakspere's lifetime are *2 Henry VI, 3 Henry VI, Romeo and Juliet, Henry V, Merry Wives, Hamlet, King Lear, Pericles, King John*, and *Richard III*, and many scholars would also include *The Taming of A Shrew*. Among other authors suffering bad editions were Greene, Beaumont and Fletcher, Marlowe, and Peele. However, not one of these other writers suffered more than two bad issues, leaving Shakespeare by far the most frequent victim after "Anonymous."

The inferiority of texts such as the first editions of *Hamlet* or *Romeo and Juliet* makes it difficult to postulate an authorized sale by either the acting company or the author. In a lecture titled "Exeunt Pirates," Peter W. M. Blayney exonerated the printers in these transactions (in private communication with the author), but as far as anyone knows, the agent or broker who sold the texts to the printers remains unidentified.

An agent or broker may very well have "prepared" a text for sale, but there is little agreement on the question of *how* texts became corrupt. Some have argued for faulty memorial reconstruction, some for stenographic transcription, others for deliberate vulgarization. However, numerous scenarios are possible, and many could involve multiple agencies of transmission. Adele Davidson enumerated alternative and often compound sources of corruption, for example, "attending multiple performances of the same play in order to improve [stenographic] transcription; . . . using stenography to record material dictated by actors . . . or by the author; or, most importantly, using stenography to copy a manuscript directly (whether from authorial, theatrical, or some other source)" (80). Other possible combinations might not have included stenography. Whatever the causes of corruption, the spate of inaccurate and unauthorized publications during Shakspere's lifetime is difficult to reconcile with his financial acumen.

Shakspere was a shrewd businessman, yet the flow of unauthorized editions went unchecked. Although copyright laws existed to serve licensing procedures and the stationers rather than to protect the author, it is not as though writers, even those who had less business savvy than Shakspere, had to tolerate unauthorized publications. Lodge and Daniel protested against unauthorized texts, Chapman printed a play to preempt possible piracy (Sheavyn, 78, 80), and Nicholas Breton complained that his verses had been published "altogether without my consent or knowledge" (Lee, *Facsimile, PP*, 16). In 1608, Heywood published several corrected texts, explaining apologetically that "some of my Plays have (unknown to me, and without any of my direction) accidentally come into the Printer's hands (and therefore so corrupt and mangled, copied only by the ear) that I have been as unable to know them, as ashamed to challenge them" (Chambers, *Stage*, 3:344). These writers protested, even if their protests came to naught. Shakspere did nothing.

In 1599, an unauthorized collection of poetry, including some attributed to Shakespeare, was published under the title *The Passionate Pilgrim*. In 1612, it was reissued with additional material by Heywood. Both editions were published over the name of "W. Shakespeare." In 1612, Heywood protested in print that he did not want people to think he had slid his own work into a volume with Shakespeare's name on the title page. Shakespeare's name was subsequently removed from the title page, and Heywood's protest is frequently cited to show that Shakspere himself raised an objection:

Here likewise, I must necessarily insert a manifest injury done me in that work, by taking the two Epistles of *Paris* to *Helen*, and *Helen* to *Paris*, and printing them in a less volume, under the name of another, which may put the world in opinion I might steal them from him; and he to do himself right, hath since published them in his own name: but as I must acknowledge my lines not worthy his patronage, under whom he hath published them, so the Author I know much offended with M. *Jaggard* (that altogether unknown to him) presumed to make so bold with his name. These, and the like dishonesties I know you to be clear of; and I could wish but to be the happy Author of so worthy a work as I could willingly commit to your care and workmanship. (*Apology*, last leaf)

The wording is dense, filled with troublesome pronouns. W. W. Greg pronounced it to be "a strangely worded and punctuated sentence," although he assumed that it was Shakspere who objected (*Folio*, 9 n). However, during the thirteen years between the two editions, Shakspere did nothing, nor does Heywood's "strangely worded" sentence make it clear that Shakspere himself objected.[*]

Shakspere's apparently passive attitude toward unauthorized publication contradicts his otherwise aggressive attitude toward money. As a shareholder in the company that presumably benefited from the sale of its plays, Shakspere personally stood to lose if plays were sold surreptitiously to a publisher. He would forfeit his share of the profit, and the script would then be freely available to rival companies.[†] Shakspere was never passive when other vested interests were at risk.

[*]See an analysis by Downs (an anti-Stratfordian) and rebuttal by Chandler.
[†]*King Lear* was first printed in 1608, and *Pericles* in 1609. Sir Richard Cholmeley's players performed both plays from the published quartos when they toured Yorkshire in late 1609 (Sisson, "Quartos," 138–39).

His various tactical maneuvers to safeguard his real estate investments in Stratford are well documented, as are his lawsuits to recover moneys owed. One would think that a man whose business records reveal a penchant for financial self-interest would not leave any source of his rightful revenue to thieves. Had Shakspere's biographical trail been unencumbered by evidence of persistent financial ambition, the incidence of play piracy would not stand out as such a fundamental contradiction. But Shakspere was clearly a man who would not find any loss of income acceptable.

A second contradiction concerns the corruption of the play texts. Shakespeare, the writer, was confident that his literary output was good enough to live through the ages. The dramatist described plays as "the abstracts and brief chronicles of the time," not merely as ephemeral entertainments. In the sonnets, Shakespeare told us more about how he viewed his literary work:

> Not marble, nor the gilded monuments
> Of Princes shall out-live this powerful rhyme. (Sonnet 55)

> You still shall live—such virtue hath my Pen—
> Where breath most breathes, even in the mouths of men.
> (Sonnet 81)

> And thou in this shalt find thy monument,
> When tyrants' crests and tombs of brass are spent.
> (Sonnet 107)

This author respected the integrity of his works and believed in their immortality, yet we are asked to believe that he did not care whether they were left to posterity as he wrote them, if they were left to posterity at all. Many biographers explain, as did Bentley, that "Shakespeare's indifference to his plays outside the medium of the theater for which they were written is the normal attitude of the time" (*Handbook*, 169). If so, why do so many plays show evidence of revision for the printed page?* Dutton thought it likely that Shakespeare expected his plays to "be read as well as acted," and that, "like Jonson, he had a sense of them as 'literary texts' " ("Birth," 83).

---

*Some texts, such as *Hamlet* and *King Lear*, would have exceeded the normal two-hour playing time in the theater, suggesting that their composition was intended for the printed page (e.g., see Greg, *Folio*, 2; Shakespeare, *Arden, Hamlet*, 56–61, 65, 75).

Bradbrook concluded—largely on the basis of its "complex and strange vocabulary, and the great variety of sources"—that *Troilus and Cressida* was "designed to be read as Literature" (*"Troilus,"* 311). On that basis, most of the Shakespeare plays would qualify as literature, intended to be read.

It is therefore surprising that some of the early published texts were so garbled that many scholars initially thought they were entirely different plays, and four corrupt texts remained garbled until better ones were published in the posthumous *First Folio*. If Shakespeare believed his powerful rhyme could outlive marble, why did he allow his works to appear in such offensively corrupt form and to remain uncorrected during his lifetime? Indeed, Harold Bloom wondered how there could "have been a writer for whom the final shape of *King Lear* was a careless or throwaway matter" (52).

So, the *shareholder* Shakspere stood to lose financially from plays stolen from his company's repertoire, and the *dramatist* Shakespeare stood to lose his literary reputation by leaving a legacy of garbled play texts. Both problems remain inconsistent with, and unresolved in, the traditional biography.

However, the theory that Shakespeare was the pen name of a courtier could explain the trail of unauthorized or corrupt Shakespeare plays. Unlike the professional writer, the Elizabethan gentleman wrote primarily for his friends and social circle, not for publication. In fact, the Elizabethan gentleman "shunned print" because it was socially degrading. His aversion to publication was mandated by the social caste system emanating from the court, but his privately circulating manuscripts presented an opportunity for printers—or brokers—who were "able to take unscrupulous advantage of a Court poet by piracies which could not with dignity be prevented" (Saunders, 140). A gentleman could not protest if his work was vulgarized or otherwise corrupted in print, lest he be seen to be interested in publication himself. If he sold a play to a Battillus or printer, even on condition of anonymity, the matter was then out of his hands.

CONTEMPORARY ALLUSIONS

As noted before, allusions to Elizabethan writers can be personal, impersonal, or ambiguous. Personal allusions provide evidence of acquaintance, whereas impersonal ones do not. If an allusion could have been written solely on the basis of having read or heard an author's work or heard about his reputation, then it does not qualify as personal. This verse, written by George Wyther, makes it clear that not every tribute to literary achievement qualifies as a *personal* testimonial:

> Oh Daniel, Drayton, Jonson, Chapman, how
> I long to see you, with your fellow Peers
> That are the only glory of these years.
> *I hitherto have only heard your fames*
> *And know you yet but by your works and names.*
> (221Q, emphasis added)

John Weever's sonnet *Ad Gulielmum Shakespeare* begins "Honey-tongued *Shakespeare* when I saw thine issue, / I swore *Apollo* got them and none other." According to Honigmann, "The many poems in praise of living poets inserted in [Weever's] *Epigrammes* were probably a hit-and-miss campaign; some of these eminent contemporaries he may have known personally, but some must have been strangers, and Weever no doubt hoped that a little of the praise that he let fly in all directions would return with interest" (*Weever*, 21). Weever's allusion to Shakespeare does not qualify as personal, because he could have written it after reading or seeing Shakespeare's work.

In contrast, as we saw, Davies addressed an epigram to his "well-accomplish'd friend Mr. Ben Jonson." That one qualifies as personal evidence; these two men knew each other. It remains to be seen who of those who praised Shakespeare's poetry or plays necessarily knew the dramatist personally.

The first allusion to Shakespeare as writer appeared in 1594, when a pseudonymous poet mentioned him as the author of *The Rape of Lucrece* ("*Shake-speare*, paints poor *Lucrece* rape"). Over the next four years, a few writers exhibited familiarity with *Lucrece* or *Venus and Adonis*, such as one who mentioned "Sweet Shak-speare."

Between 1594 and 1598, a number of Shakespeare plays were published anonymously, but it was not until 1598 that William Shakespeare was named in print as a dramatist. In that year, an obscure writer, Francis Meres, published *Palladis Tamia*. One chapter out of Meres's otherwise undistinguished volume is famous, the chapter entitled "A comparative discourse of our English Poets." It was the breakthrough both for classifying dramatic works as literature and for establishing the name "William Shakespeare" as a dramatist:

As the soul of *Euphorbus* was thought to live in *Pythagoras*: so the sweet witty soul of *Ovid* lives in mellifluous & honey-tongued *Shakespeare*, witness his *Venus* and *Adonis*, his *Lucrece*, his sugared Sonnets among his private friends, &c.

. . . so *Shakespeare* among the English is the most excellent in both kinds for the stage; for Comedy, witness his *Gentlemen of Verona*, his *Errors*, his *Love labor's lost*, his *Love labour's won*, his *Midsummers night dream*, & his *Merchant of Venice*; for Tragedy his *Richard the 2. Richard the 3. Henry the 4. King John, Titus Andronicus* and his *Romeo* and *Juliet*.

. . . so I say that the Muses would speak with *Shakespeare's* fine-filed phrase, if they would speak English. (281v–282r)

By 1598, Shakespeare had presumably written about seventeen plays, of which Meres named twelve. Five of those twelve plays had not been published, and six had been printed without author attribution. *Romeo and Juliet* had been published in a corrupt and anonymous edition, and the text of *King John* had been so corrupted that many scholars do not accept it as Shakespeare's at all. So while Meres extolled Shakespeare's literary output, he named one and possibly two plays that had been published in embarrassingly bad editions. Perhaps he had heard better versions performed onstage. Meres's source remains unknown.

Meres's often-quoted passage is useful for the literary historian, because it names several play titles, but it is not as useful for the biographer who seeks evidence of personal relationships. Meres could have written his commentary based on what he had been reading, seeing, or hearing around town. In contrast, one could claim that Meres knew the poet Barnfield, because he described him as his "friend master Richard Barnfield." But Meres named dozens of writers in his section on English poets, and no one would suppose that he personally knew every single one of them. The editor of the 1938 reprint of *Palladis Tamia*, Don Cameron Allen, considered the book "the work of a hack who had a contracted obligation to fulfill," one who relied on literary critics such as Puttenham and William Webbe for some of his information (vii–viii). Another commentator likewise supposed that Meres's "information about them must have come, not from his own direct knowledge, but from a reliable outside source" (Thomas, "Dating," 188).

Meres reported that Shakespeare shared "his sugared Sonnets among his private friends," but he did not tell his readers who the lucky sonnet recipients were. Perhaps he knew, perhaps not. One can only speculate. So while Meres was the first to praise Shakespeare as both a poet and dramatist, nobody knows whether Meres and Shakespeare ever met each other. Meres's comments on Shakespeare do not qualify as personal allusions.

In that same year, 1598, Shakespeare's name appeared as a byline on editions of *Love's Labour's Lost, Richard II,* and *Richard III,* and references to him as a dramatist started to surface (e.g., "Friendly Shake-speare's Tragedies"). Over the next eighteen years, until the year of Shakspere's death, over a dozen explicit references were made to Shakespeare as a writer. But when people wrote about Shakespeare, they did one of two things. Either they confined their comments to his literary works, or they used ambiguous language.

As we saw in Chapters 5 and 6, Davies and the authors of the *Parnassus* plays used ambiguous language when they wrote about Shakspere or Shakespeare. Most other writers, such as Meres, alluded to Shakespeare's works without giving their readers any firsthand information about the author himself. Yet many biographers tell us that Shakspere was *personally* recognized by his colleagues as an affable, well-liked, gentle, and sweet man. What is their evidence? There is none.

Honigmann showed that Shakspere's "sweet" disposition is erroneously grounded in comments about Shakespeare's *literary style*:

Such allusions to a writer's style tell us no more about his personality than in the case of Sir Nicholas Bacon of whose "sweete and sugred eloquence" we hear in 1585. It was a hackneyed formula, used of many others. . . .

All the allusions to "sweet" Shakespeare recorded in his life-time refer back to his "vein," or poetic style. Only after his death was Shakespeare the man described as "sweet"—"Sweet Swan of *Avon!*" (Jonson)—but so were many others after their deaths, for the word is one of the conventions of elegy. (*Impact,* 15)

Honigmann painstakingly demonstrated that "the myth of 'sweet Shakespeare' " has misled many readers about his supposed personality and, by extension, about his supposed circle of personal friends.

Nevertheless, biographers have persisted for nearly three centuries in reporting that Shakspere was known to be sweet-natured. In the first biographical account of Shakspere (1709), Nicholas Rowe described the poet's "sweetness in his Manners" and "good-natur'd" disposition (Chambers, *Facts*, 2:266). Sidney Lee characterized Shakspere as "a sympathetic friend of gentle, unassuming mien" who had earlier been "apostrophised as 'sweet Master Shakespeare' " (*Life*, 286–87). More recently, Samuel Schoenbaum concluded that "almost everyone seems to have thought well of Shakespeare" (*Documentary*, 205).

Schoenbaum's biography purported to be a "documentary" life, but his conception of the mild-mannered and well-liked Shakspere is not supported by the allusions that he quoted. For example, he mentioned the author of *Daiphantus* (1604) who "remarks on 'Friendly Shakespeare's Tragedies'. Did the two men know one another, as the phrase suggests?" (*Documentary*, 205). But the phrase is from a satirical epistle. Taken in context, "friendly" conveys the idea, not that Shakspere himself was known to be affable, but that Shakespeare's plays are accessible or user-friendly:

come home to the vulgar's Element, like Friendly Shake-speare's Tragedies, where the Comedian rides, when the Tragedian stands on Tip-toe: Faith it should please all, like Prince Hamlet.

Schoenbaum cited Davies's epigrammatic reference to "good Will" as evidence of Shakspere's affable disposition (205), but as we saw, the epigram is cryptic, satirical, and most importantly, impersonal.

Schoenbaum quoted William Barksted, a lesser poet and playwright, who referred to "Shakespeare" as "so dear loved a neighbour" (205). Schoenbaum was discussing what Shakspere's supposed circle of friends thought about him personally, and what testimony they left to posterity to prove it. But again, this quote is an impersonal literary allusion found in Barksted's 1607 narrative poem, *Mirrha, the Mother of Adonis*. It describes events leading up to Mirrha's death, at which point Adonis grows up, and Venus prepares to pursue him. Barksted begins the story of Shakespeare's *Venus and Adonis*, then stops in his tracks and apologizes for encroaching on the adjoining literary territory:

But stay my Muse in thine own confines keep,
    & wage not war with so dear lov'd a neighbor
But having sung thy day song, rest and sleep
    preserve thy small fame and his greater favor:
His Song was worthy merit (*Shakspeare* he)

> sung the fair blossom, thou the withered tree
> *Laurel* is due to him, his art and wit
> hath purchased it, *Cypress* thy brow will fit. (65)

In other words, Barksted's Muse is not going to wage war with Shakespeare's Muse. Barksted is clearly distinguishing his "neighbor" in the sense of adjoining literary subject matter, one story abutting another, one muse poised to compete with another. There is nothing in the verse to suggest that Barksted and Shakespeare were neighbors or even personally acquainted.

To sum up, Schoenbaum first invested Shakspere with civility and an "uprightness of dealing" by quoting Chettle's apology to somebody else. He then piled one impersonal or cryptic allusion (such as "good Will") onto another, as though they constituted reliable evidence of Shakspere's friendly personality and gentle conduct.* But Schoenbaum was only following his predecessors. For years, biographers have used impersonal allusions to Shakespeare's sweet poetry as personal evidence of a gentle, sweet man.

Most of the explicit literary allusions to Shakespeare, set down during Shakspere's lifetime, could have been written after reading or seeing one of Shakespeare's works. Allusions such as those by Weever, Barksted, or Meres tell us only that these writers knew Shakespeare by his works and name. The principal ambiguous allusions, such as those by Davies and those in the *Parnassus* plays, have been considered in earlier chapters, and none confirms a personal acquaintance with the author. In the end, there is no contemporary reference to Shakespeare remotely comparable to Marston's dedication to "his frank and heartfelt friend, Benjamin Jonson, the weightiest and most finely discerning of poets." Contrary to the impression created in traditional biographies, none of the contemporaneous Shakespearean allusions qualify as personal literary paper trails for Shakspere of Stratford.

*Schoenbaum's treatment of this evidence did not change over time. Earlier, in 1971, he described Shakespeare, the man, in similar terms: "Apart from Greene, none of his contemporaries seems to have uttered a malicious word about Shakespeare. Chettle . . . praised his civil demeanour and uprightness of dealing. From others, we hear of good Will, sweet Shakespeare, friendly Shakespeare, so dear loved a neighbor" ("Life," 14).

CURIOUS OVERSIGHTS

The allusions to Shakespeare that perhaps speak the loudest are the ones that are not there. A recent biographer of Nashe acknowledged the problem when he observed that "by a curious oversight, the greatest of Nashe's literary contemporaries is the one never mentioned by name in his pamphlets" (Nicholl, 203). Shakespeare, the playwright and poet, was obviously in the thick of things in literary London. It is therefore incredible that no colleagues wrote about him as though they knew him. In addition, several surveys of writers of the day overlooked him entirely.

For example, in *Wit's Miserie* (1596), Thomas Lodge singled out the "Divine wits" of Lyly, Spenser, Daniel, Drayton, and Nashe, but failed to mention the published author of *Venus and Adonis* and *The Rape of Lucrece*. Lodge's omission of Shakespeare is particularly odd, because on the preceding page, he made a reference to *Hamlet*: "this fiend . . . looks as pale as the Vizard [mask] of the ghost which cried so miserably at the Theater like an oyster wife, *Hamlet, revenge*" (4: 56). According to legend, one of two roles that Shakspere may have played was the Ghost in *Hamlet*. T. W. Baldwin speculated that "if Lodge were alluding to Shakspere's play, he would be 'ribbing' Shakspere both as author and as actor. . . . Here is pretty certainly one contemporary impression of Shakspere as the ghost in *Hamlet*, whether his own play or the *Old Hamlet*" (*Literary*, 25).* So, Lodge mentioned *Hamlet* on one page, and omitted Shakespeare from his address to the "Divine wits" on the next. Yet immediately after singling out these "Divine wits," Lodge paid tribute to "unnamed professors, or friends of Poetry (but by me inwardly honoured)." Here is an Elizabethan complimenting certain fellow writers, but this time, not naming names.

In 1599, Weever published his sonnet in praise of Shakespeare's "Honey-tongued" poetry and plays. As we saw, Weever was one of many writers who wrote about Shakespeare's works but not about the man himself. Many years later, when researching his book *Ancient Funeral Monuments*, Weever transcribed Shakspere's Stratford epitaphs into his notebook, but oddly, he did not include either epitaph

---

*Most traditional biographers assign Shakespeare's *Hamlet* to 1598–1601 and therefore assume that Lodge was referring to somebody else's *Hamlet*, usually called the *Ur-Hamlet*, although Baldwin dubs it the *Old Hamlet*. See Chapter 16 for additional discussion of the *Ur-Hamlet*.

when he published his book in 1631. Weever's omission is even more inexplicable if one accepts the assumption that Weever himself wrote "Will[ia]m Shakespeare the famous poet" in the margin of his notebook next to the transcriptions (Honigmann, *Weever*, 70). In other words, Weever failed to publish the epitaphs supposedly commemorating a poet he himself had praised in print back in 1599. It is another curious oversight.

In 1598, the author of an anonymous satire titled *Skialetheia*, later attributed to Everard Guilpin, censured Chaucer, John Gower, Spenser, Daniel, Gervase Markham, Drayton, and Sidney, but made no mention of the poet Shakespeare. In 1603, the antiquarian and historian William Camden, in his *Remains Concerning Britain*, included "William Shakespeare" as one of the "most pregnant wits of these our times, whom succeeding ages may justly admire" (294). Yet Camden omitted Shakespeare when discussing the worthies of Stratford-on-Avon in his later work of 1607, *Britannia*.

The author of *The New Metamorphosis* (1600–1615) named over thirty poets and playwrights of the day in a fairly comprehensive listing. Even though the author was familiar with *Venus and Adonis* and theatregoing, he failed to name Shakespeare (Lyon, 61–64). Wyther's 1613 defense of poetry in *Abuses Stript, and Whipt* (preface "To the Readers," 221Q) praised Spenser, Daniel, Sidney, Drayton, Jonson, and Chapman, but not Shakespeare.

Many years after Shakspere's death, Jonson wrote a prose piece, *Timber, or Discoveries*, in which he advised students to "read the best authors" first. Jonson named five Englishmen (Sidney, John Donne, Gower, Chaucer, and Spenser), but left out the man whom he had eulogized in 1623 as the "Star of Poets." In fact, Jonson did not write once about Shakespeare during the Stratford man's lifetime, and his silence is particularly deafening. Jonson's personal impressions of Shakspere, recorded long after the man from Stratford had died, are considered in Chapter 11.

Why did all these writers overlook Shakespeare in places where logically they should have included him? Were all of them just careless or indiscriminate? Did they think he wasn't worth mentioning? Or were they aware, directly or at second hand, that "Shakespeare" was the pen name of a gentleman of the upper class, and thus omitted him out of courtesy?

Most people would rank Shakespeare with the major figures of his day, such as Francis Bacon, Spenser, Jonson, Sir Francis Drake, or Sir

Walter Raleigh. Historical records prove that these men interacted with each other or were personally recognized for the activities with which their names are linked. If Shakespeare personally interacted with any of the opinion-setters, decision makers, or influential personages of the time, the historical record is inexplicably and uncharacteristically silent.

DEDICATIONS AND COMMENDATORY VERSES

"William Shakespeare" dedicated his two narrative poems, *Venus and Adonis* and *The Rape of Lucrece*, to Henry Wriothesley, the earl of Southampton. *Venus and Adonis* was published in 1593, the year after *Groatsworth of Wit*. Apparently, the conceited "Upstart Crow," the one who thought he could bombast out blank verse with the best of them, then found his Sunday manners and wrote with gracious humility:

To The Right Honorable Henry Wriothesley,
Earl of Southampton, and Baron of Titchfield.

Right Honorable, I know not how I shall offend in dedicating my unpolished lines to your Lordship, nor how the world will censure me for choosing so strong a prop to support so weak a burden, only if your Honor seem but pleased, I account myself highly praised, and vow to take advantage of all idle hours, till I have honoured you with some graver labor. But if the first heir of my invention prove deformed, I shall be sorry it had so noble a godfather: and never after eare so barren a land, for fear it yield me still so bad a harvest, I leave it to your Honorable survey, and your Honor to your heart's content, which I wish may always answer your own wish, and the world's hopeful expectation.

Your Honor's in all duty,
William Shakespeare.

The poet wrote his 1594 dedication to *The Rape of Lucrece* in an equally formal tone:

To The Right Honorable, Henry Wriothesley,
Earl of Southampton, and Baron of Titchfield.

The love I dedicate to your Lordship is without end: whereof this Pamphlet without beginning is but a superfluous Moiety. The warrant I have of your

Honorable disposition, not the worth of my untutored Lines makes it assured of acceptance. What I have done is yours, what I have to do is yours, being part in all I have, devoted yours. Were my worth greater, my duty would show greater, meantime, as it is, it is bound to your Lordship; To whom I wish long life still lengthened with all happiness.

Your Lordship's in all duty,
William Shakespeare.

These two dedications have fueled theories that Shakspere was the recipient of Southampton's generosity, that he succeeded in obtaining patronage from an important member of the aristocracy. While they can be used to argue that "Shakespeare" sought patronage, there is no evidence to show that he obtained it. In fact, the dedications to Southampton provide no evidence that the two men were even acquainted.

Numerous historians have demonstrated that "patrons often were not apprised of dedications before publication." As one scholar put it, the patrons' connections or relationships with an author were often "slight or nonexistent and their names mainly functioned as (misleading) signs of celebrity-endorsement" (E. H. Miller, 110–11; Marotti, "Patronage," 2).

In the dedication to *Lucrece*, Shakespeare wrote that "the warrant I have of your Honourable disposition" made his poem "assured of acceptance." In other words, Shakespeare had heard reports of Southampton's presumably generous disposition. Writers often made overtures to potential patrons by professing that they had been assured of this lordship's disposition or that ladyship's generosity.

Greene fully described his efforts to identify a likely patron in his epistle for *The Spanish Masquerado*, in which his consideration of the ancient tradition of patronage "emboldened me to make choice of your worship as a *Mæcenas*, fittest for a work of such grave import, persuaded thereunto by the report of a friend, whose opinion I craved, for the choice of a Patron: and made the more resolute by the general Censure that Fame sets down, emblazoning your virtuous disposition." When Greene made a bid to the countess of Derby for patronage (*The Myrrour of Modestie*), he wrote that "the fame . . . of this your virtuous life, and the report of your Ladyship's surpassing courtesy, encouraged me to present this pamphlet to your honor's protection." He made another bid to Gervis Clifton (*Perimedes*), having been "spurred forward by the report of your courtesy, and fame of your virtues." No evidence survives to show whether any of these attempts to obtain patronage succeeded.

Greene's formulaic dedication for *Planetomachia* (1585) to the earl of Leicester refers to the earl's reputation as "a Mæcenas of learning . . . whose courteous favor towards learning, hath forced [scholars] to discover their skill for your Lordship's private pleasure. . . . Yet the dutiful and humble affection wherewith I find myself bound to such a worthy patron of good letters, hath emboldened me to present your Honor with this Pamphlet . . . which *if your Honour shall accept*, my travail shall be so requited" (emphasis added). In this case, we know Greene succeeded in gaining patronage, not because of any subsequent dedication with a profusion of gratitude, but because Leicester's account book records his payment to Greene for "a book." Greene's dedication shows that his pamphlet was not accepted in advance, and while the payment provides a direct link between poet and patron, one could not necessarily conclude from Leicester's account book that Greene actually met his benefactor in person.

Generally, when patronage had been obtained, writers tended to tell their readers with explicit expressions of gratitude, often couched in language that confirms personal acquaintance. John Florio dedicated his Italian-English Dictionary, *A Worlde of Wordes*, to the "most Honorable Earl of Southampton, in whose pay and patronage I have lived some years." Greene dedicated *Never Too Late* to Thomas Burnaby, to whom he was indebted "for sundry favors." In a second epistle to Burnaby, Greene acknowledged "having received many friendly, nay fatherly favors at your hands," having previously "emboldened myself to present you with a pamphlet of my penning . . . *which your Worship so gratefully accepted*" (emphasis added). After Thomas Nashe received a reward from Lady Carey for *Christ's Tears* (1593), he dedicated *Terrors of the Night* (1594) to her daughter, paying tribute to her "worthy . . . Mother . . . whose purse is so open to her poor beadsmen's distresses. Well may I say it, because I have tried it, . . . [and have] found in her extraordinary liberality and bounty" (3:213–15).

Shakespeare's two dedications to Southampton make no mention of "bounty" received or "pay and patronage." Instead, his second dedication tells us that after his first try with *Venus and Adonis*, he was still writing that he had merely *heard* about, or been assured ("the warrant I have") of Southampton's disposition.* Gary Taylor thought that "one might as reasonably say that the dedications express a desire/hope/expectation that the chosen patron" (Wells et al., 2) would take note of the poems. The two dedications fail as evidence that "Shakespeare" and Southampton ever met each other.

After the two poems were published, Shakespeare dedicated nothing to anyone else ever again, which was uncharacteristic behavior for a man who lived by his pen. While no one has successfully explained how the two dedications came to be written, it remains more of a mystery that Shakespeare wrote only those two dedications—and no commendatory verses.

Most writers were recognized explicitly by their literary peers as personal friends. As we saw, Marston dedicated a play to "his frank and heartfelt friend, Benjamin Jonson, the weightiest and most finely discerning of poets." Other writers who contributed or received such explicit tributes include Beaumont, Chapman, Chettle, Daniel, Davies, Dekker, Drayton, Drummond, Fletcher, Florio, Greene, Harvey, Heywood, Lodge, Lyly, Massinger, Middleton, Mundy, Spenser, Watson, and Webster. As far as the record shows, Shakespeare had no literary friends. Honigmann found it "astonishing" that unlike all these writers, not one commendatory verse by Shakespeare has survived (*Impact*, 51).

Honigmann is not alone in his surprise. Another critic who noticed the same phenomenon suggested a possible reason: "Habitual writers of commendatory verses were, as one might suspect, mainly literary professionals. *With the curious exceptions of Sidney and Shakespeare*, all the chief poets (including Spenser and Milton) wrote puffs. . . . Few other generalizations can be made about puff writers except that *the practice seems to have been beneath the dignity of members of the peerage*" (Williams, 6, emphasis added; see also 14).

There are no commendatory verses from Shakespeare, and there are none to him. This gap is difficult for the traditional biographer to explain. It is not so difficult for those who postulate an author of high birth maintaining a safe distance from the profession of writing.

---

*William Burton dedicated his translation of *Clitophon and Leucippe* to the earl of Southampton, in which he wrote that he was "assured your honor will well like of" the pamphlet. In his introduction to *Clitophon*, Gaselee was unable to determine from the dedication "whether Burton had any intimate relations with [Southampton], or whether he merely chose him as the recipient of the *Epistle Dedicatorie* as one known to receive favourably the efforts of young men of letters" (xviii).

OUR EVER-LIVING POET

Shake-speares Sonnets was published in 1609 with the following dedication:

TO . THE . ONLIE . BEGETTER . OF.
THESE . INSVING . SONNETS.
M^r. W. H. ALL.HAPPINESSE.
AND . THAT . ETERNITIE.
PROMISED.
BY.
OVR.EVER-LIVING.POET.
WISHETH.
THE. WELL-WISHING.
ADVENTVRER. IN.
SETTING.
FORTH.

                    T. T.

Thomas Thorpe, the publisher whose initials are subscribed to the dedication, chose an extraordinary word to describe Shakespeare. That word is "ever-living," a word that is generally ignored in Shakespearean biographies.

An "ever-living" poet is a dead poet. The adjective is synonymous with the term "immortal" and is used to describe deities, nonhuman entities, or dead persons. Donald W. Foster researched the term extensively but failed to find "any instance of *ever-living* used in a Renaissance text to describe a living mortal, including, even, panegyrics on Queen Elizabeth, where one should most expect to find it—though it does appear sometimes in eulogies for the dead, as in *Henry VI, Part I*" (46). Indeed, the lines from Shakespeare's *1 Henry VI* provide the *Oxford English Dictionary*'s first illustration of the term "ever-living," as applied to a human being ("our scarce-cold conqueror, / That ever-living man of memory, / Henry the Fifth"). In his 1640 epistle to Shakespeare's *Poems*, John Benson referred to the author's "ever-living Works" (Chambers, *Facts*, 1:557). Richard Brome addressed his commemorative poem in Beaumont and Fletcher's *Comedies and Tragedies* (1647), "To the memory of the deceased but ever-living *Author* in these his Poems, Mr. John Fletcher."

There are two possibilities. Either Thorpe used the term "ever-living" incorrectly, or the poet Shakespeare was dead by 1609. William Shakspere of Stratford died in 1616.

SHAKSPERE'S WILL

Shakspere left a will and it survives today. The will that was presented for probate at the Prerogative Court at Canterbury is now the property of the Public Record Office in London. A copy was made in the court register at the time of probate. Transcripts of the register copy were made later for legal purposes, most likely relating to subsequent litigation over Shakspere's property bequests. One such transcript now resides at the Shakespeare Birthplace Trust in Stratford. (That copy, not the original, was used by the Rev. Joseph Greene to make two more transcripts around 1747.)

The Public Record Office reports that the will was dictated to lawyer Francis Collins or to his scribe. In the will, Shakspere made detailed provisions for the disposition of his assets, paying particular care to keep his estate relatively intact for a male heir, should either daughter produce one after his death.

However, Shakspere's will makes no mention of papers or manuscripts. Most biographers conclude that he no longer owned his plays, because they had all been purchased by the King's Men. Yet, as far as anyone knows, some of the plays had never been performed and could still have been in the author's study. Likewise, any unpublished poetry would still have been in his possession, but his will makes no mention of any such treasures.

Shakspere's will makes no mention of books. This is especially odd when one considers, as did the authors of *Playhouse Wills*, that "the 'bookishness' of the profession is visible: quite a few actors and one widow, Elizabeth Condell, bequeathed books" (Honigmann and Brock, 4). Those historians were commenting, not even on the *literary* profession, but on the *acting* profession. Actors such as Alleyn, Thomas Downton, and William Bird specified books in their wills, as did actor-dramatist Samuel Rowley, and Heminges bequeathed money to buy books for his grandchild.

Most traditional biographers avoid such embarrassing comparisons, explaining instead that Shakspere's books would have been covered by the catch-all clause mentioning his "goods" and "household stuff." Gibson (175) vigorously defended that position by pointing out, for example, that neither poet Samuel Daniel nor the scholarly theologian Richard Hooker specified books in their wills, so why all the fuss over no books in Shakspere's will? Gibson neglected to add that Daniel named his publisher as an overseer of his will, and the inventory filed with Hooker's will valued "his books, chests, [and] hampers . . . to put them in" at £300 (Keen, 232). The absence of books in Shakspere's will is not offset by any such comparable compensating evidence. (Biographers point out that one of the overseers for Shakspere's will was Thomas Russell, a man of property who is occasionally described as a "literary figure." But Russell was not a writer, and his relationship with Shakspere is limited to the will.)

Shakspere's will does not express any enlightened interest in matters educational. In contrast, Marston left money to educate the sons of one of his friends. Actors such as Heminges, Condell, John Bentley, and John Underwood provided for their children's education, sometimes specifying their daughters' education. Jacob Meade, who helped Henslowe and Alleyn manage the bear pits, provided for the education of his granddaughter. Shakspere left no comparable bequests for his eight-year-old granddaughter or anyone else.

Shakspere's will does confirm his theatrical associations. He bequeaths money for mourning rings to his "fellows" Heminges, Condell, and Burbage. This bequest, made in an interlineation, proves that Shakspere was a "fellow" actor or shareholder, but it does not prove that he wrote any plays.

Shakspere remembers no one in the literary profession, but he does remember someone else. He leaves his sword to Thomas Combe, nephew of the usurer, John Combe, who had left Shakspere £5 when he died.

Shakspere's will reinforces many documented facts of his life: That he was a professional associate of the King's Men, that he was on personal terms with the Combe family, and that he made a lot of money and provided for its prudent disposition. Yet the three signatures (fig. 15) display an awkward, insecure, and inconsistent hand, and Shakspere's concern for legal process and estate preservation obviously exceeded his interest in the art of expression. Certainly any powers of eloquent composition or dictation failed him at the last, even when his administrative skills did not.

If Shakspere of Stratford was a successful businessman, theatre shareholder, investor, entrepreneur, and broker, there is no conflict whatsoever between the substance and appearance of the will and the man's life history. But if Shakspere of Stratford was the greatest writer in the English language, you would never in 400 years guess it from the will's content and presentation.

EULOGIES AND DEATH

"His death evoked no great outpouring of homage. That was reserved for his rival Jonson, who was accorded, six months after he expired, an entire volume of eulogy." So stated Schoenbaum, as though that made sense (*Lives*, 27).

Over twenty years after Shakspere died, Jonson was buried in Westminster Abbey. Spenser was buried there in 1599, Beaumont in 1616, and Drayton in 1631. We know from *Parnassus 3* (I.ii.227–28) that by 1601, it was already an honor to be interred in the abbey near Chaucer in what is now called Poets' Corner. By 1623, Jonson and William Basse had suggested that Shakespeare deserved the honor of burial in the abbey, but the statue of Shakespeare in Poets' Corner was not installed until 1740.

The most celebrated writers of their time, Spenser, Jonson, even Marlowe, were either buried in Westminster Abbey or mourned in print at death, and we are always told that Shakspere achieved celebrity as a writer during his own lifetime. It is remarkable, therefore, that nothing marked Shakspere's demise until seven years after his death. Not one poet noted the event. However, the silence in the historic record makes sense if he was recognized, not as the poet, but as a successful businessman whose death was no loss to the literary community. (Chapters 9 and 10 take a closer look at the circumstances surrounding Shakspere's death and the posthumous tributes of 1623.)

THE FAMOUS WITNESS

A 1612 document reinforces the nonliterary Shakspere found thus far. The document is the Mountjoy lawsuit, a domestic dispute in which Shakspere testified as witness and alleged broker for a marriage negotiation dating back to 1604.

By the time of the 1612 depositions, Shakespeare's literary reputation had long since been established. Yet Shakspere testified as "William Shakespeare of Stratford upon Avon . . . gentleman of the Age of 48 years or thereabouts," not as a poet. Back in 1604, Shakspere was still a member of the King's Men, and at least two-thirds of the Shakespeare plays had been written. One witness testified that in 1604, "Mr. Shakespeare was employed by the defendant about that business" to negotiate the marriage, but Shakspere's regular occupation was not specified (Wallace, "Associates," 282, 292).

The Mountjoy deposition is a legal document, but even legal documents can reveal something about the professional activities of the parties involved. In a deposition of 1608, Chapman was described as someone who "hath since very unadvisedly spent the most part of his time and his estate in fruitless and vain Poetry." Another witness, testifying in 1617, identified Chapman as someone who "hath made diverse plays and written other books. But whether he may be termed a Poet or not this deponent . . . doth not know" (Eccles, "Chapman's," 184; Sisson and Butman, 185). In contrast, Shakspere apparently went from play broker to marriage broker, but in no place was he identified as a maker of plays or vain poetry.

EVIDENCE FOR THE PLAYWRIGHT

McManaway wrote an essay in which he defended Shakspere's literary credentials. He did so in part by arguing that fewer biographical records have survived for most other writers of the day, such as Marlowe, Peele, Dekker, and Daniel. But McManaway missed his own point. Some of the personal evidence he cited for those poorly documented writers was *literary*. When McManaway argued that only a fragment of poetry in Daniel's handwriting survives, he was arguing the case for the anti-Stratfordian. A literary fragment survives for Daniel. No such literary fragment survives for Shakspere. *All* of Shakspere's undisputed personal records are nonliterary, and that is not only unusual—it is bizarre. Statistically, it is also a virtual impossibility.

Over seventy historical records survive for Shakspere, but not one reveals his supposed primary professional occupation of writing. Indeed, the only evidence that proves Shakspere wrote anything is six shaky signatures. Shakspere's documentary evidence further suggests that he was ill-suited to a literary career. He is a man of no recorded education. He appears to have been uncomfortable using a pen. His documentary trail is bookless, and his will has not a trace of literary sensibilities in composition or content.

All the Shakespearean *literary* allusions are either impersonal, confined to literary criticism, or ambiguous. The few allusions purporting to tell the reader something more about "Shakespeare," the writer, are cryptic or inconclusive. The dedication introducing the 1609 edition of *Shake-speares Sonnets* tells us that by then, the poet was already dead. In short, the Shakespearean literary allusions fail any reasonable test that would qualify them as personal records belonging to Shakspere.

In *Shakespeare: A Biographical Handbook*, Bentley organized the personal documents for Shakspere's history into different phases of his life, putting all the Stratford-based records in one chapter, theatrical activities in another, and so on. In his chapter entitled "The Actor," for example, Bentley cited Augustine Phillipps's 1605 will and its bequest to his "Fellowe Shakespeare." But in his chapter entitled "The Playwright," Bentley cited not one personal document for William Shakspere. Not one.

Some biographers have concluded that Shakespeare was the most celebrated writer of his day. Others have placed him second to Jonson in popularity and renown. And yet Shakspere is the *only* alleged writer of any consequence from the period who left *no* personal contemporaneous records revealing that he wrote for a living. In contrast, the literary fragments left behind by Shakespeare's lesser contemporaries yield more than a name on a title page, a disembodied name in a list, or a play review. The comparative chart in the Appendix shows that the biography of Shakspere *as a man of letters* is unsupported by the sort of personal literary documentation found for *any* of his lesser contemporaries.

Scholars have retrieved literary fragments for those lesser contemporaries with far fewer man-hours and fewer research grants behind them. Still, in *every* case, the personal documents reveal writing as a vocation for the individuals in question. If we had the sort of evidence for Shakspere that we have for his colleagues—that is, straightforward, contemporaneous, and *personal* literary records for the man who allegedly wrote Shakespeare's plays—there would be no authorship debate.

PART THREE

MISLEADING AND MISSING EVIDENCE

Chapter Nine

A Moniment Without a Tomb

A doubt, perhaps not unworthy of notice, has arisen among some whether the old monumental bust of Shakespeare in the Collegiate Church of Stratford upon Avon Warwickshire, had any resemblance of the Bard.
—The Rev. Joseph Greene, letter to *Gentlemen's Magazine*,
June 1759

Most in the academic community are convinced that Shakspere of Stratford wrote the plays attributed to "William Shakespeare." Why? Simply put, they have posthumous evidence. In 1623, the man from Stratford was identified as the dramatist in the *First Folio*, when Ben Jonson dubbed Shakespeare the "Sweet Swan of Avon" and another poet referred to Shakspere's "Stratford moniment." This chapter investigates Shakspere's burial and Stratford monument.

Material in this chapter, previously published as "Reconsidering Shakespeare's Monument" in *The Review of English Studies* (May 1997), appears here by permission of Oxford University Press.

THE UNMARKED GRAVE

When Shakspere bought the tithes in 1605, he automatically became a lay rector, entitled to burial in the church chancel. But in 1616, the vicar of Holy Trinity Church in Stratford would have had to point out Shakspere's tombstone to visitors, because he was buried in an unmarked grave. The following doggerel appears on a stone slab in the floor of the chancel:

> GOOD FREND FOR JESUS SAKE FORBEARE,
> TO DIGG THE DUST ENCLOASED HERE
> BLESTE BE THE MAN THAT SPARES THES STONES
> AND CURST BE HE THAT MOVES MY BONES

An early biographer, Charles Knight, noted that "it is very remarkable, we think, that this plain free-stone does not bear the name of Shakspere—has nothing to establish the fact that the stone originally belonged to his grave" (535). In 1737, someone identified the grave for the visiting artist, George Vertue, who sketched the chancel and labeled the grave "no. 1," referenced in his marginal note (fig. 21).

Today's gravestone was installed in the 1700s to replace the original slab. The doggerel on that slab had been chiseled in an "uncouth mixture of small and capital letters" (Shakespeare, *Plays*, 2:506). This doggerel—poorly chiseled on an anonymous slab—was all the respect that Shakspere received until a monument was installed, sometime before 1623.

THE STRATFORD MONUMENT

The monument of Shakspere (fig. 16) is mounted on the wall of the chancel in Holy Trinity Church, and it is accepted by biographers as a commemoration of William Shakespeare, the dramatist. The monument was first referred to in the 1623 collection of Shakespeare's plays, and its epitaph was first transcribed around 1626 by the antiquarian John Weever. Another antiquarian, Sir William Dugdale (1605–86), also transcribed the epitaphs and made the first known sketch of the monument (fig. 17) around 1634, while preparing *Antiquities of Warwickshire*, first published in 1656.

Many details in Dugdale's sketch are missing or wrong, yet overall his sketch corresponds to the bust. Dugdale drew the tassels of the cushion and correctly positioned Shakspere's hands, but conspicu-

Figure 16. Shakspere's funerary monument, installed in Holy Trinity Church some time before 1623. *Courtesy of The Cleveland Public Library.*

In the north wall of the Quire is
this monument fixed for william
shakespeare the famous poet

Iudicio Pylium &c.

Figure 17. Sir William Dugdale's sketch, ca. 1634, of the
monument of William Shakspere, Holy Trinity Church,
Stratford-upon-Avon. *Photograph by Gerald E. Downs. By
permission of Sir William Dugdale.*

ously missing from his sketch are the quill and paper. Records show that over the years, the quill was as often missing as not. Reference was made to a missing quill in 1748, and a new one was inserted in 1790 (Halliwell-Phillipps, *Outlines*, 1:259). Engravings published in 1827 and 1856 show the monument without a quill (Wivell, frontispiece; Shakespeare, *Dramatic*, frontispiece). So does an oil painting of about 1828 (Fox, *Honour*, 81). In 1908, a biographer wrote that the "fingers of the right hand are disposed *as if* holding a pen" (Lee, *Life*, 286, emphasis added). The pen was evidently missing on the day Dugdale brought his sketchpad.

If there was no pen, Dugdale could have missed the paper. He was sketching in a badly lit chancel, and the condition of the paint at that time is unknown (the bust was repainted in 1649), so the paper may not have stood out in a contrasting color. Alternatively, Dugdale may have left out the paper when modifying the position of the cushion. When he inked in the cushion (pencil marks beneath the ink are still visible), he apparently picked the lesser of two evils. Rather than extend Shakspere's already elongated doublet, he evidently chose to draw the cushion on end to fill up the space and may therefore have chosen to omit the paper.

Dugdale's flawed sketch served as the model for the published engraving (fig. 18), which is attributed to Wenceslaus Hollar but is possibly the handiwork of one of his assistants. Hollar's lumpy cushion has been interpreted by some as "suspiciously resembling a woolsack" (Stopes, *Environment*, 109). That interpretation has fueled anti-Stratfordian theories that the original monument commemorated a sack-holding commodity trader, and that today's bust is a substitute that was supposedly installed around 1748–50 (Ogburn, 212–13; Whalen, *Who Was*, 20–21, and "Problem," 10–11). On the other hand, in his 1691 *An Account of the English Dramatick Poets*, Gerard Langbaine described the monument's "cushion," and he had probably seen Hollar's engraving rather than the monument itself. Some anti-Stratfordians consider the cushion itself a suspicious accoutrement, but just such a cushion appears in a 1620 monument of Bishop Goodwin at Oxford (fig. 19).

Most importantly, Hollar's substantial improvisations necessarily render his engraving unreliable as evidence of the monument's original appearance. Because Hollar was working from Dugdale's sketch rather than the monument itself, he had to invent many details. For example, the sketch offered no facial likeness to go on, so Hollar made one up. He could not have looked too closely at the corners

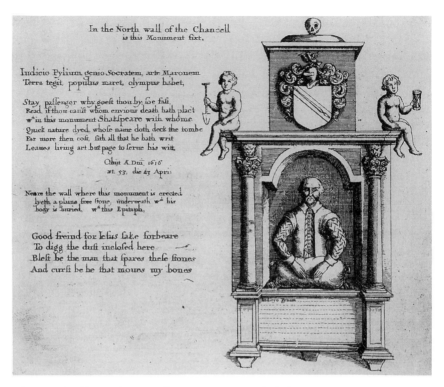

Figure 18. Wenceslaus Hollar's engraving of Shakspere's monument, published in Sir William Dugdale's *Antiquities of Warwickshire* in 1656 and in the revised edition of 1730. This engraving was adapted for Nicholas Rowe's edition of Shakespeare in 1709 and John Bell's in 1786. *Courtesy of The Cleveland Public Library.*

of the "sack," where Dugdale drew the tassels of a cushion, not the twisted ends of a sack. Ultimately, Dugdale's rendering shows sufficient correspondence with the monument to confirm that in 1634, he was looking at the same one seen today.

Two images by Vertue also predate the alleged monument substitution. His engraving (fig. 20), based on a drawing no longer extant, was published in 1725 and was the first to represent Shakspere's monument with relative accuracy. The architectural details are correct, and although Vertue fashioned the bust after the so-called "Chandos" portrait—right down to the earring—his artistic license is comparable to that of other engravers of his day, given the lax attitude toward fidelity in the years before photography. In addition, his drawing of 1737 (fig. 21), made on-site (F. Simpson, 56), corresponds to his earlier engraving.

Figure 19. The 1620 monument of Bishop Goodwin in Christ Church Cathedral, Oxford. The architecture of this and of Shakspere's monument are similar, and like Shakspere's, this monument has a cushion. *Courtesy of the photographer, Derran Charlton.*

By 1746, the monument was in a state of disrepair, and a Stratford schoolmaster, the Rev. Joseph Greene, wrote to various correspondents about plans to restore "the original monument."* Accordingly, in 1748–49, the monument was repaired and beautified, and other

*Throughout his correspondence, the Rev. Greene consistently referred to Shakspere's monument as "the original" to distinguish it from the recently installed (1740) Shakespeare cenotaph in Westminster Abbey.

Figure 20. George Vertue's engraving, published in Alexander Pope's edition of Shakespeare in 1725. *Courtesy of The Cleveland Public Library.*

Figure 21. George Vertue's 1737 sketch of Shakspere's monument in the chancel of Holy Trinity Church. *Courtesy of The Cleveland Public Library.*

restoration projects were undertaken in the late 1830s and in 1861 (Stopes, *Environment*, 113, 121). Years later, J. Dover Wilson made his much-quoted pronouncement that Shakspere's effigy still looked like a "self-satisfied pork butcher" (*Essential*, 6). So while the pudgy effigy may have its detractors, its integrity is intact.

HERE LIES SHAKSPERE

The published images of Shakspere's monument have prompted questions about its authenticity, but fewer questions have been raised about its inscription (fig. 22). If this epitaph commemorated a cryptographer, it could not be more baffling. But biographers tell us that it commemorated a celebrated playwright, and it is therefore all the more baffling. Although the death date at the bottom corresponds to within two days of the date recorded in the burial register, little else in this epitaph makes sense. Indeed, it fails as a tribute to a recognized writer.

The first two lines translate into "In judgment a Nestor, in intellect [or wit] a Socrates, in art a Virgil; the earth encloses, the people mourn, and Olympus holds." Nestor was wise, and Socrates was a great thinker, but neither had anything to do with writing, much less dramatic literature. The poet Virgil is the only name that comes close to being appropriate for a literary epitaph, but it was not a particularly

JVDICIO PYLIVM. GENIO SOCRATEM, ARTE MARONEM,
TERRA TEGIT, POPVLVS MÆRET, OLYMPVS HABET.

STAY PASSENGER, WHY GOEST THOV BY SO FAST,
READ IF THOV CANST, WHOM ENVIOVS DEATH HATH PLAST
WITH IN THIS MONVEMENT SHAKESPEARE: WITH WHOME,
QVICK NATVRE DIDE WHOSE NAME DOTH DECK y^s [THIS] TOMBE,
FAR MORE, THEN COST: SIEH ALL, y^s [THAT] HE HATH WRITT,
LEAVES LIVING ART, BVT PAGE, TO SERVE HIS WITT.

OBIT ANO DO^I 1616
ÆTATIS 53 DIE 23 AP^R

Figure 22. Inscription from Shakspere's monument.

good choice. Virgil was not one of Shakespeare's principal sources.
When Jonson searched for big-name authors from antiquity to keep
company with "Shakespeare" (see Jonson's eulogy in Chapter 10) he
chose Euripides, Plautus, and others famous for dramatic literature.
No comparable names appear in Shakspere's epitaph. The dramatist's
favorite source, Ovid, is not mentioned, either. In addition, Mount
Parnassus, sacred to the Muses, would have been the preferable
choice for a poet, rather than Olympus, generic home to all the Greek
gods.

Considering the principal part of the epitaph, death cannot literally
have placed the deceased "with in this monument," because the monument itself is too small to hold a corpse. J. O. Halliwell-Phillipps
considered this statement evidence that the epitaph was written off-
site by someone who never saw the monument. Maybe it was, but
there is a more logical explanation. The wording ("with in this monument") and the monument's architecture suggest that it was originally designed, not for wall mounting, but to sit directly on top of
the tomb itself. The monument in *Antiquities of Warwickshire* most
closely resembling Shakspere's sits directly on such a commodious
sarcophagus (fig. 23).

In addition, Shakspere's monument is not supported by ornate cor-
bels (wall brackets) typical of old monuments. The three stubby
blocks at the bottom (see fig. 16) look like afterthoughts, tacked on,
as if wall-mounting was a substitute arrangement. They therefore also

Figure 23. The Peyto monument from Sir William Dugdale's *Antiquities of Warwickshire*. The architecture of the upper half of this monument is similar to that of Shakspere's (see fig. 16). *Courtesy of The Cleveland Public Library.*

support the theory that the original plan was to place the monument over the tomb itself.

Similarly, the absence of certain factual details in the epitaph supports this theory. Whoever wrote the epitaph left out Shakspere's Christian name, as well as the usual family information such as "William, husband of." These omissions make no sense. Shakspere was a common surname in Warwickshire, and William was the last existing male in his line. Anybody who had anything to do with erecting the monument—whether Shakspere himself, family, or friends—would surely have been concerned about his first name. The epitaph tells us that his "name doth deck this* tomb," but there is no full name elsewhere, and there is no attached tomb. The likeliest explanation, again, is that the full name and family details were originally supposed to appear in a second epitaph on the bottom half of the monument, but for some reason, that plan was never carried out.

In final support of this theory, note that there is hardly any room left at the end of the epitaph for the date of death (fig. 16). The two lines appear to be unplanned afterthoughts, carved in small cramped letters in order to fit. They, too, were probably originally intended to appear somewhere else nearby. If Shakspere's monument was originally designed to sit on top of the sarcophagus, then at least the fourth, fifth, and sixth lines would make sense.

Most importantly, the epitaph does not commemorate a dramatist. The phrase "Since all, [that] He hath writt, Leaves living art, but page, to serve his witt"[†] is almost incomprehensible, and the abundance of commas does not help. Few biographers attempt to paraphrase it, and they generally pass up the opportunity to quote those who do. Stanley Wells interpreted the epitaph as "a cryptic remark which I take to mean that everything that he has written leaves an art that lives, if only on the page, to demonstrate his genius, with perhaps a pun on page as 'side of a sheet of paper' and 'pageboy' " (10). Halliwell-Phillipps read the epitaph as recognition of Shakespeare's ability to interpret nature (*Outlines*, 1:260). These attempts fail to satisfy. Although an apologist could read the whole epitaph as an inferior or cryptic version of "Here lies Shakespeare," an objective

---

*The symbol Y in the inscription is a "thorn," an engraver's shortcut for the sound "th."

†Most commentators interpret "sieh" as a misspelling of "sith," an archaic form of "since."

reader would have to admit that it does not pay explicit tribute to Shakespeare, the celebrated dramatist and poet.

Why isn't Shakspere's epitaph straightforward and eloquent, perhaps quoting one of the sonnets, for example,

> Here lies William Shakespeare, our great dramatist.
> Not marble, nor the gilded monuments
> Of princes, shall outlive his powerful rhyme.

Instead, the epitaph fails as testimony to a recognized man of letters. The three impressive but irrelevant classical names from ancient history, and the dense passage including the words "writt," "page," and "art" do not constitute satisfying or even coherent praise for a poet.

Physician John Hall's epitaph of 1635 reads, from the Latin, "most celebrated in the medical arts," and the burial register described him as the "most skillful of physicians." It is ironic that Hall elicited more explicit professional recognition at his death than did his supposedly more illustrious father-in-law. Shakspere's epitaph also compares poorly with those for Edmund Spenser ("with thee our English verse was rais'd on high"), Francis Beaumont ("He that can write so well"), Michael Drayton ("a Memorable Poet of his Age"), John Taylor ("Here lies the Water Poet"), or George Chapman ("a Christian Philosopher and Homericall Poet") (Pettigrew, 406, 407; Le Neve, 150).

A few other stray facts and posthumous legends are known about the inception of Shakspere's monument. One tradition, reported seventy or more years later, tells us that Shakspere wrote tombstone doggerel for himself and for usurer John Combe. While most biographers would cringe at the very idea, some accept those legends. *The Norton Shakespeare* editors, for example, introduced the jingle about the bones as "an epitaph he is said to have devised. . . . The verses are hardly among Shakespeare's finest, but they seem to have been effective" (Shakespeare, 45). But whether or not Shakspere had anything to do with his own or Combe's epitaph, Combe's funerary monument does have something in common with Shakspere's. Dugdale noted that the same stonemason, Gheerart Janssen, made both monuments. Janssen's shop was in Southwark, the precinct in which the Globe theatre was situated. Shakspere's and Combe's choice of the same stonemason is probably not merely a coincidence.

Combe died in 1614. In 1619, someone reported that Combe had arranged for his monument during his lifetime. Combe's will confirms that report; his will provided £60 for his monument (Chambers, *Facts*, 2:137, 139). Thomas Pope, another shareholder whose coat of arms prompted an official complaint, provided for a monument in his will. Preparing a monument to yourself was generally the prerogative of the titled classes and those of means. Combe, a baseborn usurer but one of the richest men in town, arranged for his. Perhaps, not to be outdone, Shakspere also arranged for his monument during his lifetime.* If Shakspere made such arrangements, his behavior is consistent with others who were as socially ambitious.

In *Every Man Out of His Humour*, Sogliardo planned for his own tomb, and one of his acquaintances suggested that he adorn the tomb with a hobby-horse costume. According to Halliwell-Phillipps's *Dictionary of Archaic Words*, the "hobby-horse" was "an important personage in the morris dance. . . . The hobby-horse consisted of a light frame of wicker-work, fastened to the body of the person who performed the character. . . . Thus equipped, he performed all sorts of antics, imitating the movements of a horse and executing juggling tricks of various kinds." The prop strikes Sogliardo as a suitable memorial to himself.

SOGLIARDO: The horse hangs at home in my parlor. I'll keep it for a monument, as long as I live, sure.

CARLO BUFFONE: Do so; and when you die, 'twill be an excellent trophy, to hang over your tomb.

SOGLIARDO: Mass, and I'll have a tomb (now I think on't) 'tis but so much charges.

CARLO BUFFONE: Best build it in your life time then, your heirs may hap to forget it else.

SOGLIARDO: Nay, I mean so, I'll not trust to them. (II.i.67–76)

Did Shakspere not trust to his relatives either? If only the top section of the monument was in progress or completed before he died, per-

---

*Shakspere may have taken the unusual step of signing all three pages of his will in another attempt to keep up with the Combes. According to Eccles, "John Combe had declared [in his will] that he had 'unto every sheet hereof written my name' "; likewise, Combe's brother Thomas (d. 1609) had placed his mark "unto every sheet" of his will. The same attorney, Francis Collins, witnessed both Combe's and Shakspere's wills (*Warwickshire*, 142; on will-signing procedures, see Honigmann and Brock, 12).

haps his family failed to follow his instructions and instead econo-
mized by scrapping the bottom part of the tomb.

We *know* that Shakspere had pretensions to gentility, and his documented social climbing makes him the sort of person who, like
Combe—or Sogliardo—would arrange for his own monument during
his lifetime. This explanation could account for the doggerel, the monument, and the epitaph. Shakspere's grammar school education and
native wit would have equipped him to write both the doggerel and the
epitaph. In fact, it is entirely in character to find him bombasting out
his own epitaph. He would think it great verse, while sophisticated
readers would find it inferior. And think again about the line, "Since
all, [that] He hath writ, / Leaves living art, but page, to serve his witt."
These lines sound as though they came out of the mouth of Dogberry, the constable from *Much Ado about Nothing* who fractures the
English language. Like Dogberry or Sogliardo, the epitaph writer tries
to sound impressive, but ends up sounding incoherent and ultimately
ridiculous. Recall that Sogliardo was concerned with the sound of his
own name. Perhaps the epitaph writer was trying to call attention to
the "name" of the deceased, a name "far more" important to the
memorial "than cost" or expense. If the writer of the epitaph, whoever he was, seriously intended to commemorate "Shakspeare" as a
great poet and playwright, then words failed him.

To sum up, neither the monument nor the epitaph satisfies as a
memorial to a recognized poet. Louis Untermeyer wrote that "the
flabby hand that holds a quill pen might be that of an accountant
rather than a poet" (104), and Untermeyer may not have been too
far off. If the monument commemorates a businessman, theatre
shareholder, and play broker who was sometimes mistaken for the
author of the Shakespeare plays, then the Stratford monument cap-
tures the man. An opportunist who brazenly accepted ignorant praise
meant for someone else, and who procured or vulgarized texts for
theatre companies or publishers, might very well have designed a
monument of himself holding a quill. But with his untutored "natural
wit," he would have been incapable of inventing anything better than
a bombastic epitaph.

Nobody knows the precise circumstances surrounding the commission of Shakspere's monument. No one even knows exactly when
the monument was installed, but we do know it was erected by 1623,
because a poet named Leonard Digges referred to it in that year in
the *First Folio*.

Chapter Ten

The *First Folio*

> The First Folio was first and foremost a commercial undertaking
> from which virtually everybody involved would have expected
> some kind of financial gain.
> —Peter W. M. Blayney, "Introduction to the Second Edition,"
> *The Norton Facsimile: The First Folio of Shakespeare* (xxix)

The *First Folio* is the name given by posterity to the first edition of
Shakespeare's collected plays, published in 1623 under the title *Mr.
William Shakespeare's Comedies, Histories, & Tragedies.* The book
contains thirty-six of his thirty-seven known plays (*Pericles* was ex-
cluded), eighteen of which had not been previously published. It also
contains two formal introductory letters, a frontispiece accompanied
by a poem, and several tributes in verse. It is in this prefatory material
that Shakspere of Stratford is identified as the dramatist for the first
time in the historical record. However, as we will see, some of that
prefatory material also points, not to Shakspere, but to an anonymous
man of rank. Anyone who reads through *all* the prefatory material to
the *First Folio* has to choose between two sets of signposts, those
pointing to Shakspere of Stratford and those pointing to an aristocrat.

HEMINGES, CONDELL, AND JONSON

John Heminges and Henry Condell were Shakspere's fellow share-holders and actors, and they are generally credited as the driving forces behind the *First Folio*. In the two epistles that appear in the *Folio* over their names, they claim to have collected Shakspere's manuscripts, not for profit, but as homage to so "worthy a Friend, & Fellow . . . as was our Shakespeare." Such a statement supports the conclusion that these two actors personally recognized Shakspere of Stratford as the dramatist. Samuel Schoenbaum considered their *Folio* testimony "the most crucial single document in the annals of authorship attribution" (*Evidence*, 167). Since Shakspere remembered both actors in his will, Heminges and Condell are critical links between *Shakespeare's Comedies, Histories, & Tragedies* and Shakspere of Stratford. Therefore, the information appearing in the epistles warrants serious scrutiny.

In the epistles, Heminges and Condell claim responsibility for producing the *Folio*, and most biographers assume they edited the book as well. Yet it is unlikely that Heminges and Condell played these pivotal roles. One authority on the *Folio*, W. W. Greg, pointed out that the actors' names subscribed to the dedicatory letters "might be supposed to imply that it was the players who were primarily responsible for the publication, were it not that in the Beaumont and Fletcher collection of 1647 the epistle—to Philip, Earl of Pembroke and Montgomery, the survivor of the two brothers to whom the Shakespeare Folio was dedicated—is similarly signed by ten members of . . . the King's company, although it is plain from the bookseller's address that it was Mosely [the publisher and bookseller] who was the moving spirit" (*Folio*, 1 n). If the Beaumont and Fletcher anthology is anything to go by, then the publishers, not the two actors, were the entrepreneurs behind the *First Folio*. From a strictly commercial standpoint, it is also far more likely that the publishers undertook the project, because they stood a good chance of making money on it (see McKenzie, 32–40, esp. n. 61; Blayney, "Second," xxviii–xxix).

Moreover, it is highly unlikely that Heminges and Condell composed either epistle themselves. Neither was a writer, and the particular language and style employed in both epistles has led some authorities, such as Malone and Greg, to conclude that they were written primarily or entirely by Ben Jonson (Shakespeare, *Plays*, 2:

674; Greg, *Folio*, 17–21, 26–27, and "Publishers," 151–52). The case for Jonson's authorship begins with the professional quality of the language and continues with numerous stylistic parallels with Jonson's attributed works. The author borrowed or paraphrased from *Bartholomew Fair*, and, most tellingly, from Jonson's then-unpublished translation of a tract by Pliny (Shakespeare, *Plays*, 2:661–74; Platt, 103–6). Chambers decided that "Jonson's claim seems to me on the whole the better" (*Facts*, 1:142). Since there are no writing samples from either Hemings or Condell with which to make comparisons, it is impossible to base a judgment on their compositional style. However, based on similarities to or outright borrowings from his other works, Jonson's authorship of the two epistles is not only plausible, it is a virtual certainty. And there is more evidence.

As we will see, Jonson's hand in the epistles can also be traced directly through the claim that Shakspere supposedly drafted his manuscripts with "that easiness, that we have scarce received from him a blot in his papers." That is an improbable statement when laid alongside the six labored and blotchy Shakspere signatures. It is not inherently plausible, either. Can anyone seriously imagine that Shakespeare penned straight through all thirty-seven plays without making mistakes or changes? Moreover, the statement would insult any professional writer. Marveling at a clean manuscript may have been the actors' naïve idea of a tribute, but it hardly squares with the notion of a writer struggling for perfection in draft after draft. Jonson knew full well that the actors' "compliment" was an ignorant insult, wrote it down anyway, and then *admitted to the deed* years later in his journal.

THE EPISTLES

Biographers have persisted in representing the *Folio* epistles as straightforward testimony by Heminges and Condell, yet the testimony is neither straightforward nor that of the two actors. We are dealing here with critical evidence of Shakspere's presumed literary career, so the issues are important. The full significance of Jonson's authorship of these two epistles will become clearer when we have examined the rest of his Shakespearean testimony.

The evidentiary value of the epistles is further undermined by factual inconsistencies, exaggerated claims, and outright misinformation. For example, we read that Shakspere did not have "the fate, common with some, to be executor to his own writings." The next epistle expands on this claim: "but since it hath been ordain'd otherwise, and he by death departed from that right, we . . . have collected and publish'd them." In other words, Shakspere was prevented by fate and death from publishing his plays. Yet biographers tell us that he spent the last years of his life in Stratford in affluent retirement. One thing he was *not* doing in his presumably copious spare time was making certain that his plays were published. According to Greg, "it is foolish to suppose that Shakespeare was indifferent to the fate of his own works" (*Folio*, 2). Foolish, yes, but the fact remains that the dramatist, whoever he was, exhibited no interest in publishing his plays. As we saw in Chapter 8, Shakspere did not even object when others pirated or corrupted the plays.

Note the reference to Shakspere's *right* to publish his plays ("he by death departed from that right"). This statement conflicts with received wisdom. We are always informed that Shakspere no longer had any rights, because he did not *own* the plays that had been purchased by the acting company. Even supposing that he had no legal right to publish, what was stopping him from supervising publication? Why did he not ensure that his plays were left to posterity as he wrote them? Surely he would have wanted any corrupt texts replaced with good ones, but as far as the record shows, he did nothing. Ironically, the author of the *Folio* epistle expressed indignation, even if Shakspere did not:

as where (before) you were abused with diverse stolne, and surreptitious copies, maimed, and deformed by the frauds and stealths of injurious imposters, that exposed them: even those, are now offered to your view cured, and perfect of their limbs; and all the rest, absolute in their numbers, as he conceived them.

The epistles further claim that the actors themselves collected Shakspere's plays for publication, but nobody knows how all thirty-six play texts got to the printers. Heminges and Condell, on behalf of the King's Men, might have provided some of the twenty-two plays registered at the time of publication, although it is likely that such an outright contribution would have left the company at a disadvantage.

Acting companies did not make a habit of selling, much less giving away, plays from their repertory to publishers, and the steps they took to prevent publication indicate that it was not generally in their best interest. Many scholars assume that the acting company was respon-

sible for blocking the publication of *Henry V* and *Much Ado* and
otherwise "safeguarding most of their Shakespearean plays" (Chambers, *Facts*, 1:146). In 1599, Henslowe's agent paid forty shillings to
"stay the printing" of *Patient Grissell*, which had gone into production two months earlier (Foakes and Rickert, 130, 132). A 1608
contract involving one of the boy companies (The Children of the
King's Revels) contained a provision penalizing any partner who
would "cause to be put in print, any manner of play book now in
use" (Hillebrand, "Child," 224). As we have seen, *King Lear* and
Pericles were both performed in the provinces by Cholmeley's Players
shortly after the plays were published (Sisson, "Quartos," 138–39).
According to Hillebrand, Martin Slater was sued for staging a play
using a script that had belonged to an actor with a rival company
("Child," 224). Concerning the 1623 *First Folio* in particular, Heminges paid £5 to the Revels office in 1627 to prevent a rival company
from performing plays published in the *Folio* (Ingleby, *Centurie*,
157). Clearly, if the King's Men released texts from their repertory
for publication, it was not to their long-term benefit. Yet biographers
such as Schoenbaum and Richard Dutton accept the claim that the
actors voluntarily provided the playbooks out of sheer admiration for
their late colleague.

However, the King's Men could not possibly have provided all the
Shakespeare plays for publication, because they did not own all of
them. No records survive to show how the *Folio* publishers obtained
those plays (at least eight, perhaps as many as fourteen) already owned
by printers and publishers outside the *Folio* syndicate. It would have
been the publishing syndicate, not the actors, who negotiated for
permission to print previously registered or published material. Blayney supposed that two of the five named publishers in the *First Folio*
syndicate "chose to join the venture as proportional shareholders
rather than to sell or lease" their copyrights ("Second," xxviii). According to bibliographer Leo Kirschbaum, "the whole matter of temporary publishing rights . . . in the 1623 Shakespeare folio is clouded
and obscure (that is, there must have been some deal between the
individual owners of the copies and the publishers)" ("Copyright,"
246).* In addition, as far as anyone knows, three plays had never

---

*Greg alluded to the matter of temporary rights in Jonson's 1616 collected *Works*,
in which the publishers of two earlier single editions were given title-page credit
(*Folio*, 14 n). Stansby owned copyright to many of Jonson's masques but published
most of the rest of Jonson's works without any recorded transfer of copyright from
previous owners, and without entry. For a summary of copyright issues involved in
Jonson's 1616 folio, see Jonson, *Ben Jonson* (9:13–15).

been performed and might still have been sitting on the author's desk. The claim that Heminges and Condell collected all thirty-six plays cannot be taken literally.

In another misleading statement, the epistles claim that the *Folio* was typeset from the author's manuscripts "as he conceived them." There is hardly a scholar around who believes that statement. The claim was obviously made to promote the edition as though it were based on the author's original manuscripts. Most of the plays were in fact typeset from earlier editions, transcripts by parties unknown, or theatrical promptbooks. The claim is merely one of several instances of promotional hype in the epistles (e.g., "what ever you do, Buy").

It must now be evident that the *Folio* epistles are largely advertising copy and exaggeration. Moreover, they show signs of being deliberately misleading, particularly on those points that cross-reference with Jonson's later testimony (discussed in the next chapter). Gary Taylor expressed caution about taking the "ambiguous oracles of the First Folio" at face value (Wells et al., 18). Therefore, any authorship conclusion based on those ambiguous oracles must likewise be questioned.

"GENTLE" SHAKESPEARE

Martin Droeshout created the most famous image purporting to be William Shakespeare (fig. 24). It is the face that sells postcards, books, and souvenirs. According to Charlton Hinman, "the Droeshout engraving, apparently based on a line drawing by some other and now unknown artist, is not very skillfully executed and can scarcely be thought either especially pleasing or a good likeness" (ix). The engraving is, after the Stratford bust, the only image of Shakspere with any claim to authority, yet its claim is tenuous.

Droeshout was a Flemish artist whose reputation today is little known beyond this assignment. He was born in 1601 and was therefore twenty or twenty-one years old when commissioned for the *Folio* engraving. If Droeshout ever met his future subject in living flesh, he would have been no more than fifteen at the time.

Nobody knows what Droeshout used as his model, but it could not have been the dead body. It could have been a death mask, the engraver's six-year-old memories, a portrait of Shakspere that no longer exists, a picture of somebody else, or a figment of the artist's

Figure 24. Martin Droeshout's engraving from the 1623 *First Folio. Courtesy of The Cleveland Public Library.*

imagination. Whatever inspired it, it has not filled all Shakespeare lovers with a sense of satisfaction.

Among the observations that have been made about the Droeshout engraving are that the "horrible hydrocephalous" head is dispropor-tionately large for the body and looks like it is sitting on a plate; the asymmetrical Dutch-cut hair looks like a bad wig; the mouth is too small and too far to the right; the eyes and nose "are too small for the face"; the ear is malformed; the face has a five o'clock shadow; the eyes are too close together; one eye is lower than the other; there is a distracting white crescent beneath the right eye; the lighting comes from more than one source; the doublet is disproportionately small, the sections are asymmetrical, and the shoulder "wings" are "grotesquely large and vilely drawn" (Lewis, 2:555–56; Spielmann, 32–38). Bear in mind that Droeshout was a Jacobean engraver, not Pablo Picasso.

The following lines, attributed to Jonson, accompanied the Droeshout engraving into print:

> To the Reader.
>
> This Figure, that thou here seest put,
>   It was for gentle Shakespeare cut;
> Wherein the Graver had a strife
>   with Nature, to out-do the life:
> O, could he but have drawn his wit
>   As well in brass, as he hath hit
> His face; the Print would then surpass
>   All, that was ever writ in brass.
> But, since he cannot, Reader, look
>   Not on his Picture, but his Book
>   B. I.

As one scholar dryly observed, "it is lucky these metrical commendations are not required to be delivered upon oath" (Boaden, 11).

One ambiguity appears in the phrase "hit his face," which refers to the engraver who cuts the image into the metal plate. However, "hit" is also a past tense of "hide." So the line also reads, "the engraver has hidden the face of the author." The author may be hidden, figuratively speaking, behind the harlequin portrait, not unlike an author who hides behind a made-up name.* Authors who needed to hide behind made-up names were usually men of social rank, avoiding the stigma of print.

The prefatory material in the *Folio* is littered with hints that the poet was a man of rank, and the word "gentle" in the second line is one of those hints. In this poem, Jonson became the first person to

---

*Some anti-Stratfordians have interpreted the black line at the jaw, up to the tabular ear, as the outline of a mask (Ogburn, 224; Whalen, *Who Was*, 53, 54). However, a seventeenth-century engraving of King James shows the same highlighted line at the jaw and the same tabular ear (Bennett, 157).

write about "gentle Shakespeare," but he was not the last. The epithet has stuck. Biographers have routinely used this adjective to construct Shakspere's gentle-mannered reputation. For example, we read in *The Riverside Shakespeare* that "the recurrent word in the testimonials of Shakespeare's friends and acquaintances is 'gentle.' It characterizes an engaging but self-effacing person" (Levin, 4).

Probably much to the dismay of his colleagues, Honigmann called attention to the "curious fact, apparently forgotten by those who are attracted to a 'gentle Shakespeare', that open, unequivocal tributes to his gentleness only appeared in print after his death, in the Folio, in two poems signed by Ben Jonson" (*Impact*, 16). As Ian Donaldson added, "thus launched into the critical vocabulary, the word 'gentle' recurs repeatedly in later tributes to Shakespeare and forms an important ingredient in the eighteenth-century concoction of the dramatist's personality" ("Tother," 122). Yet nothing can be found in the contemporary record to describe a gentle-*mannered* Shakespeare.

Jonson coined the epithet "gentle Shakespeare," not during his colleague's lifetime, but seven years *after* Shakspere had died in Stratford. What did Jonson mean by it? Schoenbaum accepted the epithet as a "fitting designation for the innate gentleman who was not gently born" (*Documentary*, 205), but Jonson was more likely alluding to a Shakespeare who was indeed gently born. Back then, a "gentle" person not specifically engaged in gentle behavior was someone of aristocratic birth. The word "gentle" is one of several that send out mixed signals about the dramatist.

In the epistles, Jonson referred to Shakespeare's plays three times as "trifles." The gentleman dramatists, as distinct from the paid professionals, "tended to speak of plays, including their own, as trifles or baubles" (Bentley, *Dramatist*, 25). In contrast, a few pages later in the *Folio*, Leonard Digges referred to Shakespeare's "Works," and the next page announced "The Works of William Shakespeare." Jonson certainly considered his own plays to be "works." The words "trifles" and "works" send out another set of mixed signals, one pointing to a gentleman-amateur, the other to a commoner and paid professional. In addition, Droeshout dressed Shakespeare in a doublet generally associated with a "gentleman of 'the better sort' " (Spielmann, 34).

Such visual and textual ambiguities suggest that the deficiencies in the Droeshout portrait were not accidental. If the deficiencies were due to the engraver's inexperience, then why did the publishers commission him in the first place? If Droeshout was sufficiently experi-

Figure 25. Portrait of Ben Jonson by Robert Vaughan, engraved around 1627 and published in Jonson's 1640 *Works. Courtesy of The Cleveland Public Library.*

enced, then why the clumsy and inept rendering? It is difficult to dismiss the distortions simply as unintentional or beyond anyone's control.

Finally, compare the engraving of Shakespeare to those of Drayton, Chapman, Jonson, Weever, and Florio (figs. 25–30). These other

Figure 26. Engraving of Michael Drayton, published in the 1619 edition of his *Poems. Courtesy of The Cleveland Public Library.*

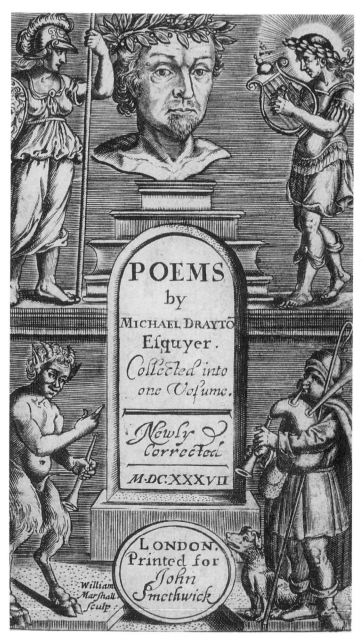

Figure 27. Title page of Michael Drayton's *Poems* published in 1637, several years after Drayton had died. *Courtesy of The Cleveland Public Library.*

Figure 28. Engraving of George Chapman, published in his 1615 translation of Homer. *Courtesy of The Cleveland Public Library.*

portraits are more skillfully executed, have more expression, and have a feel of individuality, and most include a symbol of the literary profession, that is, the laurel wreath or books. As David Riggs concluded, "nothing in [Droeshout's] engraving would lead one to suppose that Shakespeare was a poet" (278).

JONSON'S EULOGY

Jonson's *First Folio* eulogy to "William Shakespeare" is generally accepted by biographers as a fitting tribute requiring little comment,

Figure 29. Engraving of John Weever, published in *Ancient Funeral Monuments*, 1631, the year before the antiquarian died. *Courtesy of the Ohio State University Libraries, Rare Books and Manuscripts.*

Figure 30. Engraving of John Florio published in *Queen Anna's New World of Words*, 1611.

although it contains the most critical information used to prove the traditional authorship attribution. While the title itself suggests that Jonson personally knew Shakespeare, one critic has remarked that "subsequently we learn very little about Shakespeare either as a man . . . or as a poet" (Lipking, 142). Moreover, according to Alexander Leggatt, it is "one of Jonson's best known, most puzzling and most hotly debated poems" (227). Yet most of that hot debate is to be found in books about Jonson or in academic journals, rather than in Shakespearean biographies.

T.J.B. Spencer categorized the eulogy in the "genre of 'Commendatory Poems,' the kind of thing assembled . . . to support the sales of a book. . . . The financial outlay on the [*Folio*] venture was heavy, and it was necessary for [the publishers] to do everything possible to ensure its success" (24–25). Under those circumstances, Jonson presumably would have fulfilled his assignment by writing a glowing encomium. Yet in this poem, ostensibly promoting the Shakespeare plays, we find mixed messages, conflicting information, and disparaging remarks.

Like his two *Folio* epistles, Jonson's eulogy is factually inconsistent and unreliable. The following seventeen lines begin the eulogy, but Jonson never really gets started. He gets bogged down in double talk:

To the memory of my beloved,
The AUTHOR
MR. WILLIAM SHAKESPEARE:
And what he hath left us.

To draw no envy (*Shakespeare*) on thy name,
　Am I thus ample to thy Book and Fame:
While I confess thy writings to be such,
　As neither *Man*, nor *Muse*, can praise too much.
'Tis true, and all mens suffrage. But these ways
　Were not the paths I meant unto thy praise:
For seeliest [blindest] Ignorance on these may light,
　Which, when it sounds at best, but echoes right;
Or blind Affection, which doth ne're advance
　The truth, but gropes, and urgeth all by chance;
Or crafty Malice, might pretend this praise,
　And think to ruin, where it seem'd to raise.
These are, as some infamous Bawd, or Whore,
　Should praise a Matron. What could hurt her more?

But thou art proof against them, and indeed
  Above th'ill fortune of them, or the need.
I, therefore will begin.

Pause before proceeding. What was Jonson dispensing with when he wrote "I, therefore, will begin"? He was signaling that he made a false start. He may as well have written, "Well, folks, now I'm done with my opening double-talk. I've given you fair warning, and I will now get on with the eulogy." Jonson also predicted that less discerning readers would miss the point. "Blind affection" is going to supersede common sense and the search for truth.

C. M. Ingleby paraphrased the opening lines:

"To draw no envy," &c., certainly does not mean . . . [that] Ben thought to lower Shakespeare by extravagantly praising him. He meant to say, that while Ignorance, Affection, or Malice, by excessive, indiscriminate or unjust praise, would be sure to provoke the detraction of Envy,

"these ways
Were not the paths I meant unto thy praise;"

for he [Jonson] could with full knowledge and strict impartiality award him the highest praise that could be expressed. (*Centurie,* 151)

Ingleby was not looking for a second layer of meaning, and he had the good taste to avoid commenting on the hookers.

What kind of eulogy drags in comparisons with bawds or whores, and why? One Jonsonian critic, Richard S. Peterson, found an echo of Jonson's favorite poet, Horace, in this dubious imagery:

the passage may owe the vivid terms in which it is cast to an unnoticed Horatian source. In his description of Lollius's aversion to parasitic friendship in *Epistles* I.18 Horace observes: "As matron and strumpet will differ . . . so will the friend be distinct from the faithless parasite" . . . a striking combination of elements which Jonson has rearranged here to stigmatize a false friend as an "infamous Baud, or Whore" praising a "Matron." (176)

In other words, Jonson was deploring worthless or damaging praise from Shakspere's parasitic false friends, a striking admission in itself. But there is more in it than that.

Jonson was also dropping a not-so-subtle hint about Shakespeare's aristocratic credentials by defining opposite ends of the social spectrum. At one extreme is low life, and at the other is the upper crust of society. A "matron" is "a married woman, usually with the accessory idea of (moral or social) rank or dignity" (*OED*), but Jonson elevated Shakespeare above the matron to a position of complete immunity and unimpeachable honor. His "gentle Shakespeare" was thus far above those who might insult him with cheap or ignorant flattery. However, Shakspere of Stratford was not in any such exalted social class. He died an armigerous gentleman by purchase on the lower rung of the gentry.

According to this passage about whores and matrons, any praise coming from riffraff and directed to someone from the upper class was at best worthless, and at worst injurious. (In his commonplace book, Jonson echoed this sentiment when he wrote that "it is as great a spite to be praised in the wrong place, and by a wrong person, as can be done to a noble nature.") A few pages earlier in the *Folio*, he had given his readers an example of insulting praise from ignorant admirers, specifically the actors' "compliment" about the unblotted manuscripts. Then he alerted the reader to look out for insults masquerading as praise ("crafty Malice, might pretend this praise").

The poem thus begins with seventeen lines that anti-Stratfordians would call a tip-off. Here is an unorthodox paraphrase:

I am up to the challenge of dealing with those who would heap malice on, or envy your name and reputation, although it is impossible to praise your works too much. That is the truth, and everybody says so. But that is not what I intend to say in your honor. The ignorant will read into these lines what they want to, if it sounds good but is actually wrong ("but echoes right"). Or they will be blinded to truth by their idolatry and will flail around for explanations to rationalize their admiration.

There are those who purport to sing your praises but by so doing actually insult you. If a whore or person of low degree praised a respectable lady from the upper class, the lady would be insulted, not complimented. But you can withstand insulting "praise" from unworthy and ignorant admirers. Not only are you above them, you don't need them. You are above the need to protect yourself.

After the false start, Jonson began his tribute to the dramatist William Shakespeare:

I, therefore will begin. Soul of the Age!
  The applause! delight! the wonder of our Stage!
My *Shakespeare*, rise; I will not lodge thee by
  Chaucer, or *Spenser*, or bid *Beaumont* lie
A little further, to make thee a room:
  Thou art a Moniment, without a tomb,
And art alive still, while thy Book doth live,
  And we have wits to read, and praise to give.
That I not mix thee so, my brain excuses;
  I mean with great, but disproportion'd *Muses*:
For, if I thought my judgment were of years,
  I should commit thee surely with thy peers,
And tell, how far thou didst our *Lily* out-shine,
  Or sporting *Kid*, or *Marlowe's* mighty line.
And though thou had small *Latin*, and less *Greek*,
  From thence to honour thee, I would not seek
For names; but call forth thund'ring *Aeschylus*
  Euripides, and *Sophocles* to us,
Paccuvius, Accius, him of *Cordova* dead,
  To life again, to hear thy Buskin tread,
And shake a Stage; Or, when thy Socks were on,
  Leave thee alone, for the comparison
Of all, that insolent *Greece* or haughty *Rome*
  Sent forth, or since did from their ashes come.
Triumph, my *Britain*, thou hast one to show,
  To whom all scenes of *Europe* homage owe.
He was not of an age, but for all time!
  And all the *Muses* still were in their prime,
When like *Apollo* he came forth to warm
  Our ears, or like a *Mercury* to charm!
Nature herself was proud of his designs,
  And joyed to wear the dressing of his lines!
Which were so richly spun, and woven so fit,
  As, since, she will vouchsafe no other Wit.
The merry *Greek*, tart *Aristophanes*,
  Neat *Terence*, witty *Plautus*, now not please;
But antiquated, and deserted lie
  As they were not of Nature's family.
Yet must I not give Nature all: Thy Art,
  My gentle *Shakespeare*, must enjoy a part.
For though the *Poet's* matter, Nature be,
  His Art doth give the fashion. And, that he,
Who casts to write a living line, must sweat,

(Such as thine are) and strike the second heat
Upon the *Muses'* anvil: turn the same,
(And himself with it) that he thinks to frame;
Or for the laurel, he may gain a scorn,
For a good *Poet's* made, as well as born.
And such wert thou. Look how the father's face
Lives in his issue: even so, the race
Of *Shakespeare's* mind, and manners brightly shines
In his well-turned, and true-filed lines:
In each of which, he seems to shake a Lance,
As brandished at the eyes of Ignorance.
Sweet swan of *Avon*! what a sight it were
To see thee in our waters yet appear,
And make those flights upon the banks of *Thames*
That so did take *Eliza*, and our *James*!
But stay, I see thee in the *Hemisphere*
Advanced, and made a Constellation there!
Shine forth, thou Star of *Poets*, and with rage,
Or influence, chide, or cheer the drooping Stage;
Which, since thy flight from hence, hath mourned like night,
And despair's day, but for thy Volume's light.

When Jonson dubbed Shakespeare the "Sweet swan of Avon," he forged an all-important link to Shakspere of Stratford. There are many English towns "upon-Avon," but only one of them was home to a William Shakspere with a London theatre career.

However, Jonson's allusion to the Avon gave readers only half of the information necessary to make an identification. The other half appears a few pages later in another tribute in which Digges wrote:

> *Shake-speare*, at length thy pious fellows give
> The world thy Works: thy Works, by which, out-live
> Thy Tomb, thy name must: when that stone is rent,
> And Time dissolves thy *Stratford* Moniment,
> Here we alive shall view thee still.

"Thy Stratford Moniment" points to Shakspere's hometown. The explicit reference to "thy Stratford Moniment" on one page, plus "Sweet swan of Avon" on another, point to Stratford-upon-Avon, where there is a monument to Shakspere, plain as day. To many, that constitutes proof positive: The man from Stratford-upon-Avon is the poet William Shakespeare.

Yet, these geographic references that tie down the identification of the dramatist introduce more ambiguities. Neither Jonson nor Digges came right out and said "Stratford-upon-Avon," nor did they use the word "monument." Digges wrote "thy Stratford Moniment," and Jonson wrote "Thou art a Moniment, without a tomb." Both chose the word "moniment," a word ignored by traditional biographers.

Bear with some minutiae here. Two references were made to "moniment," both times spelled with an *i*. It is an archaic word, and in the literature of the day, it was not exactly synonymous with "monument." Edmund Spenser used the word as synonymous with a body of written work.* So while at first glance, Jonson and Digges simply referred to the Stratford monument, they were also referring to the Shakespearean canon. These two poets were pushing a pun. In particular, Jonson's line, "Thou art a Moniment, without a tomb," suggests a double meaning. The line can mean that (*a*) Shakespeare is memorialized by his body of work, not by a tomb—witness Shakespeare's own Sonnet 81: "Your monument shall be my gentle verse"; and (*b*) Shakspere's Stratford monument was originally supposed to sit on top of the tomb itself, but since it does not, it is a monument without a tomb.

The wordplay on monument and moniment is important as an example of deliberate ambiguity. In particular, Jonson's wordplay serves as an early signal to the reader to proceed with care, to beware of double meanings. And those who consider this an unsupported theory may have difficulty explaining why, in first editions of the *Folio*, the letter *i* of "Moniment" in Jonson's eulogy was set in bold face type (R. L. Miller, 8 n). Was Jonson looking over the compositor's shoulder to make sure the spelling was not overlooked by future readers?

Jonson dropped another hint that the dramatist Shakespeare was not Shakspere of Stratford. Jonson would "commit" Shakespeare with his peers, Lyly, Kyd, and Marlowe. These lines sit in a time warp, and Jonson suggested as much when he told his reader that this part of

---

*Anti-Stratfordian R. L. Miller (10) cited Spenser's use of the word "moniment" from *The Faerie Queen*:

> Then as they gan his Library to view,
> And antique registers for to avise,
> There chanced to the Princes hand to rise
> An ancient book, hight Briton *moniments*,
> That of this lands first conquest did devise. (II.ix.59)

his critique concerns, or is "of years." The three literary "peers" predate Shakspere's presumed period of creativity by nearly a decade. Lyly flourished 1579–90, but wrote very little after 1590. Marlowe died in 1593, and Kyd in 1594. The careers of these three "peers" were over by the time Shakspere was supposedly first establishing himself in literary London. By suggesting that Shakespeare's literary career was at its zenith during the heydays of Lyly, Kyd, and Marlowe, Jonson undermined his own identification of Shakspere as the "swan of Avon."

Overall, Jonson's authorship testimony is simply too ambiguous and self-contradictory to accept without qualification. As for Digges's testimony, it is impersonal and therefore of no use as personal literary evidence. He addresses "*the* deceased Author" and "*our* Shakespeare" (emphasis added).

Biographers point out that Digges at about age twelve became a stepson to Thomas Russell, the overseer of Shakspere's will, which puts the two men at two degrees of separation. If this link is to be extrapolated into a personal relationship between Digges and Shakspere, then there should be some trace of their friendship. There is none. However, Digges did leave a trace of his friendship with Edward Blount, one of the publishers of the *Folio*. In 1622, Blount published one of Digges's translations, and extant correspondence confirms a personal relationship (Hotson, *I, William*, 255), but any relationship between Digges and Shakspere remains conjectural. Digges's poems to Shakespeare in the *First* and *Second Folios* and in the 1640 poetry anthology are confined to literary praise. Even his reference to the Stratford moniment is not necessarily at firsthand. Digges mentions the dramatist one more time in his note on the flyleaf of Lope de Vega's sonnets, in which he wrote that the Spanish regarded Lope as "in England we should of our Will Shakespeare." Like John Davies, Digges used the impersonal "our" to describe Shakespeare.

BETWEEN THE LINES

The connecting links in the chain between the *First Folio* of Shakespeare's plays and William Shakspere of Stratford, therefore, are (*a*) the allusion to "thy Stratford Moniment," (*b*) the allusion to "Sweet swan of Avon," (*c*) the funerary monument in Stratford-on-Avon, and (*d*) the conclusion that Heminges, Condell, Jonson, and Digges all recognized the actors' "friend and fellow" Shakspere as the author. The cumulative strength of that chain depends on the strength of each link. Those links are not sound.

Most important, Jonson's testimony is not consistent, self-explanatory, or accurate. One Jonsonian critic discusses "the debate over the sincerity of Jonson's praise," while another thinks the poem conveys an "ambiguity of attitude" (Peterson, 158; Trimpi, 148; see also Lipking, 140). Various Jonsonian commentators have grappled at length with that ambiguity. Many quote the seventeenth-century poet John Dryden who regarded Jonson's eulogy as "an insolent, sparing, and invidious panegyric" (2:75), but rarely is Jonson's eulogy the subject of an extended critical analysis in the Shakespearean biography. However, Dryden's opinion alone should prompt a thorough dissection of this most critical of testimony, and it certainly proves that Jonson's eulogy is capable of more than one interpretation. In other words, Dryden's opinion proves, if any further proof were needed, that *Jonson's eulogy is ambiguous.* It cannot be taken at face value, a point on which at least the Jonsonian scholars agree. Incidentally, John Benson, the publisher of the 1640 edition of Shakespeare's poems, did not take the *First Folio* testimony at face value either. The frontispiece and accompanying verse (fig. 31) are blatant take-offs on the Droeshout engraving and Jonson's eulogy.

Jonson's poems alternated between ambiguous and straightforward, as the occasion demanded. Uncomplimentary or satiric verse demanded ambiguity, so Jonson used "convenient pseudonymic labels" (Dutton, *Folio*, 78). Conversely, he usually saluted personal friends, fellow writers (e.g., Chapman and Joshua Sylvester), and benefactors in straightforward language. On at least one occasion, though, Jonson exercised restraint in a complimentary verse to someone who might be compromised by brushing elbows too closely with him:

> *To one that desired me not to name him*
> Be safe, nor fear thy self so good a fame,
> That, any way, my book should speak thy name:
> For, if thou shame, rank'd with my friends, to go,
> I am more ashamed to have thee thought my foe.
> (Epigram 77)

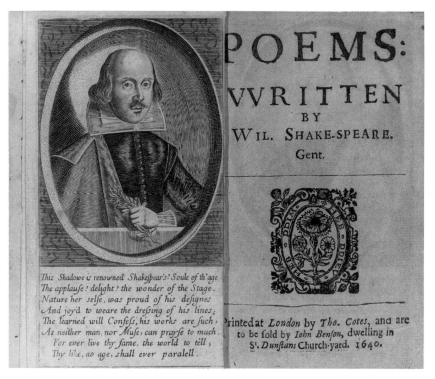

This Shadowe is renowned Shakespear's? Soule of th'age
The applause? delight? the wonder of the Stage.
Nature her selfe, was proud of his designes
And joy'd to weare the dressing of his lines,
The learned will Confess, his works are such,
As neither man, nor Muse, can prayse to much.
For ever live thy fame, the world to tell,
Thy like, no age, shall ever paralell.

POEMS:
VVRITTEN
BY
WIL. SHAKE-SPEARE.
Gent.

Printed at *London* by *Tho. Cotes*, and are
to be sold by *Iohn Benson*, dwelling in
St. *Dunstans* Church-yard. 1640.

Figure 31. Frontispiece and title page to the 1640 anthology of Shakespeare's poetry. Like the two anthologies that preceded it (*Shake-speares Sonnets* of 1609 and the *Folio* of 1623), this edition was prefaced with ambiguous, tongue-in-cheek, or blatantly satiric material. The "Shadow" of Shakespear and the poem are direct take-offs on the *First Folio*, and question marks, irreverently sprinkled throughout the first two lines, confirm the satire. This edition was unauthorized, but it is obvious that not everyone took the *First Folio* prefatory material seriously. *Courtesy of the Ohio State University Libraries, Rare Books and Manuscripts.*

Jonson seems to be protecting the anonymity of someone who would be disgraced by an overt association with him, a professional writer. Jonson did not want to embarrass this friend with any explicit praise. That friend may or may not be Shakespeare, but the epigram shows that Jonson took care for some reason not to identify in print a person whom he admired.

Jonson used ambiguity to camouflage targets of satire, and he exercised restraint out of respect for those of social rank, so *why* did he mix ambiguity with straightforward praise in his *Folio* eulogy? If the commoner Shakspere was the author, there was no need for ambiguity. If Jonson's tributes were entirely complimentary and sincere, there was no need for ambiguity. On the other hand, if an aristocrat was the author, there was *every* reason for ambiguity. And finally, if Shakspere of Stratford was *not* the author, then any satirical or unflattering comments likewise would be blurred. One Jonsonian commentator, Sara van den Berg, came surprisingly close to pinpointing this phenomenon in her analysis of the *Folio* eulogy:

In poems to fellow artists and to the aristocracy Jonson relies heavily on such conventions [i.e., explicit use of the poet's name, the metaphorical compliment, and so on]. Because he can assume intimacy and equality when writing to artists but not when addressing the aristocracy, Jonson uses different conventions in the two situations. *Only in the poem for Shakespeare does he combine both methods.* (215, emphasis added)

Jonson was supposedly extolling a respected colleague and a commoner, long dead, something he was free to do and usually did in straightforward language. Jonson's *Folio* "testimony" is suspicious simply *because* he used ambiguous language. He even suspected his doubletalk might be lost on posterity, and that his pun on "Moniment," for example, despite the giveaway boldface *i*, might be overlooked, because he said so in his poem: "For seeliest Ignorance on these may light, / Which, when it sounds at best, but echoes right." *For ignorant folk may read these lines which sound right but are actually wrong.* You will read what you want to read.

The sheer number of misleading or contradictory statements in the *First Folio* strongly suggests that traditional biographers have been following a false scent. Those who accept statements in the *Folio* as "hard facts" supporting Shakspere's authorship are ignoring the signposts that contradict those "hard facts" and point in a different direction.

The irregularities in the *First Folio*'s front matter cumulatively provide strong evidence that the attribution to Shakspere is both unreliable and incomplete. The nominal nature of Heminges and Condell's involvement, Jonson's pervasive ambiguities, his earlier parodies of Shakspere, and the extraordinary absence of explicit references to the dramatist in Jonson's earlier work, together prompt anti-Stratfordians to reject the signposts in the *First Folio* pointing to

Shakspere of Stratford, and to choose instead the signposts pointing to a gently born Shakespeare.

The authorship attribution in the *Folio* constitutes the first historical evidence identifying Shakspere in personal terms as the dramatist. The evidence is posthumous, and for no other writer of Shakespeare's time period are we asked to trust such ambiguous and belated information, uncorroborated by any solid documentation left during the author's life, as evidence of authorship.

Chapter Eleven

Shakspere's Drinking Buddies

> Shakespear, Drayton, and Ben Jonson, had a merry meeting, and
> it seems drank too hard, for Shakespear died of a fever there
> contracted.
>
> —John Ward, *Diary* (ca. 1661–63)

Ben Jonson and Michael Drayton are the two writers most frequently
portrayed as personal friends of Shakspere, and John Ward's report
has a certain romantic attraction. However, the "merry meeting" at
the pub is a legend (Chambers, *Facts*, 2:250). So are stories of Shakspere's tippling with Jonson at the Mermaid tavern. According to one
historian:

Shakespeare's membership of a club of dramatists, poets and wits which met
at "the Mermaid tavern" is one of the most popular and widely disseminated
legends about "Elizabethan" England. It is also one of the most improbable,
notwithstanding Leslie Hotson's demonstration that the William Johnson
who was joined with Shakespeare in the purchase of the Blackfriars Gate-
house in March 1613 was the landlord of the Mermaid in Bread Street. This
proves only that Shakespeare at the very end of his working life was acquainted with the keeper of one of the best-known London taverns, which
is neither surprising nor in itself significant, especially as Shakespeare's purpose in associating Johnson and two others with himself in this transaction

remains obscure. Acquaintance with a tavern-keeper does not imply acquaintance with his guests, and is certainly not evidence that Shakespeare associated with those known to have belonged to the "Mermaid Club." Of this there is none. (Shapiro, 6)

There *is* evidence that Jonson frequented the Mermaid tavern. A surviving letter addressed to the "right Worshipful Fraternity . . . that meet the first Friday of every Month, at the sign of the Mermaid" named Jonson (Shapiro, 8). Neither Shakspere nor Drayton was named.

In fact, nobody thinks of Drayton as a barfly. On the contrary, Francis Meres described him as "a man of virtuous disposition . . . and well-governed carriage, which is almost miraculous among good wits in these declining and corrupt times" (281). In addition, the third *Parnassus* play tells us that Drayton did not fit the stereotype of a poet, being disinclined to drink and carouse.

Even so, was there a grain of truth in the story about the "merry meeting"? Were Shakspere, Jonson, and Drayton all personal friends?

There is evidence that Jonson and Drayton knew each other. Jonson wrote a poem to "his friend" Drayton, whom he addressed familiarly as "Michael" before acknowledging some past affront. In conversation, Jonson told William Drummond that "Drayton feared him, and he esteemed not of him" (Newdigate, 136). However, there is nothing quite so clear-cut with respect to Jonson's or Drayton's relationship with Shakspere.

DE SHAKESPEARE NOSTRATI

All of Jonson's testimony concerning "Shakespeare" was recorded *after* Shakspere had died in 1616. As the anti-Stratfordian J. Thomas Looney stated, "During the eighteen years [i.e., 1598–1616] of implied intimacy with Shakespeare the biography of Jonson is indeed real and substantial. His activities, his associates, his friendships, his quarrels, are all there, as open as daylight. There is, however, one mystery in it: one stupendous gap. It contains no Shakespeare" ("Jonson," 64). The gap is indeed mysterious. While Shakspere was alive, Jonson never once mentioned him by name.

In addition, Shakespearean biographers generally quote from Jonson's testimony as though it was all reasonably straightforward. Yet most of what Jonson had to say about Shakspere is anything but self-explanatory, and as many Jonsonian critics have pointed out, it is self-contradictory (e.g., Riggs, 277).

Jonson eulogized Shakespeare in 1623, but his satirical caricatures, Sogliardo and the "Poet-Ape," exhibit no literary respect. Did or did not Jonson respect Shakespeare? Anti-Stratfordians have to ask that question twice, depending on which Shakespeare they are talking about: that is, Shakespeare, the pseudonymous dramatist, or Shakspere, the wheeler-dealer from Stratford. A close analysis of the rest of Jonson's testimony suggests that Jonson deliberately bequeathed to posterity two Shakespeares, two distinct and inherently incompatible *personas*, one whom he respected, and another whom he made fun of. The analysis also shows *how* Jonson conflated the two into one and blurred the outlines.

The first of Jonson's posthumous allusions to Shakspere is minor. In his 1619 conversations with poet William Drummond, he complained that Shakespeare wrote of a seacoast in landlocked Bohemia (in *The Winter's Tale*), and that Shakspere "wanted Art." He also denigrated the Greek play on which Shakespeare based *Comedy of Errors*. These are literary, not personal complaints. Jonson could have made these comments after having seen or read the plays.

Another of Jonson's allusions to Shakspere, however, is personal. Sometime between 1630 and 1637, up to two decades after Shakspere died, Jonson wrote a paragraph in his commonplace book:

De Shakespeare nostrat. [of the native Shakespeare]

I *remember*, the Players have often mentioned it as an honour to *Shakespeare*, that in his writing, (whatsoever he penned) he never blotted out line. My answer hath been, Would he had blotted a thousand. Which they thought a malevolent speech. I had not told posterity this, but for their ignorance, who choose that circumstance to commend their friend by, wherein he most faulted. And to justify mine own candor (for I loved the man, and do honour his memory (on this side Idolatry) as much as any.) He was (indeed) honest, and of an open, and free nature: had an excellent *Phantsie*; brave notions, and gentle expressions: wherein he flow'd with that facility, that sometime it was necessary he should be stopped: *Sufflaminandus erat*

Augustus in Hat.

[the brake needed to be applied]; as *Augustus* said of *Haterius*. His wit was in his own power; would the rule of it had been so too. Many times he fell into those things, could not escape laughter: As when he said in the person

of *Caesar*, one speaking to him; *Caesar, thou dost me
wrong.* He replied: *Caesar did never wrong, but with just
cause*: and such like; which were ridiculous. But he redeemed his vices, with his virtues. There was ever more in
him to be praised, than to be pardoned. (8:583–84)

Recall that in the *First Folio* epistle, the actors (or rather, Jonson,
on their behalf) boasted that they had "scarce received from him a
blot in his papers." Here in his commonplace book, Jonson acknowledged that he "had not told posterity" about his role in putting over
the insult about the unblotted manuscripts. It was Jonson's admission—for Greg, it was "confirmation" ("Publishers," 152)—of his
authorship of those two epistles.

Most biographers give this outright admission—indeed the entire
allusion—short shrift, and that should raise an eyebrow or two. In
essence, Chambers noted that Jonson's testimony "shows both admiration for the poet and affection for the man," and Chambers's
slight attention to the passage is extraordinary (*Facts*, 1:70, see also
1:235, 397–98). He spent four pages dissecting a lawsuit concerning
real estate belonging to Shakspere's mother, over eight pages on the
Welcombe enclosures, and nearly three pages on Shakspere's purchase
of tithes, but he devoted barely four sentences to an allusion that he
personally viewed as Jonson's testimony "to Shakespeare's authorship
of [*Julius Caesar*]." Dennis Kay's commentary was similarly brief. For
him, the passage confirmed Shakspere's "easy and felicitous grace in
composition" and his "generous and witty nature," and it explained
Jonson's "scorn of the players' compliment that Shakespeare never
blotted a line" (271). Few biographers have done much more with
the passage.

First let us put the allusion in context. The journal or commonplace
book in which it was written was published under the title *Timber,
or Discoveries* in 1641, four years after Jonson's death.* *De Shakespeare nostrati* is part of a larger section of literary criticism in which
Jonson ridicules the masses for choosing jingles over poetry and hack
writers over good ones. He derides the second- and third-rate writers

---

*Over 80% of *Timber* is unoriginal. The majority of entries are translations from
Seneca, Cicero, Quintilian, and other ancients, frequently adapted with some mod-
ification, and often conflated or intermixed. Castelain concluded that Jonson was
setting down themes, ideas, and source material for future verses or plays. Passages
in the commonplace book do in fact turn up in plays and poetry, for example, in his
"Address to the Readers" in *The Alchemist*.

who flourish and make money, even though their compositions are
so bad that if you tried to correct them by blotting out the bad bits,
you would be left with nothing but one big blot. In Jonson's own
words:

Nothing in our Age, I have observed, is more preposterous, than the *running Judgments* upon *Poetry*, and *Poets*. . . . And those men almost named
for *Miracles*, who yet are so vile, that if a man should go about, to examine,
and correct them, he must make all they have done, but one blot. . . .
   Yet their vices have not hurt them: Nay, a great many they have profited;
for they have been loved for nothing else . . . because the most favour common vices. . . .
   . . . In these things, the unskillful are naturally deceived. (8:581–83)

The "sordid multitude" prefers vice to virtue, has no taste or aesthetic
judgment, and that multitude specifically includes actors. Jonson's
ultimate examples of "the unskillful" were, in fact, the players.
   Jonson segued into *De Shakespeare nostrati* with "I remember, the
Players have often mentioned it as an honour" that Shakspere delivered unblotted manuscripts. He inserted the business about the blots
into the *Folio* and then brought up the subject again many years later.
Of all the things that Jonson might have said about Shakspere, why
was he so obsessed with the blots?
   Manuscripts marked up with corrections and revisions were the
author's so-called "foul papers." Foul papers were then transcribed
into "fair copy" for the acting company. Fair copies are the ones
without the blots. If Shakspere's papers contained no blots, *then they
were not the author's foul papers.* By implication, Shakspere never delivered an authorial set of foul papers to the acting company.
   Technically, the degree to which blotted foul papers differed from
fair or at least fairer copy is less relevant to Jonson's *Folio* remarks
than are the conceits about them that he promotes. Jonson intended
an uncritical reader to picture Shakespeare, like the Wolfgang Mozart
as portrayed in the play *Amadeus*, merely transcribing onto paper the
ideas that magically popped, fully developed, into his head. This conceit carried through to Beaumont and Fletcher's 1647 *Comedies and
Tragedies* in which the publisher, Humphrey Moseley, expressed similar amazement at Fletcher's unblotted pages: "What ever I have seen
of Mr. *Fletcher's* own hand, is free from interlining; and his friends
affirm he never writ any one thing twice. It seems he had that rare

felicity to prepare and perfect all first in his own brain; to shape and attire his *Notions*, to add or lop off, before he committed one word to writing, and never touched pen till all was to stand as firm and immutable as if engraven in Brass or Marble" (*Works*, 1:54). Moseley's dedicatory epistle, similarly presented over actors' names, also refers to the "flowing compositions of the then expired sweet Swan of Avon Shakespeare" (*Works*, 1:50). The front matter in the Beaumont and Fletcher *Folio* is clearly indebted to and derivative of that in the Shakespeare *Folio*. In particular, Moseley's fulsome praise of Fletcher's facility is obviously based on Jonson's conceit, as set forth in the Shakespeare *First Folio*, about unblotted papers.

In *De Shakespeare nostrati*, Jonson disparaged the ignorant players who mistook the clean copies that Shakspere delivered for the author's originals ("but for their ignorance, who chose that circumstance to commend their friend by, wherein he most faulted"). For Jonson, unblotted verse was artless, ignorant verse. In his translation of Horace's *Art of Poetry*, we read that the author of inferior verse should "blot all, and to the anvil bring / Those ill-turn'd Verses, to new hammering. . . . A wise and honest man will cry out shame / On artless Verse . . . [and] / Blot out the careless" (8:333, 335). These images of blots, anvils, and turned lines recur in Jonson's eulogy to Shakespeare, who struck the second heat on the Muse's anvil to perfect his "well-turned" lines. This Shakespeare, the poet in whom "Art" *must* play a part, is at odds with Jonson's *De Shakespeare nostrati*.

THE HAPPY IMITATOR

The information in the *Folio* and Jonson's commonplace book are linked by the cross-reference to the blots, and any analysis of the commonplace book requires some shuttling back and forth between it and the *Folio*. Let us go back for a moment to check the wording in the *First Folio*:

His mind and hand went together: and what he thought, he uttered with that easiness, that we have scarce received from him a blot in his papers.

Put aside the blots for a moment. We have just encountered a remarkable phrase. The author of this epistle referred to Shakspere as someone who *uttered*, not someone who *wrote* "with that easiness."

An etymological digression is required here. In 1623, the word "utter" was in use in the sense most common today, that of exercising the faculty of speech. But it had several other meanings in vogue at the time. The first definition in the *Oxford English Dictionary* reads, "to put (goods, wares, etc.) forth or upon the market . . . ; to vend, sell. In very frequent use from c. 1540 to c. 1655." Jonson used the word in this sense in *Every Man In His Humour* (III.iv.63). Another definition reads, "to give currency to (money, coin, notes, etc.); . . . esp. to pass or circulate (base coin, forged notes, etc.) as legal tender."* "Utter" is still used in this sense today in England. And two other definitions read, "to produce or yield; to send out, supply, or furnish," and "to issue by way of publication; to publish." These last usages are found in the Star Chamber Decree of 1584 governing publishing (*OED*), the 1586 Privy Council order concerning unlawful books (Arber, 2:811), and the 1616 Enlarged Grant by James I to the Stationers (Arber, 3:317–18).

These multiple definitions suggest another pun, but note that the word "utter" is not synonymous with "write." In that sense, "utter" is unlike the words "say" or "speak," which have been used to quote the written word since the Middle Ages. Shakspere may speak, he may sell, he may commit forgery, and he may supply or publish—but in this section, he does not *write*. Yet the word "utter" is juxtaposed with the unblotted papers. Does "utter" refer here, even obliquely, to piracy, or to the oral reporting sometimes used to patch together play texts? Did it merely convey fluent verbal delivery? Or was Jonson just being sloppy in his choice of words? The latter is unlikely.

Jonson used the word "utter" at least fifteen times in *Timber*, occasionally to mean exercising the faculty of speech, and once to mean producing or publishing. He used "utter" three times to condemn glib critics or duplicitous parasites. Most frequently, he used "utter" when berating those who babble ignorantly or arrogantly. Jonson hammered home the opinion that empty-headed fast talk is not the same as educated and eloquent discourse. When taken in the larger Jonsonian context, his choice of the word "utter" in the *Folio* sends up a red flag. It is another example of Jonsonian ambiguity.

One literary critic discussed Jonson's capacity for backhanded compliments and advised readers not to "underestimate Jonson's finesse,

*See also the editor's note in *Arden, Love's Labour's Lost*, V.ii.316.

his ability to insinuate misgivings even while he seems to commend" (Lipking, 141), and the *Folio* provides numerous instances of this finesse. Another example appears in one of the epistles, where Jonson wrote that Shakspere "was a happy imitator of Nature." That was not much of a compliment, because elsewhere in *Timber*, Jonson made it clear that while "Imitation" of the masters was the path to literary excellence, "to Nature, Exercise, Imitation, and Studie, *Art must be added*, to make all these perfect" (8:639, emphasis added). David Riggs is one of many Jonsonian biographers who commented on Jonson's "exacting craftsmanship." In his conception of "the ideal poet Jonson dwells upon the importance of 'Study': 'Indeed, things, wrote with labour, deserve to be so read, and will last their Age' " (Riggs, 238). Clearly, Jonson had no respect for undisciplined artless composition, and in his view, "Nature" and "Imitation" were not by themselves enough to warrant commendation. Therefore his allusion to Shakespeare as an "Imitator of Nature" is, in Jonson's universe, an insult disguised as a compliment.

In his eulogy, Jonson wrote that "Nature," "Art," and "sweat"— note the word "sweat," as opposed to uttering with "that easiness"— were all required to produce Shakespeare's "true-filed lines." This Shakespeare, the admired perfectionist, is the diametric opposite of the spontaneous "natural" creator who issued forth extempore, with no blots, relying only on that talent with which he was born. It is a fundamental contradiction.

ART VS. NATURE

Shakespeare has long been touted as a "natural wit." We read that he "excelled in the natural vein." Leonard Digges wrote that "Nature only helped him," and there are many similar assessments to be found in *The Shakspere Allusion-Book* (see Ingleby et al.). This untutored Shakspere, the one who lacked "Art," has survived to the present day. The fact is, Shakspere's reputation as a natural-born genius was built on the backhanded "testimonials" of Jonson, and subsequently handed down through his extended circle of literary associates. With Jonson's eulogy, the classical debate over "Art versus Nature" came into renewed vogue. As Brian Vickers noted, "reactions to Jonson's criticism form one of the centres of the Art-Nature controversy over the next two hundred years. . . . The founding viewpoints were not only taken literally but were exaggerated" (1:1, 12; see also Doran, 62).*

However, the words "nature" and "natural," as Jonson used them, are semantic minefields. For example, Jonson used "nature" to convey the idea of being unsullied by education in his sarcastic description of Sogliardo: "For his other gifts of the mind, or so, why they are as nature lent him them, pure, simple, without any artificial drug or mixture of these two threadbare beggarly qualities, learning and knowledge" (*Every Man Out*, IV.viii.10–14). Jonson used the word "naturals" in the same sense in paragraphs following *De Shakespeare nostrati*:

Ingeriorum discrimina. [difference of wits]

And some, by a cunning protestation against all reading, and false venditation [ostentatious display] of their own naturals, think to divert the *sagacity* of their Readers from themselves, and cool the scent of their own *fox-like* thefts; when yet they are so rank, as a man may find whole pages together usurp'd from one Author. . . .

. . . *But* the Wretcheder are the obstinate contemners of all helps and Arts: such as presuming on their own *Naturals* (which perhaps are excellent) dare deride all diligence, and seem to mock at the terms, when they understand not the things; thinking that way to get off wittily, with their Ignorance. . . . And they utter all they can think, with a kind of violence, and *indisposition*; unexamined. . . . and the more willful, and stubborn, they are in it, the more learned they are esteemed of the *multitude*, through their excellent vice of Judgment: who think those things the stronger, that have no Art. (8:586–87)

In this passage, Jonson has returned to the sordid multitude and the undeserving recipients of their admiration. Notice that Jonson associated the undisciplined "natural" wit with inferior, plagiarized, or pirated ("fox-like thefts," "usurp'd") writing. And in the passages immediately preceding *De Shakespeare nostrati*, he had ridiculed the unskillful who are "naturally" deceived in matters of literary judgment. In the midst of all this discussion about uneducated "natural" wits, Jonson labeled his paragraph about Shakspere *De Shakespeare nostrati*.

*For a discussion of the art-nature debate prior to Jonson's eulogy, see Baldwin's *William Shakspere's Small Latine and Lesse Greeke* (1:4–14).

Herford and Simpson translated "De Shakespeare Nostrati" as "our fellow Shakespeare," but "*nostrati*" means, literally, "of our country" or "native." One might assume that Jonson was claiming Shakspere as a famous native son. Jonson certainly expressed a sense of national pride when he wrote in his eulogy, "Triumph, my Britain, thou hast one to show, To whom all Scenes of Europe homage owe." But in *Timber*, he did not elaborate on Shakspere's home-grown qualities, and there is nothing in the paragraph to suggest that Jonson was reflecting on national pride. Elsewhere in his commonplace book, Jonson recommended the best English writers for study, but Shakespeare is not among them. So "nostrati," in the sense of native English, is not a good fit here.

Jonson's classical sources illuminate his intentions. According to one editor of *Timber*, Jonson's "borrowings are made with almost unvarying consistency, to illustrate and confirm certain leading principles which he held clearly in mind," and he condemned such extensive borrowing only by "those who did not genuinely share the sentiments expressed in their sources" (R. Walker, 5, 6). In his passage about "Naturals," he was translating Quintilian's comments about untrained orators who presumed on their own "Naturals," here meaning "natural gifts" or "native powers," as opposed to trained skills (e.g., see Quintilian, 1:281). Underlying the passage is more of Quintilian, who wrote that "if natural talent alone were sufficient, education might be dispensed with" (1:267).*

Jonson's paragraph on Shakspere is but one in a series about the uneducated who "are *naturally* deceived." If we now take on board the seventeenth-century definitions of "natural," Jonson's marginal annotation *De Shakespeare nostrati* assumes a new dimension.† The casual reader would think of Shakspere as home-grown or native, whereas the classically educated reader would think of Shakspere as untrained, of merely native intellect. We now turn to the section of *De Shakespeare nostrati* featuring the orator known for his native powers.

*See Donaldson (*Jonson*, xiv–xv). Baldwin quoted *The First Part of the Elementarie* (1582) by Richard Mulcaster to illustrate the influence of Quintilian on the subjects of "Nature and Art," and untrained "natural abilities" vs. trained perfection (*Latine*, 1:10–11).

†Seventeenth-century Latin-English dictionaries (EMEDD) confirm Jonson's various uses of these words; they define "native" as synonymous with "natural," and "natural" as synonymous with "fool." See B. Gibbons's note (Shakespeare, *Arden, Romeo*, II.iv.91) for Shakespeare's use of "natural."

IN THE PERSON OF CAESAR

Critical information about *Shakespeare nostrati* as the alleged dramatist appears in the allusion to Caesar. The line that Jonson recorded ("As when he said in the person of *Caesar*, one speaking to him; *Caesar, thou dost me wrong*. He replied: *Caesar did never wrong, but with just cause*") is similar to Caesar's line from Shakespeare's *Julius Caesar* (III.i.47–48), "Know, Caesar doth not wrong, nor without cause / Will he be satisfied," but is not quite accurate. Yet the words "did never wrong, but with just cause," must have been said, and moreover, must have made some impact, because Jonson recycled them in *The Staple of News*. Was this a joke or a famous mistake?

This reference to Caesar, traditionally accepted as a personal literary allusion, should provoke intense interest from the Shakespearean biographer. It has, however, generated relatively little interest (but see Furness, *Caesar*, 136–40). It is again the Jonsonian commentators, such as Herford and Simpson (*Jonson*, 11:232), who have wrestled with the quoted—or misquoted—lines. They noted that Jonson made the "explicit statement that the mistake was Shakespeare's," although in this instance, Shakspere had *spoken*, but not necessarily *written* the line in question. This brings us to a fundamental error in a traditional assumption about this passage.

Biographers routinely assume that Jonson was criticizing *Shakespeare nostrati*'s fluency *as a writer*, but the evidence tells us otherwise. In the lead-in to the anecdote about Caesar, Jonson introduced the analogy, "as Augustus said of Haterius." According to *The Oxford Classical Dictionary*, Haterius was an orator "noted for facility of improvisation and impetuous delivery . . . which called forth Augustus' remark 'Haterius needs a brake.' " Seneca explained that "his eloquence not only ran, but it ran down-hill." When Jonson wrote that Shakspere "flow'd with that facility," he was describing Shakspere's facility, not as a writer, but as an extemporaneous and impulsive talker. And it was this verbose fellow who "fell into those things, could not escape laughter." This Shakspere talked at a great rate (cf. "uttered with that easiness"), and his improvised speechifying provoked laughter. Once again, Shakspere is held up as the object of ridicule. And are we not meeting up with another Shake-scene, the "gentleman player," Gullio, or Sogliardo, each of whom mistakenly thought of himself as eloquent?

Jonson tells us that Shakspere, impersonating Caesar, spoke the lines in question. Perhaps Shakspere performed the role of Caesar, although no contemporaneous historical evidence survives to show that he did. Perhaps he recited an inferior version of the play or flubbed the line. Perhaps Shakspere, the paymaster, was sometimes greeted informally as Caesar and misquoted the line in casual conversation. Whichever, it is clear from the allusion to Haterius that Jonson was not commenting on Shakspere's "facility" as a *writer*. Nor was he complimenting Shakspere. In another section in *Timber* devoted to "Talking Overmuch," Jonson criticizes "too much talking [as] ever the *Indice* [indication] of a fool" (8:574).

Those who remain skeptical of this interpretation will perhaps be convinced by one other piece of evidence: The fuller text of Jonson's source. Jonson lifted more than just the analogy to Haterius; he lifted an entire chunk of *De Shakespeare nostrati* almost verbatim out of a passage by Seneca. Compare the following to *De Shakespeare nostrati*.

Haterius used to let the public in to hear him declaim extempore. Alone of all the Romans I have known he brought to Latin the skill of the Greeks. His speed of delivery was such as to become a fault. Hence that was a good remark of Augustus': "Haterius needs a brake"—he seemed to charge downhill rather than run. He was full of ideas as well as words. He would say the same thing as often as you liked and for as long as you liked, with different figures and development on every occasion. He could be controlled—but not exhausted.

But he couldn't do his own controlling. . . . He had his talents under his own control—but the degree of their application he left to another's.

. . . In his anxiety to say nothing that was not elegant and brilliant, he often fell into expressions that could not escape derision. I recall that he said, while defending a freedman who was charged with being his patron's lover: "Losing one's virtue is a crime in the freeborn, a necessity in a slave, a duty for the freedman." The idea became a handle for jokes, like "you aren't doing your duty by me" and "he gets in a lot of duty for him." . . .

. . . And many things of this sort were brought up against him. There was much you could reprove—but much to admire: he was like a torrent that is impressive but muddy in its flow. But he made up for his faults by his virtues, and provided more to praise than to forgive. (1:428–433)

This passage is about a loquacious orator, not a writer.

When Jonson wrote elsewhere in *Timber* about writers or orators, he thought of appropriate professional counterparts. He applauded Francis Bacon's gift for oratory using Seneca's words about another orator and rhetorician, Cassius Severus. In the section in which he advised students to read the best authors first, he plugged in Quintilian's recommendation to read Homer and Virgil in addition to his own preferred authors.

What is important, then, is the significance of Jonson's source. On the one occasion outside of the *Folio* when Jonson put pen to paper to write about Shakspere, he plugged in Seneca's description of Haterius to fill out his reminiscence. When Jonson thought about Shakspere, he didn't think of Aeschylus or Euripides or other great dramatists. He thought of an ancient senator whose extemporaneous speeches often provoked unintended derision.

JONSON'S SHAKSPERE

Following is a paraphrase of *De Shakespeare nostrati*, as if written by Jonson and liberally augmented with some authorial bombast:

Of our home-grown and intellectually deficient Shakspere

I scorn those who choose mediocre writing over good, thereby enriching the hack writers. The "sordid multitude" has no literary taste, which reminds me of the actors whose letters I wrote for the *First Folio*.

Heminges and Condell thought it a compliment to marvel over Shakspere's unblotted manuscripts. Their "praise" illustrates how the ignorant "are naturally deceived." Everybody knows that foul papers are filled with corrections. So when I would hear Heminges and Condell gushing over Shakspere's unblotted manuscripts, I knew they'd received fair copies, not the author's foul papers.

Years later, when they read the line that I had written for them—the one about the blots—they thought it was terrific. However, in an unguarded moment, I informed them that their "compliment" was really an insult, because they had failed to distinguish between foul papers and fair copies. They thought that was a destructive comment and accused me of being spiteful. They also didn't want me to expose their "compliment" for the uninformed flattery that it was. I did not reveal any of this at the time to the public.

To reconcile myself to them, and to attest to my fair and open mind, I professed admiration of Shakspere—while actually stating the opposite—by paying tribute to an Idol, a false god.

Let me explain "idolatry." I consider it the ultimate form of insincere flattery. In Epigram 65, I berated my Muse for making me "commit most fierce idolatry" in praise of a "worthless lord." When I praised Sir William

Uvedale, I stopped short of insincere praise: "Which (would the world not mis-call't flattery) I could adore, almost t'idolatry." So, when I chose the word "idolatry," I was expressing disdain disguised as a compliment. But it squared things with Heminges and Condell.

To say that Shakspere "was (indeed) honest" may seem like a sincere compliment, but I have previously sneered at the dishonest "Poet-Ape" and the slippery pretender Sogliardo. Notice the word "indeed" inside parentheses. I frequently used excessive punctuation to signal satiric asides.* My interjection of "indeed" may as well have been an "ahem." You might also be interested in my sarcastic Epigram 115, "On the Town's Honest Man":

> Describ'd, it's thus: Defin'd would you it have?
> Then, The town's honest Man's her errant'st knave.

Recall that the phrase "as I am an honest gentleman" was understood to mean the opposite. Likewise, Shakspere was the opposite of honest.

However, he had an extroverted disposition, an active imagination—especially when it came to his own self-image—and lots of ideas. He was garrulous, (and here I started borrowing from Seneca) and "of an open, and free nature." He used flowery and polite phrases in an attempt to sound genteel and articulate, but he always overdid it. Sometimes, like Haterius, he did not keep himself under control. In fact, you often had to shut him up. He had a sense of humor but no self-restraint.

In his over-reaching efforts to be eloquent, Shakspere had a tendency to make a fool of himself. Many of us remember the time when he garbled the line from *Julius Caesar*. Everyone standing around knew the correct line, but Shakspere thought he had demonstrated his thespian skills.

Like Haterius, Shakspere "redeemed his vices, with his virtues. There was ever more in him to be praised, than to be pardoned." Seneca had written of "faults." I wrote of "vices" to tie the passage to my earlier criticism of vice and the sordid multitude.

Those men who "were almost named for miracles" in the field of letters had not been in the least disadvantaged by their vices. On the contrary, "a great many have *profited*" from them. Those with vices were loved by the sordid multitude, indeed "loved for nothing else." And the most preposterous object of that adulation was Will Shakspere.

---

*According to an editor of *The Yale Ben Jonson*, Jonson used parentheses to "signal shifts to and from a different tone of voice. These semi-asides can create extremely funny interruptions of thought; their humor is vitiated if they are incorporated into the sentence" (*Every Man In*, 217). In a book on Jonson and his collected plays and epigrams, Dutton retained "Jonson's characteristic punctuation because it is often the key to his sense. . . . Jonson usually punctuates for the speaking voice" (*Folio*, xi).

Nothing in *De Shakespeare nostrati* describes a writer. When Jonson referred to literary men, he used explicit terminology, for example, of John Donne: "thy language, letters, arts, best life"; of Beaumont: "For writing better, I must envy thee"; of John Selden: "Your book, my Selden, I have read"; of Nicholas Breton: "So with this Author's readers will it thrive"; and of Drayton: "Of all that read thy *Poly-Olbion*." In the *First Folio* eulogy, Jonson chose similarly explicit terms: "while thy Book doth live, And we have wits to read." However, *De Shakespeare nostrati* is devoid of any such *literary* terminology. The closest Jonson gets is denigrating what the two actors used to say about Shakspere's unblotted papers.

In *Timber*, Jonson delivered a nonliterary man who was the butt of ridicule. To complete the impression that the credited source of the Shakespeare texts was lacking in literary sensibilities himself, Jonson gave an example of a line corrupted from a Shakespeare play, as it came out of Shakspere's mouth. There was certainly nothing in *De Shakespeare nostrati* about Shakespeare's "well-turned" lines. Jonson cannot have been speaking of the same man whom he extolled in the eulogy as "thou Star of Poets."

MOULDY TALES

Even during the years when he was silent on Shakspere the man, Jonson took swipes at Shakespearean texts in several of his own plays. And when Jonson's allusions are considered together, they suggest that he was rankled by something in particular. But was he irritated with Shakespeare, the dramatist, or Shakspere, the play broker and businessman?

It is surely odd that Jonson never explicitly complimented the majestic tragedy of a *Lear*, or the refined wit of a *Twelfth Night*, or the disciplined art in Shakespeare's poetry. Instead, he made fun of Shakspere, found trivial faults with the plays, or referred to some of their unsavory characters.

As we saw in *Every Man Out of His Humour*, Sogliardo is a relative of Silence, the rural justice in *2 Henry IV* who gets inebriated, won't stop singing, and has to be carried to bed. Sogliardo bought a silly coat of arms with the silly motto "Not Without Mustard," a parody of Shakspere's supposed motto. Jonson closed his play with the line, "you may in time make lean Maciente as fat as Sir John Falstaff." In *Epicene*, Jonson made a brief mention of Doll Tear-sheet, Falstaff's whore. In the Induction to *Bartholomew Fair* (1614), Jonson made it clear that playgoers who would "swear *Jeronimo* or *Andronicus* [were] the best plays," showed that their taste was woefully out-of-date. In the same Induction, a "Servant-monster in the Fair" is thought to be a derogatory reference to Caliban in *The Tempest*. None of these allusions suggests literary admiration.

In his prologue, written for the 1616 folio version of *Every Man In His Humour*, Jonson satirized several Shakespeare plays, and various critics have identified his targets as *The Winter's Tale*, the *Henry VI* trilogy, *Henry V*, and either *The Tempest* or *Cymbeline*. The Prologue closes with Jonson's exhorting the audience to laugh at the "popular errors" in all these plays. This error-prone dramatist is, presumably, the same Shakespeare whom Jonson eulogized in 1623 as better than the best of the ancient classical dramatists. Again, it is a fundamental contradiction.

In *The Staple of News*, Jonson paraphrased the same misquoted line from *Julius Caesar* found in *De Shakespeare nostrati*: "Cry you mercy, you never did wrong, but with just cause." And finally, in "Ode to Himself" (1629), we read:

> No doubt some mouldy tale,
> Like *Pericles*, and stale
> As the Shrieve's crusts, and nasty as his fish—
>   scraps, out [of] every dish
> Thrown forth, and rak't into the common tub,
> May keep up the Play-club:

The shrieve's or sheriff's tub was placed outside a prison to receive charitable handouts of crusts and scraps for prisoners. Here, Jonson associated *Pericles* with scraps, play scraps, an image evocative of the "Poet-Ape," whose "works are e'en the frippery of wit." *Pericles* was not included in the *First Folio*. It was registered in 1608 by Edward Blount, but published by Henry Gosson in 1609 in a corrupt edition patched together in part with a reported text* (Mowat, 218; Edwards, esp. 34–35, 43). Jonson was not so much putting down the author of *Pericles* as he was putting down the scavengers who produced the corrupt text.

In Jonson's own plays, then, we find pet peeves, such as contempt

---

*Maguire doubts that memorial reconstruction was the principal agency of corruption, although she considers *Pericles* largely "wrecked verse" (295).

for Shakspere's social pretensions, throwaway allusions to a few of Shakespeare's lower-class characters, and sneers at play-patching, trivial errors, and corrupt lines. In other words, over the years Jonson alluded to or ridiculed specific aspects of Shakespeare's plays and, outside of the *Folio*, found not one word of commendation for Shakespeare's "true-filed lines." Jonson's ridicule and nit-picking everywhere else stand in diametric opposition to his literary praise in the *Folio*.

JONSON'S BEQUEST

One of the pettifogger's tactics is to find fault with a minor detail and use it to discredit the larger argument. Jonson's complaints were petty but plausible. Taken together, they come across as contrived and deliberate. When it came to Shakspere/Shakespeare, Jonson regularly contradicted himself or complained about trivial matters. He belittled Shakespeare's small Latin and less Greek, yet two lines later eulogized him as better than the best of the ancient dramatists. He wrote that Shakspere's manuscripts contained no blots and then testified that Shakespeare reworked and revised by striking the second heat on the Muse's anvil.

Jonson's two conceptions of Shakspere/Shakespeare are *inherently incompatible*, but his conflated testimony makes sense if he recognized Shakspere and Shakespeare as two different people. Jonson knew better than to comment explicitly in print on the professionally performed plays of an aristocrat. When he took aim at the opportunistic and bombastic play-scavenger who associated himself with Shakespeare's works, he took care to encrypt his satire. Jonson juxtaposed both images in the *Folio*, and went part way toward explaining himself in his anecdotal entry in *Timber*. Jonson was at the center of, not a conspiratorial government cover-up, but a misinformation campaign.

As far as the record shows, Shakspere's reputation as a nonscholar began around 1613,* when Jonson's friend "F. B.," probably Francis Beaumont, began to circulate the story about a natural-born genius unsullied by education. F. B. would "from all Learning keep these

---

*For discussion on the most likely date of this verse letter, that is, summer or fall of 1613, see Moore, "F. B.'s Verse." Later dates have been proposed (e.g., 1615 by Chambers, *Facts*, 2:223–24), but Finkelpearl argues that Beaumont suffered a stroke no later than October 1613 (*Beaumont*, 42, 68–69 n, Appendix B), which would support Moore's dating. Finkelpearl proposes 1608–9.

lines as clear / as Shakespeare's best are, which our heirs shall hear / Preachers apt to their auditors to show / how far sometimes a mortal man may go / by the dim light of Nature, t'is to me / an help to write of nothing; and as free, / As he, whose text was, god made all that is, / I mean to speak." In other words, future generations are going to *hear* how much a man may accomplish using only untrained God-given talent, *or so F. B. intends to say.* This statement appears to be a deliberate crossing of wires in the Shakespearean commentary, a first allusion to a rumor mill about the "natural" playwright. Furthermore, F. B.'s lines foreshadow Jonson's report that Shakspere was "a happy imitator of Nature," had "small Latin and less Greek," and "Nature herself was proud of his designs."

Shakspere's reputation was handed down through Jonson's literary circle, and three lines from a prologue of 1662 suggest a typical line of transmission:

> Yet Gentle *Shakespear* had a fluent Wit,
> Although less Learning, yet full well he writ;
> For all his Plays were writ by Nature's light.

This verse was published by Margaret Cavendish, duchess of Newcastle (Ingleby, *Centurie*, 335). Jonson wrote two masques for her husband, and poems to members of her family. Cavendish's opinions on Shakespeare are clearly influenced by Jonson. She repeats all the major themes: Gentle; fluent; less learned; and "writ by Nature's light" echoing F. B.'s "dim light of Nature." In a surviving letter, she writes of Shakespeare, the "natural poet."

A second example of Jonson's influence is even more illuminating. Around 1657–63, Thomas Plume recorded some gossip in his notebook: "One told Ben Johnson—Shakespeare never studied for any thing he wrote. B. J. said—the more to blame He—said—Caesar never punishes any but for a just cause & another time makes Athens in Bohemia" (Jonson, *Ben Jonson*, 1:185). This entry tells us something about Plume's source. Jonson had been dead at least twenty years before Plume put pen to paper, so the stories were hardly new. The anecdote about *Julius Caesar* had been in print for at least fifteen years. However, we know about the supposed geographical blunder in *Winter's Tale* from Jonson's conversations with Drummond. But Drummond's notes were not published until the next century (1711), so we must conclude that Jonson had *told* somebody who passed it on along to Plume. This story about Bohemia got around, and the road leads back to Jonson.

Taken together, these allusions, which could be augmented with many others from *The Shakspere Allusion-Book* (see Ingleby et al.), show that Jonson sent out mixed messages concerning Shakspere/Shakespeare, that he conflated two reputations, and then handed them down through his immediate circle. Finally, the epistle by F. B. tells us that the rumor mill started during Shakspere's lifetime.

SHAKSPERE'S NEIGHBOR

Like Shakspere, Michael Drayton was born in Warwickshire. He was primarily a poet, but Henslowe recorded numerous payments to him as a collaborating dramatist. Though based in London, Drayton was a regular visitor to Warwickshire throughout his life. Shakspere's son-in-law, physician John Hall, treated Drayton for an illness and described him in his medical journal as "an excellent poet." It is no wonder, then, that biographers suppose that Drayton and Shakspere were well acquainted, even drinking buddies. But there is no evidence to support those assumptions.

Drayton wrote about "Shakespeare" by name only once but gave no indication of a personal friendship. The poem in question was published with *Elegies upon Sundry Occasions* in 1627, although its date of composition is unknown. Some have dated it prior to the publication of the *First Folio* (Ingleby, *Centurie*, 168). Drayton's lines about Shakspere occur in the middle of a critical assessment of "*Poets & Poesie*":

> and be it said of thee,
> *Shakespeare* thou hadst as smooth a Comic vein,
> Fitting the sock, and in thy natural brain,
> As strong conception, and as Clear a rage,
> As any one that traffic'd with the stage. (*Works*, 3:229)

The "sock" is the traditional footwear of the comic actor on the ancient Greek or Roman stage. If one assumed that these lines identified Shakespeare, the dramatist, one might paraphrase them:

Shakespeare, you had as good a knack for writing comedy, and in your talented God-given brain, as good an imagination and as much inspiration, as anyone who worked in the theatre.

That interpretation seems reasonable on the surface, and it is probably what Drayton intended at first glance. The passage is, after all, taken from Drayton's assessment of writers and is similar in some ways to his earlier lines in praise of Christopher Marlowe ("which made his verses clear, / For that fine madness still he did retain / Which rightly should possess a poet's brain.") But the verse to Shakspere is lukewarm praise. Moreover, under closer inspection, the interpretation is a stretch.

To begin with, Drayton described some other writers in this poem as "my dear companions whom I freely chose / My bosom friends." Drayton made no such personal reference to Shakspere. Drayton spoke of Jonson's sock and buskin, referring to both comedy and tragedy, yet he associated Shakspere only with the "sock" of comedy, not with tragedy, history, or poetry. Drayton wrote of "learned" Jonson's "poems rightly dramatic," Marlowe's "verses," Lyly's "writing," and Drummond's "poesy," all explicit literary terms. Yet Drayton omitted any unambiguous literary terms when he described Shakspere.

Shakspere's "Comic vein" brings to mind a flair for writing comedy, but Drayton's selective emphasis on his comic "vein" need not refer to the Shakespeare comedies. Shakspere's "vein" (*OED*, def. 9a) could just as easily refer to his legendary "natural wit" and propensity for jesting. If so, Drayton anticipated *Shakespeare nostrati*, whose "wit was in his own power." Drayton described Shakspere's "strong conception," an image that likewise corresponds to *Shakspere nostrati*'s "brave notions."

Drayton chose several words associated with acting and play brokering. "Trafficking," for example, is generally associated with trading in commodities, negotiating, and bargaining. "Fitting the sock" also means "as befits a comedian," with the connotation of wearing the comedian's or clown's costume. While "smooth" was routinely used to describe flowing or polished verse, including Shakespeare's, it also implies glib insincerity as in a smooth talker (see *OED*, def. 7b). Similarly, "rage" was used regularly to signify poetic passion or inspiration, but "rage" also denotes anger, sexual passion, a foolish act, or jesting talk. That last definition resonates the most with the "Comic vein" and "sock" images. Drayton's lines about Shakespeare are, like Jonson's, ambiguous. Here, then, is an unorthodox paraphrase:

Shakspere, you had a slick sense of humor, as befits a clown; and in your unschooled brain, as many big ideas and confident jests as anyone who traded in stage commodities.

Drayton, a fellow Warwickshireman, referred only once to Shakspere, and then not in personal terms. He ostensibly complimented Shakspere, not for *Hamlet* or *Lear* or narrative poetry, but for his flair for comedy. At best, Drayton damned Shakspere with faint praise, and at worst he described Shakspere in terms that point to the *factotum*. Drayton, like Jonson, seems to have pointed in two directions at once. He referred to Shakespeare, the writer, while describing Shakspere, the entrepreneur. And there is more.

In the same poem, Drayton admitted that he had not named certain poets who chose to circulate their manuscripts privately rather than publish. Some of those poets had written successfully for the stage. But just as Thomas Lodge did not name everyone whose writing he admired, Drayton was not going to name any names, either. The relevant lines at the end of the poem are

> For such whose poems, be they ne'er so rare,
> In private chambers, that encloistered are,
> And by transcription daintily must go:
> As though the world unworthy were to know,
> Their rich composures, let those men that keep
> These wondrous relics in their judgment deep,
> And cry them up so, let such Pieces be
> Spoke of by those that shall come after me,
> I pass not for them: nor do mean to run,
> In quest of these, that them applause have won,
> Upon our Stages in these latter days,
> That are so many, let them have their bays
> That do deserve it; let those wits that haunt
> Those public circuits, let them freely chant
> Their fine Composures, and their praise pursue. (*Works,* 3:231)

Drayton was describing dramatic verses that had been performed but not yet published. These plays circulated only in manuscript, in privileged circles. Drayton implies he is not in a position to extol ("cry them up") either the plays or their authors. He writes, "I pass not for them," meaning that he writes in public and as a professional, not as a gentleman amateur. He leaves it to others to talk about these plays, and presumably to expose them to a wider audience by publishing them. It is tempting to speculate that Drayton wrote the poem sometime before 1623, and that he had in mind those Shakespeare plays that had yet to be published.

Drayton and Jonson are the two writers that legends associate per-

sonally with Shakspere, and they are the two men who should have
been able to tell us the most about their supposed celebrated colleague. Instead, they told us very little. Their words do not confirm
their legendary friendship with Shakspere, nor do they square with
the traditional biography. Jonson conflated the reputations of two
men, one whom he respected as a dramatist, and another whom he
scorned as a pretentious and garrulous play broker. Drayton told us
much less than we should have expected, especially since he was
known personally to Shakspere's son-in-law. His four-and-a-half lines
in faint praise of "Shakespeare" were packed with words suggestive
of an actor and play broker. To cap it off, he concluded the poem
by talking about aristocratic poets who had written for the stage, but
whose names he would not reveal.

Chapter Twelve

Conspiracies and Chicanery

> And then one must reckon with the amateurs, the eccentrics, the cranks with theories. Of these the worst would be the heretics, alert to conspiracies, who saw a sinister plot to take away the plays from their true progenitor, Bacon or Marlowe or some Earl or other, and bestow them instead on the Stratford boor.
> —Samuel Schoenbaum, *Shakespeare's Lives* (viii)

Most anti-Stratfordians believe that "William Shakespeare" was the pen name of a maverick nobleman. Various scenarios have been developed to explain how and why his anonymity was maintained, and conspiracy theories have certainly been proposed.

Proponents of conspiracy theories argue that a playwright who could be recognized as a court insider was not only exposed to social disgrace but also posed a security risk, because many of the plays contained politically charged material. If the courtier-playwright remained anonymous, then at least some of the satire would be lost on the general public. Some theorists are therefore convinced that the state erased certain records and set up elaborate schemes to divert attention away from the highborn author. Less drastic versions propose that the author simply paid Shakspere of Stratford to take the credit, as Woody Allen did in *The Front*, or that Shakspere was tapped as a stand-in by the dramatist's family, perhaps sometime after the real author had died.

Traditional biographers, however, think that *any* stratagems to conceal the true author are positively laughable. They express astonishment that Ben Jonson, with the tacit collusion of Heminges and Condell, could be persuaded to commit perjury in the *First Folio* testimonials. Above all, how could any conspiracy have taken place? Too many people would have to have been in on the plot. Samuel Schoenbaum, quoted in the epigraph, denigrates the "heretics" and their covert plots, but he is ignoring the most important factor: Elizabethan mores.

In Elizabethan England, no conspiracy was necessary to prevent overt reference on the printed page to a courtier or an aristocrat whose plays were performed on the public stage. Social convention and state censorship already prevented it. The combination of legislation and social convention was potent, and it is probably impossible to establish precisely where the statutes left off and convention began. But people simply did not embarrass courtiers or aristocrats in print.

THE "STIGMA OF PRINT"

Any courtier or nobleman good enough to write professionally could not be seen to be doing so. He could not accept payment or publish under his own name. Sir Philip Sidney, regarded by many as the quintessential courtier-soldier-poet of the day, never published, and after his death his sonnet cycle was pirated. Gentlemen in Shakespeare's England consciously avoided what J. W. Saunders dubbed "The Stigma of Print."* Elizabethan gentlemen wrote for others in their social circle with no thought of seeing their compositions in print. Custom prohibited the upper class gentleman from having or appearing to have any profession at all, writing included. To publish for public consumption was the business of the paid professional, not the gentleman. This "horror of professionalism" dictated that the gentleman be skilled, but never "a narrow specialist, never a professional (which suggested the artisan, the hired servant)" (Vale, 3). An

---

*Helgerson discusses some of the conditions under which "the amateurs avoided print" in "The Elizabethan Laureate" (201). Marotti cites Helgerson in his discussion of the gentleman's need to "reject such literary trifles [i.e., poetry or erotic novellas], allowing himself only to appear in print as the author of pious and didactic works" ("Patronage," 12 n).

Elizabethan commentator described a literary value system quite different from that of later centuries:

For as well Poets as Poesie are despised. . . . Among the Nobility or gentry . . . especially in making or Poesie, it is so come to pass that they have no courage to write, &, if they have, yet are they loath to be . . . known of their skill. So as I know very many notable Gentlemen in the Court that have written commendably, and suppressed it again, or else suffered it to be published without their own names to it: as if it were a discredit for a Gentleman to seem learned. . . .
   . . . And in her Majesty's time . . . are sprung up another crew of Courtly makers [writers], Noblemen and Gentlemen of Her Majesty's own servants, who have written excellently well, as it would appear if their doings could be found out and made public. (G. G. Smith, 2:19, 22, 63)

Some members of the court wrote extremely well, but they were not writing publicly. Some poetry attributed to courtiers was published during their lifetimes, but generally without their knowledge or consent.

THE GENTLEMAN POET IN PRINT

Editors, publishers, and gentlemen poets employed a variety of methods "to protect the author from social condemnation" (Saunders, 143). Some authors substituted initials or adopted pseudonyms. Others hid their names in acrostics or other types of puzzles. Many verses were published with no attribution whatsoever. Misattributions, both deliberate and inadvertent, were common and sometimes compounded by suspicious circumstances of publication.

Songs and Sonnets (1557), today referred to as *Tottel's Miscellany*, was the first anthology of published poetry. Two major contributors were the earl of Surrey and Sir Thomas Wyatt, but the collection was "unauthorized by the authors, most of whom were dead" (*Tottel's*, 2:93 n). Many of the contributors have never been identified, and Hyder Edward Rollins explained that "for a gentleman to publish original lyrics was at this time regarded as distinctly bad form" (*Tottel's*, 2:88).

Some gentlemen signed their verse with a "posy," or motto. In George Gascoigne's *The Posies* (1575), for example, some poems were subscribed with the words "Si fortunatus infoelix." Gabriel Harvey's marginal note in his copy of the book identified that motto as "lately the posie of Sir Christopher Hatton" (G.C.M. Smith, 166). Harvey's annotation provides one of the few positive identifications of a high-ranking man behind a motto.

The title page of *The Phoenix Nest* (1593) claims that its verses were written by "Noble men, worthy Knights, gallant Gentlemen, Masters of Arts, and brave Scholars." According to Rollins, "more impressive names, more really fine poets, were connected with *The Phoenix Nest* than with any previous anthology." But *none* of them was named. A few poems were subscribed with initials or titles, such as "Sir W. H.," but most were anonymous. Among the "impressive names" then living, and identified by modern editors as contributors, were Sir Edward Dyer and the earl of Oxford (*Phoenix*, xvi, xviii, xx).

Not every poet personally consented to be published in these poetry collections. Oxford and Dyer appeared as contributors to *England's Helicon* (1600), but in the preface the publisher Nicholas Ling claimed that each poem "was delivered by some especial copy coming to [the editor's] hands." Of course, Ling did not name his sources. He also anticipated that some gentlemen poets might be offended to be seen in the company of professional writers, and his preface continues:

No one man, that shall take offense that his name is published to any invention of his, but he shall within the reading of a leaf or two, meet with another in reputation every way equal with himself, whose name hath been before printed to his poem, which now [if] taken away were more than theft: which may satisfy him that would fain seem curious, or be entreated for his fame.

. . . Further, if any man whatsoever, in prizing of his own birth or fortune, shall take in scorn that a far meaner man in the eye of the world shall be placed by him, I tell him plainly, whatsoever so excepting, that that man's wit is set by his, not that man by him. (4–5)

There is evidence that Ling took steps after the pages came off the press to placate some disgruntled contributors. He originally printed three poems over the initials "S.W.R." (presumably Sir Walter Raleigh), but these initials were then covered over by a slip of paper pasted on top and imprinted with the word "Ignoto." Similar slips were pasted over several other subscriptions. In the later edition (1614), all these attributions reverted to "Ignoto" or were replaced with different initials. These deliberate alterations indicate that some objections had been lodged (*Helicon*, xxi–xxix).

In his preface to another anthology, *A Poetical Rhapsody* (1602), Francis Davison likewise anticipated objections to "the mixing . . . of diverse things written by great and learned Personages, with our mean and worthless scribblings." Davison lamely protested that his own efforts to maintain everyone's anonymity had been thwarted by the printer.

One of the more complicated Elizabethan authorship problems concerns *Willobie His Avisa*, a scandalous poem that satirized "persons of great importance" (*Willobie*, 186). *Avisa* was published in 1594 and was popular enough to warrant editions in 1596 and 1599. In 1596, an apology *cum* disclaimer, published in *Penelope's Complaint*, gratuitously insisted that *Avisa* was pure fiction, not libelous satire. No one was deceived. Despite the censors' attempt in 1599 to ban the book, *Avisa* escaped into print again in 1605 and 1609. In the case of *Avisa*, then, the motive to cloak the identity of the author was compounded by the more practical matter of avoiding a confrontation with the censors.

The author of the title was ostensibly Henry Willobie, a student at Oxford. Many critics have accepted Willobie as the author, but G. B. Harrison showed that the relevant identifying facts disqualify him (*Willobie*, 222–26). Moreover, the attribution rests solely on the dubious authority of "Hadrian Dorrell," who wrote the preface for Willobie, his "chamber-mate" at Oxford. Willobie had supposedly gone overseas, entrusting his papers to Dorrell, who subsequently came across *Avisa* and assumed Willobie had written it. Dorrell decided it should be published. He also claimed not to know whether *Avisa* was written as fact or fiction, but in his disclaimer two years later, he contradicted many of his statements and protested that *Avisa* was fiction. Dorrell's story is transparent nonsense.

More to the point, "Hadrian Dorrell" is itself a pseudonym.* As far as anyone knows, the Henry Willobie who entered Oxford in 1591 was an innocent bystander, and he was never even summoned to explain himself. In addition, the author of *Avisa* knew better than to lampoon the aristocracy explicitly. He encrypted his satire and then passed on the blame to Willobie.

*There is no record of Dorrell at Oxford. The 1997 International Genealogical Index does not list anyone named "Hadrian Dorrell" (Dorral, Durrell, Darrell, etc.) in the sixteenth or early seventeenth centuries.

THE GENTLEMAN PLAYWRIGHT IN PRINT

The poetry anthologies and *Avisa* demonstrate some methods used to deflect or avoid recognition as a published poet, but writing overtly for the public stage would have been doubly degrading to a courtier's reputation. Plays were not considered respectable literature, and the public theatres were associated with whorehouses and vice. One might therefore anticipate more difficulty identifying any courtiers who regularly wrote plays, but two of them left vestigial traces.

In 1599, a Jesuit spy reported that the "Earl of Derby is busy penning comedies for the common players." That stray remark turned up in two letters intercepted by Elizabeth's secret service.* Nobody knows what name, if any, Derby may have written under, or if any extant plays are his, but the letters prove that Derby wrote plays. The reference to "common players" leads to the inference that Derby was writing, at least in part, for the public stage. Derby's own company was touring the provinces throughout the 1590s and performed at court early in 1600.

The author of *The Arte of English Poesie* (1589) named the earl of Oxford along with Richard Edwards of Her Majesty's Chapel as deserving of praise for "comedy and Enterlude," linking Oxford to respectable court plays (G. G. Smith, 2:65). In 1598, Francis Meres, author of *Palladis Tamia*, listed Oxford as one of the "best for comedy," but in the same paragraph, Meres also named the same Richard Edwards, as well as Doctor Gager of Oxford University, before listing some of the paid professionals. Private or academic entertainments did not carry the social stigma of the public stage.

A spy's covert remarks about Derby's activities as a dramatist were intercepted and thereby preserved in the state records. Nobody in Derby's social circle recorded that information. The two Elizabethan authors who reported that Oxford wrote plays juxtaposed his name with references to court performances and academia, allowing their readers to associate an earl with respectable entertainments. Nobody else mentioned either peer as a playwright in any other known written records, but it is difficult to describe that state of affairs as the result of a conspiracy. Did state officials hold rapiers to everyone's throats to prevent them from jotting down remarks about Derby's or Ox-

*Letters are by George Fenner, 30 June 1599 (*Calendar of State Papers, Domestic*). Two letters by the Jesuit Henry Garnet were written on the same date to Fenner's Venetian correspondents.

ford's playwriting into letters or journals? They didn't need to. Everyone had the tact, common sense, and respect for authority not to embarrass an earl by writing about his déclassé activities.

Neither peer published his plays, at least not under his own name, although aristocrats *could* have written some of the plays published anonymously or with initials. To this day, many writers remain anonymous or deliberately concealed behind pen names such as *Cygnus* and *Peter Picks*, and nobody thinks that those unsolved mysteries smack of conspiracy. It is certainly possible that "William Shakespeare" is just another of those unsolved mysteries. There would have been no good options open to a courtier or nobleman consumed with a passion to write and compulsively attracted to the theatre. A pen name, whether chosen by author, publisher, or agent, would have been the only solution.

THE CODE OF CONSENT

On a 1989 PBS *Frontline* program, Schoenbaum compared Shakespearean conspiracy theories to those concerning the number of gunmen at Dallas in 1963, insisting that there was no "grassy knoll" in Shakespeare. However, the parallel is found, not in assassination theories, but in the code of silence among the U.S. Secret Service staff, which kept John F. Kennedy's philandering out of the public eye until after his death. One of Kennedy's biographers wrote that "the logistics of Kennedy's liaisons with Judith Campbell and dozens of other women in the White House and in hotels, houses, and apartments around the country and around the world required secrecy and devotion rare even in the annals of the energetic service demanded by successful politicians" (Reeves, 290). The Secret Service protected a highly-placed individual out of respect for his office and position. During the Roosevelt administration, there was a "code of consent" between the press corps and the White House staff to refrain from public comment on Franklin Roosevelt's physical handicap.

These codes of consent, involving hundreds to thousands of individuals, were effective. Moreover, when they are discussed in public decades later, nobody expresses disbelief. Even though they were conducted under the glare of the media, such codes are completely plausible. Despite the changing political climates and technological advances, social codes have effectively protected privileged individuals from the disgrace or embarrassment of public exposure.

If a courtier's work was performed and published under the name of "William Shakespeare," then some of the court and *literati* had to have been "in the know." The sheer number of people on the inside track, or privy at second hand to some of the facts, makes a state conspiracy implausible. Then why didn't all these people talk about it? Among themselves, they probably did talk about it. They just didn't *write* about it, at least not in plain English. When contemporaries wrote about the dramatist Shakespeare, either they confined their remarks to comment on his literary output, or they encrypted their allusions.

EARLY AUTHORSHIP DOUBTS

An early indication of a question concerning Shakespeare's authorship appeared in 1595, when Thomas Edwards published *Cephalus and Procris. Narcissus,* two poems each followed by an envoy. In *L'Envoy* to *Narcissus,* Edwards praised several Elizabethan poets, introducing each one with an allegorical nickname (e.g., "Collyn" for Edmund Spenser) or reference to a work for which they were known (e.g., *Rosamund* for Samuel Daniel). "Adon" signifies Shakespeare:

> Adon deafly [deftly] masking through
> Stately tropes rich conceited,
> Shewed he well deserved to,
>   Loves delight on him to gaze,
> And had not love her self entreated,
>   Other nymphs had sent him bays.
>
> Eke in purple robes distained,
> Amidst the Center of this clime,
> I have heard say doth remain,
>   One whose power floweth far,
> That should have been of our rhyme
>   The only object and the star.
>
> Well could his bewitching pen,
> Done the Muses objects to us,
> Although he differs much from men,
>   Tilting under Friaries,
> Yet his golden art might woo us,
>   To have honored him with bays.

In the second stanza, with the reference to privileged "purple robes," Edwards became the first to imply that the poet of *Venus and Adonis* was an aristocrat. Nineteenth-century scholars were puzzled, but they variously identified the purple-robed poet as Lord Buckhurst, the earl of Oxford, the earl of Essex, or by virtue of his legal profession, Francis Bacon. They also had understandable difficulty reconciling the author of *Venus and Adonis* in the first stanza with a purple-robed aristocrat in the second. In his 1882 edition of *Cephalus* for the Roxburghe Club, the Rev. W. E. Buckley got around the problem by considering the second two stanzas as separate from the first, even though the second failed to introduce a new poet. At least one of Buckley's scholarly correspondents thought all three stanzas described Shakespeare (T. Edwards, 333–46). The editors of *The Shakspere Allusion-Book* (Ingleby et al.), however, followed Buckley and severed the second two stanzas from the first, expressing similar mystification.

While Edwards implied that an aristocrat wrote *Venus and Adonis*, the *Parnassus* authors seemed to think that Samuel Daniel wrote *Romeo and Juliet*. In *Polimanteia* (1595), "W. C." placed a marginal allusion, "All praise / worthy. / Lucrecia / Sweet Shak-/speare. / Eloquent / Gaveston. / Wanton / Adonis," adjacent to a passage extolling not Shakespeare's, but Daniel's works. Satirists Joseph Hall and John Marston implied that Bacon wrote Shakespeare's two narrative poems (Gibson, 59–65). Around 1598–1601, Gabriel Harvey guessed that Dyer might be the poet:

The younger sort takes much delight in Shakespeare's Venus, & Adonis: but his Lucrece, & his tragedy of Hamlet, Prince of Denmark, have it in them, to please the wiser sort. Or such poets: or better: or none. [following appear the Ovidian lines from the title page of *Venus and Adonis*]

> Vilia miretur vulgus: mihi flavus Apollo
> Pocula Castaliæ plena ministret aquæ:

quoth Sir Edward Dyer, between jest, & earnest. Whose written devises far excel most of the sonnets, and cantos in print. (G.C.M. Smith, 232–33)

Whoever wrote "A never writer to an ever reader" in the 1609 epistle for *Troilus and Cressida* brought to mind the earl of Oxford's probable posie, "Ever or Never." All these writers were either misinformed, genuinely puzzled about the authorship, or deliberately cryptic or misleading.

These allusions were written at a time when writers used "a system of communication in which ambiguity [became] a creative and necessary instrument" to encode their material (Patterson, 11). These writers were not part of a conspiracy. They were products of their time, schooled in the art of ambiguity. While it is commonplace to find poetry, prose passages, and dialogue that defy deciphering, it is highly unusual, if not unique, to find one particular writer for whom *all* the literary allusions with some hint of personal information are ambiguous or cryptic. Any other writer of consequence from Shakespeare's day can be clearly and personally identified in some of his literary paper trails. Yet all that remains in Shakespeare's file are allusions that read as though everyone avoided explicit identification of the man. Just as the Secret Service and the press corps did not broadcast the facts about Kennedy or Roosevelt, Shakespeare's professional colleagues did not write explicitly about a gentleman dramatist in their midst. Their discretion suggests that they held "Shakespeare" at a respectful distance, safe from the taint of the literary, theatrical, and publishing professions.

MISINFORMATION

No conspiracy was required to persuade Jonson and his tribe to push the myth of Shakspere as natural wit and presumed author. In Shakespeare's England, diversions, deliberate ambiguities, and misinformation were encouraged by social convention and censorship regulations. Nevertheless, some traditional scholars occasionally express disbelief or even shock to find "Honest Ben" Jonson or Heminges and Condell accused of making fraudulent statements about Shakespeare's authorship in the *First Folio* (e.g., I. Wilson, 401).

Any incredulity or outrage is entirely misplaced. Misleading poetry is not perjury. Jonson would hardly have flinched at writing ambiguous or misleading verses or letters, something he did just about every working day. For Jonson's own admission of the practice, see his epigrams "To My Muse" or "To All, to Whom I Write." Jonson was conditioned to write between the lines on sensitive subjects, in this case confusion between the pen name of a man of rank and the name of a braggart shareholder and broker.

Shakspere of Stratford was unquestionably an opportunist, and it is likely that he exploited the similarity between the two names. It is also probable that he bought or appropriated some of the Shakespeare texts and sometimes took credit for them. Not only did nobody interfere, but Jonson and others in his circle actively promoted Shakspere's borrowed literary reputation.

Customs and regulations in Shakespeare's England prevented exposure in print of privileged persons engaged in socially compromising activities. The theory that Shakespeare was the pen name of a courtier explains why Shakespeare is the only playwright of consequence from the period who left behind no personal literary paper trails, why William Shakspere was able to fill the void, and why Jonson and others could so easily cross the wires that posterity has yet to untangle.

SKULLDUGGERY

Every other writer of consequence from the Elizabethan and Jacobean eras left a few personal paper trails that prove he was capable of writing what posterity attributes to him. The unique absence of comparable evidence for Shakspere has been so frustrating that some enterprising researchers have gone that extra mile and created new records where the archives have left off.

The most notorious of these villains was John Payne Collier (1789–1883) whose forgeries still contaminate Shakespeareana. He fabricated documentation concerning theatre shareholding, counterfeited entries in Henslowe's papers, and planted various "discoveries" in repositories such as the Bodleian Library and the Dulwich Archives, where he had unrestricted access and unlimited borrowing privileges. Collier's disrespect for precious historical records is appalling, and we probably do not yet know the extent of his sabotage.

Collier's friend and colleague, Peter Cunningham (1816–69), came under suspicion when he tried to sell the 1604–5 and 1611–12 Revels Accounts to the British Museum in 1868. The accounts were at first pronounced forgeries, then pronounced genuine, then questioned again. A. E. Stamp's 1930 *The Disputed Revels Accounts* continues to be quoted as the ultimate vindication of the disputed documents, but Samuel A. Tannenbaum's analysis of their irregularities, *Shakspere Forgeries*, leaves lingering doubts.

In his self-appointed role as Stratford tour guide, John Jordan (1746–1809) invented a number of legends about Shakspere. In 1784, he published John Shakspere's supposed "spiritual will" (a testament of faith in Catholicism) found by a workman in the house where the Shaksperes had lived. The will disappeared. Some biographers have rejected the will as spurious, while others have tentatively accepted it. (This questionable evidence continues to loom large in debates about Shakspere's hypothetical Catholicism.)

William Henry Ireland (1777–1835) forged an "original" manuscript of *King Lear* and parts of *Hamlet*. Ireland's most outrageous fabrication was an entire "lost" Shakespeare play, *Vortigern*, which was produced in London's West End (1796) and closed after one disastrous performance. Ireland's phony letters, receipts, deeds, and a catalogue of Shakespeare's library fooled many celebrated nineteenth-century bardolators, including the Prince of Wales. After Edmund Malone exposed some of the forgeries, Ireland made a full confession.

The Shakespeare forgeries not only taint the documentation. They give one nightmares about an even more hideous crime. If Collier was unprincipled enough to contaminate documents with fake information to corroborate his latest research paper, then one has to wonder what he might have destroyed.

MISSING EVIDENCE

Shakspere's biographers wring their hands in dismay over missing records. Evidence that historians might have expected to find includes:

- Registers of marriage ceremonies in Warwickshire towns where Shakspere might have been married. In one register in Worcester, the pages covering the dates in question have been cut out (Gray, 235).
- The inventory exhibited with Shakspere's will.
- The Revels Accounts for 1589–1604, critical years for Shakespearean dramatic activity. The 1604–5 accounts that break the silence may be forgeries.
- The dramatist's papers, correspondence, or books.
- The first of John Hall's (Shakspere's son-in-law) two medical casebooks.

Hall's second casebook, now in the British Library, was published in 1657 as *Select Observations on English Bodies*. Shakspere is nowhere mentioned in this casebook. Hall's earliest dated case is from 1617, the year after Shakspere died, but the cases do not appear in chronological order, and the majority are undated. An editor of *Select Observations* admitted that "there is no way of knowing if undated cases come from an earlier or later time [than 1617]. It would be reasonable to assume that a doctor, who started practicing medicine around 1600, might have selected cases from clinical data of the first seventeen years of his practice" (Joseph, 35). Hall's first casebook has been lost, and historians will always wonder whether it contained any mention of William Shakspere.

Furthermore, the casebook that does survive raises a question. Hall described his patient Michael Drayton as "an excellent poet" and noted the learned accomplishments of several other patients, among them Lady Rainsford ("devoted to sacred literature and conversant in the French language"), Baronet Puckering ("very learned, much given to study"), and a "Mr. Queeny," probably one of Hall's in-laws ("a man of good wit, expert in tongues, and very learned") (Joseph, *91, 124, 60*). But one of the most telling entries describes "the only Son of Mr. *Holy-oak* (which framed the Dictionary)" (154). The patient's father, Francis Holyoake had written the *Dictionarium Ethmologicum Latinum*. Although Hall recorded cases for his own relatives, including his wife Susanna, he failed to make note anywhere of his own family's supposed literary heritage.

It is also worth mentioning that the man who translated Hall's casebook from Latin into English, James Cooke, is one man who *did* see Hall's other notebook. If Hall *did* record anything about his remarkable father-in-law (and many biographers suppose that Hall attended Shakspere's final illness), Cooke was oddly silent on the matter. Yet in his preface, Cooke described his meeting with Hall's widow, Susanna. He also described Hall's clientele, which included some of the "most eminent Persons" in Warwickshire, and Hall's facility in the French language. Cooke had nothing to say in his preface about the good physician's supposedly eminent father-in-law.

Other papers relating to Shakspere survived long enough to have been examined by eighteenth- and nineteenth-century investigators but have since vanished, prompting more debate about the nature of the information they may or may not have contained. The Rev. James Wilmot (b. 1726) combed Warwickshire looking for books, papers, and other documentation with which to prepare a life of Shakspere. He found some relevant papers but no books. By 1785, he concluded that someone else had written the plays and burned all the papers.

Some of Henslowe's playhouse inventories were examined by early scholars but are no longer extant. Edmund Malone inspected two documents that convinced him that Shakspere moved to Southwark in 1596 and remained there for twelve years, but both documents have been lost.

Some of the missing records, such as a marriage register, would have augmented the personal documentation for Shakspere of Stratford, while others could have related to his professional activities. The literary records concerning Shakspere's supposed writing career, if indeed they ever existed, seem to have been subjected to a thorough housecleaning, and that phenomenon is unique. How is this unusual gap in the historical record to be explained?

Robert Bearman, senior archivist for The Shakespeare Birthplace Trust, explained that for many years, archival records were not prized as they are today, and security was lax. The plot thickened when unscrupulous men like Collier entered the picture and gained unlimited access to various archives. Like many eighteenth- and nineteenth-century scholars, Collier took possession of numerous historical documents. He doctored some of them, while others have since disappeared. Most historians remain cautious when considering any documentation that Collier is known to have handled, and he is known to have handled much.

However, the absence of any personal *literary* records for "Shakespeare" is a most suspicious phenomenon, and the laws of probability argue against a total absence of such documentation. Even if someone like Collier did attempt to sweep the archives clean, he could never have known what else might remain to be discovered. However, if Shakespeare was a gentleman of rank, then social custom and legislation would have kept him out of the written record *in the first place*. Once again, the theory that Shakespeare was the pen name of a courtier would explain why there are no personal literary paper trails.

PART FOUR

OVERWHELMING EVIDENCE

Chapter Thirteen

Shakspere's Education

> The sons and daughters of John and Mary Shakespeare were
> brought up in an illiterate household—neither parent witnessed
> except with a mark. . . .
> . . . The immense range of Shakespeare's language—his in-
> ventiveness, his facility, his power of recall to just the right level
> of conscious use—was his unique endowment, but it was fos-
> tered in the fortunate situation of good regular schooling against
> the background of oral training in a not unintelligent home.
> —Muriel C. Bradbrook, *Shakespeare: The Poet
> in His World* (10, 14)

An early editor of the German Shakespeare Society's *Jahrbücher*, Karl
Elze, observed that "the poetic imagination . . . bestows upon no one
a knowledge of facts" (278). Nobody knows how Shakspere learned
any of the facts and information so abundant in the plays. Unless the
dramatist had access to advanced education, books, and cultured society, one has to visualize a sort of literary clairvoyant who acquired
all his knowledge and culture by some process other than learning.

With few exceptions, the biographies of Elizabethan and Jacobean
writers cite educational records, or as in Ben Jonson's case where no
institutional record survives, personal testimony to an academic

mentor. But in Shakspere's case, we hit a snag: No biography can account for his education. The Stratford grammar school records for the years in question do not survive, so no one can prove whether Shakspere did or did not attend. So when a biographer refers, for example, to "the rhetorical training he received in school" (Bate, *Genius*, 328), he is presenting guesswork as fact. The best that can be inferred is that *if* Shakspere wrote the plays, then he *must* have attended the Stratford grammar school.

A MAN OF GENIUS

Most men of genius, such as Wolfgang Amadeus Mozart, Albert Einstein, and John Milton, left records of their education or the professional training that prepared them for their life's work. Even the geniuses who precede Shakespeare by a century or two left behind some sort of documentation relating to their education. For example, Dante's tribute to his mentor is similar to Jonson's tribute to William Camden (see Chapter 8). Dante introduced a Florentine scholar and statesman, Brunetto Latini, in his *Inferno* and wrote:

> my mind is etched . . .
> with your kind image, loving and paternal,
> when, living in the world, hour after hour
>
> you taught me how man makes himself eternal.
> And while I live my tongue shall always speak
> of my debt to you, and of my gratitude. (Canto XV)

Francesco Petrarch and Lodovico Ariosto both studied law before pursuing their literary careers. In the company of those dating from the Renaissance onward, Shakspere stands alone as a presumed literary giant with no visible means of educational support.

The biographer quoted in the epigraph to this chapter supposed that Shakspere's upbringing partly compensated for any inadequacies in his formal education. According to her theory, Shakspere got off to a good start in his "not unintelligent home"—filled with illiterate people. Then Shakspere was supposedly sent to the grammar school.

Tradition tells us that Shakspere attended the grammar school but dropped out at around age thirteen, due to his father's waning fortunes. Tradition is probably right, because later evidence attests to Shakspere's basic literacy. As an actor, he had to be able to read his roles. The "gentleman player," the satirical incarnation of Shakspere in *Groatsworth of Wit,* had been "a Country author, passing at a Moral" before hiring other playwrights to write for him. Patching together old morality plays would have required basic literacy. So would (possibly) play brokering and (certainly) the vulgarization of texts. Shakspere negotiated many legal documents, and it is more likely that he could read those documents, rather than always having to rely on a scrivener. We know of three letters written to him, one about borrowing money, and two others, no longer extant, concerning the Welcombe pasture enclosures. We know he could sign or at least scrawl his name. However, while Shakspere's biographical trails suggest that he attended grammar school, they do not suggest that he became an intellectual, much less a literary giant.

In fact, Shakspere's presumed incomplete grammar school training stops far short of anything that could account for a spectacular Renaissance education. Since the surviving records for Oxford, Cambridge, and the Inns of Court show no trace of any William Shakspere, biographers logically conclude that he did not have a university education. Some conclude, less logically, that he didn't need one. T. W. Baldwin supposed it "a piece of the greatest good fortune that Shakspere had no better an education to waste his time upon things which were for him unimportant" (*Latine,* 2:493). Peter Levi agreed that "luckily for us he left school early" (32; see also 27).

It is difficult to square Shakspere's probable but incomplete grammar school training with the works of Shakespeare—works that attest to a highly educated mind. One measure of that highly educated mind is Shakespeare's command of the English language:

Much more has been written about the verbal audacity and word-creativeness of Shakespeare than about another power of his, more remarkable even than his gift of formal invention—I mean his genius in the manipulation and development of meaning. . . . Shakespeare possessed this power in a degree never approached before or since by any Englishman, or perhaps by any individual mind. (Gordon, 266–67)*

*The *Oxford English Dictionary* credits Shakespeare with coining 1,904 words; his nearest rivals are Francis Bacon, with 866, Sir Thomas Browne with 849, Jonson with 838, George Chapman with 802, Thomas Nashe with 665, and Edmund Spenser with 606. But Schäfer's critical analysis of the methodology used to compile the *OED* suggests that the "preferential treatment" given to the Shakespeare corpus tends "to inflate his innovation rate which, when properly adjusted, is not so exceptional" (62).

Shakespeare's mastery of the English language reveals an education far beyond what any grammar school could offer. Grammar schools did not teach English. The traditional biography deals with this dilemma by assuming that Shakspere attended the Stratford grammar school for up to six years; by endowing that grammar school with educational capabilities equivalent to the best in all of England; by interpreting selected literary references to Shakspere's "natural" talents as testimony to his limited formal training, despite the inherent contradiction with his astonishing grammar school training; and by citing his genius to explain away any other educational gaps.

According to many biographers, the Stratford grammar school was an extraordinary institution. Some boast that the quality of schoolmasters at Stratford was exceptionally high and point to the comparatively generous salary of £20 per year. However, job turnover was high. From 1564, when Shakspere was born, to 1579, when he was fifteen, there were six different schoolmasters. The higher salary may have been necessary to entice someone to take the job. Levi acknowledged that "this swift succession of schoolmasters does not create confidence in the school" (30).

Nor did the Stratford grammar distinguish itself as a preparatory school. Again, according to Levi, "none of Shakespeare's exact contemporaries at school went on to Oxford or Cambridge; at least none has been traced" (32). Historian Mark Eccles traced one (*Warwickshire*, 58–59).

Distinguished Elizabethan and Jacobean academics, such as Roger Ascham and Henry Peacham, deplored the conditions in provincial grammar schools. Most of them were one-room schoolhouses with all levels taught by one schoolmaster and perhaps an assistant, using a minimum of learning tools. According to Virgil K. Whitaker, students were "taught by methods that developed before the multiplication of printed textbooks, when writing materials were too scarce and expensive for much note-taking and men relied primarily upon their memories" (37). Alfred Harbage described the dreaded grammar schools as "places where Latin grammar was instilled by means of rote recitation and the rod in sessions of eight hours a day, six days a week, all months of the year" (34). Yet biographers believe that Shakspere dropped out of grammar school and somehow made the leap to erudite author without any further formal training. Or as Baldwin put it, "he began to swim where he fell in, from the grammar school wharf" (*Literary*, 499).

In the absence of any concrete evidence supporting Shakspere's schooling, some authorities have embraced the theory of education by osmosis. Harbage assured his readers that "the creative artist absorbs information from the surrounding air" (25). Baldwin was convinced that it was "relatively unimportant whether Shakspere became acquainted with these materials through formal drill in grammar school or whether he merely absorbed them from the air" (*Latine*, 2:664), and offered the following rationale:

If William Shakspere had the grammar school training of his day—or its equivalent—he had as good a formal literary training as had any of his contemporaries. At least, no miracles are required to account for such knowledge and techniques from the classics as he exhibits. Stratford grammar school will furnish all that is required. The miracle lies elsewhere; it is the world-old miracle of genius. (*Latine*, 2:663)

Another commentator concluded that "the ways of genius have always been inexplicable" (Campbell, "Himself," 179).

Inexplicable, perhaps. But the development of a genius should not be completely *untraceable*, and Shakspere's supposed progress from incipient genius to productive creative artist remains completely untraceable.

There is more jarring evidence. Shakspere's daughter Judith grew up illiterate; she signed with her mark. His eldest daughter, Susanna, made a "painfully formed signature, which was probably the most that she was capable of doing with the pen" (Thompson, 1:294), and she was unable to recognize her own husband's handwriting. If, against all odds, the man from Stratford did overcome the obstacles presented by a rural market town and go on to write plays and poetry considered pinnacles of expression in the English language, would he so devalue basic literacy as to allow any of his children to grow up unable to read and write? Even if he was absent from Stratford during his children's formative years, would he not have insisted *in absentia* that Susanna and Judith be tutored? While it is true that Elizabethan girls were generally not educated and female literacy was found mostly in the upper classes, it is ironic to find Shakespeare's heroines and their ladies-in-waiting literate, even erudite. But Shakspere's closest distaff relatives are, without exception, functionally illiterate.

An ultimate irony in the traditional biography is that John Shakspere, the illiterate glover who rose to positions of civic responsibility, wanted better for his son and sent him to grammar school, or so we are told. William, having presumably acquired his spectacular education and gentrification, evidently did not share his father's enlightened perspective, because he did not insist on properly educating his own children.

SMALL OR LARGE LATIN

Jonson's *First Folio* eulogy is largely responsible for Shakspere's reputation as the natural-born genius, unsullied by any formal advanced education. Recall these lines:

> I should commit thee surely with thy peers,
> And tell, how far thou didst our *Lily* out-shine,
>   Or sporting *Kid*, or *Marlowe's* mighty line.
> And though thou had small *Latin*, and less *Greek*,
>   From thence to honour thee, I would not seek
> For names; but call forth thund'ring *Aeschylus*
>   *Euripides*, and *Sophocles* to us

Jonson's reference to Shakspere's "small Latin, and less Greek" has caused no end of trouble. The traditional biographer usually infers from that line that Jonson did not consider Shakspere much of a classical scholar, and that the modicum of Latin that he would have learned at grammar school was more than adequate preparation for his life's work.

Entire books have been written to rationalize Jonson's denigration of Shakspere's minimal classical training, the most famous being Baldwin's *William Shakspere's Small Latine and Lesse Greeke*:

It is much more sensible to let Shakspere acquire in grammar school the "small Latine, and lesse Greeke" with which Ben Jonson endowed him. It accounts quite satisfactorily for Shakspere's scholarly acquirements. Nothing which has been observed so far would indicate that these acquirements were anything more than the smattering supposed to be absorbed by the ordinary "well-beaten, learned-grammarian." (2:675)

Another critic claimed that "it is no exaggeration to say that any adult who possessed the competence in Latin that Shakespeare must have had before he left school could read in two months all the books that Shakespeare studied" (Whitaker, 36). Another scholar assumed that "seven years at school are enough to enable a lad to read easy passages

in Latin fluently and to puzzle out the harder bits" (Stapfer, 102).
Yet many books in Latin that Shakespeare drew from were much
"harder bits," far beyond the scope of any Elizabethan grammar
school.

Other scholars have had understandable difficulty reconciling the
traditional interpretation of "small Latin" with the overwhelming evidence in the plays of Shakespeare's mastery of both the Latin language and classical literature. In 1891, quite early in his career,
Chambers wrote that "Shakespeare's knowledge of classics and philosophy has always puzzled his biographers. A few years at the Stratford Grammar School do not explain it." He then speculated that
Shakespeare's command of the classics was probably the result of university training, despite the lack of evidence (*Gleanings*, 144).

According to one Latin specialist, C. S. Montgomery, the number
of Shakespeare's "Latin derived words varies considerably. In the earlier plays there are between two and three hundred in each play, while
in the later plays the numbers are more than trebled." Further,
"Shakespeare's knowledge of Latin construction is unique. In fact,
with him it becomes an additional sense." And "Shakespeare's most
inspired passages are the results of his subconscious assimilation of
the Latin language and Latin Literature" (13, 33, 40). Montgomery's
analysis suggests that the typical representation of Shakespeare as a
nonscholar is the result either of a misreading of Jonson's reference
to "small Latin, and less Greek," or that Jonson's complaint was misleading.

Did Jonson intend the line as an insult, even though it is found in
a eulogy? Certainly readers from his own circle interpreted it as derogatory. In the preface to the 1659 edition of plays written by Jonson's former amanuensis, Richard Brome, we read that Jonson "threw
in his [Shakespeare's] face—small Latin and less Greek." Leonard
Digges was at pains to counter some of those perceived slurs in his
own later tribute to Shakespeare.

Nevertheless, as with the first seventeen lines of his eulogy, Jonson's words turn out to be ambiguous. They can be read—or mis-
read—in more than one way, and he could have defended his words
as complimentary. A plausible complimentary interpretation was advanced by Ian Donaldson, who suggested that Jonson borrowed a
technique from an ancient orator:

to praise another person: begin (says Quintilian) by mentioning the person's
disadvantages, then go on to say how he overcame them: as for example,

he was a small man, but very brave. Jonson is saying: Shakespeare was not a classical scholar, did not aim to outgo the ancients, but despite this, he exceeded them all. It is a serious and profound tribute. ("Tother," 125)

Another critic read the lines "how far thou didst our Lily out-shine, / Or sporting Kid, or Marlowe's mighty line. / And though thou had small Latin, and less Greek, / *From thence* to honour thee" (emphasis added) as critical of John Lyly, Thomas Kyd, and Christopher Marlowe:

In the case of an unlearned author, the fair comparison would be with his contemporaries, not with the classics of antiquity. But this limitation does not apply to Shakespeare. Although Shakespeare was comparatively unlearned, Jonson does not need, in order to praise him, to turn to such authors as Lyly, Kyd and Marlowe (*From thence*) for a standard of achievement. Shakespeare can stand up to the comparison with the dramatists of Greece and Rome. (T.J.B. Spencer, 34)

According to this interpretation, then, Jonson was referring to Lyly's, Marlowe's, and Kyd's standard of achievement, presumably *their* "small Latin, and less Greek"—not Shakespeare's.

These various readings jostle with each other, but they again prove that Jonson's testimony is ambiguous, capable of multiple interpretations. Yet most of these modern interpretations conflict with the prevailing opinion in the seventeenth century, that is, that Jonson's remark *was* derogatory. Jonson was a methodical writer, and surely, he knew what he was doing. At the least, he sent out mixed messages and at most, he undermined his own testimony.

THE DIM LIGHT OF NATURE

Some biographers use the lines by "F. B.," addressed in 1613 to Jonson, as evidence that Shakspere was regarded as a nonscholar who got where he did on the strength of his natural abilities:

Here I would let slip,
(If I had any in me) scholarship,
And from all Learning keep these lines as clear
as Shakespeare's best are, which our heirs shall hear
Preachers apt to their auditors to show
how far sometimes a mortal man may go

by the dim light of Nature, t'is to me
an help to write of nothing; and as free,
As he, whose text was, god made all that is,
I mean to speak.
                    F. B.

Chambers thought the lines were "full of admiration and discriminating kindliness" (*Facts*, 1:70). But F. B. was hardly admiring Shakspere by describing him as a nonscholar to Jonson, a man known to
prize scholarship above almost anything else. F. B. was insulting Shakspere if he reported that he had gone only as far as the "dim light of
nature" would permit.

Why did F. B. write about "Preachers apt to their auditors"? That
line is the key to this passage. Preachers "apt to their auditors" are
preachers who tell their listeners what they want to hear. And F. B.
intends to be one of those preachers, to speak of such "free" and
God-given texts. Here is a paraphrase:

I'd release* scholarship from these lines, if I had any to begin with. Then
these lines would be free from erudition, just as Shakespeare's best works
are. At least that's what future generations are going to hear from preachers
who know what their audiences want. They'll hear how much a man may
accomplish using only natural, untrained talent. They'll hear how easy it is
to write something as free from erudition as his whose plays were created
solely on the strength of his God-given talent, or so I intend to say.

F. B.'s lines reinforce Jonson's eulogy:

> For seeliest [blindest] Ignorance on these may light,
>   Which, when it sounds at best, but echoes right;
> Or blind Affection, which doth ne're advance
>   The truth, but gropes, and urgeth all by chance;

For ignorant folk may read these lines that sound right but are actually wrong. Both F. B. and Jonson were "apt to their auditors."
Both wrote about promoting the "natural" Shakespeare to a receptive
audience.

*To "let slip," a term used in the sport of coursing, is to release the dogs from their
leash. Shakespeare uses the term figuratively in *Julius Caesar* (III.1.273), *1 Henry
IV* (I.3.272) and *Coriolanus* (I.6.38–39).

SHAKESPEARE'S LEARNING

The extent of Shakespeare's erudition is a subject that divides the experts. Harbage confidently asserted that the plays merely "*looked* learned," especially "to the less literate public" (50). According to Frederick S. Boas, who specialized in the classics, Shakespeare "was not a learned man, and all the fantastic theories based upon the assumption that the plays could only have been written by such a one may be given short shrift" (*Drama*, 71). On the other hand, Paul Stapfer, another classical scholar, thought the opposite: "If we take the word 'learning' in its large and liberal sense, and no longer reduce the question to a miserable pedantic wrangling over his more or less of Greek and Latin, then, of all men that ever lived, Shakespeare is one of the most learned" (105). Was Shakespeare learned, or an untutored natural wit? One measure would be the size and substance of his reading list.

Over the years, scholars have identified many books that influenced Shakespeare. The following is a list of authors that Shakspere could have read at the Stratford grammar school:

Æsop

Aphthonios, Aelius Festus

Aristophanes

Buchanan, George

Caesar, Julius

Camerarius, Ioachimus

Cicero, Marcus Tullius

Culmann, Leonhard

Du Bartas, Guillaume De Salluste

Erasmus, Desiderius

Horace (Quintus Horatius Flaccus)

Juvenal (Decimus Junius Juvenalis)

Lily, William

Livy (Titus Livius)

Lucan (Marcus Annaeus Lucanus)

Mantuan (Battisti Spagnuoli)

Ovid (Publius Ovidius Naso)

Palingenius
Persius Flaccus, Aulus
Plautus, Titus Maccius
Quintilian (Marcus Fabius Quintilianus)
Seneca, Lucius
Terence (Publius Terentius Afer)
Virgil (Publius Virgilius Maro)
Wilson, Thomas

But various scholars have also proposed that Shakespeare read the
following authors, none of whom was included in a provincial grammar school curriculum:

Achilles Tatius
Aelianus, Claudius
Alberti, Leon Battista
Alciatus, Andreas
Ammianus Marcellinus
Appian
Apuleius, Lucius
Aretino, Pietro
Ariosto, Lodovico
Athenaeus
Aurelius Antoninus, Marcus (Caracalla)
Averell, William
Bandello, Matteo
Barnes, Barnaby
Belleforest, François de
Boaistuau, Pierre
Boccaccio, Giovanni
Boiardo, Matteo Maria
Bright, Timothy
Brooke, Arthur
Camden, William
Cardano, Girolamo

Castiglione, Baldassare
Catullus, Gaius Valerius
Caxton, William
Cecchi, Giovammaria
Cervantes, Miguel de
Chapman, George
Chaucer, Geoffrey
Cinthio (Giambattista Giraldi)
Claudianus, Claudius
Constable, Henry
Créton, Jean
Daniel, Samuel
Day, Angell
Day, John
Dolce, Lodovico
Drayton, Michael
Eden, Richard
Edwards, Richard
Eliot, John
Elyot, Sir Thomas
Fabyan, Robert
Florio, John
Foxe, John
Froissart, Jean (tr. by Berner)
Gallus, Gaius Cornelius
Gascoigne, George
Geoffrey of Monmouth
Giovanni Fiorentino
Golding, Arthur
Goslicius, Laurentius Grimaldus
Gower, John
Grafton, Richard
Grammiticus, Saxo
Greene, Robert

Groto, Luigi

Guazzo, Stefano

Hakluyt, Richard

Hall, Edward

Harington, Sir John

Harsnett, Samuel

Heliodorus (tr. by A. Fraunce)

Henryson, Robert

Heraclitus

Hesiod

Holinshed, Raphel

Homer

Hooker, Richard

Hurtado de Mendoza, Diego

Isocrates

James I

Jonson, Ben

Jourdain, Silvester

Kyd, Thomas

LeFevre, Raoul

Leo Africanus

Leslie, Bishop John

Lewkenor, Sir Lewes

Lodge, Thomas

Lucretius Carus, Titus

Luscianus (Lucian)

Lydgate, John

Lyly, John

Marianus

Marlowe, Christopher

Marston, John

Martire, Pietro

Massuccio, Salernitano

Mexía, Pedro

Spenser, Edmund
St. Bernard of Clairvaux
Sterling, William Earl of
Stow, John
Strachey, William
Straporola, Giovanni Francesco
Surrey, Henry Earl of
Susenbrotus
Swinburne, Henry
Tacitus, Cornelius
Tasso, Torquato
Theocritus
Thomas, William
Twine, Lawrence
Vega, Lope de
Vespucci, Amerigo
Warner, William
Watson, Thomas
Whetstone, George
Wyatt, Sir Thomas

Faced with such a prodigious reading list, traditional scholars have to work both sides of the street, on the one side citing Shakespeare's extensive reading and evident erudition, and on the other, rationalizing his supposedly minimal learning without seriously reducing his capacity to write.

For example, many critics sidestep Shakespeare's evident command of languages not taught at the grammar school. H. N. Gibson defended the Shakespeare of biography as a man who knew no more "than any other moderately well-educated man of his period" (180). But the "moderately well-educated man of his period" was fluent in two or three languages, not five or six. Shakespeare must have been able to read in French, Italian, and Spanish, in addition to Latin and Greek, because some of his literary sources had not yet been translated from those languages into English. Schoenbaum acknowledged that François de Belleforest's *Histoires tragiques*, Ser Giovanni Fiorentino's *Il Pecorone*, and Cinthio's *Epitia* and *Hecatommithi* had not yet been translated into English (*Lives*, 103; see also Shaheen, 161–69). Those works were primary sources for *Hamlet, Merchant of Venice, Othello*, and *Measure for Measure*. Among other books for which Shakespeare would have had no English translation were Luigi da Porto's *Romeus and Juliet* (Italian) and Jorge de Montemayor's *Diana* (Spanish) for *The Two Gentlemen of Verona*. While biographers agree that this Italian story or that French essay or the other Spanish novel inspired various Shakespeare plays, they do not explain how Shakespeare became such a linguist.

Here are various scholars, summarized by a bibliographer, trying to come to grips with Shakespeare's sources, his acccss to them, and his linguistic capabilities*:

- Since Shakespeare was not a linguist and Young's translation did not appear until 1598, there is no justification for suggesting that *Midsummer Night's Dream* was influenced by [Montemayor's] *Diana.*

- Although other versions of *Diana* were available to Shakespeare, he probably used Wilson's translation (which was never printed and which is not extant) for the Proteus-Julia plot of *Two Gentlemen of Verona.*

- O. J. Campbell errs in suggesting the lost English play, *Felix and Philiomena*, as the source of *Two Gentlemen of Verona*. Shakespeare's source was *Diana* of Montemayor.

- In four instances in which Shakespeare's important characters deviate from [Arthur] Brooke's poem, *Romeo and Juliet* agrees with the original version of Luigi da Porto of which no known English or French translation was in existence. Although one may either ignore this indebtedness to da Porto or assume a lost intermediary play, Shakespeare had, probably, direct or indirect contact with Luigi da Porto's own version of the tale.

- If Shakespeare used Homer's *Iliad* at all [as a source for *Troilus and Cressida*], he obtained it in some translation other than Chapman's. Perhaps Shakespeare found all this material in an old English play, which is no longer extant.

When the earliest known English translation postdates the relevant Shakespearean play or poem, scholars often minimize or discredit Shakespeare's reliance on the source, or they divert attention to another favorite catchall solution: The lost intermediary source. These

*In *The Foreign Sources of Shakespeare's Works*, Guttman summarized these views of Hector Genouy (132), R. L. Ashhurst (131), T. P. Harrison, Jr. (132), O. H. Moore (121–22), and J.S.P. Tatlock (68).

lost sources are hypothetical adaptations or translations into English of foreign-language books on which the dramatist supposedly relied.

Shakespeare's reliance on *Il Pecorone* in the original Italian for *The Merchant of Venice* illustrates the problem perfectly. *Il Pecorone* was published in Milan in 1554 but had not been translated into English or French in Shakespeare's time:

> The first Novel of the fourth Day contains the first account of the Jew demanding a pound of flesh from his Christian debtor and also mentions the incident of the ring and the name "Belmonte." A similar story was told in the *Gesta Romanorum*, a collection of medieval tales which was translated into English and ran through several editions between 1579 and 1600, but that version does not have the story of the ring nor the name, so that Shakespeare must have followed Giovanni either directly, or through the medium of some play now lost, for some incidents of *The Merchant of Venice*. (Bartlett, *Editions*, 92)

Shakespeare's reliance on books in foreign languages puzzles the experts, so they suppose all sorts of things rather than conclude the obvious. If Shakespeare regularly relied on books not yet translated from Italian, French, and Spanish, then he must have been able to read in Italian, French, and Spanish.

Although few commentators ask how he could have acquired the linguistic skills that fell outside any grammar school curriculum, occasionally one will speculate. One critic supposed that Shakspere hired foreign-language tutors in London during the Lost Years (1585–92) for which no biographical records exist (Gibson, 174). Another explained that Shakspere would have acquired "a good working knowledge of French" while lodging in the Mountjoy household in 1604 (I. Wilson, 292), because the Mountjoys were French Huguenots. Yet Shakspere's physical presence in the Mountjoy household provides no evidence of French lessons. Moreover, his tenancy there postdates several plays, including *Henry V* and *Hamlet*, that relied on French.

Shakespeare's multilingualism is not confined to his ability to read in the various languages. Some scholars have noted that he was so facile with foreign vocabularies that he imported words from abroad or expanded the meaning of an English word with the sense used only in its foreign context. Joseph Hunter put forth the following example from *Othello*:

> But that I love the gentle Desdemona,
> I would not my unhoused free condition
> Put into circumscription and confine
> For the sea's worth. (I.ii.25–28)

Unhoused . . . is no English word to express the idea which it here represents. *Unhoused* conveys to English ears the suggestion of no state or condition which a man would not willingly resign for a less worthy prize than the gentle Desdemona. But the case is different in Italy. There *cassare* denotes both *to go to housekeeping* and *to marry*, so that *unhoused* is there equivalent to *unmarried*. This is the sense which the passage requires. But it is unlikely that it would have been so used except by a writer who was acquainted familiarly with the double Italian sense of the expression. (*Illustrations*, 2:320; Roe, private correspondence with the author)

Yet most biographers sidestep Shakespeare's evident command of Continental languages. Instead, they allow Shakspere his smattering of "small Latin," "less Greek" if any, and just enough French, picked up from the Mountjoys, backstage, or who-knows-where, to let him squeak through some of the most critical material not yet translated into English.

Shakespeare's sophisticated command of foreign languages remains unsupported by the traditional biography. By way of comparison, Eccles was interested in tracing poet Thomas Watson's Continental travels, in part because "Watson's experience of foreign countries is a matter of some interest in accounting for the unusual breadth of his reading in Italian, French, and neo-Latin poetry." Eccles succeeded in finding some fragments of Watson's training at the English College at Douai in France, fragments that provide at least a smidgen of support for Watson's multilingual skills (*Marlowe*, 129, 137–38). How Shakespeare developed as a creative artist remains a complete mystery because, for him, there is no comparable evidence.

Chapter Fourteen

Country Lad or Courtier

> The anti-Stratfordian position is a summary judgment about the curse of provincial origins and barbarian rusticity, one that radically underestimates the classical rigors of Tudor public education and overestimates the scope of aristocratic learning. It is pernicious doctrine.
>
> —Gail Kern Paster, "The Sweet Swan" (38–39)

Most anti-Stratfordians have searched for the true author in the court of Elizabeth, even though literary giants rarely turn up among the aristocracy. That is partly because there are not that many aristocrats to start with and partly because writing at a professional level is supposed to be beneath their dignity. But being of high birth does not automatically disqualify one from being a literary giant, any more than does being of low birth—witness Count Leo Tolstoy, Lord Byron, and Sir Walter Scott.

However, many Shakespeare scholars, such as the editor of the *Shakespeare Quarterly* quoted in the epigraph, have accused anti-Stratfordians of being snobs. According to another scholar, Jonathan Bate, "anti-Stratfordians cannot abide the thought of Shakespeare resembling an untutored Romantic genius of low origins" (*Genius*, 92). Stanley Wells thought that skeptical inquiries into Shakespeare's authorship were "usually the result of snobbery—reluctance to believe that works of genius can be produced by a person of relatively humble birth or by one who did not enjoy a university education—or of the desire for self-publicity, or of both" (3). These anti-Stratfordian publicity-seeking snobs have the effrontery to find outright contradictions between the contents of the plays and what is known of Shakspere's humble beginnings and subsequent experiences. Worse, they hypothesize that the real Shakespeare was an aristocrat.

Wells, Bate, and Paster were avoiding the issue with a misplaced appeal to egalitarian sensibilities. Any snob would need look no further than Robert Burns to find a poetic genius who came from humble surroundings. But historians have evidence to trace Burns's literary progress. Moreover, Burns wrote about what he knew—the Scottish countryside. In contrast, Shakspere supposedly came from the humble environs of Stratford-upon-Avon but wrote about the upper classes, and historians have *no* evidence to trace his literary progress or to support his exposure to an aristocratic lifestyle.

THE SNOB PREJUDICE

According to Richard Helgerson, "Shakespeare had stood, as he still stands today, for Royal Britain, for a particularly anachronistic state formation based at least symbolically on the monarch and an aristocratic governing class." This upper-class perspective sets Shakespeare apart from other dramatists of his day. Again, according to Helgerson, "Shakespeare's history plays are concerned above all with the consolidation and maintenance of royal power. The history plays [that other dramatists wrote] give their attention to the victims of such power. Kings and their aristocratic rivals are what the audiences at Shakespeare's history plays see most. In the work of Munday, Chettle, Heywood, Dekker, and their collaborators, common people and their upperclass champions occupy the central place." Unlike Shakespeare, then, these other playwrights wrote "from a commoner's point of view" (Helgerson, *Forms*, 244, 234, 237). Another critic, David Shelley Berkeley, found that Shakespeare's plays are "thematically concerned with the problem of righting the misfortunes of those of high blood and with reducing the external importance of churls" (97). According to Richard Dutton, Shakespeare's comedies follow the ideals of courtly romance, "far removed from the practicalities of trade or the realistic need to make a living. . . . Indeed, the courtly provenance of Shakespearean comedy as a whole is underlined if we compare it with the characteristic works of slightly later contemporaries, like Dekker, Jonson and Middleton, whose attention is on the low-life of London streets rather than on never-never worlds of Belmont and Illyria" (*Life*, 96–97). According to Northrop Frye, "Shakespeare seems to have had the instincts of a born courtier." He was "interested in chronicle, the personal actions and interactions of the people at the top of the social order. . . . Shakespeare's social vision is a deeply conservative one" (10, 59–60).

According to these commentators, the works of Shakespeare reflect an aristocratic perspective, but Shakspere's documentary evidence reflects the opposite. The man from Stratford left plenty of footprints but not one in an aristocratic environment. Even writers with documented access to upper-class or court life, such as Edmund Spenser or Samuel Daniel, were in no position to describe the aristocratic life as insiders, only as outsiders looking in (May, *Courtier*, 33–34, 39–40). Yet Helgerson identified in Shakespeare a singular upper-class ideology, "as though he wanted to efface, alienate, even demonize all signs of commoner participation in the political nation" (*Forms*, 214).

In *Blood Will Tell*, David Shelley Berkeley discovered the biggest snob of all—William Shakespeare. Berkeley demonstrated that superior blood gives Shakespeare's characters powerful advantages over their inferiors. Hamlet is mortally wounded with the poisoned rapier before turning the weapon on Laertes, but Hamlet, the one with royal blood, still expires last. It takes two snake bites to kill Cleopatra, but only one to kill her hand-maiden. The princess Perdita (*Winter's Tale*) has not had a day's schooling in her life, yet she is an educated lady (13). Similarly, Orlando is "gentle, never schooled, and yet learned" (*As You Like It*, I.i.164–65). Shakespeare consistently emphasizes the virtues of the well-born and the deficiencies of the base-born, magnifying any such distinctions found in his source material (Berkeley, 7). In addition, Shakespeare's consistent caricaturing of the lower classes as butts of jokes and comic relief, and the names he gives his baseborn characters, Bottom, Dull, Mistress Overdone, and so on, all indicate his attitude toward the lower orders. Ben Jonson, in contrast, gives some of the silliest names, like Sir Epicure Mammon and Sir Amorous La-Foole, to the upper classes. As Berkeley concluded, there is "very little satire in Shakespeare of the gentle classes as perceived by the base-born" (58).

One could flip through the catalogue of Shakespeare's baseborn characters and be hard pressed to find fully developed three-dimensional individuals. Even the entertaining rustics in *A Midsummer Night's Dream* are caricatures. Only in *Henry V* can a baseborn soldier improve his social status; otherwise none in the lower classes can make the transition upward. Shakespeare's attitude toward social mobility differs significantly from that of other playwrights such as Marlowe, Dekker, and Webster, who are concerned with "the ability of plebeians to rise rapidly to positions of eminence through merit" (Berkeley, 96, 8).

While we know nothing of Shakspere's personal experiences in the world of the aristocrat, we do know of his pretensions to gentility. But Berkeley pointed out that Shakespeare, the dramatist, had an "aversion to gentling by purchase, by self-creation, and by marriage" (7). By this reckoning, Shakspere must have thoroughly despised himself. He bought his coat of arms, was certainly a self-made success, and attempted to upgrade his coat of arms using his mother's non-existent social connections.

It is difficult to argue that the author of Shakespeare's plays was a commoner with, at the very most, occasional opportunities to observe at a distance the manners, behavior, tastes, and activities of the upper class. Think of the cultured wit-combats of *Love's Labour's Lost* or *Merchant of Venice*. All but three plays (*Merry Wives, Comedy of Errors*, and *Taming of the Shrew*) were written about the upper classes and from their point of view. In fact, the commercial class of which Shakspere of Stratford was a member seems almost unknown to the poet Shakespeare. Only a few characters, such as those in *Merry Wives, Errors*, and *Shrew*—and Shylock—fill that slot.

Mrs. C. C. Stopes spent years looking for one document, any document, to link Shakspere to the earl of Southampton, to whom the two narrative poems were dedicated. She failed in her endeavor. A later biographer, G.P.V. Akrigg, gained access to newly discovered Southampton family archives, but he didn't find anything, either. To date, nothing has been found to support Shakspere's presence in any upper-class household. (The 1595 payment to the Lord Chamberlain's Men for performing at court is not evidence of social interaction between the players and the court.) He does not even show up in the home of Sir Henry Rainsford, a friend of Drayton, and Rainsford lived just two miles south of Stratford.

Shakspere of Stratford stood on one of the lower social rungs, looking up. Shakespeare the dramatist wrote as though he stood on one of the top rungs, looking down. How did the dramatist gain access to and interact with the upper classes *without leaving any tracks?*

THE ELASTIC LOST YEARS

No biographer has been able to bridge the gulf between Shakspere's historical records and the educational training and culture evident in his plays without resorting to unsupported speculation. Shakspere left Stratford no earlier than 1585 and *Venus and Adonis* was published in 1593. Nobody knows what he was doing during these so-called Lost Years, the run-up to his presumed debut as a published writer. So everybody guesses, and theories abound.

Never in recorded literary history has any one man presumably packed so much into such a short time without leaving a single footprint. These Lost Years in Shakspere's life must equip him for a literary debut that otherwise has him springing, like the goddess Athena, fully armed from the head of Zeus. Not only did the polished *Venus and Adonis* emerge in 1593, but by 1594 when he turned thirty, he had also written *The Rape of Lucrece, Comedy of Errors*, all three parts of *Henry VI*, and probably *Love's Labour's Lost, Two Gentlemen of Verona*, and *Romeo and Juliet*. Collectively, these works reveal a thorough classical education, detailed familiarity with parts of Italy and France, and exposure to the cultured life of the upper classes, all acquired after 1585 and before 1593.

Hundreds of scholars have attempted to invest Shakspere with the proper credentials and allow him sufficient time to write without overloading him during these seven years. For example, concerning the years 1592–94, one scholar wrote in the *Shakespeare Quarterly:*

The strongest probability is that Shakespeare was [an actor but] did not tour in the plague years, and thus had time to produce his two long poems, *Venus and Adonis* and *The Rape of Lucrece*. These poems run to 1,194 and 1,855 lines respectively, and so are equal in length to about one and a half plays. I judge them to be about a year's work, and they certainly could not have been written by an actor plodding an average of fifty miles a week along unpaved Elizabethan roads. . . . If we assign Shakespeare *Titus Andronicus* and one other play—perhaps *The Comedy of Errors*, or work on *The Taming of the Shrew*—to write in these two years, 1592–94, we shall have given him plenty to do without acting as well. (George, 320)

This scholar has acknowledged the severe pressure on the Lost Years to allow Shakspere sufficient time to train, apprentice, produce, and flourish as a writer.

Many suppose that Shakspere spent most of the Lost Years in a law office, because the plays and poems are full of legalese. Some biographers are convinced that he traveled to the Continent, because the Italianate plays reveal a firsthand sense of geography. Some have made a case for his interim career as a country schoolmaster. Others have argued that Shakspere spent those undocumented years as an acting apprentice, a soldier, a sailor, a medical student, a printer, a gardener, a bookworm, a spy, or a secretary or tutor in a noble household.

The Lost Years are not infinitely elastic, yet the various conjectural assignments, when laid end to end, stretch decades beyond the available seven years. Each conjecture, however, is supported with convincing evidence of the playwright's familiarity with this vocation or that activity. One could hypothesize that Shakspere spent the Lost Years as a law clerk, but if he did, then he could not have been the Continental traveler or the country schoolmaster. Each hypothetical career leaves him deficient in other critical areas.

Yet by 1593, Shakspere emerged from behind the curtain as a genius in full flower, a supernova on the literary scene, already the quintessential Renaissance man. It is the greatest of mysteries that he could accomplish this feat without leaving a single track to show how he did it.

SHAKESPEARE AND RENAISSANCE ITALY

Shakespeare's familiarity with matters Italian also sets him apart from other dramatists. Jonson, for example, sprinkled *Volpone* with Italian words, bits of local color, Venetian details, and tourist attractions—all probably the result of John Florio's coaching (Levith, 15–16). Jonson's biographers cannot cite evidence to show that he spent any time in Italy, but they can support his relationship with Florio, a translator who published an Italian-English dictionary. Jonson inscribed a copy of *Volpone* (fig. 6) to his "worthy Friend Mr. John Florio: *The aid of his Muses*" (emphasis added).

On the other hand, Shakespeare's plays reveal a specific knowledge of Italy. Mario Praz summed up the options: "There are two possible alternatives: either Shakespeare travelled to the North of Italy, or he got this information from intercourse with some Italian in London.

There is no evidence for the first alternative" (104). There is no evidence for the second alternative, either. But since no records show that Shakspere ever set foot out of England, Praz went on to postulate that Florio coached Shakspere, as Florio had coached Jonson on *Volpone*. Needless to add, no book inscription from Shakspere to Florio survives.

Ernesto Grillo (1876–1946), an Italian professor of language and literature at the University of Glasgow, argued for the first alternative, that Shakespeare's familiarity with Italy came from firsthand travel: "When we consider that in the north of Italy he reveals a more profound knowledge of Milan, Bergamo, Verona, Mantua, Padua and Venice, the very limitation of the poet's notions of geography proves that he derived his information from an actual journey through Italy and not from books" (146).

Where did the dramatist become intimately familiar with the Italian *commedia dell' arte*, an art form that profoundly influenced some of his earliest plays? The last recorded visit by any Italian players in England was in 1577–78 (Chambers, *Stage*, 2:262–63), well before Shakspere could have seen them. Where did he read Italian sculptor Giulio Romano's tombstone epitaph? He paraphrased it in *The Winter's Tale*, but the only book containing the epitaph, a 1550 book by an Italian historian, Giorgio Vasari, was not published in English until the nineteenth century. One specialist noted that "in order to glean effectively from Vasari, the reader would need a polished level of Italian to match the sophistication of the writer's prose" (Talvacchia, 43). Either Shakespeare had "a polished level of Italian" and read Vasari, or he saw the epitaph in Italy, but the traditional biography supports neither conclusion. How did he know how far it was from Montebello to Padua? How did he correctly identify obscure Veronese buildings, traditions, and topographical features in *Romeo and Juliet*? Did Shakespeare pick up all these seemingly unimportant details—not found in his primary literary sources—from returned travelers? Given the vast number of accurate tidbits and facts, it is highly unlikely that he routinely relied on returned travelers, expatriates, travel books, or any such sources at second hand.

Nevertheless, in spite of every indication to the contrary, biographers continue to argue that Shakespeare got his factual information secondhand rather than from personal experience (e.g., Schoenbaum, *Documentary*, 127). Schoenbaum admitted that foreign travel would have equipped Shakespeare to write knowledgeably about Italian culture, topography, and traditions, but could cite no evidence to support the theory. He got around the problem by asserting that "Shakespeare's grasp of Italian topography is not all that secure" (*Compact*, 170), a conclusion with which at least three experts on Renaissance Italy disagree.*

PRIVILEGED PASTIMES

It is an old saw that writers write most convincingly about what they know. They delve into their warehouse of personal experiences, both consciously and subconsciously, and haul out the best words they own to give expression to an idea. According to Ian Lancashire, "most linguists today believe that a person's speaking or writing is routinely exercised semiblindly and that we are unselfconscious of the process that creates it" (177). If so, then Shakespeare's subconscious influenced his choice of expressions, including expressions drawn from aristocratic pursuits. Novelist Robertson Davies countered this line of reasoning, saying that "Shakespeare had a few telling details which he injected into his plays that made them seem realistic, and I have done the same in my novels" (Epstein, 287).

Davies's rationale won't hold up, because he failed to distinguish between book-learned or secondhand information and firsthand experience. There is a difference between researching or boning up on a subject in order to add "a few telling details," and employing terminology in a way that reveals intimate familiarity. Shakespeare effortlessly used the terminology from privileged pastimes to create imaginative figures of speech and dramatic imagery, whereas other writers of the day inserted "telling details" in literal ways, such as using book-learned hunting terms when writing a scene about hunting.

For example, J. W. Fortescue caught Jonson using and misusing hunting terms, lifted straight out of a handbook, in *Sad Shepherd*. Fortescue concluded that "Jonson . . . must have copied the whole of the words out of a book of sport, probably *The Noble Arte of Venerie*. No man who knew anything of harbouring [i.e., identifying the deer to be hunted] would have adduced all the possible signs of woodcraft in reference to a single deer" (2:338). Jonson added a few

---

*Besides Grillo, see Magri's "No Errors in Shakespeare." Her research tallies with lectures given by Richard Paul Roe, whose book on the subject is forthcoming.

"telling details" even when he got some of them wrong. In contrast, Fortescue concluded that the author of *Hamlet* (III.ii.337–38) and *Julius Caesar* (III.i.204–6) was a "man who has seen a large field, stained, as was the custom, with the blood of the hunted stag, not the man of books, Jonson, who gives perfectly correct details about making the first cut into a deer's brisket" (2:342–43).

Caroline F. E. Spurgeon compared Shakespeare's imagery to that of Marlowe, Jonson, Chapman, Massinger, and Dekker, concluding that "with Shakespeare, the greatest number of images within this group [of imagery drawn from 'daily life'] are those drawn from 'sport' and he is the only one of the six with whom this subject comes first . . . thus emphasising his love of country and outdoor life and occupations. He has more images of riding and of bird-snaring and falconry than of any other forms of outdoor sport, and in both these groups *there is evidence of personal experience*" (30–31, emphasis added). Spurgeon noted that instances of Marlowe's sports imagery were "very few, and they show no sign of personal experience." Neither did Jonson's, except for his fencing terms (32).

Shakespeare's use of falconry terms is especially striking in this passage from *Othello*, in which the Moor suspects Desdemona of infidelity:

> If I do prove her haggard,
> Though that her jesses were my dear heart-strings,
> I'd whistle her off, and let her down the wind,
> To prey at fortune. (III.iii.264–67)

From James Edmund Harting's *The Birds of Shakespeare*, we learn that a "haggard" is "a wild-caught and unreclaimed mature hawk." "Jesses" are the leashes fastened to the hawk's legs by the falconer. When "a useless bird was to be dismissed, her owner flew her 'down the wind;' and thenceforth she shifted for herself, and was said 'to prey at fortune' " (57–59). Most playgoers or readers would miss the complexity of this imagery.

Maurice Pope wrote that Shakespeare's unerring and unusually liberal use of falconry terms "could in theory be explained by saying that he did his homework thoroughly. The easier explanation is that it was home territory." After consulting the courtesy books that were available to Shakespeare, Pope categorically ruled out the idea that he cribbed from manuals on falconry (135).

Shakespeare's creative use of falconry terminology differs dramatically from that of other writers. G. Blakemore Evans pointed out that Thomas Heywood's dialogue for *A Woman Killed with Kindness* was "a little shaky on technical hawking terms, which he lifts from Gervase Markham's *The Gentlemans Academie*" (157). Heywood's use of book-learned falconry terminology is comparable, therefore, to Jonson's book-learned use of hunting terminology in *Sad Shepherd*. Most other playwrights used falconry terms when writing about the sport itself or recycled a few familiar textbook phrases (e.g., "stoop to a gaudy lure"). But even Michael Drayton, who wrote a convincing description of a falconry outing in *Polyolbion*, was not so familiar with falconry that he could use the technical jargon to create complex metaphors.

Falconry has never been a cheap pastime, and in Shakespeare's day, "hawking necessarily remained a mainly aristocratic sport" (Vale, 42). Yet it was Shakespeare, alone among the Elizabethan dramatists, who revealed an intimate and unlabored familiarity with the privileged sport of falconry, just as though he'd grown up with it.

He seems to have been trained as an equestrian as well. In *Love's Labour's Lost*, two lords compare notes about their encounter with the ladies:

BOYET: Full merrily
     Hath this brave manage, this career, been run.

BEROWNE: Lo! he is tilting straight. (V.ii.481–83)

"Manage" is "a term from the riding-school" and "career" is "a term in horsemanship. . . . Both terms belonged specially to the tilting-yard" (Shakespeare, *Arden*, 158). Shakespeare used technical terms associated with the tilting yard and the riding schools—both the province of the gentleman of means—to describe the wooing of women. So he must have been intimately familiar with those equestrian environments.

In Henry V's speech to the French ambassador, Shakespeare demonstrated a rather stunning virtuosity with the technical terms of royal tennis, a "popular game among the Elizabethan nobles." But Shakespeare was not writing about a tennis match; he was writing about Henry V's challenge to France:

When we have match'd our rackets to these balls,
We will in France, by God's grace, play a set
Shall strike his father's crown into the hazard.
Tell him he hath made a match with such a wrangler
That all the courts of France will be disturb'd
With chases. (I.ii.261–66)

The lines are dense with tennis terms, used figuratively and in skillful puns; the *Arden* editor required six footnotes to explain them all. The word "crown" puns on the French throne, on the coin, and on the "method of scoring in royal tennis." "Chases" is used as a three-way pun, one meaning being "points in tennis" (25–26). Evidently Shakespeare was completely at home with the finer points of royal tennis.

In these examples, Shakespeare's command of his subjects extended beyond commonplaces in everyday usage. Did he rummage through falconry or equestrian handbooks or take a cram course in royal tennis in order to write these kinds of passages? On the contrary, such details reveal personal experience.

Moreover, it is highly unlikely that Shakespeare dropped these "details" into his plays to "make them seem realistic," as Robertson Davies argued. Far from adding that convincing atmosphere of verisimilitude, these sorts of images would more likely go right past the majority of theatregoers. The vocabulary, puns, and figures of speech would be understood and appreciated by only a fraction of Elizabethan audiences: The educated and privileged élite.

Shakespeare regularly went for the privileged activities instead of the common ones. He preferred music that required written notation over music learned by ear, which Berkeley took as another indicator of his social bias. For Shakespeare, music was a "social discriminant. Gentles were trained to sing ayres, madrigals, and motets—in general, such music as was reduced to notational form—whereas base-borns . . . sang, impromptu and by ear, ballads, folk-songs, and catches" (49). Shakespeare's musical knowledge far exceeded that of his contemporaries, and his passion for dancing, especially society dancing, inspired some of his best puns.

While many writers drew terminology from popular amusements and pastimes, such as fencing, chess, dice, card playing, or the less expensive sorts of hunting, it is Shakespeare's easy familiarity and versatility with the upper-class sports and privileged pastimes that set him

apart from the others. He is unique in the way he *uses* that terminology, in nonliteral senses, such as using hunting terms to describe
Caesar's death (III.i.204–10) or Queen Gertrude's distress (*Hamlet*,
IV.v.109–10). Here is where the traditional scholar's explanation of
Shakespeare's specialized terminology disintegrates. Shakespeare used
technical terms, figuratively, to create imagery. Writers don't exhaus-
tively research a subject for the sole purpose of tossing off a well-
turned metaphor when describing something else; they draw directly
from their personal knowledge and experience.

Specialists in various fields have documented Shakespeare's detailed
knowledge of ancient history, archery, art, astrology, astronomy, the
Bible, botany, the classics, court politics, coursing, dancing, falconry,
fencing, France, heraldry, horsemanship, hunting, Italy, languages,
law, literature, medicine, music, ornithology, politics, seamanship,
royal tennis, and tournaments. About half those subjects were the
exclusive province of the Elizabethan upper classes, but Shakspere left
no footprints in any upper-class household.

Although few biographers venture to guess how Shakspere could
have found either the leisure or the means to pursue such activities,
occasionally a biographer will speculate on his access to stately homes
and lifestyles. Some, such as Bradbrook, postulate his retreat to
Southampton's country estate, supposing that there "he would have
had access both to country pursuits and to the intimate ways of a
noble household. It is one thing to learn the manners of the great
from courtesy books and another to take a close part in the wit-
combats, the flirtations and the sudden enmities of the life of privi-
lege" (*Poet*, 78). There is not a shred of evidence to support
Bradbrook's hypothesis. As Bentley pointed out, "many fine imaginative stories of Southampton's introduction of Shakespeare into
noble and courtly circles . . . have been invented and retailed with
conviction," adding a few pages later, that "in spite of the thousands
of pages that have been written on the Earl of Southampton as the
poet's patron, the only *facts* so far established are Shakespeare's dedication of two long poems to him in 1593 and 1594" (*Handbook*,
150, 155).

Biographers cannot cite any evidence that links Shakspere personally with any upper-class household. But historians have discovered
evidence to link Drayton to Sir Henry Willoughby (fig. 8); Jonson
to Lord D'Aubigny; Daniel to the Pembrokes; Lodge to the Earl of
Derby; Massinger to Sir Francis Foljambe; Spenser to Sir Walter Ra-

leigh; Marlowe to Sir Thomas Walsingham; Nashe to Sir George Carey; Mundy, Lyly, and Watson to the Earl of Oxford; and Peele to the earl of Northumberland. Shakspere is, once again, odd man out.

SHAKESPEARE'S AUDIENCE

Records show that Shakespeare's plays were performed at public theatres such as the Globe, at more privileged venues such as the Blackfriars theatre, and at the most privileged venue, the court. But did Shakespeare write primarily for the man in the street, or for the educated élite? If he wrote primarily for the general public over at the Globe, and as one of their number, what is all that culture and erudition doing in the plays? Some of the experts are baffled.

Shakespeare's thorough command of classical literature illustrates the difficulty. Like Lancashire, Boas assumed that a writer's subconscious influences his choice of expression: Shakespeare's "subliminal" use of classical knowledge "had seeped into his subconscious self, and thence, as he wrote, it welled forth at any moment on to his manuscript." Boas was therefore puzzled when he considered the people for whom Shakespeare supposedly wrote:

What did the audiences in the Globe and the Blackfriars make of it all? This is to me a constant enigma. The young gallants of the Inns of Court who, like Ovid in Jonson's *Poetaster*, were devotees of poetry instead of law, may have appreciated such echoes of their humanist studies. But how about the citizens and 'prentices, the groundlings? What was Hecuba "and all that" to them, or they to Hecuba? (*Drama*, 99–100)

Boas concluded that typical playgoers could not understand most of the classical allusions, because they did not have the educational background. Gibson took the other side, writing that "if Shakespeare, whoever he might be, had insisted on filling his plays with allusions and references which his audiences could not understand, he would soon have ceased to have any audiences" (178). They cannot both be right. Either Shakespeare wrote over the heads of the average playgoers, or the average playgoers were steeped in classical education and Renaissance culture. Who were these playgoers?

Essentially, "anyone with the price of admission" could attend a play (Cook, 8). But an Elizabethan with enough disposable income to pay for theatre admission was not necessarily an educated and cultured Elizabethan. Andrew Gurr, the author of *Playgoing in Shakespeare's London*, assumed that "playgoing must have had a special appeal as a leisure activity to the illiterate, since the playgoer's involvement with the written word need have gone no further than the playbills posted to advertise performances. The high proportion of women at the playhouses testifies to the popularity of playgoing for the illiterate, since few women of any class, even in London, could write their names" (55).

If a substantial percentage of Shakespeare's audience was uneducated and uncultured, how did they grasp the layers of meaning that today still go past many, if not most, playgoers and require scholarly footnotes and hundreds of books to explain? Considering the extensive use that he made of the classics, language, literature, and aristocratic pursuits, Shakespeare could not have had the average playgoer foremost in mind when he wrote the plays. While the groundlings could enjoy *Hamlet* for its characters and action, they would miss the significance of Hecuba or French falconers. Only the educated and privileged élite could appreciate most of the levels on which Shakespeare wrote.

Bate assumed that "Shakespeare's ideal spectator would have shared the dramatist's own grammar-school education" (*Ovid*, 12), but the plays presume a cultural awareness and sophisticated appreciation far beyond any grammar school training. Shakespeare wrote as though he were independent of the tastes and education of the average playgoer. As we saw, Shakespeare's command of the sport of falconry as a means of expression was sufficiently technical to have demanded a working knowledge of the sport from his audience. Then, as today, most playgoers would miss such references unless they consulted annotated editions. It is more likely, therefore, that Shakespeare's plays were written primarily for the educated aristocracy and the court.

J. Dover Wilson inferred as much: Shakespeare "succeeded in securing . . . the admiring patronage of a powerful circle of cultivated noblemen at court. For them he wrote his poems, and chiefly for them too, as I believe, he wrote his comedies, his early tragedies, and histories. And though he wrote to please, he did so to please himself quite as much as his patrons; for he admired them as much as they admired him. Their tastes were his own" (*Essential*, 68). This Shakespeare is a far cry from the legendary commercial man of the theatre who penned plays strictly for financial gain.

Walt Whitman wrote that Shakespeare's plays were "conceiv'd out of the fullest heat and pulse of European feudalism—personifying in unparallel'd ways the mediæval aristocracy, its towering spirit of ruthless and gigantic caste, with its own peculiar air and arrogance" (2: 404). In an age of such "ruthless and gigantic caste," it is difficult to believe that the Shakspere of traditional biography came from the world of the baseborn yet wrote about the world of the aristocrat.

Chapter Fifteen

Autobiographical "Echoes"

> There is no biographical point of entry to his works comparable
> to that which we have with Marlowe, Jonson or Donne.
> —Richard Dutton, *William Shakespeare: A Literary Life* (5)

Writers give themselves away even when they don't intend to. Arthur
Miller remained unaware for some time that he had based Maggie,
the leading character in his play *After the Fall*, on his famous wife,
Marilyn Monroe. After Monroe died, Miller's producer told him that
everyone would see Maggie as "a portrait, purely and simply, of Marilyn," and only then did he realize that he had been "blinding
[him]self to the obvious" (Miller, 527). Miller's experience reinforces
the notion that creative writers cannot help but reveal themselves in
their work.

However, most analyses of Shakespeare's plays find few parallels to
Shakspere's documented life. In their search for personal "echoes,"
biographers scrape up a smattering of references to gloving, schooldays, and life in the countryside, but nothing with any autobiographical substance.

The editors of *A Textual Companion* enumerated a handful of possible "echoes," such as a caricature of Sir Thomas Lucy, from whose
apocryphal deer park Shakspere supposedly poached; the character Sir

James Blunt in *Richard III* ("the Blunts owned land in Stratford, and were related by marriage to the Combes" [Shakespeare, *Arden*, 302 n]); and a parallel between Shakspere's coat of arms and a speech by the Fool in *King Lear* (Wells et al., 77).

Almost any description of sylvan settings or the great outdoors is cited as evidence of Shakspere's affinity with picturesque Warwickshire. Park Honan thought the sheepshearing scenes in *Winter's Tale* "so closely evoke Warwickshire that it might well have been penned at New Place" (369). Honan finds more "autobiographical aspects" in the plays than most biographers. In one of his longer reaches, he found a connection between the composition of Pyramis and Thisbe's famous wall from *Midsummer Night's Dream* and repairs to the wall outside the Stratford grammar school (214–15). For Honan, *Comedy of Errors* is "a many-layered comedy with hints of Stratford's life," and he compared John Shakspere to one of the characters: "like the dramatist's father, [Egeon] has lacked money at a crucial time, and also faced a law as arbitrary as the Tudor usury statutes which affected John Shakespeare" (165).

Another batch of "echoes" refers to schoolmasters and schoolboys. Much is made of speeches from *Taming of the Shrew* and *Love's Labour's Lost* as reminiscent of Shakspere's presumed attendance at the Stratford grammar school. Many quote the lines from *As You Like It* about "the whining school-boy . . . creeping like snail unwillingly to school." Many biographers have found an "echo" of the death of Shakspere's father in the death of Hamlet's father. Some have found Shakspere's grief over his son Hamnet, who died in 1596, reverberating in a passage from *King John*.*

Finally, biographers have looked for parallels to Shakspere's professional training—in the glover's workshop. The antiquary Edgar I. Fripp quoted lines from *Hamlet* ("Is not parchment made of sheepskins?") and *Romeo and Juliet* ("a wit of cheveril, that stretches from an inch narrow to an ell broad"), among others, to demonstrate Shakespeare's familiarity with "technical language, borrowed from his father's business" (1:80). Likewise, for Honan, "a wealth of gloving images in the plays suggests that William knew his father's craft well" (28–29).

---

*The *Arden* editor assigns the composition of *King John* to 1590–91, six years before Hamnet's death.

Biographers take pains to explain the glovers' technical jargon and its relevance to Shakspere's upbringing. At the same time, alarm bells don't go off with respect to the sheer volume and range of Shakespeare's technical or specialized knowledge evident throughout the plays. If biographers expanded their rationale to account for the many subjects with which the playwright was conversant, they would inevitably conclude that Shakespeare spent most of his time in privileged social circles and environments. But, of course, Shakspere's biography does not support that conclusion.

AUTOBIOGRAPHICAL THEMES

The traditional biographers' analyses of "personal" reflections in the Shakespeare plays, such as the sheepskin reference in *Hamlet*, leave one with the impression that the plays must be mostly intellectual or historical abstractions, independent of the author's life. Yet the very intensity and sincerity of the writing argue against that conclusion.

Many books have addressed the broad issues with which the author grapples in play after play. Some themes are universal, but some are more particular to Shakespeare. Consider the themes of wrongful or ambiguous accusations of infidelity (*Winter's Tale, Othello, Much Ado,* and *All's Well*), the obligations of royalty and nobility (*Hamlet* and *Measure for Measure*), and social ostracism (*King Lear*, the aristocratic outcasts in *As You Like It*, and Prospero in *Tempest*). Biographers find no convincing parallels between these thematic concentrations and Shakspere's life.

Shakespeare's sonnets provide us with the most personal information about the poet himself, but that information does not square with Shakspere's documented life history, either. One series encourages some young man of rank to beget heirs to ensure his family line. Most commentators identify that young man as the earl of Southampton. Conventional chronology dates those sonnets between 1592–96, and in 1592 Southampton was resisting pressure to marry a lady of the court. But Elizabethan England was class-conscious, and a social barrier prohibited any man of base birth from addressing an earl on matters of such personal and political importance as marrying and begetting heirs. How did Shakspere, a man of base birth, vault over that barrier? Most biographers do not tell us; a few have proposed that Southampton's mother hired Shakspere to write persuasive

poems in an avuncular tone. However, anti-Stratfordians postulate
that the poet was one of the upper class and that there was no social
barrier.

In a cluster of sonnets supposedly written sometime before 1599,
the poet described himself growing old, for example, "when my glass
shows me myself indeed / Beated and chopp'd with tann'd antiquity"
(Sonnet 62), and "as I am now / With time's injurious hand crush'd
and o'er-worn" (Sonnet 63). In the 1590s, Shakspere was still in his
thirties.

The poet evidently wrote Sonnet 77 as a sort of gift card to ac-
company the presentation of a commonplace book to an unidentified
recipient:

> Look what thy memory cannot contain,
> Commit to these waste blanks, and thou shalt find
> Those children nursed, deliver'd from thy brain,
> To take a new acquaintance of thy mind.
> These offices, so oft as thou wilt look,
> Shall profit thee, and much enrich thy book.

Despite the poet's obvious interest in encouraging someone to keep
a journal, Shakspere's own children grew up functionally illiterate.

Sonnet 134 is full of imagery created out of legal jargon, and Sonnet 116 is so full of nautical terminology that the author of *Shakespeare and the Sea* nicknamed it "A Navigational Sonnet" (Falconer,
154–55). As far as is known, Shakspere never studied law and never
set sail out of England.

Sonnet 125 contrasts sincere respect for authority with the outward
shows of those who curry favor, and the first two lines, "Were 't aught
to me I bore the canopy, / With my extern the outward honouring,"
point to a courtier as their author. Shakespeare cannot mean a canopy
used in a performance or a canopy used in a religious service, as has
been suggested. The sonnet is concerned with authority, power, and
the toadies who compete with genuinely loyal supporters. The canopy
in question is the canopy of state carried by courtiers in processions
over the ultimate symbol of authority, the monarch. It is difficult to
explain why Shakespeare would ponder the symbolic honor of holding the canopy unless he was entitled to carry it himself on some
occasion.

Shakspere's documented life leads away from, not toward, the emotional and factual content of the plays and sonnets. Unlike Shakspere, the poet suffered humiliating reversals of fortune. In Sonnet 25, the author suggests that he fell from favor at court, where "public honour and proud titles" were much in evidence. In Sonnet 90, he is in despair over a more general reversal, "Now while the world is bent my deeds to cross, / Join with the spite of fortune, make me bow." In Sonnet 37, he seeks relief from being "poor" and "despised." Biographers cite no events in Shakspere's documented life to which those lines could refer. According to the traditional story, Shakspere was successful, rich, and well liked.

The sonnets that most contradict Shakspere's life story are those about shame and disgrace to name and reputation. The poet tells us that he was "in disgrace with fortune and men's eyes" mourning his "outcast state" (Sonnet 29). He agonizes that "fortune" "did not better for [his] life provide, / Than public means which public manners breeds. / Thence comes it that [his] name receives a brand" (Sonnet 111). How could "public manners" have so stigmatized a man of common birth? In Sonnet 110, Shakespeare wrote:

> Alas 'tis true, I have gone here and there,
> And made myself a motley to the view,
> Gored mine own thoughts, sold cheap what is most dear,

Samuel Schoenbaum explained that Shakspere wrote these lines because he "chafed at the social inferiority of actors" (*Documentary*, 148). But if Shakspere had been so utterly humiliated by the theatre profession, why did he continue as a member of the acting company for years after the "motley" sonnet was presumably written? He was still with the King's Men in 1604, long after he had made lots of money and had the financial freedom to escape from the profession that he supposedly found so degrading. Furthermore, the brazen and opportunistic Shakspere of record is at odds with the humiliated and socially disgraced poet.

The plays and poems pose many questions that beg for solution, yet Shakspere's life gives the biographer nothing to go on. Many have tried but none have identified the Dark Lady of the sonnets. Most scholars agree that the Fair Youth is the earl of Southampton, but they disagree as to the nature of his relationship with the poet and fail to locate any corroborating evidence. No one knows the identity of the Rival Poet. Was either Sir Christopher Hatton or Sir William

Knollys the prototype for Malvolio? Was Sir Walter Raleigh or John Florio satirized in *Love's Labour's Lost*? Just how autobiographical is *Hamlet*? Does *Hamlet* suggest an insider's perspective at court? Were Polonius's precepts for his son Laertes really based on the precepts written by Lord Burghley for his son (see Schoenbaum, *Lives*, 493)? If so, how would Shakspere, a commoner, have dared to take the liberty of caricaturing Burghley onstage?

Those who have constructed the Shakespearean biography are stuck with such unanswered questions. It is likely that they have been researching the wrong man and that the answers lie instead in the biography of an Elizabethan courtier.

A GLIMPSE OF WARWICKSHIRE

Two plays in the canon make specific reference to Shakspere's Warwickshire environs and neighboring shires. One is *2 Henry IV*:

DAVY: I beseech you, sir, to countenance William Visor of Woncot against Clement Perkes of the hill.

SHALLOW: There are many complaints, Davy, against that Visor; that Visor is an arrant knave, on my knowledge. (V.i.34–37)

Here is a fleeting and uncomplimentary reference to an offstage character named "William Visor" (*viz.* mask) "of Woncot." Whether Woncot refers to Woodmancote, in Gloucestershire, or Wincot, about six miles south of Stratford, the village of Wincot does turn up in the only Shakespeare play with a solid set of Warwickshire allusions. That play is *The Taming of the Shrew*. The *Arden* editor stated that "no other play in the canon refers so specifically and extensively to the county of his birth" (Shakespeare, 63). However, if the allusions are read as reflections of the author's impressions of his native environs, it creates a problem of a surprising sort. The principal Warwickshire character in *Shrew*, Christopher Sly, is a boor and a drunk. If the man from Stratford was describing what he thought of his neighbors, relatives, or worse yet, himself, one can only hope his nearest and dearest never saw the piece.

Christopher is "old Sly's son of Burton-heath, by birth a pedlar, by education a card-maker [one who makes cards for combing wool], by transmutation a bear-herd, and now by present profession a tinker." Sly is thus characterized as a rogue and vagabond, as defined in the Elizabethan statutes that outlawed jugglers, peddlers, tinkers, and bear-herds, as well as common players. Sly's family is from Burton-Heath. Shakspere's aunt, Mary Arden's sister, lived in Barton-on-Heath, sixteen miles south of Stratford. Sly mentions Marian Hacket, "the fat ale-wife of Wincot." Shakspere's mother came from Wilmcote.

The scene opens with Sly passing out drunk near a country manor house. A nobleman, returning from the hunt with his hounds and retinue, trips over him and decides to play a practical joke. He instructs his staff to lug Sly up to the best bedroom, clean him up, and provide him with a boy in costume to pose as his wife. Sly wakes from his stupor to find himself clothed in finery, surrounded by the appointments of an aristocratic household, and catered to with food and wine. Attendants convince him that he is lord of the manor and that his own troupe of players will entertain him. The masquerade then gives way to the play proper of *Taming of the Shrew*.

Three places named in the scene fall within a twenty-mile radius of Stratford-upon-Avon. Based on this intimate sense of geography, one is tempted to conclude, as did the *Arden* editor, that the dramatist was thinking of his home turf. But Sly is a comical Warwickshire denizen who is duped into thinking himself a nobleman. With one hand, the author points to Warwickshire and to a tinker who could be identified with William Shakspere of Stratford, and with the other he suggests the substitution of the tinker for a nobleman. If, however, the Warwickshire allusions are brushed off as fiction or nonspecific satire, out the door go the only scenes with local color specific to Shakspere's family and hometown environs. All that is left after that are references to leather, schooldays, bucolic snapshots, and general family events as the "echoes" of Shakspere's life in the plays.

Chapter Sixteen

Chronological Disorder

> The fact is that the chronology of Shakespeare's earliest plays is
> so uncertain that it has no right to harden into an orthodoxy.
> —F. P. Wilson, *Marlowe and the Early Shakespeare* (113)

Over the years, scholars have attempted to sort Shakespeare's plays
into chronological order and to determine when they were written.
Although they are far from unanimous on the details, there is today
a rough consensus as to what got written when. *The Arden Shakespeare* chronology assigns to the period between 1589 and 1613 the
writing of all 37 known plays, 154 sonnets, 2 narrative poems, and
several miscellaneous poems.

   The play chronology is particularly fragile in the early sequence.
Biographers generally assign the *Henry VI* trilogy, *Titus Andronicus*,
Comedy of Errors, and *King John* (a play causing particular dissension)
to 1589–91, but attempts to date other plays before 1591 create
serious problems. The rock solid date of 1592 for the "Upstart
Crow" reference in *Groatsworth* and the equally immovable date of
1593 for *Venus and Adonis* are used respectively as evidence of Shakespeare's emerging success in London theatre and his professional debut as a published writer. His debut needs to come late enough in
the timetable to allow the Lost Years to equip him for it. Pushing

more plays back to 1590 or earlier starts to unravel the entire structure.

A date of 1589 for *Taming of the Shrew* is therefore potentially troublesome for the *Arden* editor, Brian Morris:

> If we add to this that J. C. Maxwell (Arden edn, 1953) prefers a date of 1589–90 for *Titus Andronicus*, and that Honigmann (Arden edn, 1954) argues strongly for a date of "winter/spring of 1590/91" for *King John*, we find that the years before 1592 are becoming uncomfortably full. Either Shakespeare wrote with great speed and industry or his career as a playwright began earlier than Chambers believed. Chambers's date of 1590–1 for the start of Shakespeare's career is based on the earliest known reference to Shakespeare as a dramatist in Greene's *Groats-worth of Wit* (1592) where the reference to his "Tyger's hart wrapt in a Players hyde" parodies a line from *3 Henry VI.* . . . But Shakespeare may quite possibly have left Stratford for London as early as 1585, and we simply do not know where he was or what he was doing in the period 1585–90. He might, as Aubrey [the gossip] reports, have been "a Schoolmaster in the Country"; he might have been writing *The Taming of the Shrew*. (59)

This passage illustrates the pressure on orthodox Shakespeareans to squash the playwriting into an uncooperative container.

CHRONOLOGY AT RISK

It may already be evident that the chronological ordering of Shakespeare's plays is an exercise in circular reasoning, because dating the plays is essentially the result of two processes: (*a*) identifying in the archival records the dates for publication of, registrations of, performances of, and allusions to certain plays; and (*b*) shoehorning those dates, and dates for the balance of all the other plays, into what has been constructed of Shakspere's known or possible years in London, or as Chambers put it, "into the time allowed by the span of Shakespeare's dramatic career" (*Facts*, 1:253). Stylistic and metrical tests have been developed as well, but they are generally used to corroborate rather than identify dates.

The order in which the plays were written is only part of the problem. Equally critical is the date when Shakespeare began to write. One commentator referred to the moment "when the period of regular authorship arrived" (Thompson, 1:299), as though it suddenly pulled into the Shakespeare Station like a train, but nobody knows when Shakespeare's first lines of poetry or drama issued forth. The Stratford grammar school cannot be considered much of a cultural kick-start, so Shakspere's serious intellectual development begins around 1585–86, when we lose track of him in Stratford, and ends in 1593, when *Venus and Adonis* is published. But there is a problem.

When undisputed biographical facts are integrated into the scenario, Shakspere's available preparation time starts to shrink. The year before he supposedly bursts forth from the laboratory of enlightenment with his published poetry, he has already established himself in several other fields. By 1592, he was already an actor, paymaster of writers, theatrical *factotum*, and moneylender. Those emerging careers encroach on the time in which Shakspere was supposedly cramming information into his head, gaining access to aristocratic circles, and reading like crazy.

The Lost Years have been subjected to further pressure. Various prominent scholars have themselves proposed earlier dates for a number of Shakespeare's works, and if these proposals were accepted, the predebut chronology could look like this:

1581–82	*Romeo and Juliet*
1582–89	some of the sonnets
1584–89	*The Comedy of Errors*
1586	*The Phoenix and the Turtle*
1587	*The Two Gentlemen of Verona*
1588	*Love's Labour's Lost*
1588–89	*Hamlet*
1589	*The Taming of the Shrew*
1589–90	*Titus Andronicus*
1590	*1 Henry VI*
——	*2 Henry VI*
1590–91	*King John*
1591	*3 Henry VI*
——	*Richard III*

This sequence* is obviously unworkable for Shakspere. Even if one ignores, as most orthodox scholars do, A. S. Cairncross's tentative theory that *King Lear* and *Twelfth Night* were also written by 1593 (182–83), the Lost Years would be utterly inadequate to equip Shakspere for his debuts in 1592–93, because by that time, he would be already a third of the way through his writing career. (However, this revisionist approach to chronology has one advantage: It delivers a Shakspere who is a precocious self-starter, as opposed to the late bloomer of tradition.)

Most surprising are proposals that certain sonnets, poems, *Romeo and Juliet*, or even the sophisticated *Love's Labour's Lost* could have been drafted before Shakspere ever left Stratford. Usually these proposals are based on topical allusions perceived in the texts or verbal echoes found in literature of the day. These proposals put an impossibly heavy demand on the Stratford grammar school, and an even heavier demand on the boy whom legend describes as dropping out of grammar school at about age thirteen in order to apprentice in his father's workshop. Yet despite such seemingly insurmountable difficulties, some scholars have found sufficient reason to risk postulating earlier dates. Such proposals, however, do not fare well with mainstream editors.

There is a further problem of selectivity. Not every historical reference to a possible Shakespeare play is admitted into the lineup, and *Hamlet* is a case in point. *Hamlet* is generally assigned to 1598–1601, a suitable time in the alleged creative period for such a mature work. But a decade earlier, in 1589, Thomas Nashe made a reference to "whole Hamlets . . . of tragical speeches" (G. G. Smith, 1:312). Henslowe's papers show that in 1594 a play called *Hamlet* was in production, and in 1596, Thomas Lodge referred to a performance of *Hamlet* at the Theatre (4:56). Scholars cannot reconcile such a mature play to Shakspere's early years in London, so most of the time,

---

*Scholars postulating radically early dates are J. Hunter for *Romeo and Juliet* (*Illustrations*, 2:120–21; see also Shakespeare, *Arden, Romeo*, 27); Gurr ("First Poem," 221–26) and Hotson (*Sonnets*, 33) for certain sonnets; Peter Alexander for *Comedy of Errors* (Shakespeare, *Arden, Errors*, xvii n. 2; see also Honigmann, "*Lost*," 128); R. G. White for *Love's Labour's Lost* (Furness, 332, 341); Honigmann for *Phoenix and the Turtle, Two Gentlemen* ("*Lost*," 128), and *King John* (Shakespeare, *Arden*, lviii); and Cairncross for *Hamlet* (73). The chronology of plays dated from 1589 onward is generally accepted (see *Arden* editions for *Shrew*, 65; *Titus*, xxiv; *1 Henry VI*, xxxviii; *2 Henry VI*, xlvi; *3 Henry VI*, xlv; and *Richard III*, 61).

we are told that those are references to somebody else's *Hamlet*, not Shakespeare's, and that this other *Hamlet*, the so-called *Ur-Hamlet* ("ur" meaning original or earliest), is now lost. Then we are subjected to theoretical exercises about *Ur-Hamlet*, possibly written by the obscure Thomas Kyd from whom Shakespeare supposedly borrowed. A few orthodox scholars believe that "Shakespeare's *Hamlet* and no other is the play mentioned by Nashe in 1589 and Henslowe in 1594" (Cairncross, 73), but they are in an unpopular and largely ignored minority. Other proposed lost source plays are dubbed *Ur-Tempest*, *Ur-Shrew*, *Ur-Titus*, *Ur-Henry VIII*, and *Ur-Pericles*. No other corpus by an Elizabethan dramatist is so derivative of *Ur* titles.

Haphazard titles add to the uncertainty. In Shakespeare's day, dramatists and producers played fast and loose with titles, and historians have wrestled with similar-sounding titles to determine if they refer to the same play or to separate entities. For example, the 1594 Henslowe accounts refer to *The Venetian Comedy*, *The Love of an English Lady*, *The Love of a Grecian Lady*, *The Grecian Lady*, and *The Grecian Comedy*. These entries probably refer to only two separate plays (Knutson, *Repertory*, 21–22; see also "Repertory," 466). Shakespeare's *Henry VIII* was known by an alternate title, *All Is True*. Henslowe recorded seven Shakespearean-sounding titles during the early 1590s, that is, *Hamlet*, *Harry V*, *King Lear*, *Troilus*, *Harry VI*, *Titus*, and *Taming of a Shrew*. Neil Carson, the author of *A Companion to Henslowe's Diary*, approached these entries with a degree of caution:

> Only the last three [*Henry VI*, *Titus*, and *a Shrew*] conform to the orthodox notions concerning Shakespearian chronology. Consequently, it is probable (although not, by the nature of the evidence, absolutely certain) that *Hamlet* and *Troilus* are lost plays which Shakespeare may have known, and that *Henry V* and *King Lear* refer to the old Queen's Men's plays preserved as *The Famous Victories of Henry V*, and *King Leir*. Until the complicated relationship between *a Shrew* and *the Shrew* is fully understood, it is impossible to know if Henslowe's title refers to a source play or to Shakespeare's version of the story. Similar uncertainties surround both *Henry VI* and *Titus Andronicus*. (68)

King Lear is usually dated 1604–6. But Cairncross proposed that the 1594 *King Leir* listed in the Henslowe diary was derivative of Shakespcare's earlier *King Lear,* rather than the other way around. His theory was not well received.

Other play titles turn up in all sorts of records that *could* be Shakespeare plays under alternative titles, if only the dates were not so early. *The History of Agamemnon and Ulysses,* presented at court in 1584, could be *Troilus and Cressida. Felix and Philiomena,* presented in 1585, could be *Two Gentlemen of Verona.* But these records are too early to fit into Shakspere's timeline, so the most that biographers can allow is that they might be lost plays that Shakespeare used as sources. Chambers's commentary on *Two Gentlemen of Verona* serves as a good example of the syndrome:

The only clear source is the story of Felix and Felismena in Jorge de Montemayor's *Diana Enamorada.* If Shakespeare could not read Spanish, he may have used the translation of Bartholomew Yonge, printed in 1598 but finished sixteen years earlier, or the French translation of Nicolas Collin (1578, 1587), or the play of "Felix & Philiomena" given at court by the Queen's men in 1585. (*Facts,* 1:331)

You will notice that Chambers also had difficulty dealing with Shakespeare's reliance on a source not yet translated from Spanish, but assumed that Shakespeare was somehow capable of reading French. He also relegated *Felix and Philiomena* to the safe status of a possible source play.

Scholars who try to push back the invisible 1589 barrier encounter the most resistance. For example, the *Arden* editor of *Romeo and Juliet* stated that "the earliest date that has been *seriously* proposed for first performance is 1591" (Shakespeare, 26, emphasis added), brushing aside as frivolous any proposals to date the play any earlier. It is not hard to figure out why such proposals are generally given short shrift or ignored altogether. Honigmann explained that a "date as early as 1591 for *Romeo* would bring the early Shakespeare chronology toppling down, so it must be resisted at all costs" (*Impact,* 67). Joseph Hunter's radically early date of 1581 for *Romeo and Juliet* would mean that Shakspere wrote an Italianate play at age seventeen before he had ever set foot out of Stratford. Shakspere's supposed scholarly accomplishments by 1581 are undocumented, not to say doubtful.

Such tampering with conventional chronology is therefore risky for the orthodox scholar, and any play chronology that starts much before 1589 is potentially explosive. If Shakspere of Stratford was incapable of writing sophisticated plays in the early or mid-1580s, but evidence supported the earlier date anyway, scholars would be forced to consider someone else as the playwright.

CHRONOLOGICAL COMPATIBILITY

The method used to date *The Tempest* raises serious questions about the validity of the established chronology. *The Tempest* is considered a late play, usually assigned to 1610–11. That date hinges upon Shakespeare's presumed reliance on an actual shipwreck in the Bermudas, reported by William Strachey in 1610. Strachey's report, sometimes referred to as one of the Bermuda pamphlets, remained unpublished until 1625, so Shakspere would have had to read it in manuscript in London. If it can be proved that Strachey's report was indeed a source for *The Tempest*, then Shakespeare could not have written the play before 1610. (Incidentally, shipwrecks occur in *Merchant of Venice*, *Twelfth Night*, and other plays, but critics have not found it necessary to identify real shipwrecks as Shakespeare's sources for them.)

Edmond Malone (1741–1812) was the first biographer to construct and publish a chronology, and he identified Strachey's Bermuda shipwreck report as a source for *The Tempest*. However, Joseph Hunter (1783–1861) argued that the play was written in 1596, a comparatively early date in the traditional chronology. To support his hypothesis, he identified Lodovico Ariosto's *Orlando Furioso* as Shakespeare's primary source, pointing out that Ariosto was not only popular, but had, "of all the Italian poets . . . the greatest influence on [English] literature" (*Disquisition*, 35). His influence on Shakespeare has been detected in *Much Ado about Nothing* and *Taming of the Shrew*.

Ariosto's epic includes a storm at sea and a Mediterranean island, Lampedusa, that is inhabited by an old hermit who lives in a cell. After further investigation, Hunter concluded that Lampedusa, a real island reputed to be enchanted, was the prototype for the setting of *The Tempest*. Finally, Hunter found in Shakespeare's play some topical allusions to Sir Walter Raleigh's 1596 report of an expedition to Guiana, and he tied the date of *The Tempest* to that topical report.

Hunter's research is all but ignored by today's scholars. The *Arden* editor asserted that "none of Hunter's arguments amounts to much"

(Shakespeare, xv n). Geoffrey Bullough, whose *Narrative and Dramatic Sources of Shakespeare* is considered authoritative, did not mention Hunter's analysis or Ariosto's epic, although he did make a fleeting reference to Raleigh's report, old hat as it would have been by 1610. Instead, Bullough further developed Malone's rationale for dating *The Tempest* in 1610–11.

Yet Malone, Hunter, and Bullough shared a common method for dating *The Tempest*. All three tied the date of the play to allusions drawn from a sensational topical report. Malone and Bullough cited Strachey's report and Hunter cited Raleigh's.

Bullough accepted Malone's later date of 1610–11. Why? Because *The Tempest* "was prompted to some extent by the excitement caused by the disappearance at sea in 1609 of Sir Thomas Gates . . . and the subsequent publication of pamphlets describing his shipwreck in the Bermudas" (8:237–38). Yet Hunter claimed that news of Raleigh's 1595 expedition, published in a pamphlet, "could not but excite great attention at the time" (*Illustrations*, 1:140). In fact, Raleigh's pamphlet went through three printings in 1596.

According to Bullough, Shakespeare "certainly" read the Strachey report and "used its phrasing to good effect" (8:239). Bullough stated that "to Strachey the dramatist owed specific details" about "the roaring and darkness . . . ; the fear, amazement, prayers, and utter weariness of the passengers and crew; their common toil; the St. Elmo's fire on mast and rigging . . . ; the safe harbour . . . ; the recurrent storms . . . ; the birds caught on the rocks . . . ; a drink made of berries . . . ; a gentleman carrying wood . . . ; [and] a plot against the governor's life" (8:240). Yet Hunter quoted passages from Ariosto that provided most of the same details. Compare both possible sources in the following examples, cross-referenced to the relevant lines in *The Tempest*:

Possible source: Strachey's report (Bullough, 8:275–78, emphasis added)

a dreadful storm . . . which swelling, and *roaring* as it were by fits . . . at length did beat all light from heaven; which like an *hell of darkness turned black* upon us . . . the *heavens look'd so black* upon us

Possible source: Ariosto's *Orlando Furioso* (41.11 & 12, emphasis added)

With weather so tempestuous and *so dark,*
And *black thick clouds . . .*
. . . .
Nor less, nor much less fearful is the *sound*
The cruel tempest in the tackle makes

Lines in *The Tempest* (I.ii.2–3, emphasis added)

MIRANDA: Put the wild waters in *this roar,* allay them.
   The *sky, it seems, would pour down stinking pitch*

* * *

Possible source: Strachey's report (Bullough, 8:276, 278, emphasis added)

Prayers might well be in the heart and lips . . .
. . . who gave her now up, rent in pieces and *absolutely lost.*

Possible source: Ariosto's *Orlando Furioso* (41.14, Moral, emphasis added)

Then thought they *all hope past,* and down they kneel,
And unto God to take their souls *they pray*
. . . .
. . . Rogero in his extremity of danger . . . hath recourse to
   God *by prayer*

Lines *in The Tempest* (I.i.51–53, emphasis added)

MARINERS: *All lost! to prayers, to prayers! all lost!*
BOATSWAIN: What, must our mouths be cold?
GONZALO: The King and Prince at *prayers!* let's assist them

* * *

Possible source: Strachey's report (Bullough, 8:283, emphasis added)

the *Berries,* whereof our men seething, straining, and letting stand some three or four days, made a kind of pleasant drink: these Berries are of the same bigness and color of Corynthes, full of little stones

Possible source: Ariosto's *Orlando Furioso* (41.57, emphasis added)

> But eating *berries*, drinking water clear

Lines in *The Tempest* (I.ii.335–36, emphasis added)

CALIBAN: . . . wouldst give me
  Water with *berries* in't

Ariosto's epic has some details not found in Strachey, such as the ship master's whistle, and Strachey has some not found in Ariosto, such as mariners catching birds on the rocks, but *The Tempest* lines cross-referenced are no more specific than any of the previously given examples. Yet Hunter's case for Ariosto and Raleigh, and with it the case for 1596, has been brushed aside.

Today, biographers routinely rely on Malone's and Bullough's arguments for dating *The Tempest* in 1610–11. The *Arden* editor (Shakespeare, xxviii) is one of many who cite parallels, for example, between the descriptions of St. Elmo's fire in the Bermuda pamphlets and Ariel's report of the "electric display during the storm (I.ii.196)." But Kenneth Muir noted that such details were, in fact, generic to most shipwrecks:

> The extent of the verbal echoes . . . has, I think, been exaggerated. There is hardly a shipwreck in history or fiction which does not mention splitting, in which the ship is not lightened of its cargo, in which the passengers do not give themselves up for lost. . . . Both Strachey and Erasmus mention a ball of fire at the masthead; but as both mention that it used to be called Castor and Pollux, it is likely that Strachey consulted Erasmus to eke out his memories. (*Plays*, 280)

So far, it would appear that parallels between *The Tempest* and either Strachey's report or Ariosto's epic are inconclusive. While there are many similarities, there is no evidence of direct dependence on either.

There is, however, another factor to be considered: The *Ur-Tempest*. No one has ever seen this hypothetical *Ur-Tempest*, but some scholars suppose it existed, because it could explain similarities between Shakespeare's play and an obscure German play, *The Fair Sidea* by Jacob Ayrer, who died in 1605. *The Fair Sidea* "contains a dethroned magician, a prince who is made to carry logs, whom Sidea pities and marries, and a spirit-servant. As Ayrer adapted foreign plays this one may be based on one brought to Germany by an English touring company" (Muir, *Plays*, 279). The rudiments of the plot sound similar to those in *The Tempest*, but 1605 is too early for Shakespeare's *The Tempest* to have toured Germany. Of course, if it had toured Germany before 1605, then obviously it had to have been written by then, and the case for anchoring the date of *The Tempest* in Strachey's report would be thrown overboard. However, most scholars either dismiss any parallels between Ayrer's play and *The Tempest*, or they assume that both Ayrer and Shakespeare relied on a common source. Chambers, for example, wrote that "use of a common source is a more plausible explanation than borrowing on either hand" (*Facts*, 1:493). That common source, a hypothetical lost play, is dubbed the *Ur-Tempest*, and with that explanation, the need to consider an earlier date for *The Tempest* is presumably eliminated.

What are the primary factors in these sorts of chronology decisions? Strachey's "specific details" were no more "specific" to lines in *The Tempest* than those in Ariosto, an author whom Shakespeare is known to have read. Raleigh's report was, like Strachey's, topical and sensational. The case that Hunter advanced had at least as much substance as did Malone's and Bullough's. Yet Hunter's research has been dismissed because his arguments did not "amount to much."

The deciding factor in dating *The Tempest* in 1610–11 appears to be compatibility with Shakspere's active years in London. Just as a date of 1591 "for *Romeo* would bring the early Shakespeare chronology toppling down" (Honigmann, *Impact*, 67), so a date of 1596 for *The Tempest* would topple the later chronology. Orthodox scholars agree that *The Tempest* was a late play, but if it was written in 1596 instead of 1610–11, then the accepted Shakespearean chronology falls apart. Either *The Tempest* was not a late play after all, meaning that various stylistic evaluations have been seriously flawed, or the entire Shakespearean chronology has to be adjusted backward by at least a dozen years. That adjustment would force an intolerably early date, perhaps 1580, onto Shakespeare's first play. In 1580, Shakspere was sixteen years old. Since the fixed dates of Shakspere's life rule out such an early start to the playwriting, no biographer can entertain the possibility that the chronology is seriously out of alignment.

A BORROWER OR A LENDER

On one hand, Shakespeare strikes most people as the inventor, the originator, the trendsetter. On the other hand, this creative genius, this innovator of expression, this man of letters who reshaped the English language, has been reduced by academia to a literary rag-picker. Biographers deliver a Shakespeare who was barely capable of an original idea, who constantly scavenged from others and followed fashions invented by playwrights otherwise considered second-rate. The little known Thomas Kyd, for example, is often credited with inventing the revenge tragedy on which *Hamlet* was patterned.

The dating of the Shakespeare plays is integral to the question of who was the borrower and who was the lender, and *Winter's Tale* presents an interesting case in point. Scholars identify Robert Greene's 1588 romance novel *Pandosto* as the inspiration of *Winter's Tale*, traditionally dated 1610–11. The author of *Shakespeare's Sources* wrote that "there are more verbal echoes from *Pandosto* than from any other novel used by Shakespeare as a source" (Muir, 247). The *Arden* editor went even further:

To anyone reading romance [*Pandosto*] and play [*Winter's Tale*] consecutively, or even comparing [specific] passages, the picture is inescapable of a Shakespeare who, having closely studied the story and made his plot, had *Pandosto* at his elbow as he wrote, and *as he wrote from time to time turned to the book to refresh his memory, using it sometimes almost verbatim,* sometimes with little change, and sometimes with much, and sometimes departing from it altogether, but finding there the constant source for most of his material. (Shakespeare, xxxi, emphasis added)

The above editor is describing Shakespeare as a plagiarist. Yet Greene was a chronic literary pickpocket. *Arden* editor Cairncross dubbed Greene the "arch-plagiarist" (Shakespeare, *2 Henry VI*, xliii), and Robert W. Dent showed that "Greene, by the standards of any age, was a plagiarist, and a plagiarist by the carload in his first novels" (151). Nevertheless, Shakespeare has been cast in the role of borrower, in this case borrowing from a lesser writer notorious for plagiarism. (Although he supposedly wrote *Winter's Tale* in 1610, Shakespeare apparently plagiarized from an early edition of *Pandosto*, passing up the more recent 1607 edition, a choice that raises the

question from yet another standpoint.) Did Shakespeare really plagiarize the arch-plagiarist, Greene?

It is often difficult for literary critics to distinguish the borrower
from the lender. In his articles on *Love's Labour's Lost*, H. B. Charlton
proposed that Shakespeare "seems deliberately to echo verbal and
stylistic peculiarities of Lodge's *Rosalynde* (1590), Sidney's *Arcadia*
(printed 1590), and Puttenham's *Arte of English Poesie* (1589). Of
course, if these echoes are accepted, an argument based on them cuts
both ways, when it is not demonstrably certain which is the original,
which the echo" (394). If such arguments cut both ways, then there
would seem to be some scope for challenging the extent of Shakespeare's indebtedness to his literary inferiors. A 1614 poem praised
Shakespeare's plays whence "needy new-composers borrow more"
(Ingleby, *Centurie*, 106), suggesting that other writers borrowed
from Shakespeare, rather than the other way around.

Yet many critics have demoted Shakespeare from master craftsman
to master cobbler and scavenger. This Shakespeare "habitually followed his sources as closely as he could, taking from them everything
possible—plot structure, characterization, even whole passages that
he merely versified" (Whitaker, 4). Honan described Shakespeare as
"an accomplished parasite" who "lifts part of the story" from here
and "numerous details" from there (117). Others imagine Shakespeare constantly rummaging through books, looking for good plots
or "telling details." In his discussion concerning the sources for
Othello, Muir supposed that "Shakespeare was presumably scanning
Cinthio's book [*Hecatommithi*] in his search for plots in the early
years of the seventeenth century" (*Plays*, 182). (Note that Cinthio's
Hecatommithi had not yet been translated from Italian into English.)
Bullough supposed that "the playwright in search of a plot found in
the Virginian [i.e., Bermuda] pamphlets promising features, including
a tempest" (8:242). Levin assumed that Shakespeare's "dialogue of
The Taming of the Shrew, in particular, is sprinkled here and there
with Italian words and phrases, polite clichés which might well have
been acquired from John Florio's conversational handbook" ("Italians," 21).

According to critics, when Shakespeare needed a plot, a classical
allusion, an Italian reference, or some "telling detail," he went to
somebody's bookshelf to look one up, consulted with a fellow actor,
plagiarized from a hack writer, or headed for the pub to find a recently returned traveler. Biographers have conjured up a Shakespeare

who put the literary pieces together like a patchwork quilt, cutting and pasting, and filling in any blanks as one might solve a crossword puzzle.

The anti-Stratfordian is free to conjure up a different Shakespeare, a poet who read widely and drew from his knowledge so subtly and pervasively that scholars are still hard pressed to track down all the allusions and sources in his works. This Shakespeare was not a hack borrower but a learned writer distilling and synthesizing his knowledge and experience into immortal literature from which other writers borrowed.

The principal cause of the dichotomy between these two conceptions of the playwright is Shakspere's dates. His year of birth, 1564, and his presence in Stratford through 1585 preclude any serious literary achievement much before 1589–90. If only Shakespeare had started writing at least a decade earlier, biographers would not have to cast him into the role of borrower and plagiarist. But if Shakespeare was usually the innovator, biographers would be forced to abandon any idea that Shakspere was Shakespeare, for the innovator must precede the borrowers, and the borrowers would have begun borrowing before Shakspere had departed Stratford.

Chapter Seventeen

A Playwright by Any Other Name

> The question *How did he or she do it?* takes, in the case of William Shakespeare, the more drastic form, *Did he do it?* . . .
>
> . . . There is an embarrassing disproportion between the meager verifiable biographical events and the tremendous literary events associated with Shakespeare's name.
>
> —John Updike, "One Cheer for Literary Biography" (4)

The biography of William Shakspere is deficient. It cites not one personal *literary* record to prove that he wrote for a living. Moreover, it cites not one personal record to prove that he was *capable* of writing the works of William Shakespeare. In the *genre* of Elizabethan and Jacobean literary biography, that deficiency is unique. While Shakspere left over seventy biographical records, not one of them tells us that his occupation was writing. In contrast, George Peele's meager pile of twenty-some personal biographical records includes at least nine that are literary. John Webster, one of the least documented writers of the day, left behind fewer than a dozen personal biographical records, but seven of them are literary.

Scholars do not identify this most glaring of deficiencies in Shakspere's biography—the absence of contemporaneous personal literary paper trails. Those who express dismay at the paucity of evidence nevertheless imply that there is *some* legitimate literary peg on which to hang Shakspere's biographical skeleton. There is no such literary peg. One can make a case for Shakspere as a shareholder, actor, moneylender, broker, entrepreneur, real estate investor, or commodity trader, but one cannot make a case, based on the biographical evidence, for Shakspere as a writer.

FAMOUS YET UNKNOWN, EDUCATED YET UNSCHOOLED, GENTLE YET BELLIGERENT, HERE YET THERE

Although the documented facts about Shakspere are nonliterary, they present a coherent and consistent character. Those same facts lose their coherence when combined with other facts that emerge from the literary works themselves. When biographers try to fit the two sets of facts together, they find them incompatible. Their solution has been to put the conflicting information into the same book, but into different chapters.

Few biographers have attempted a life story of Shakspere that unfolds in strict chronological order. Most segregate theatrical activities and Stratford business dealings into separate chapters, regardless of the chronological sequence. Schoenbaum admitted that the greatest Shakespearean biographers were unable to construct a coherent narrative for the life of the dramatist:

It is after all a melancholy truth that the three greatest of all contributions to the biographical tradition—Malone's posthumous biography, Halliwell-Phillipps's *Outlines*, Chambers's study of facts and problems—abandon continuous narrative. Perhaps we should despair of ever bridging the vertiginous expanse between the sublimity of the subject and the mundane inconsequence of the documentary record. (*Lives*, 568)

Schoenbaum's own biographies failed to bridge that "vertiginous expanse."

Louis Untermeyer understated the case when he wrote that the Shakespeare of biography "seems to have lived a life of complex paradox. Never in the history of literature has there been so strange a union of genius and businessman, of the superlatively natural creator, the accommodating workman, and the small-town citizen" (105–6). Honigmann put his finger on another inherent contradiction: "For, having stumbled through the mists of sentimentality and tradition, we discover that the sign-posts always point two ways at once. Some thought him a hoarding miser, others 'open, and free' " (*Impact*, 23).

Indeed, scholars have crammed the world's greatest dramatic genius inside a straitjacket named William Shakspere, constraining him with the known facts of an unintellectual life. The constraints have forced biographers to create an abnormal noncharacter with no discernible personality. What is known of Shakspere's character is canceled out by the attempt to splice his life onto Shakespeare's literary output. The manipulation of data to obscure or rationalize the more flagrant contradictions reduces the Shakespeare of biography to an amorphous nonentity.

In fact, the playwright of biography makes no sense as a human being. Shakspere deserted his family whenever he was in London, yet biographers picture him "raising a family" or suppose he was committed to strong family values (Schoenbaum, *Lives*, 14; see also Honan, 231, 236). This supposed paragon of literacy let his children grow up functionally illiterate, while he himself was a man of no recorded education. He left no trace of having been a precocious student, and legend tells us that he dropped out of grammar school. According to Schoenbaum, "almost everyone seems to have thought well of Shakespeare" (*Documentary*, 205), but the first time he turned up in print, he was lambasted as the untrustworthy and arrogant "upstart Crow." The *Parnassus* authors called him "shrewd," that is, calculating. The Shakspere of record was obsessed with financial self-interest and was accused of being a callous skinflint, yet we are told he was "gentle Will." We are also told that this mild-mannered "Shakespeare lived quietly, unobtrusively, for the most part" (McManaway, 181), or that he was "a relaxed and happy man, almost incapable of taking offense" (Chute, 134), but the historical records show that he was accused of assault in 1596, that he hauled people into court to recover debts, and that he hoarded grain during famine. Ben Jonson seems to have considered him a thief, a man who liked to hear himself talk, and, at times, a laughingstock.

Playwriting paid far less than did Shakspere's documented activities, yet we are told that he wrote plays to make money. As far as we know, nobody paid him to write anything. He was supposedly the leading light of "his" theatre company, but business records show that his primary roles with the acting company were that of financier and entrepreneur. Moreover, he was in Stratford, not London, during certain performance seasons and lucrative holiday assignments at court, so he could not always have been present with the company. This man with a head for money and an ambition for social status then turned his back on the opportunity of his life, when James I assumed patronage of the King's Men. Alvin Kernan cited the 1603 warrant for the letters patent that elevated the Lord Chamberlain's Men to the King's Men:

With this warrant, the resident playwright of the King's Men, William Shakespeare, also became official playwright to the prince. . . . The social status of Shakespeare's acting company escalated greatly when its members became grooms of the chamber and servants to his majesty. (xvi)

The statement that Shakespeare became "the official playwright to the prince" is an extreme one for which there is no evidence. Nevertheless, if Shakspere really was a playwright with an exceptional nose for opportunity, why did he shift his attentions away from the theatre profession and toward business investments in Stratford, when he was at the height of his supposed London career? His 1602 purchase of the Stratford freehold property had already placed him "among the local landed gentry and . . . in the position of landlord to many tenant farmers"; his 1605 purchase of tithes, while lucrative, required additional work to administer the numerous subleases (Lewis, 2:335; see also 2:380–83).

It was not the only time he walked away from opportunities offering real social advancement. In *The Norton Shakespeare*, we are told that "in Elizabethan England, aristocratic patronage, with the money, protection, and prestige it alone could provide, was probably a professional writer's most important asset" (Shakespeare, 52). We are told by another biographer that Shakespeare "was a professional in constant search for aristocratic buttering on his bread" (Thomson, 175). But the records suggest otherwise. Despite the importance of literary patronage, Shakespeare, whoever he was, apparently gave up looking for patrons after just two dedications.

Shakspere, the man, is an unbelievable conflation of a self-effacing nonentity and an aggressive wheeler-dealer. Ian Wilson found it "notable" that when actor Augustine Phillipps drew up his will, he appointed "as his legal overseer trusty book keeper Heminges . . . significantly not choosing for this [responsibility] an arguably dreamy writer like Shakespeare." In his next chapter, Wilson described the "hard-headed clique of businessmen, Shakespeare among them, making commercial decisions" (311, 342). Wilson's conception of "Shakespeare" alternated between "dreamy" and "hard-headed," and that contradictory character is indicative of a hybrid person. No consistent traits can emerge from the artificial splicing together of two distinctly different personalities.

The two writers whom historians most closely associate with Shakespeare—Jonson and Drayton—never wrote about him by name during his lifetime. Shakespeare, whose sensitivity to human relationships and conflicts is the marvel of every playgoer, apparently had *no* literary friends—or enemies—or if he did, as far as we know, they inexplicably failed to invite him to contribute commendatory verses, never exchanged letters with him, and never mentioned him as though they knew him.

Traditional biographers rarely inquire into the temperament of the creative genius, but if they did, Shakspere of Stratford would not fit the mold. Certainly no contemporary described him as an artist driven by his Muse. The playwright was surely a man of consuming passion and artistic compulsion, yet Shakspere supposedly stopped writing abruptly at the top of his career. Then this presumed towering intellectual deserted literary London at the height of his powers to return to the illiterate environs of Stratford. Commentators suppose that he was just plain tired, or that Shakspere, the "family man," wanted to retire to his hometown.

Shakspere was supposedly a skilled writer, but his will was utterly unliterary, and his handwriting was practically illegible. Shakespeare the poet believed his verses were powerful enough to outlive marble, yet Shakspere, a man of documented self-interest, did nothing to ensure their accurate preservation through supervised publishing. Schoenbaum accepted the incompatible attitudes without blinking: "If Shakespeare was indifferent to the ultimate fate of the plays that immortalized him, he showed no similar nonchalance about assembling and passing down intact his estate" (*Documentary*, 161). Schoenbaum further speculated that Shakspere died without knowing, and "possibly not caring" (130) whether his plays would be preserved in print. Shakspere, the parsimonious operator, was supposedly nonchalant even when the Shakespeare plays were published surreptitiously, despite the fact that piracy hit him and his fellow shareholders in the pocketbook.

Shakespeare's poetry had earned him considerable fame and respect, yet not one writer of the day noted Shakspere's death in 1616. The Stratford bust and epitaph supposedly represent the best anyone could produce at the time to memorialize an eminent poet and dramatist. Some biographers even swallow the idea that England's greatest dramatist wrote doggerel for his own tombstone.

Instead of highlighting these outrageous conflicts in schedule, temperament, activity, and so on, biographers attempt to put credible spins on them all. They romanticize hard facts, avoid the worst of the information, separate inherently conflicting material into different chapters, and then manipulate Shakspere's motives, personality, and presumed creative flow to manufacture a synthetic literary biography. In so doing, they neutralize or contradict the solid information found in Shakspere's historical dossier. Harold Bloom, author of *The Western Canon*, would undoubtedly be horrified to think that he reflected a nonconformist's view:

It is as though the creator of scores of major characters and hundreds of frequently vivid minor figures wasted no imaginative energy in inventing a persona for himself. At the very center of the Canon is the least self-conscious and least aggressive of all the major writers we have known.

There is an inverse ratio, a little beyond our analytical skills, between Shakespeare's virtual colorlessness and his preternatural dramatic powers. (55)

Similarly, Park Honan's Shakespeare "seems to have flourished with a certain annihilation of the sense of himself" (118).

SHAKSPERE, GENT.

Shakspere's documentary records are not those of a literary genius but those of a man with financial acumen and a mediocre intellect. If all the Shakespeare plays had been published anonymously, *nothing* in William Shakspere's documented biographical trails would remotely suggest that he wrote them. Shakspere of Stratford is not, in fact, a viable authorship candidate, and if he were discovered today as a new contender, his candidacy would not be taken seriously.

Who, then, was William Shakspere of Stratford? The records tell us. The uncontested documentation proves that he was a successful businessman who invested shrewdly and made a lot of money. That documentation, augmented by satirical allusions, supports the career of an entrepreneur who brokered plays, costumes, frippery, loans, a marriage, and probably an *impresa* assignment.

One personality trait that is particularly well documented is tight-fistedness. Robert Bearman, author of *Shakespeare in the Stratford Records*, pointed out that Shakspere bought New Place from an owner who was "pressed for cash. . . . In these circumstances he would have been well placed to strike a bargain" (25). Thomas Whittington's will of 1601, specifying Mrs. Shakspere's outstanding debt of 40s to Whittington, suggests that Shakspere did not provide sufficient funds to support his family, because his wife was reduced to borrowing from a former employee. Whittington pressed for collection from "the said William Shaxpere" as a matter of principle; his will specified that moneys recovered be given to the poor. Shakspere's avaricious *persona* is reinforced by the outstanding debt of £20 "owing by Mr. Shakespre" in Ralph Hubaud's will of 1608; Hubaud was the man from whom Shakspere bought the tithes in 1605. It is reinforced again by the tax rolls listing Shakspere in default. During the very years that he was a tax delinquent, Shakspere was busy investing in real estate, hoarding grain, and being approached for financing. Lewis concluded that "certainly his defaulting cannot well have been the result of not having funds" (1:270). From those records and those of his court cases, Shakspere seems to have been quick to sue to recover debts, but slow to pay off his own obligations.

Honigmann (a committed Stratfordian) touched on the same subject, bringing in yet more reasons to question the traditional biography:

If one lists all of these various [business or financial] activities in chronological order it appears that there were major financial negotiations in almost every year from 1594—and that refers only to those that were concluded successfully. Add the unsuccessful ones (for example, *Shakespeare v. Lambert*, 1597 . . .); add deeds or decisions that must have been made, but are now lost (for example, Susanna's marriage settlement in 1607); add other opportunities or dangers that had to be carefully considered (whether or not to oppose the Welcombe enclosures), and one wonders how the dramatist found time to go on writing plays. He clearly did not need to write, financially speaking, after the accession of King James. ("Businessman," 44–45)

Shakspere was one of the *nouveaux riches*, and his business transactions consistently reflect his ambitions. For example, his purchase of New Place, the second largest house in Stratford, smacks of social climbing, because he took the unnecessary step of obtaining a certified copy of the transaction. Bearman speculated that Shakspere, "like the other 'new' gentry of his time, was indulging in a little harmless snobbery. There are many other examples of middle-class families who invested their money in lands. . . . They then had their title to these secured by elaborate certified copies of their deeds, and kept the College of Heralds busy by making tenuous claims to a right to bear a coat of arms in order to secure entry into the élite band of gentry. We cannot assume that Shakespeare was above such things" (18). Indeed, it is difficult to attribute Shakspere's decision to seek certification to anything other than social posturing. It cannot have been indicative of cautious business acumen. Not only was the document legally redundant, but Shakspere is known to have handled other property transactions quite casually. In 1602, he acquired property in Chapel Lane but the documents were never fully executed (Bearman, 38).

If Shakspere was motivated by social ambition when he certified his purchase of New Place and when he applied for the coat of arms, his behavior is consistent with the caricatures of Sogliardo, Gullio, or the "gentleman player." It is noteworthy that in the rare instances when Shakespeare the dramatist concerns himself with social climbing, he is found "laughing at the pretensions of the lower classes" (Berkeley, 97).

In fact, an intensive examination of the Stratford-based records led Bearman to a bourgeois Shakspere whose records bore almost no resemblance to the poet of legend. In these records, Bearman found "little, if anything, to remind us that we are studying the life of one who in his writings emerges as perhaps the most gifted of all time in describing the human condition. Here in Stratford he seems merely to have been a man of the world, buying up property, laying in ample stocks of barley and malt and, when others were starving, selling off his surpluses and pursuing debtors in court, and conniving, as it seems, at the Welcombe enclosures" (76). Shakspere was lampooned early in his career as a miserly Ant, greedy for gain, and his documentary records are consistent with that portrayal.

Shakspere's last will vividly exhibits his preoccupation with the physical trappings of the newly gentrified. Its terms show that he was primarily concerned with preserving his real estate empire for a future male heir. His mean streak is found in his most infamous bequest, that of the second-best bed to his wife. Whereas most wills of the day made bequests to well-beloved wives, or appointed them as executors, Shakspere humiliated his wife from beyond the grave. The provision of the second-best bed is not even in the body copy; it is an interlineation stuck in at the end of the section in which Shakspere bequeathed all his real estate holdings to his daughter and son-in-law. The bed is Shakspere's one and only bequest to his wife, whom he did not even mention by name. Many biographers assure their readers that Shakspere was confident that his wife would be sufficiently provided for under a law that automatically granted widows one third of the estate. However, the authors of *Playhouse Wills* found that "there is, inconveniently, no evidence that [the law] was observed in Warwickshire" (Honigmann and Brock, 14). Therefore, upon Shakspere's demise, his widow became a dependent, tenant, or enforced guest in her own home. Nor did he leave anything to anyone on her side of the family, leaving clothes to his sister and bequests to other blood relatives. Nor could he remember the name of his own sister's son; the will shows a blank space where the name was to be written.

Shakspere's predilection for moneylending at interest filtered down into his last wishes. He specified that a 10% penalty be levied should the bequests to his two daughters not be paid in a timely fashion. Since Susanna was one of the executors, Shakspere "in effect ordered one daughter to pay interest to the other" (Honigmann, "Businessman," 41). It is difficult to sustain a case for Shakspere the gentle family man in the face of such cold, impersonal, and incontrovertible evidence.

Most of the legatees named in the will, Shakspere's "inner circle," were upwardly mobile wealthy landowners or business associates. Shakspere left bequests to William Reynolds "gent.," who owned property in Welcombe and became "one of the largest landowners in Stratford"; Anthony Nashe "gent.," who witnessed some of Shakspere's property transactions, was involved in the tithes that Shakspere bought, would obtain a coat of arms in 1619, and was "one of the wealthiest men in Stratford"; Anthony's brother, John, who managed and farmed the tithes that Shakspere had leased from the Hubaud family; Thomas Russell, "Esquire," an extremely wealthy landowner who bought a manor in nearby Droitwich after an unsuccessful attempt to purchase Clopton House in Stratford; and Francis Collins, "gent.," Shakspere's attorney (Campbell and Quinn, *Encyclopedia*,

686, 581, 728; Eccles, *Warwickshire*, 123, 121–22, 117). Shakspere left his sword to Thomas, the nephew of moneylender John Combe. He also named neighbor Hamnet Sadler, baker and money collector, and, as a witness, Julius Shaw, wool trader and maltster. As we have seen, Shakspere left small bequests to three of his London colleagues, Burbage, Heminges, and Condell, but he remembered no one in the literary profession.

All the documentary evidence shows that Shakspere was a shrewd negotiator at the bargaining table, manipulative, sometimes involved in shady deals, and pretentious. Those characteristics are amply reinforced by the satirical allusions that biographers reluctantly introduce, only to drop like hot potatoes. Again and again, the satirical portraits deliver the same bombastic operator with an overblown opinion of himself, but none of them points to a writer.

The theatrical documentation shows that his role with the Chamberlain's/King's Men was not that of dramatist but that of entrepreneur and financier. The records also point to an opportunist who was associated with some of the published Shakespeare plays, and with a number of inferior texts. Shakspere's vocation as play broker could account for a number of plays, known today to be somebody else's, but published then over the name of William Shakespeare or over the initials "W. S." Honigmann observed that in the 1600s, "unscrupulous men used [Shakespeare's] name to sell plays that, as all the world now agrees, could not have come from his pen" (*Impact*, 46). The evidence suggests that one of those unscrupulous men was William Shakspere. Richmond Crinkley wrote in the *Shakespeare Quarterly*:

There is certainly external evidence, in that Shakespeare's initials were applied to a number of works printed during the time he flourished—works which he did not disown and to which indeed he could well have done what he was initially said to have done, "overseen." *Locrine* appeared in 1595 as "Newly set forth, over-seen and corrected by W. S." The traditional theory that the printer was trying to capitalize on Shakespeare's name is surely implausible, since Shakespeare's name was not by then widely printed. It is more likely that Shakespeare as a producer and *procurer of plays* did exactly what the title page said he did. It is no discredit to him that he did so, it being then something of a producer's prerogative. (519, emphasis added)

The Shakespeare whom Crinkley identified as the producer and procurer of plays conjures up the familiar images of the "gentleman player," the acquisitive Ant whose "thrift is theft," the paymaster of playwrights, and the "Poet-Ape."

Any financial interest in play scripts that Shakspere retained as a theatre shareholder was subverted by the theft of the Shakespeare plays. Shakspere therefore stood to lose hard cash from any unauthorized sale of the Shakespeare plays *unless Shakspere himself stood to gain by that sale.* In other words, either this aggressive businessman with a financial stake in the Shakespeare plays inexplicably did nothing to stop the piracy—or he *was* the play pirate. In 1593, he may have hit an unanticipated bonanza. If indiscriminate or uninformed readers occasionally mistook him for the pseudonymous author of *Venus and Adonis,* Shakspere may well have capitalized on the similarities of the two names. It is even possible that the pen name derived from the name of the broker.

LOOKING FOR SHAKESPEARE

No biographer has successfully integrated the life of Shakspere with the works of Shakespeare. Although the synthesis of what we know about the writer is the antithesis of what we know about the man from Stratford, biographers nevertheless have attempted to merge these mutually incompatible entities, forcing a marriage of convenience filled with chronological disorders. What we know of Shakspere's business activities encroaches too much on his presumed playwriting time, and what we do *not* know of his education and cultural enlightenment precludes his having gotten the necessary preparation. If Shakspere had acquired the education and cultural experiences to write the plays, he would have left at least a few footprints behind to prove it. Shakspere's extant records are not only devoid of personal literary evidence, they point *away* from a literary career and toward other vocations. The footprints that he did leave lead to a literary dead end.

The contradictory and incompatible evidence has prompted anti-Stratfordians to search for an alternative author. When the hard evidence is examined, what emerges is an overwhelming weight of probability that William Shakspere of Stratford did *not* write the plays of William Shakespeare, and an equally overwhelming weight of probability that a gentleman of rank did. The idea that "William Shakespeare" was the pen name of an Elizabethan aristocrat is ultimately less fanciful than ascribing to an alleged grammar school dropout the most exquisite dramatic literature in the English language. And which scenario is more plausible: A code of silence that prevented or obscured written references to an aristocratic writer, or an inexplicable conspiracy to eradicate *all* the personal literary paper trails for the commoner William Shakspere? Unfortunately, scholars tacitly accept the statistically impossible scenarios: That Shakspere left no personal records revealing his profession as a writer, or that if he left any, they have *all* been lost or destroyed.

Shakespeare's chroniclers should be able to write a biography that has a rational relationship to the literary output of the man. The fact that biographers have failed after countless attempts strongly suggests that they are writing about the wrong man. It is a pity that no comparable efforts have been expended to find the foot that fits the literary glass slipper. If the effort were made and a solution were found, readers and playgoers would reap immense rewards. Passages that continue to confound scholars would be closer to solution. Works that have captured the imagination of generations of playgoers would increase in their fascination if we knew more about the real life events that inspired them. A biography of a Shakespeare whose life story meshes with the Shakespearean literature is bound to be more illuminating than the litany of property transactions sandwiched in between the writing of *Hamlet* and *King Lear*. How exciting it would be if we knew something about Shakespeare's personality, his relationships, his loves, his demons, and his Muses. Unfortunately, until the authorship question gains legitimacy in academic and literary circles, we will all be stuck with a biography out of joint with the plays.

Schoenbaum had this to say about the good folk of Stratford-upon-Avon:

What did fellow townsmen make of the distinguished playwright of the Chamberlain's company and admired poet of love's languishment who sojourned each year in their midst? They probably troubled their heads little enough about the plays and poems. Business was another matter; they saw Shakespeare as a man shrewd in practical affairs. (*Documentary*, 178)

Certainly the historical record attests to Schoenbaum's description. Nobody in Stratford had anything to say about any famous poet in their midst. It is enough to make one think there was no poet in their midst.

Appendix: Chart of Literary Paper Trails

Just as birds can be distinguished from turtles by characteristics peculiar to the species, so writers can be distinguished from doctors, actors, or financiers, by the types of personal records left behind. This chart compares *personal* and *literary* records left by Elizabethan and Jacobean writers during their lifetimes, with at least one record extant for any category checked. Category 10 includes evidence dating up to twelve months following death, to allow for eulogies or reports of death. Documentation follows.

	Ben Jonson	Thomas Nashe	Philip Massinger	Gabriel Harvey	Edmund Spenser
1. Evidence of education	Yes	Yes	Yes	Yes	Yes
2. Record of correspondence, especially concerning literary matters	Yes	Yes	Yes	Yes	Yes
3. Evidence of having been paid to write	Yes	Yes	Yes	-	-
4. Evidence of a direct relationship with a patron	Yes	Yes	Yes	Yes	Yes
5. Extant original manuscript	Yes	Yes	Yes	Yes	-
6. Handwritten inscriptions, receipts, letters, etc. touching on literary matters	Yes	Yes	Yes	Yes	-
7. Commendatory verses, epistles, or epigrams contributed or received	Yes	Yes	Yes	Yes	Yes
8. Miscellaneous records (e.g., referred to personally as a writer)	Yes	Yes	Yes	Yes	Yes
9. Evidence of books owned, written in, borrowed, or given	Yes	Yes	-	Yes	Yes
10. Notice at death as a writer	Yes	-	-	-	Yes

Samuel Daniel	George Peele	Michael Drayton	George Chapman	William Drummond	Anthony Mundy	John Marston	Thomas Middleton
Yes	Yes	-	-	Yes	-	Yes	Yes
Yes	Yes	Yes	Yes	Yes	-	-	-
-	Yes	Yes	Yes	-	Yes	Yes	Yes
Yes	Yes	Yes	Yes	-	Yes	-	-
Yes	Yes	-	-	Yes	Yes	-	Yes
Yes	Yes	Yes	Yes	Yes	Yes	Yes	Yes
Yes	-	Yes	Yes	Yes	Yes	Yes	Yes
Yes	Yes	Yes	Yes	Yes	Yes	Yes	Yes
-	-	-	Yes	Yes	-	Yes	-
-	-	Yes	-	-	Yes	-	-

	John Lyly	Thomas Heywood	Thomas Lodge	Robert Greene	Thomas Dekker
1. Evidence of education	Yes	-	Yes	Yes	-
2. Record of correspondence, especially concerning literary matters	Yes	-	Yes	-	Yes
3. Evidence of having been paid to write	-	Yes	-	Yes	Yes
4. Evidence of a direct relationship with a patron	Yes	-	Yes	Yes	-
5. Extant original manuscript	-	Yes	-	-	-
6. Handwritten inscriptions, receipts, letters, etc. touching on literary matters	Yes	Yes	-	-	Yes
7. Commendatory verses, epistles, or epigrams contributed or received	Yes	Yes	Yes	Yes	Yes
8. Miscellaneous records (e.g., referred to personally as a writer)	Yes	Yes	Yes	Yes	Yes
9. Evidence of books owned, written in, borrowed, or given	-	-	Yes	-	-
10. Notice at death as a writer	-	Yes	-	Yes	-

Thomas Watson	Christopher Marlowe	Francis Beaumont	John Fletcher	Thomas Kyd	John Webster	William Shakspere
Yes	Yes	Yes	-	Yes	-	-
-	-	-	-	Yes	-	-
-	-	-	Yes	-	Yes	-
Yes	Yes	-	-	Yes	-	-
-	-	-	-	-	-	-
-	-	-	-	-	-	-
Yes	-	Yes	Yes	-	Yes	-
Yes	Yes	Yes	Yes	Yes	Yes	-
-	-	-	Yes	-	-	-
Yes	Yes	Yes	-	-	-	-

Abbreviations used:

ELA   *English Literary Autographs: 1550–1650.* W. W. Greg, in col-
           laboration with J. P. Gilson, Hilary Jenkinson, R. B. Mc-
           Kerrow, and A. W. Pollard.
HS   *Ben Jonson.* Edited by C. H. Herford and Percy Simpson.

Ben Jonson (1572–1637) 1 epigram 14 to William Camden and dedication to *Every Man In His Humour* (HS, 8:31, 3:301); **2** letter to the
earl of Salisbury from prison, mentioning "George Chapman, a learned,
and honest Man" and the cause of their imprisonment, "a play" (HS,
1:194–96); **3** payments for city entertainments and plays (HS, 11:586;
11:307–8); **4** royal patent of 1630, increasing Jonson's pension in consideration of "those services of his wit & pen" (HS, 1:245–46); **5** *The
Masque of Queenes* (see fig. 5); **6** book inscriptions (HS, 1:262–71); **7**
verse to "my worthy and honour'd friend Mr. George Chapman" for
his translation of *Hesiod* (HS, 8:388–89); **8** Merchant Taylors' Company record "to conferr with Mr Benjamyn Johnson the Poet, aboute
a speeche" (HS, 11:587); imprisonment for writing *The Isle of Dogs*
(HS, 1:Appendix III); **9** over 120 books catalogued (HS, 1:250–71,
11:593–97); John Selden's 1614 preface to *Titles of Honor*, referring
to a book "in the well-furnisht Librarie of my beloved friend that singular Poet M. Ben: Jonson" (HS, 1:250); **10** elegies on Jonson's death
(HS, 11:421–94).

Thomas Nashe (?1567–?1601) 1 Cambridge, BA degree (Nicholl, *Nashe*,
23, 35, 36); **2** letter to William Cotten (see fig. 7), referring to "an
after harvest I expected by writing for the stage and for the press"
(*ELA*, XX); **3 & 4** letter by Sir George Carey to his wife: "nashe hath
dedicated a booke unto you with promis of a better, will cotton will
disburs v^{li} or xx nobles in yowr rewarde to him and he shall not finde
my purs shutt to relieve him out of prison there presently in great
missery malicied for writinge against the londoners" (Duncan-Jones,
15); **5** Latin verse while a Cambridge scholar (Nicholl, *Nashe*, 36); **6**
letter to Cotten (see fig. 7); **7** preface to *Menaphon* (1589) refers to
the author Robert Greene as his "sweet friend" (Greene, 6:10); **8** action by the authorities against the authors of *The Isle of Dogs* (a raid
"to peruse soch papers as were fownd in Nash his lodgings") (Nicholl,
Nashe, 244); **9** signature on flyleaf and marginalia in John Leland's
Principum in Anglia Virorum Encomia (Nicholl, *Nashe*, 97); **10** no
evidence; an epitaph, probably by Jonson, is undated (Duncan-Jones,
"Epitaph," 4–6); another epitaph by Charles Fitzgeffrey may also have

been written within twelve months of Nashe's death, but the exact date of Nashe's death is not known.

Philip Massinger (1583–1640) 1 St. Alban's Hall, Oxford (Dunn, 10–11); **2** letter to Philip Henslowe around 1612–15 regarding payment for "the play of Mr. Fletcher and ours . . . Rec . . . for the use of Mr. Daborne, Mr. Feeld, Mr. Messenger" with a postscript written by Massinger (Beaumont, 1:25); **3** playwright Robert Daborne wrote to Henslowe around 1613–14 concerning his "earnings in the play," requesting that he be paid "as much as Mr. Messenger" (Dunn, 16); **4** dedication to Sir Francis Foljambe for *The Maid of Honor*: "That you have been . . . for many years . . . patrons to me and my despised studies. . . . I was supported by your frequent courtesies and favours" (Dunn, 19); **5** autograph manuscript of *Believe as You List*, 1631 (*ELA*, XIV); **6** inscription to Sir Francis Foljambe in a presentation copy of *The Duke of Milan*, 1623 (*ELA*, XIV); **7** "To my judicious and learned Friend the Author [James Shirley] upon his ingenious Poem, the Grateful servant" (Massinger, 4:365); **8** James Shirley's "To my honoured Friend, Master Philip Massinger, upon his Renegado," 1630 (Massinger, 1:ciii); **9** & **10** no evidence.

Gabriel Harvey (1550–1630) 1 Cambridge (Stern, 10, 12, 50); **2** letters to Burghley "to obtain the Orators place," and another regarding the master of Trinity Hall post (Stern, 53, 77; *ELA*, LXXI); **3** no evidence; **4** letter by William Fulke, master of Pembroke Hall stating, "Whereas my lorde, the Earle of Leycester hath made earnest request for the continuance of Mr. Harveyes fellowshipp" and Harvey's letter to Leicester about obtaining an academic position (Stern, 48–50); **5** Latin verses written for Audley End (Stern, 40); **6** marginalia (Stern, plates); **7** Edmund Spenser's sonnet "To the right worshipfull my singular good frend, M. Gabriell Harvey" (Stern, 77); **8** marginalia regarding John Florio and John Eliot, "mie new London companions for Italian and French" (Stern, 43); **9** catalogue of Harvey's books (Stern, Part 3); see also Spenser no. 9; **10** no evidence.

Edmund Spenser (1552–1599) 1 Merchant Taylors' and Pembroke Hall (Judson, 15; *Spenser Encyclopedia*, 669); **2** letter to Gabriel Harvey, mentioning his poem, written from Leicester House, published as one of *Three Letters* (Stern, 66–68); letter to Harvey discussing "English Hexameters" (Stern, 55); **3** no evidence; **4** dedication of *Colin Clouts Come Home Againe* to Sir Walter Raleigh referring to his "infinite debt" owed for "singular favours and sundry good turns" (Judson, 139); **5** no evidence; **6** in his capacity as secretary to Lord Grey, Spenser scribed letters, but these do not relate to his literary career; **7** sonnet "To the right worshipfull my singular good frend, M. Gabriell Harvey" (Stern, 77); **8** Lodowick Bryskett's report of a gathering around 1585, in which Spenser describes his "*heroical verse*, under the title of a *Faerie Queene*" (*Spenser Encyclopedia*, 119); **9** Spenser gave books to Harvey (Stern, 49 n, 203, 237); **10** John Chamberlain's letter to Dudley Carleton: "Spenser, our principal poet, coming lately out of Ireland, died at Westminster on Saturday last (Judson, 203).

Samuel Daniel (1562–1619) 1 Magdalen Hall, Oxford (Eccles, "Daniel," 148–49); dedication (*Defence of Rhyme*) to the earl of Pembroke, acknowledging his debt to the countess of Pembroke, having "received the first notion for the formal ordering of these compositions, at Wilton, which I must ever acknowledge to have been my best school" (Daniel, 1:xv–xvi); **2** letter to Robert Cecil, Viscount Cranbourne (1605), apologizing for "making the stage the speaker of my lines" (Daniel, 1:liii); letter to the earl of Devonshire, 1604 (see fig. 13): "in this matter of Philotas . . . first I told the Lordes I had written 3 Acts of this tragedie the Christmas before my L. of Essex troubles" (Daniel, 1:xxiii); **3** no evidence; **4** 1604 letter to the earl of Devonshire (as in no. 2): "I had read some part of [*Philotas*] to your honor: and this I said having none else of power to grace me now in Court" (Daniel, 1: xxiii); **5** portions of *Hymen's Triumph*, around 1614 (*ELA*, XXI); **6** inscription for *Hymen's Triumph* to Jean Drummond, Lady of Roxborough (*ELA*, XXI); **7** verse "To my good friend, M. [Joshua] Sylvester" for his Du Bartas translation (Daniel, 1:281); John Davies's Epigram 155 "To my worthily-disposed friend Mr. Sam. Daniell," regarding "thy Muse" from *The Scourge of Folly* (1611) (Davies, 2:26); **8** March 1618 "License to Samuel Daniel, groom of the Q.'s privy chamber, to print *The Collection of the Historie of England*, compiled by himself" (*"Rymer's Foedera,"* 2:841); **9** & **10** no evidence.

George Peele (1556–96) 1 Oxford (Ashley, 15, 23); **2** letter to Lord Burghley (see fig. 14) to present "the history of Troy in 500 verses" (*ELA*, XVI); **3** & **4** record of the earl of Northumberland's payment "to one Geo. Peele, a poett, as my Lord's liberality 3£" (Ashley, 182–83); **5** *Anglorum Feriae*, poem of 1595 (ELA, XVI); **6** see no. 2; **7** no evidence; **8** see no. 3; **9** no evidence; Ashley (23) states that the school at Christ's Hospital granted him "extra books for the study of Erasmus, Cicero, Terence, Horace, and Ovid," but does not cite the source; **10** no evidence.

Michael Drayton (1563–1631) 1 no evidence; **2** letters discussing poetry, including his *Polyolbion*, to and from William Drummond (Masson, 81–85); **3** numerous payments in Henslowe's papers, for example, "lent unto . . . mihell drayton in earneste of a Booke" (Foakes and Rickert,

183); **4** inscription of 1627 (see fig. 8) to his "muche honored ffrend the worthy Sr Henry willoughby one of the selected Patrons of thes my latest Poems" (*ELA*, VIII); **5** no evidence; **6** see fig. 8; **7** epigram from John Davies "To mine honest as loving friend Mr. Michael Drayton" (Davies, 2:60); "To M. John Davies, My Good Friend" (1609) for *Holy Roode* (Drayton, *Works*, 1:499); from Jonson "on the Muses of his Friend M. Drayton" (HS, 8:396–98); **8** physician John Hall described him as an "excellent poet" (Joseph, *18*); **9** no evidence; **10** letter (early 1632) to Viscount Stirling by Drummond reporting on Drayton's death and mentioning *Polyolbion, Odes*, and *Elegies* (Masson, 184–85).

George Chapman (?1559/60–1634) 1 no evidence; **2** letter to Henry Jones, to whom he also addressed his epistle for *Epicede* (Sisson and Butman, 186); if the letters copied in the Dobell manuscript are genuine, then Chapman protested in one of them against the censorship of his "owne Plaies" (MacLure, 19n–20; Clare, 142); **3** record of payment of 40s from Philip Henslowe (see fig. 10) for "a Pastorall ending in a Tragedye" (*ELA*, XII); **4** petition to the earl of Northumberland refers to a "due debt" for his translation of Homer, undertaken for the late Prince Henry ("two yeares studious writing impos'd by his highness") (Spivack, 19–20): **5** no evidence; **6** inscription to Henry Crofts in a copy of *Homer* (Eccles, "Early," 178); **7** commendatory verse "To My Worthy Friend Mr. George Chapman, and his translated *Hesiod*" from Michael Drayton (1618) (Drayton, *Works*, 1:503); his 1612 verse to "his Loved Sonne, Nat. Field, and his Wether-cocke Woman" (Greg, *Bibliography*, 438); **8** testators in a 1617 lawsuit stated that "George Chapman doth professe Poetrie" and "hath made dyvers plays and written other books" (Sisson and Butman, 185); **9** dedication to Henry Reynolds on a copy of *The Crown* (MacLure, 204); **10** no evidence.

William Drummond (1585–1649) 1 Edinburgh university (Masson, 8); **2** letters to and from Michael Drayton discussing poetry (Masson, 81–83); **3** & **4** no evidence; **5** sonnet (*ELA*, LI); **6** inscription in John Florio's *A Worlde of Wordes* (*ELA*, LI); **7** a "missive" from Ben Jonson regarding "the Friendship contracted with The Right Virtuous and Learned Mr. William Drummond" (Masson, 105); **8** the Jonson *Conversations* (HS, 1:128–78); **9** collection presented to Society of Antiquaries of Scotland and Edinburgh University (*ELA*, LI); **10** no evidence.

Anthony Mundy (1560–1633) 1 & **2** no evidence; **3** petition for payment by "Monday, the poett . . . [for] books of the late shewes and speeches" for the Lord Mayor's pageant (Turner, 163) and numerous payments in Henslowe's papers, for example, "to paye unto antony mundaye in fulle payment for a playe" (Foakes and Rickert, 206); **4** poem to the earl of Oxford for *The Mirror of Mutability*, in which Mundy looks forward to resuming their friendly discussions ("Donec præstentes sermone fruamur amico") (Ward, 185–86; Hannas, private communication); **5** part of *The Booke of Sir Thomas Moore* (*ELA*, XI) (see fig. 9); **6** dedicatory epistle and verse for *Heaven of the Mind* to John Swinnerton, sheriff of London (*ELA*, XI); **7** Henry Chettle's epistle "To his good frend M. Anthony Mundy" for *Primaleon of Greece*, 1596 (Jenkins, *Chettle*, 14–15, 267); **8** Freedom List of the Draper's Company lists Mundy as "a Poet" (Eccles, "Munday," 100); **9** no evidence; **10** monument inscription described Mundy as a "servant to the City, With his Pen" (Turner, 173).

John Marston (1576–1634) 1 Oxford and Middle Temple records (Finkelpearl, *Marston*, 84, 86); **2** no evidence; **3** "lent unto mr. maxton the new poet . . . in earnest of A booke" (Foakes and Rickert, 124); **4** & **5** no evidence; **6** signed dedication to the Ashby Entertainment, 1607 (*ELA*, XVIII); **7** dedication of *The Malcontent* to "his frank and heartfelt friend, Benjamin Jonson" (Marston, *Plays*, 195); **8** Jonson reported in *Conversations* that he "had many quarrels with Marston . . . wrote his Poetaster on him the beginning of them were that Marston represented him in the stage" (HS, 1:140); **9** draft of Marston's father's will bequeathed law books to him (Finkelpearl, *Marston*, 84); **10** no evidence.

Thomas Middleton (1580–1627) 1 Queen's College, Oxford (Barker, 5–6); **2** no evidence; **3** payment to "Thomas Middleton Gent." for "*Mask of Cupid*, and other shows lately made . . . by the said Mr. Middleton" (Middleton, 1:xxxix–xl); several payments in Henslowe's papers, for example, "paye unto mr mydelton in fulle paymente of his playe" (Foakes and Rickert, 206); **4** no evidence; **5** manuscript of *A Game at Chess* (*ELA*, XCIV); **6** dedication to "Mr. William Hammond" on a manuscript of *A Game at Chess* (*ELA*, XCIV); **7** verse from dramatist Nath. Richards "Upon the tragedy of my familiar acquaintance, Tho. Middleton" for *Women Beware Women* (Middleton, 6:235); **8** warrant following a performance of *A Game at Chess* to bring "one [Edward] Middleton sonne to Midleton the Poet" to the authorities (Middleton, 1:lxxxiii); **9** & **10** no evidence.

John Lyly (?1554–1606) 1 Oxford and Cambridge (Lyly, 1:1, 16); **2** letter to Robert Cecil (1597) regarding reversion of the Master of the Revels post, and a petition to the Queen concerning the post (Lyly, 1:68–69, 70–71); **3** no evidence; **4** 1584 correspondence ("beware of my lord of Oxenford's man called Lyly, for if he sees this letter he will put it in print or make the boys in Paul's play it upon a stage") (G. K. Hunter, 76); **5** no evidence; **6** letter to Robert Cecil of 1602 concerning his "petition" and mentioning the good offices of poet Fulke Greville (Lyly, 1:75); **7** epistle to Watson, "the Author his Friend" for *Hekatompathia* (Lyly, 1:26–27); **8** Gabriel Harvey referred to Lyly as "a playmunger, an Interluder" (Lyly, 1:44); **9** & **10** no evidence.

Thomas Heywood (?1573/5–1641) **1** & **2** no evidence; **3** numerous payments in Henslowe's papers, for example, "unto Thomas Hewode in fulle payment for his playe" (Foakes and Rickert, 224); **4** no evidence; **5** *The Escapes of Jupiter* (Francis, 51); **6** see no. 5; **7** from John Webster "To his beloved friend Maister Thomas Heywod" for *Apology for Actors*, 1612; **8** John Taylor "To my approved good friend M. Thomas Heywood" for his *Apology for Actors*; **9** no evidence; **10** burial register in Clerkenwell listing "Tho. Heywood, Poet" (Chambers, *Stage*, 3: 339).

Thomas Lodge (1558–1625) **1** Merchant Taylors', Oxford, Lincoln's Inn, University of Avignon (Walker, 423–25; Eccles, "Lives," 81, 82); **2** letter to Sir Thomas Edmondes thanking him for favors and mentioning that "Coriate the fooles booke is uppon the press" (*ELA*, XIX); **3** no evidence; **4** dedication to William, earl of Derby (*A Fig for Momus*, 1595): "as your noble father in mine infancie, with his owne hands incorporated me into your house, so in this my retired age and studie . . . shall be imployed to doe you honour and service" (Lodge, 3:3–4). **5** & **6** no evidence; **7** epistle to Michael Drayton, his "sweet friend," *A Fig for Momus* (Lodge, 3:60–63); **8** see no. 7; **9** Lodge refers to his books in two letters of 1609 (Eccles, "Lives," 83); **10** no evidence.

Robert Greene (1558–92) **1** Cambridge (Parr, 538, 540); **2** no evidence; **3** the earl of Leicester's payment to "Robert Grene that presented a booke to your lordship vli" for *Planetomachia*, 1585 (S. Adams, 259); **4** dedication of *Never To Late* (part 2) to Thomas Burnaby: "having received many friendly, nay fatherly favours at your hands," and subsequently "imboldened my selfe to present you with a Pamphlet of my penning . . . which your Worship so gratefully accepted" (R. Greene, 8:115–16); **5** & **6** no evidence; **7** commendatory sonnet from Thomas Lodge for *The Spanish Masquerado*, 1589, mentioning "Mon doux ami" and "mon Greene" (Greene, 5:240); **8** Greene's epistle for "my absent friend, M. Thomas Lodge" for *Euphues Shadow*, 1592 (Lodge, 2:7); **9** no evidence; **10** Henry Chettle's epistle to *Kind Harte's Dreame* (Chettle, 5).

Thomas Dekker (?1572–1632) 1 no evidence; 2 letter to Edward Alleyn
(see fig. 12) regarding "my Eûlogium (or Praise) of you & yor Noble
Act" (*ELA*, IX); 3 receipt of payment (see fig. 11) in Henslowe's papers
(*ELA*, IX); numerous payments from Henslowe, for example, "to lend
thomas dickers in earneste of A playe Boocke" (Foakes and Rickert,
130); 4 & 5 no evidence; 6 see figs. 11–12; 7 verse to his "deere
friend" Anthony Mundy for *Palmerin of England, Part III* (Turner,
140); 8 Jo[hn] Da[vies] to "thy friend if thine own" for Dekker's *Lan-
thorne and Candlelight*, 1609 (Dekker, *Non-Dramatic*, 3:184); 9 &
10 no evidence.

Thomas Watson (?1557–92) 1 records at the English College, Douai (Eccles, *Marlowe*, 137–38); 2 & 3 no evidence; 4 dedication of *Hekatompathia* to the earl of Oxford, who "oftentimes and earnestly called upon
mee, to put it to the presse" (Watson, 3–4); 5 & 6 no evidence; 7
epistle from John Lyly "to the author his friend" for *Hekatompathia*
(Watson, 7–8); 8 Watson and Christopher Marlowe arrested and jailed
after a street fracas (Boas, *Marlowe*, 101–4); 9 no evidence; 10 George
Peele wrote "To Watson, worthy many Epitaphs / For his sweet
Poesie" in *Honour of the Garter*, 1593 (Peele, 266).

Christopher Marlowe (1564–93) 1 Cambridge (Boas, *Marlowe*, 13); 2 &
3 no evidence; 4 Thomas Kyd's letter reporting that his "first acquaintance with this Marlowe, rose upon his bearing name to serve my Lord
although his Lordship never knewe his service, but in writing for his
plaiers" (Boas, *Marlowe*, 241); letter from Robert Sidney to Lord
Burghley, 1592 "Christofer Marly, by his profession a scholar . . . says
himself to be very well known both to the Earl of Northumberland and
my Lord Strange" (Nicholl, *Reckoning*, 234–35); 5, 6, & 7, no evidence; 8 Kyd wrote to Lord Keeper Puckering of "this Marlowe" who
had been "writing for his [Lordship's] plaiers" (Kyd, 1:cviii–cix); Marlowe died on 31 May 1593 and Kyd's letter was written after 1 June,
"probably in the summer or autumn" (*ELA*, XV); 9 no evidence; 10
George Peele's tribute to Marlowe written "about three weeks after
Marlowe's death": "unhappy in thine end, / Marley, the Muses darling,
for thy verse"; there is also evidence of an elegy, now lost, by Thomas
Nashe (Nicholl, *Reckoning*, 51–52, 58, 60–61).

Francis Beaumont (? 1584–1616) 1 Oxford, Inner Temple (Beaumont, 1:
10); 2, 3, 4, 5, & 6 no evidence; 7 commendatory verse "To my Friend
Maister John Fletcher upon his faithful Shepheardesse" (Greg, *Bibliog-
raphy*, 424); verse to "my deare friend, Mr Benjamin Jonson for *Volpone*
(HS, 11:319–20); 8 verse letter to Jonson about meeting at the Mermaid
(Beaumont, 1:25); 9 no evidence; 10 burial (without a monument) at
Westminster Abbey near Geoffrey Chaucer (Beaumont, 1:26).

John Fletcher (1579–1625) 1 & 2 no evidence; 3 Nathan Field, Robert Daborne, and Philip Massinger's letter to Philip Henslowe requesting that "the money shall be abated out of the money remaynes for the play of Mr. Fletcher and ours" (Beaumont, 1:25); **4, 5, & 6** no evidence; 7 "To his worthy friend Mr. Ben Jonson" for *Catilene*, 1611 (HS, 11:325–26); from George Chapman "To his loving friend M. Jo. Fletcher concerning his Pastorall" *The Faithful Shepherdesse* around 1610 (Greg, *Bibliography*, 424); 8 Jonson's *Conversations* that "next himself only Fletcher and Chapman could make a Mask" and that "Chapman and Fletcher were loved of him" (HS, 1:133, 137); 9 father's bequest to "Nathaniell Fletcher and John Fletcher all my books" (Beaumont, 1:8); 10 no evidence.

Thomas Kyd (1558–94) 1 Merchant Taylors' school entry (Kyd, xvi); 2 Kyd's letter to Lord Keeper Puckering from prison, following his arrest with Christopher Marlowe (*ELA*, XV); 3 no evidence; 4 letter to Puckering refers to "my Lord, whom I have servd almost theis iij. yeres now, in credit untill nowe" (Kyd, cix); **5, 6, & 7** no evidence; 8 Kyd wrote to Puckering of his "acquaintance wth this Marlowe" and of the "occasion of o^r wrytinge in one chamber twoe yeares synce" (Kyd, cviii); 9 & 10 no evidence.

John Webster (?1578/80–?1632/3) 1 & 2 no evidence; 3 several payments in Henslowe's papers, for example, "lent unto . . . John webster . . . in earneste of A playe" (Foakes and Rickert, 219); **4, 5, & 6** no evidence; 7 verse "To his beloved friend Maister Thomas Heywood" for the 1612 *Apology for Actors*; 8 William Rowley's verse "To his friend" John Webster for *The Duchess of Malfi*; 9 & 10 no evidence.

Bibliography

ORTHODOX WORKS

Abbott, Dean Eric, John Betjeman, Kenneth Clark, John Pope-Hennessy, A. L. Rowse, and George Zarnecki. *Westminster Abbey*. Radnor, PA: The Annenberg School Press, 1972.

Adams, Joseph Quincy. *Shakespearean Playhouses*. 1917. Reprint, Gloucester, MA: Peter Smith, 1960.

Adams, Simon, ed. *Household Accounts and Disbursement Books of Robert Dudley, Earl of Leicester, 1558–1561, 1584–1586*. London: Cambridge University Press, 1995.

Akrigg, G.P.V. *Shakespeare and the Earl of Southampton*. London: Hamish Hamilton, 1968.

Arber, Edward. *A Transcript of the Registers of the Company of Stationers of London, 1554–1640 A.D.* 5 vols. 1875–94. Reprint, New York: Peter Smith, 1950.

Ariosto, Ludovico. *Orlando Furioso*. Translated by Sir Joseph Harington. Edited by Robert McNulty. Oxford: Clarendon Press, 1972.

Ashley, Leonard R. N. *George Peele*. New York: Twayne Publishers, 1970.

Attridge, Derek. "Puttenham's Perplexity: Nature, Art, and the Supplement in Renaissance Poetic Theory." In Patricia Parker and David Quint, eds., *Literary Theory/Renaissance Texts*, 257–79. Baltimore: Johns Hopkins University Press, 1986.

Austin, Warren B. "A Supposed Contemporary Allusion to Shakespeare as a Plagiarist." *Shakespeare Quarterly* 6 (fall 1955): 373–80.

———. *A Computer-Aided Technique for Stylistic Discrimination. The Authorship of Greene's Groatsworth of Wit.* Washington, DC: U.S. Dept. of Health, Education, and Welfare, Office of Education, 1969.

Bald, R. C. "The *Locrine* and *George-A-Greene* Title-Page Inscriptions." *The Library*, 4th series, 15 (1935): 295–305.

Baldwin, T. W. *William Shakspere's Small Latine and Lesse Greeke.* 2 vols. Urbana: University of Illinois Press, 1944.

———. *On the Literary Genetics of Shakspere's Plays 1592–1594.* Urbana: University of Illinois Press, 1959.

Barker, Richard Hindry. *Thomas Middleton.* New York: Columbia University Press, 1958.

Barksted, William. *The Poems of William Barksted.* Edited by Alexander B. Grosart. Manchester: C. E. Simms, 1876.

Bartlett, Henrietta C. *Mr. William Shakespeare, Original and Early Editions of His Quartos and Folios, His Source Books and Those Containing Contemporary Notice.* New Haven: Yale University Press, 1922.

———. "Extant Autograph Material by Shakespeare's Fellow Dramatists." *The Library* (December 1929): 308–12.

Bate, Jonathan. *Shakespeare and Ovid.* Oxford: Clarendon Press, 1993.

———. *The Genius of Shakespeare.* London: Picador, 1997.

Bearman, Robert. *Shakespeare in the Stratford Records.* Stroud, UK: Alan Sutton Publishing, 1994.

Beaumont, Francis. *The Works of Beaumont and Fletcher.* Edited by Alexander Dyce. 2 vols. New York: D. Appleton, 1879.

Beaumont, Francis, and John Fletcher. *Comedies and Tragedies.* London, 1647.

Beckerman, Bernard. "Philip Henslowe." In Joseph W. Donohue Jr., ed., *The Theatrical Manager in England and America*, 19–62. Princeton: Princeton University Press, 1971.

Benbow, R. Mark. "Dutton and Goffe versus Broughton: A disputed contract for plays in the 1570s." *Records of Early English Drama* newsletter, University of Toronto Press (1981): 3–9.

Bennett, Martyn. *Illustrated History of Britain.* North Pomfret, VT: Trafalgar Square Publishing, 1992.

Bentley, Gerald Eades. *The Jacobean and Caroline Stage.* 7 vols. Oxford: Clarendon Press, 1941–68.

———. *Shakespeare and Jonson.* Chicago: University of Chicago Press, 1945.

———. *The Swan of Avon and the Bricklayer of Westminster.* Princeton: Princeton University Press, 1946.

———. *Shakespeare: A Biographical Handbook.* New Haven: Yale University Press, 1961.

———. *Shakespeare and His Theatre*. Lincoln: University of Nebraska Press, 1964.

———. *The Profession of Dramatist in Shakespeare's Time 1590–1642*. 1971. Reprint, Princeton: Princeton University Press, 1986.

———. *The Profession of Player in Shakespeare's Time 1590–1642*. 1984. Reprint, Princeton: Princeton University Press, 1986.

Berkeley, David Shelley. *Blood Will Tell in Shakespeare's Plays*. Graduate Studies, Texas Tech University, no. 28, January 1984.

Berry, Herbert. "Aspects of the Design and Use of the First Public Playhouse." In Herbert Berry, ed., *The First Public Playhouse: The Theatre in Shoreditch 1576–1598*, 29–45. Montreal: McGill-Queen's University Press, 1979.

———. *Shakespeare's Playhouses*. New York: AMS Press, 1987.

Bishop, Morris. *Petrarch and His World*. Bloomington: Indiana University Press, 1963.

Blayney, Peter W. M. *The First Folio of Shakespeare*. Washington, DC: Folger Library Publications, 1991.

———. "Introduction to the Second Edition." *The Norton Facsimile: The First Folio of Shakespeare*, New York: Norton, 1996.

Bloom, Harold. *The Western Canon*. New York: Harcourt Brace and Company, 1994.

Boaden, James. *An Inquiry into the Authenticity of Various Pictures and Prints, etc*. London: Robert Triphook, 1824.

Boas, Frederick S. *Queen Elizabeth in Drama and Related Studies*. London: George Allen and Unwin, 1950.

———. *Christopher Marlowe: A Biographical and Critical Study*. 1940. Reprint with corrections and a supplementary note, Oxford: Clarendon Press, 1966.

Bradbrook, Muriel C. "What Shakespeare Did to Chaucer's *Troilus and Criseyde*." *Shakespeare Quarterly* 9 (summer 1958): 311–19.

———. "Beasts and Gods: Greene's 'Groatsworth of Witte' and the Social Purpose of 'Venus and Adonis.' " *Shakespeare Survey* 15 (1962): 62–72.

———. *Shakespeare: The Poet in His World*. 1978. London: Methuen, 1980.

Bradley, Jesse Franklin, and Joseph Quincy Adams. *The Jonson Allusion-Book*. New Haven: Yale University Press, 1922.

Brome, Richard. *The Dramatic Works of Richard Brome*. 3 vols. London: John Pearson, 1873.

Brooks, Eric St. John. *Sir Christopher Hatton*. London: Jonathan Cape, 1946.

Brown, Ivor. *Shakespeare*. London: Collins, 1949.

Bullough, Geoffrey. *Narrative and Dramatic Sources of Shakespeare*. 8 vols. 1957–75. Reprint, New York: Columbia University Press, 1966.

Burford, E. J. *Bawds and Lodgings: A History of the London Bankside Brothels c. 100–1675.* London: Peter Owen, 1976.

Burgess, Anthony. *Shakespeare.* Toronto: Clarke, Irwin, 1970.

Cairncross, A. S. *The Problem of Hamlet: A Solution.* London: Macmillan, 1936.

Calendar of State Papers, Domestic Series, of the Reign of Elizabeth, 1598–1601. Edited by Mary Anne Everett Green. London: Longmans, Green, and Co., 1869.

Camden, William. *Britannia.* Oxford, 1695.

———. *Remains Concerning Britain.* Edited by R. D. Dunn. Toronto: University of Toronto Press, 1984.

Campbell, Oscar James. "Shakespeare Himself." *Harper's,* July 1940, 172–85.

Campbell, Oscar James, and Edward G. Quinn. *The Reader's Encyclopedia of Shakespeare.* New York: Thomas Y. Crowell, 1966.

Carpenter, Frederic Ives. *A Reference Guide to Edmund Spenser.* Chicago: University of Chicago Press, 1923.

Carroll, D. Allen. *Greene's Groatsworth of Wit.* Medieval and Renaissance Texts and Studies. Binghamton, NY: State University of New York at Binghamton, 1994.

Carson, Neil. "Literary Management in the Lord Admiral's Company, 1596–1603." *Theatre Research International* 2 (May 1977): 186–97.

———. "Production Finance at the Rose Theatre, 1596–98." *Theatre Research International* 4 (May 1979): 172–83.

———. *A Companion to Henslowe's Diary.* Cambridge: Cambridge University Press, 1988.

Castelain, Maurice. *Ben Jonson: Discoveries. A Critical Edition.* Paris, [1906].

Cerasano, S. P. "The 'Business' of Shareholding, The Fortune Playhouses, and Francis Grace's Will." *Medieval and Renaissance Drama in England* 2 (1985): 231–51.

Chamberlain, John. *The Letters of John Chamberlain.* Edited by Norman Egbert McClure. 2 vols. Philadelphia: American Philosophical Society, 1939.

Chambers, E. K. *The Elizabethan Stage.* 4 vols. 1923. Reprint, Oxford: Clarendon Press, 1961.

———. *Shakespearean Gleanings.* London: Oxford University Press, 1944.

———. *William Shakespeare: A Study of Facts and Problems.* 2 vols. 1930. Reprint, London: Oxford University Press, 1963.

———. *Sources for a Biography of Shakespeare.* 1946. Reprint, London: Oxford University Press, 1970.

Chandler, David. " 'Upstart Crow': Provenance and Meaning." *Notes and Queries* (September 1995): 291–94.

———. "A Further Reconsideration of Heywood's Allusion." *Elizabethan Review* 3 (fall 1995): 15–24.

Charlton, H. B. "The Date of 'Love's Labour's Lost,' " and "The Date of 'Love's Labour's Lost,' II, The Russian Masquerade." *Modern Language Review* 13 (1918): 257–66, 387–400.

Chettle, Henry. *Kind-Hartes Dreame.* Edited by G. B. Harrison. 1922–26. The Bodley Head. Reprint, London: John Lane, 1966.

Christian, Mildred G. "Middleton's Residence at Oxford." *Modern Language Notes* 61 (1946): 90–91.

Churchill, R. C. *Shakespeare and His Betters.* London: Max Reinhardt, 1958.

Chute, Marchette. *Shakespeare of London.* New York: E. P. Dutton, 1949.

Clare, Janet. *Art Made Tongue-Tied by Authority: Elizabethan and Jacobean Dramatic Censorship.* The Revels Plays Companion Library. Manchester and New York: Manchester University Press, 1990.

Clary, William W. "The Case for the Defense." In *Shakespeare Cross Examination: A Compilation of Articles First Appearing in the American Bar Association Journal,* 25–32. Chicago: The Cuneo Press, 1961.

Cohn, Albert. *Shakespeare in Germany in the Sixteenth and Seventeenth Centuries.* 1865. Reprint, New York: Haskell House Publishers, 1971.

Coleridge, Samuel Taylor. *Coleridge's Writings on Shakespeare, A Selection of the Essays, Notes and Lectures.* Edited by Terence Hawkes. New York: Capricorn Books, G. P. Putnam's Sons, 1959.

Cook, Ann Jennalie. *The Privileged Playgoers of Shakespeare's London, 1576–1642.* Princeton: Princeton University Press, 1981.

Crinkley, Richmond. "New Perspectives on the Authorship Question." *Shakespeare Quarterly* 36 (winter 1985): 515–22.

Crosse, Henry. *Vertues Common-wealth: or The High-way to Honour.* Edited by Alexander B. Grosart. London, 1878.

Crupi, Charles W. *Robert Greene.* Boston: Twayne Publishers, 1986.

Daiphantus, or The Passions of Love. An. Sc. [Anthony Skoloker]. London, 1604.

Daniel, Samuel. *The Complete Works in Verse and Prose of Samuel Daniel.* Edited by Alexander B. Grosart. 5 vols. 1885–96. Reprint, New York: Russell and Russell, 1963.

Dante's Inferno. Translated by Mark Musa. Bloomington: Indiana University Press, 1971.

Davidson, Adele. "Shakespeare and Stenography Reconsidered." *Analytical and Enumerative Bibliography* 6 (1992): 77–100.

Davies, John. *The Complete Works of John Davies of Hereford*. Edited by Alexander B. Grosart. 2 vols. 1878. Reprint, New York: AMS Press, 1967.

De Grazia, Margreta, and Peter Stallybrass. "The Materiality of the Shakespearean Text." *Shakespeare Quarterly* 44 (fall 1993): 255–83.

De Groot, John Henry. *The Shakespeares and "The Old Faith."* 1946. Reprint, New York: Books for Libraries Press, 1968.

Dekker, Thomas. *The Non-Dramatic Works of Thomas Dekker*. Edited by Alexander B. Grosart. 5 vols. London: The Huth Library, 1884–86.

———. *The Dramatic Works of Thomas Dekker*. Edited by Fredson Bowers. 4 vols. Cambridge: Cambridge University Press, 1953–61.

Dent, Robert W. "Greene's *Gwydonius*: A Study in Elizabethan Plagiarism." *Huntington Library Quarterly* 24 (1960–61): 151–62.

Donaldson, Ian. Introduction to *Ben Jonson*. The Oxford Authors. New York: Oxford University Press, 1985.

———. "Jonson and the Tother Youth." In R. B. Parker and S. P. Zitner, eds., *Elizabethan Theater: Essays in Honor of S. Schoenbaum*, 111–29. Newark: University of Delaware Press, 1996.

Doran, Madeleine. *Endeavors of Art: A Study of Form in Elizabethan Drama*. Madison: University of Wisconsin Press, 1954.

Drayton, Michael. *Poems by Michael Drayton*. London, 1637.

———. *The Works of Michael Drayton*. Edited by J. William Hebel. 5 vols. Oxford: The Shakespeare Head Press, 1931.

———. *Michael Drayton: Selected Poems*. Edited by Vivien Thomas. Manchester: Carcanet New Press, 1977.

Dryden, John. *Of Dramatic Poesy and Other Critical Essays*. Edited by George Watson. 2 vols. London: J. M. Dent and Sons, 1962.

Dugdale, Sir William. *Antiquities of Warwickshire*. London, 1656.

———. *The Antient Usage in Bearing of such Ensigns of Honour as are Commonly Call'd Arms*. London, 1682.

Duncan-Jones, Katherine. "Jonson's Epitaph on Nashe." *Times Literary Supplement*, 7 July 1995, 4–6.

———. "Nashe in Newgate." *Times Literary Supplement*, 22 March 1996, 15.

Dunn, T. A. *Philip Massinger: The Man and the Playwright*. London: Thomas Nelson and Sons, 1957.

Dutton, Richard. *Ben Jonson: To the First Folio*. Cambridge: Cambridge University Press, 1983.

———. *William Shakespeare: A Literary Life*. New York: St. Martin's Press, 1989.

———. *Mastering the Revels: The Regulation and Censorship of English Renaissance Drama*. Iowa City: University of Iowa Press, 1991.

————. *Ben Jonson, Authority, Criticism.* New York: St. Martin's Press, 1996.

————. "The Birth of the Author." In R. B. Parker and S. P. Zitner, eds., *Elizabethan Theater: Essays in Honor of S. Schoenbaum,* 71–92. Newark: University of Delaware Press, 1996.

Eccles, Mark. "Middleton's Birth and Education." *Review of English Studies* 7 (October 1931): 431–41.

————. "Sir George Buc, Master of the Revels." In Charles J. Sisson, ed., *Thomas Lodge and Other Elizabethans,* 409–506. Cambridge, MA: Harvard University Press, 1933.

————. *Christopher Marlowe in London.* Cambridge, MA: Harvard University Press, 1934.

————. "Samuel Daniel in France and Italy." *Studies in Philology* 34 (January 1937): 148–67.

————. "Chapman's Early Years." *Studies in Philology* 43 (April 1946): 176–93.

————. "Anthony Munday." In Josephine W. Bennett, Oscar Cargill, and Vernon Hall, Jr., eds., *Studies in The English Renaissance Drama, in Memory of Karl Julius Holzknecht,* 95–105. New York: New York University Press, 1959.

————. *Shakespeare in Warwickshire.* Madison: University of Wisconsin Press, 1961.

————. "Brief Lives: Tudor and Stuart Authors." Supplement to *Studies in Philology* 79 (fall 1982).

————. "Elizabethan Actors I: A–D." *Notes and Queries* 236 (March 1991): 38–49.

————. "Elizabethan Actors II: E–J." *Notes and Queries* 236 (December 1991): 454–61.

Edmond, Mary. "Yeomen, Citizens, Gentlemen, and Players: The Burbages and Their Connections." In R. B. Parker and S. P. Zitner, eds., *Elizabethan Theater: Essays in Honor of S. Schoenbaum,* 30–49. Newark: University of Delaware Press, 1996.

Edwards, Philip. "An Approach to the Problem of *Pericles.*" *Shakespeare Survey* 5 (1952): 25–49.

Edwards, Thomas. *Cephalus and Procris. Narcissus.* Edited by W. E. Buckley. London: Nichols and Sons, 1882.

Elze, Karl. *Essays on Shakespeare.* Translated by L. Dora Schmitz. London: Macmillan, 1874.

EMEDD Web site (classical dictionaries). www.chass.utoronto.ca:8080/english/emed/patterweb.html.

England's Helicon. A Collection of Lyrical and Pastoral Poems: Published in 1600. Edited by A. H. Bullen. 1887. Reprint after revision, London: Lawrence and Bullen, Ltd., 1899.

Epstein, Norrie. *The Friendly Shakespeare*. New York: Viking, 1993.

Erne, Lukas. "Biography and Mythography: Rereading Chettle's Alleged Apology to Shakespeare." *English Studies* 79 (September 1998): 430–40.

Evans, Gareth, and Barbara Lloyd Evans. *Companion to Shakespeare*. 1978. Reprint with corrections, London: J. M. Dent and Sons, 1985.

Evans, G. Blakemore, ed. *Elizabethan-Jacobean Drama: The Theatre in Its Time*. 1988. New York: New Amsterdam Books, 1990.

Falconer, Alexander Frederick. *Shakespeare and the Sea*. London: Constable, 1964.

Finkelpearl, Philip J. *John Marston of the Middle Temple*. Cambridge, MA: Harvard University Press, 1969.

———. " 'The Comedians' Liberty': Censorship of the Jacobean Stage Reconsidered." *English Literary Renaissance* 16 (winter 1986): 123–38.

———. *Court and Country Politics in the Plays of Beaumont and Fletcher*. Princeton: Princeton University Press, 1990.

First Folio. *See* Peter W. M. Blayney; Charlton Hinman.

Fletcher, John. *See* Francis Beaumont.

Florio, John. *Queen Anna's New World of Words*. 1611. Facsimile reprint, Menston, UK: Scolar Press, 1968.

———. *A Worlde of Wordes*. 1598. Facsimile reprint, New York: Georg Olms Verlag, 1972.

Foakes, R. A., and R. T. Rickert. *See Henslowe's Diary*.

Fortescue, J. W. "Hunting." In *Shakespeare's England: An Account of the Life and Manners of his Age*, 2:334–50. 2 vols. 1916. Reprint, London: Oxford University Press, 1962.

Foster, Donald W. "Master W. H., R.I.P." *PMLA* 102 (January 1987): 42–54.

Fox, Levi. "An Early Copy of Shakespeare's Will." *Shakespeare Survey* 4 (1951): 69–77.

———. *In Honour of Shakespeare*. Norwich: Jarrold and Sons in association with The Shakespeare Birthplace Trust, 1972.

———, ed. *Correspondence of the Reverend Joseph Greene*. London: Her Majesty's Stationery Office, 1965.

———, ed. *Minutes and Accounts of the Corporation of Stratford-upon-Avon and Other Records*. Vol. 5. Hertford: The Dugdale Society by Stephen Austin and Sons, 1990.

Francis, F. C. "The Shakespeare Collection in the British Museum." *Shakespeare Survey* 3 (1950): 43–57.

Freehafer, John. "Leonard Digges, Ben Jonson, and the Beginning of Shakespeare Idolatry." *Shakespeare Quarterly* 21 (winter 1970), 63–75.

Freeman, Arthur. *Thomas Kyd: Facts and Problems.* Oxford: Clarendon Press, 1967.

Fripp, Edgar I. *Shakespeare: Man and Artist.* 2 vols. London: Oxford University Press, 1938.

Frost, David. "Shakespeare in the Seventeenth Century." *Shakespeare Quarterly* 16 (winter 1965): 81–89.

Frye, Northrop. *Northrop Frye on Shakespeare.* Edited by Robert Sandler. New Haven: Yale University Press, 1986.

Furness, Horace Howard, ed. *Othello, A New Variorum Edition of Shakespeare.* 1886. Reprint, New York: Dover Publications, 1963.

———. *Love's Labour's Lost, A New Variorum Edition of Shakespeare.* Philadelphia: J. B. Lippincott, 1904.

———. *The Tragedie of Julius Caesar, A New Variorum Edition of Shakespeare.* Philadelphia: J. B. Lippincott, 1913.

Ganzel, Dewey. *Fortune and Men's Eyes: The Career of John Payne Collier.* Oxford: Oxford University Press, 1982.

Gardner, Edmund G. *The King of Court Poets: A Study of the Work Life and Times of Lodovico Ariosto.* London: Archibald Constable, 1906.

Gascoigne, George. *The Posies.* Edited by John W. Cunliffe. Cambridge: Cambridge University Press, 1907.

Gaselee, Stephen. Introduction to *The Loves of Clitophon and Leucippe.* Translated by William Burton. 1597. Stratford: The Shakespeare Head Press, 1923.

George, David. "Shakespeare and Pembroke's Men." *Shakespeare Quarterly* 32 (fall 1981): 305–23.

Gerard, John. *The Herball.* London, 1597.

Gibson, H. N. *The Shakespeare Claimants.* 1962. Reprint, New York: Barnes and Noble, 1971.

Gordon, George. *Shakespeare's English.* "Society for Pure English, Tract 29." Oxford: Clarendon Press, 1928.

Goree, Roselle Gould. "Concerning Repetitions in Greene's Romances." *Philological Quarterly* 3 (1924): 69–75.

Gray, Joseph William. *Shakespeare's Marriage and Departure from Stratford.* London: Chapman and Hall, 1905.

Greene, Rev. Joseph. *See* Levi Fox.

Greene, Robert. *The Life and Complete Works in Prose and Verse of Robert Greene, M. A.* Edited by Alexander B. Grosart. 15 vols. London: The Huth Library, 1881–86.

———. *Groatsworth of Wit. See* D. Allen Carroll.

Greg, W. W. *Henslowe Papers: Being Documents Supplementary to Henslowe's Diary.* London: A. H. Bullen, 1907.

———. "The First Folio and its Publishers." In *Studies in the First Folio, written for The Shakespeare Association,* 129–56. London: Oxford University Press, 1924.

———. "Edward Alleyn." In *A Series of Papers on Shakespeare and the Theatre. By Members of The Shakespeare Association*, 1–34. London: Oxford University Press, 1927.

———. "Three Manuscript Notes by Sir George Buc." *The Library*, 4th series, 12 (December 1931): 307–21.

———. *A Bibliography of the English Printed Drama to the Restoration. Vol. 1, "Stationer's Records, Plays to 1616: Nos. 1–349."* London: Oxford University Press, 1939.

———. *The Shakespeare First Folio*. Oxford: Clarendon Press, 1955.

Greg, W. W., in collaboration with J. P. Gilson, Hilary Jenkinson, R. B. McKerrow, and A. W. Pollard. *English Literary Autographs: 1550–1650*. [London]: Oxford University Press, 1925–32.

Grillo, Ernesto. *Shakespeare and Italy*. Glasgow: Robert Maclehose, University Press, 1949.

Guilpin, Everard. *Skialetheia or A Shadowe of Truth, in Certaine Epigrams and Satyres*. Edited by D. Allen Carroll. Chapel Hill: University of North Carolina Press, 1974.

Gurr, Andrew. "Shakespeare's First Poem: Sonnet 145." *Essays in Criticism* 21 (July 1971): 221–26.

———. *Playgoing in Shakespeare's London*. 1987. Cambridge: Cambridge University Press, 1989.

———. "Money or Audiences: The Impact of Shakespeare's Globe." *Theatre Notebook* 42:1 (1988): 3–14.

———. *The Shakespearian Stage 1574–1642*. 3rd ed. Cambridge: Cambridge University Press, 1992.

———. "Three Reluctant Patrons and Early Shakespeare." *Shakespeare Quarterly* 44 (summer 1993): 159–74.

———. *The Shakespearian Playing Companies*. Oxford: Clarendon Press, 1996.

Guttman, Selma. *The Foreign Sources of Shakespeare's Works*. Morningside Heights, NY: King's Crown Press, 1947.

Hall, Joseph. *The Works of Joseph Hall*. Edited by Josiah Pratt. 10 vols. London: C. Whittingham, 1808.

Halliday, F. E. *Shakespeare and His World*. London: Thames and Hudson, 1956.

Halliwell-Phillipps, J. O. "Complaints Against Dethick." In *The Shakespeare Society's Papers*, 4:57–62. London, 1849.

———. *Dictionary of Archaic Words*. 1850. Reprint, London: Bracken Books, 1989.

———. *Outlines of the Life of Shakespeare*. 6th ed. 2 vols. London: Longmans Green, 1886.

Harbage, Alfred. *Shakespeare Without Words and Other Essays*. Cambridge, MA: Harvard University Press, 1972.

Harmon, William, and C. Hugh Holman. *A Handbook to Literature*. 8th
    ed. Upper Saddle River, NJ: Prentice-Hall, 2000.
Hart, Alfred. "Did Shakespeare Produce His Own Plays?" *Modern Language
    Review* 36 (January 1941): 173–83.
Harting, James Edmund. *The Birds of Shakespeare*. (Also published under
    the title *The Ornithology of Shakespeare*.) London: John Van Voorst,
    1871.
Helgerson, Richard. "The Elizabethan Laureate: Self-Presentation and the
    Literary System." *ELH* 46 (summer 1979): 193–220.
———. *Forms of Nationhood*. Chicago: University of Chicago Press, 1992.
Henslowe's Diary. Edited by R. A. Foakes and R. T. Rickert. Cambridge:
    Cambridge University Press, 1961.
Heywood, Thomas. *An Apology for Actors*. Edited by Richard H. Perkinson.
    New York: Scholars' Facsimiles and Reprints, 1941.
Hillebrand, Harold Newcomb. "The Child Actors: A Chapter in Elizabe-
    than Stage History." *University of Illinois Studies in Language and
    Literature* 11 (February and May 1926).
———. "Thomas Middleton's *The Viper's Brood*." *Modern Language Notes*
    62 (1927): 35–38.
Hinman, Charlton, ed. *The First Folio of Shakespeare, The Norton Facsimile*.
    New York: Norton, 1968.
Honan, Park. *Shakespeare: A Life*. Oxford: Oxford University Press, 1998.
Honigmann, E.A.J. *Shakespeare's Impact on His Contemporaries*. London:
    Macmillan, 1982.
———. *Shakespeare: The "Lost Years."* Manchester: Manchester University
    Press, 1985.
———. *John Weever: A Biography of a Literary Associate of Shakespeare
    and Jonson, Together with a Photographic Facsimile of Weever's
    "Epigrammes" (1599)*. Manchester: Manchester University Press,
    1987.
———. " 'There Is a World Elsewhere': William Shakespeare, Business-
    man." In Werner Habicht, D. J. Palmer, and Roger Pringle, eds.,
    *Images of Shakespeare: Proceedings of the Third Congress of the Inter-
    national Shakespeare Association, 1986*, 40–46. Newark: University of
    Delaware Press, 1988.
Honigmann, E.A.J., and Susan Brock, eds. *Playhouse Wills 1558–1642*. Man-
    chester: Manchester University Press, 1993.
Hotson, Leslie. *Shakespeare versus Shallow*. 1931. Reprint, Freeport, NY:
    Books for Libraries Press, 1970.
———. *I, William Shakespeare*. New York: Oxford University Press, 1938.
———. *Shakespeare's Sonnets Dated and Other Essays*. New York: Oxford
    University Press, 1949.
———. *Shakespeare by Hilliard*. London: Chatto and Windus, 1977.

Howard-Hill, T. H. *A Game At Chess*. The Revels Plays. Manchester and New York: Manchester University Press, 1993.

Hummel, Ray O., Jr. "Henry Cross's 'Vertues Common-wealth.' " *The Papers of The Bibliographical Society of America* 43 (1949): 196–99.

Hunter, G. K. *John Lyly: The Humanist as Courtier*. London: Routledge and Kegan Paul, 1962.

Hunter, Joseph. *A Disquisition on the Scene, Origin, Date, etc. of Shakespeare's "Tempest."* London: C. Whittingham, 1839.

———. *New Illustrations of the Life, Studies, and Writings of Shakespeare*. 2 vols. 1845. Reprint, New York: AMS Press, 1976.

Ingleby, C. M. *A Complete View of the Shakspere Controversy*. London:Nattali and Bond, 1861.

———. *Shakespeare's Centurie of Prayse*. Revised with many additions by Lucy Toulmin Smith. 2nd ed. London: N. Trübner and Co., 1879.

Ingleby, C. M., Lucy Toulmin Smith, and F. J. Furnivall. *The Shakspere Allusion-Book: A Collection of Allusions to Shakspere from 1591 to 1700*. 2 vols. 1909. Reprint, Freeport, NY: Books for Libraries Press, 1970.

Ingram, William. "The Closing of the Theaters." *Modern Philology* 69 (November 1971): 105–15.

———. *A London Life in the Brazen Age: Francis Langley 1548–1602*. Cambridge, MA: Harvard University Press, 1978.

———. *The Business of Playing: The Beginnings of the Adult Professional Theater in Elizabethan London*. Ithaca: Cornell University Press, 1992.

Jenkins, Harold. *The Life and Work of Henry Chettle*. London: Sidwick and Jackson, 1934.

———. "On the Authenticity of *Greene's Groatsworth of Wit and The Repentance of Robert Greene*." *Review of English Studies* 11 (January 1935): 28–41.

Jones, Norman. *God and the Moneylenders: Usury and Law in Early Modern England*. Oxford: Basil Blackwell Ltd., 1989.

Jonson, Ben. *The Works of Ben Jonson with Notes Critical and Explanatory and a Biographical Memoir*. Edited by William Gifford. 9 vols. London: Bickers and Son, Henry Sotheran and Co., 1875.

———. *Ben Jonson's Plays*. Edited by Felix E. Schelling. 2 vols. 1910. Reprint, New York: Dutton, 1964.

———. *Ben Jonson*. Edited by C. H. Herford and Percy Simpson. 11 vols. Oxford: Clarendon Press, 1925–52.

———. *Ben Jonson's Timber, or Discoveries*. See Ralph S. Walker.

———. *Every Man In His Humour*. *The Yale Ben Jonson*. Edited by Gabriele Bernhard Jackson. New Haven: Yale University Press, 1969.

Joseph, Harriet. *Shakespeare's Son-in-law: John Hall, Man and Physician.* Hamden, CT: Archon, 1964.

Jowett, John. "Johannes Factotum: Henry Chettle and *Greene's Groatsworth of Wit.*" *Papers of the Bibliographical Society of America* 87 (December 1993): 453–86.

———. "Notes on Henry Chettle." *Review of English Studies* 45 (August and November 1994): 384–88, 517–22.

Judson, Alexander C. *The Life of Edmund Spenser.* Baltimore: The Johns Hopkins Press, 1945.

Kathman, David. "The Economics of Elizabethan Actors." Paper presented at The Shakespearean Research Symposium, Los Angeles, October 1998.

Kay, Dennis. *Shakespeare: His Life, Work and Era.* New York: William Morrow, 1992.

Keen, Rosemary. "Inventory of Richard Hooker." *Archæologia Cantiana* 70 (1956): 231–36.

Kernan, Alvin. *Shakespeare, the King's Playwright.* New Haven: Yale University Press, 1995.

Kirschbaum, Leo. "A Census of Bad Quartos." *Review of English Studies* 14 (January 1938): 20–43.

———. "An Hypothesis Concerning the Origin of the Bad Quartos." *PMLA* 60:3 (September 1945): 697–715.

———. "The Copyright of Elizabethan Plays." *The Library,* 5th series, 14 (December 1959): 231–50.

Knight, Charles. *William Shakespeare: A Biography.* London: [C. Knight and Co.], 1843.

Knutson, Roslyn Lander. *The Repertory of Shakespeare's Company 1594–1613.* Fayetteville: University of Arkansas Press, 1961.

———. "The Repertory." In John D. Cox and David Scott Kastan, eds., *A New History of Early English Drama,* 461–80. New York: Columbia University Press, 1997.

Kyd, Thomas. *The Works of Thomas Kyd.* Edited by Frederick S. Boas. Oxford: Clarendon Press, 1901.

Lancashire, Ian. "Empirically Determining Shakespeare's Idiolect." *Shakespeare Studies* 25 (1997): 171–85.

Langbaine, Gerard. *An Account of the English Dramatick Poets.* 1691. Reprint, New York: Burt Franklin, n.d.

Law, Ernest. *Shakespeare as a Groom of the Chamber.* London: G. Bell, 1910.

———. *Some Supposed Shakespeare Forgeries.* London: G. Bell, 1911.

Lee, Sidney. *"Venus and Adonis," Being a Reproduction in Facsimile.* Oxford: Clarendon Press, 1905.

———. *A Life of William Shakespeare.* 6th ed. London: Smith, Elder, 1908.

Leggatt, Alexander. *Ben Jonson: His Vision and His Art*. London: Methuen, 1981.

Leishman, J. B., ed. *The Three Parnassus Plays 1598–1601*. London: Ivor Nicholson and Watson, 1949.

Le Neve, John. *Monumenta Anglicana, Being Inscriptions on the Monuments of Several Eminent Persons Deceased in or since the Year 1600 to the End of the Year 1718*. London, 1717–19.

Levi, Peter. *The Life and Times of William Shakespeare*. London: Papermac, 1988.

Levin, Harry. "Shakespeare's Italians." In Michele Marrapodi, A. J. Hoenselaars, Marcello Cappuzzo, and L. Falzon Santucci, eds., *Shakespeare's Italy: Functions of Italian Locations in Renaissance Drama*, 17–29. 1993. Rev. ed. Manchester: Manchester University Press, 1997.

———. General Introduction to *The Riverside Shakespeare*. Edited by G. Blakemore Evans and J.J.M. Tobin. 2nd ed. New York: Houghton, Mifflin Co., 1997.

Levith, Murray J. *Shakespeare's Italian Settings and Plays*. London: Macmillan, 1989.

Lewis, B. Roland. *The Shakespeare Documents: Facsimiles, Transliterations, Translations, and Commentary*. 2 vols. Stanford: Stanford University Press, 1940.

Lipking, Lawrence. *The Life of the Poet: Beginning and Ending Poetic Careers*. Chicago: University of Chicago Press, 1981.

Lodge, Thomas. *The Complete Works of Thomas Lodge*. Edited by Edmund W. Gosse. 4 vols. Edinburgh: The Hunterian Club, 1875–88.

Lyly, John. *The Complete Works of John Lyly*. Edited by R. Warwick Bond. 3 vols. Oxford: Clarendon Press, 1902.

Lyon, John Henry Hobart. *A Study of "The Newe Metamorphosis" Written by J. M., Gent, 1600*. New York: Columbia University Press, 1919.

MacIntyre, Jean, and Garrett P. J. Epp. " 'Cloathes worth all the rest': Costumes and Properties." In John D. Cox and David Scott Kastan, eds., *A New History of Early English Drama*, 269–85. New York: Columbia University Press, 1997.

Mackail, J. W. "The Life of Shakespeare." In Harley Granville-Barker and G. B. Harrison, eds., *A Companion to Shakespeare Studies*, 1–8. Cambridge: Cambridge University Press, 1966.

MacLeod, Randall. "Spellbound: Typography and the Concept of Old-Spelling Editions." *Renaissance and Reformation* 15 (1979): 50–76.

MacLure, Millar. *George Chapman*. 1966. Reprint, Toronto: University of Toronto Press, 1969.

Maguire, Laurie E. *Shakespearean Suspect Texts: The "Bad" Quartos and Their Contexts*. Cambridge: Cambridge University Press, 1996.

Malone Society Collections. London and Oxford, 1907–.

Manningham, John. *Diary of John Manningham, of the Middle Temple, and of Bradbourne, Kent, Barrister-at-Law, 1602–1603.* Edited by John Bruce. 1868. Reprint, New York: Johnson Reprint Corp., 1968.

Marotti, Arthur F. *John Donne, Coterie Poet.* Madison: University of Wisconsin Press, 1986.

———. "Patronage, Poetry, and Print." *The Yearbook of English Studies: Politics, Patronage and Literature in England 1558–1658,* Special Number 21 (1991): 1–26.

Marston, John. *The Works of John Marston.* Edited by A. H. Bullen. 3 vols. London: John C. Nimmo, 1887.

———. *The Selected Plays of John Marston.* Edited by Macdonald P. Jackson and Michael Neill. Cambridge: Cambridge University Press, 1986.

Martin, Milward W. *Was Shakespeare Shakespeare? A Lawyer Reviews the Evidence.* New York: Cooper Square, 1965.

Massinger, Philip. *The Dramatick Works of Philip Massinger.* Edited by John Monck Mason. 4 vols. London, 1779.

Masson, David. *Drummond of Hawthornden: The Story of His Life and Writings.* 1873. Reprint, New York: Greenwood Press, 1969.

Matus, Irvin Leigh. *Shakespeare, In Fact.* New York: Continuum, 1994.

Maxwell, Baldwin. Review of *Shakespeare and His Betters,* by R. C. Churchill, and *The Poacher from Stratford,* by Frank W. Wadsworth. *Shakespeare Quarterly* 10 (summer 1959): 435–37.

May, Stephen W. *The Elizabethan Courtier Poets: The Poems and Their Contexts.* Columbia: University of Missouri Press, 1991.

McKenzie, D. F. "Printers of the Mind: Some Notes on Bibliographical Theories and Printing-House Practices." *Studies in Bibliography* 22 (1969): 1–75.

McManaway, James G. *Studies in Shakespeare, Bibliography, and Theater.* New York: Shakespeare Association of America, 1969.

McPherson, David C. *Shakespeare, Jonson, and the Myth of Venice.* Newark: University of Delaware Press, 1990.

Meres, Francis. *Palladis Tamia.* Edited by Don Cameron Allen. New York: Scholars' Facsimiles and Reprints, 1938.

Middleton, Thomas. *The Works of Thomas Middleton.* Edited by A. H. Bullen. 8 vols. London, 1885.

Miller, Arthur. *Timebends: A Life.* New York: Grove, 1987.

Miller, Edwin Haviland. *The Professional Writer in Elizabethan England: A Study of Nondramatic Literature.* Cambridge, MA: Harvard University Press, 1959.

Minutes and Accounts of the Corporation of Stratford-upon-Avon and Other Records 1553–1620. Transcribed by Richard Savage. 4 vols. London: Oxford University Press, 1929.

Montaigne, Michel de. *The Essayes of Montaigne. John Florio's Translation.* New York: Modern Library, 1933.

Montgomery, C. S. *Shakespearean Afterglow.* 1942. 3rd ed. Melbourne: Robertson and Mullens, 1946.

Mowat, Barbara. "The Theater and Literary Culture." In John D. Cox and David Scott Kastan, eds., *A New History of Early English Drama,* 213–30. New York: Columbia University Press, 1997.

Muir, Kenneth. *Shakespeare's Sources.* London: Methuen, 1957.

———. *The Sources of Shakespeare's Plays.* London: Methuen, 1977.

Nashe, Thomas. *The Complete Works of Thomas Nashe.* Edited by Alexander B. Grosart. 6 vols. London: The Huth Library, 1883–84.

Neilson, William Allan, and Ashley Horace Thorndike. *The Facts about Shakespeare.* Rev. ed. New York: Macmillan, 1961.

Nelson, Alan H. "George Buc, William Shakespeare, and the Folger *George a Greene.*" *Shakespeare Quarterly* 49 (spring 1998): 74–83.

Newdigate, Bernard H. *Michael Drayton and His Circle.* Oxford: Printed at the Shakespeare Head Press by B. Blackwell, 1941.

Nicholl, Charles. *A Cup of News: The Life of Thomas Nashe.* London: Routledge and Kegan Paul, 1984.

———. *The Reckoning: The Murder of Christopher Marlowe.* New York: Harcourt Brace, 1992.

Nungezer, Edwin. *A Dictionary of Actors and of Other Persons Associated with the Public Representation of Plays in England before 1642.* New Haven: Yale University Press, 1929.

Parnassus plays. *See* J. B. Leishman; Oliphant Smeaton.

Parr, Johnstone. "Robert Greene and His Classmates at Cambridge." *PMLA* 77 (December 1962): 536–43.

Partridge, A. C. *The Tribe of Ben: Pre-Augustan Classical Verse in English.* Columbia: University of South Carolina Press, 1966.

Paster, Gail Kern. "The Sweet Swan." *Harper's,* April 1999, 38–41.

Patterson, Annabel. *Censorship and Interpretation: The Conditions of Writing and Reading in Early Modern England.* Madison: University of Wisconsin Press, 1984.

Peele, George. *Plays and Poems.* Introduction by Henry Morley. London: G. Routledge, [1887].

Pennel, Charles A. "The Authenticity of the *George A Greene* Title-Page Inscriptions." *Journal of English and Germanic Philology* 64 (1965): 668–76.

Peterson, Richard S. *Imitation and Praise in the Poems of Ben Jonson.* New Haven: Yale University Press, 1981.

Pettigrew, Thomas Joseph. *Chronicles of the Tombs.* 1857. Reprint, New York: AMS Press, 1968.

The Phoenix Nest. 1593. Edited by Hyder Edward Rollins. 1931. Reprint, Cambridge, MA: Harvard University Press, 1969.

A Poetical Rhapsody. Edited by Hyder Edward Rollins. 2 vols. Cambridge, MA: Harvard University Press, 1931.

Polimanteia. "England's Address to her Three Daughters, etc." In Alexander B. Grosart, ed., *Elizabethan England in Gentle and Simple Life.* London, 1881.

Poole, Eric. "Shakespeare's Kinfolk and the Arden Inheritance." *Shakespeare Quarterly* 34 (fall 1983): 311–24.

Pope, Maurice. "Shakespeare's Medical Imagination." *Shakespeare Survey* 38 (1985): 175–86.

———. "Shakespeare's Falconry." *Shakespeare Survey* 44 (1992): 131–43.

Praz, Mario. "Shakespeare's Italy." *Shakespeare Survey* 7 (1954): 95–106.

Quennell, Peter. *Shakespeare: The Poet and His Background.* Readers Union. London: Weidenfeld and Nicolson, 1964.

Quintilian. *The Institutio Oratoria of Quintilian.* Translation by H. E. Butler. 4 vols. 1920–22. Cambridge, MA: Harvard University Press, 1980.

Race, Sydney. "J. P. Collier and the Dulwich Papers." *Notes and Queries* (18 March 1950): 112–14.

———. "Manningham's Diary." *Notes and Queries* (September 1954): 380–83.

Rae, Wesley D. *Thomas Lodge.* New York: Twayne Publishers, 1967.

Reeves, Richard. *President Kennedy: Profile of Power.* New York: Simon and Schuster, 1993.

Riggs, David. *Ben Jonson: A Life.* Cambridge, MA: Harvard University Press, 1989.

Robertson, J. M. *The Baconian Heresy.* New York: E. P. Dutton, 1913.

Rossi, Sergio. "Duelling in the Italian Manner: The Case of *Romeo and Juliet.*" In Michele Marrapodi, A. J. Hoenselaars, Marcello Cappuzzo, and L. Falzon Santucci, eds., *Shakespeare's Italy: Functions of Italian Locations in Renaissance Drama,* 17–29. 1997. Rev. ed. Manchester: Manchester University Press, 1993.

Rothery, Guy Cadogan. *The Heraldry of Shakespeare.* London: Morland Press, 1930.

Rutter, Carol Chillington. *Documents of the Rose Playhouse.* Manchester: Manchester University Press, 1984.

"Rymer's Foedera." Vol. 2: *1377–1654.* Edited by Thomas Duffus Hardy. London: Longman and Co., and Trübner and Co., 1873.

Sanders, Chauncey Elwood. "Robert Greene and His 'Editors.' " *PMLA* 48 (June 1933): 392–417.

———. *An Introduction to Research in English Literary History.* New York: Macmillan, 1952.

Sanders, Norman. "Robert Greene's Way with A Source." *Notes and Queries* (March 1967): 89–91.

Saunders, J. W. "The Stigma of Print: A Note on the Social Bases of Tudor Poetry." In *Essays in Criticism 1*, 139–64. 1951. Reprint, Amsterdam: Swets and Zeitlinger N.V., 1968.

Savage, Richard, ed. *Minutes and Accounts of the Corporation of Stratford-upon-Avon and Other Records 1553–1620.* Vol. 4. London: The Dugdale Society by Humphrey Milford, Oxford Univeristy Press Amen House, 1929.

Schäfer, Jürgen. *Documentation in the "O.E.D.": Shakespeare and Nashe as Test Cases.* Oxford: Clarendon Press, 1980.

Schoenbaum, Samuel. *Internal Evidence and Elizabethan Dramatic Authorship: An Essay in Literary History and Method.* Evanston, IL: Northwestern University Press, 1966.

———. "Shakespeare and Jonson: Fact and Myth." In David Galloway, ed., *The Elizabethan Theatre 2*, 1–19. Toronto: Macmillan of Canada, 1970.

———. "The Life of Shakespeare." In Kenneth Muir and Samuel Schoenbaum, eds., *A New Companion to Shakespeare Studies*, 1–14. Cambridge: Cambridge University Press, 1971.

———. *William Shakespeare: A Documentary Life.* Oxford: Clarendon Press, 1975.

———. *William Shakespeare: A Compact Documentary Life.* 1977. Revised edition with a new postscript, New York: Oxford University Press, 1987.

———. *William Shakespeare: Records and Images.* New York: Oxford University Press, 1981.

———. *Shakespeare's Lives.* Oxford: Clarendon Press, 1991.

Seneca the Elder. *Declamations.* Translated by M. Winterbottom. 2 vols. Cambridge, MA: Harvard University Press, 1974.

Shaheen, Naseeb. "Shakespeare's Knowledge of Italian." *Shakespeare Survey* 47 (1994): 161–69.

Shakespeare, William. *Poems Written by Wil. Shake-speare.* London, 1640.

———. *The Works of Shakespear.* Edited by Alexander Pope. 6 vols. London, 1725.

———. *The Dramatick Writings of Will. Shakspere: with the notes of all the various commentators.* London: John Bell, 1786–88.

———. *The Plays and Poems of William Shakspeare.* Edited by Edmond Malone. 21 vols. London, 1821.

———. *The Dramatic Works of William Shakespeare.* Edited by Samuel Weller Singer. London: Bell and Daldy, 1856.

———. *The Arden Shakespeare.* Various editors. 38 vols. London and New York: Methuen, Routledge, and University Paperbacks, 1946–91.

———. *Shakespeare's Sonnets.* Edited by Stephen Booth. New Haven: Yale University Press, 1977.

———. *The First Folio. See* Peter W. M. Blayney and Charlton Hinman.

———. *The Norton Shakespeare*. Edited by Stephen Greenblatt. New York: Norton, 1997.

———. *The Riverside Shakespeare*. *See* Harry Levin.

The Shakespeare Society's Papers. Vols. 1–4 (1844–49). London.

Shapiro, I. A. "The 'Mermaid Club.' " *Modern Language Review* 45 (January 1950): 6–17.

Sheavyn, Phoebe. *The Literary Profession in the Elizabethan Age*. Manchester: Manchester University Press, 1909.

Shelden, Michael. *Orwell: The Authorized Biography*. New York: Harper Collins, 1991.

Shield, H. A. "Links with Shakespeare IV." *Notes and Queries* (10 December 1949): 536–37.

Simpson, Frank. "New Place: The Only Representation of Shakespeare's House from an Unpublished Manuscript." *Shakespeare Survey* 5 (1952): 55–57.

Simpson, Richard. *The School of Shakspere*. 2 vols. London: Chatto and Windus, 1878.

Sisson, Charles J. "Shakespeare Quartos as Prompt-Copies." *Review of English Studies* 18 (April 1942): 129–43.

———. "The Laws of Elizabethan Copyright: The Stationers' View." *The Library*, 5th series, 15 (March 1960): 8–20.

———. *Lost Plays of Shakespeare's Age*. London: Frank Cass and Co. Ltd., 1970.

Sisson, Charles J., and Robert Butman. "George Chapman, 1612–22: Some New Facts." *Modern Language Review* 46 (April 1951): 185–90.

Slights, William W. E. *Ben Jonson and the Art of Secrecy*. Toronto: University of Toronto Press, 1994.

Smeaton, Oliphant, ed. *The Return from Parnassus or The Scourge of Simony*. London: J. B. Dent, 1905.

Smith, D. Nichol. "Authors and Patrons." In *Shakespeare's England: An Account of the Life and Manners of his Age*, 2:182–211. 2 vols. 1916. Reprint, London: Oxford University Press, 1962.

Smith, G. C. Moore. *Gabriel Harvey's Marginalia*. Stratford-upon-Avon: Shakespeare Head Press, 1913.

Smith, G. Gregory, ed. *Elizabethan Critical Essays*. 2 vols. 1904. Reprint, London: Oxford University Press, 1971.

Smith, Irwin. *Shakespeare's Blackfriars Playhouse: Its History and Its Design*. New York: New York University Press, 1964.

Somerset, J. A. "New Facts Concerning Samuel Rowley." *Review of English Studies* 17 (1966): 293–97.

Spencer, T.J.B. "Ben Jonson on His Beloved, The Author Mr. William Shakespeare." In *The Elizabethan Theatre 4*, 22–40. Hamden, CT: Archon, 1974.

The Spenser Encyclopedia. Edited by A. C. Hamilton et. al. Toronto: University of Toronto Press, 1990.

Spielmann, M. H. *The Title-page of the First Folio of Shakespeare's Plays: A Comparative Study of the Droeshout Portrait and the Stratford Monument.* London: Oxford University Press, 1924.

Spingarn, J. E. "The Sources of Jonson's 'Discoveries.' " *Modern Philology* 2 (April 1905): 1–10.

———, ed. *Critical Essays of the Seventeenth Century.* 3 vols. 1908–9. Reprint, Bloomington: Indiana University Press, 1957.

Spivack, Charlotte. *George Chapman.* New York: Twayne Publishers, 1967.

Spurgeon, Caroline F. E. *Shakespeare's Imagery and What it Tells Us.* 1935. Reprint, Boston: Beacon, 1961.

Stamp, A. E. *The Disputed Revels Accounts.* London: Oxford University Press, 1930.

Stapfer, Paul. *Shakespeare and Classical Antiquity.* Translated by Emily J. Carey. 1880. Reprint, New York: Burt Franklin, 1970.

Stern, Virginia F. *Gabriel Harvey: His Life, Marginalia, and Library.* Oxford: Clarendon Press, 1979.

Stopes, Mrs. C. C. "Mr. Shakspeare about my Lorde's Impreso." *The Athenæum* (16 May 1908): 604–605.

———. *Burbage and Shakespeare's Stage.* London: Alexander Moring, De La More, 1913.

———. *Shakespeare's Environment.* London: G. Bell and Sons, 1914.

———. "Thomas Edwards, Author of 'Cephalus and Procris, Narcissus.' " *Modern Language Review* 16 (July–October 1921): 209–23.

Streitberger, W. R. "Personnel and Professionalization." In John D. Cox and David Scott Kastan, eds., *A New History of Early English Drama,* 337–55. New York: Columbia University Press, 1997.

Strong, Roy. *The Cult of Elizabeth.* London: Thames and Hudson, 1977.

Stubbings, Hilda U. *Renaissance Spain in Its Literary Relations with England and France: A Critical Bibliography.* Nashville: Vanderbilt University Press, 1968.

Sugden, Edward H. *A Topographical Dictionary to the Works of Shakespeare and His Fellow Dramatists.* Manchester: Manchester University Press, 1925.

Talvacchia, Bette. "The Rare Italian Master and the Posture of Hermione in 'The Winter's Tale.' " *Elizabethan Review* 1 (spring 1993): 40–57.

Tannenbaum, Samuel A. *Shakspere Forgeries in the Revels Accounts.* 1928. Reprint, Port Washington, NY: Kennikat Press, 1966.

———. *More about the Forged Revels Accounts.* Shakspere Studies No. 3. New York: The Tenny Press, 1932.

———. *Shaksperian Scraps and Other Elizabethan Fragments.* New York: Columbia University Press, 1933.

Tayler, Edward William. *Nature and Art in Renaissance Literature.* New York: Columbia University Press, 1964.

Taylor, Gary. *See* Stanley Wells.

Thomas, David, and Jane Cox. *Shakespeare in the Public Records.* Public Record Office. London: Her Majesty's Stationery Office, 1985.

Thomas, Sidney. "The Printing of *Greenes Groatsworth of Witte* and *Kind-Harts Dreame.*" *Studies in Bibliography* 41 (1988): 196–97.

———. "On the Dating of Shakespeare's Early Plays." *Shakespeare Quarterly* 39 (summer 1988): 187–94.

Thompson, Edward Maunde. "Handwriting." In *Shakespeare's England: An Account of the Life and Manners of His Age,* 1:284–310. 2 vols. 1916. Reprint, London: Oxford University Press, 1962.

Thomson, Peter. *Shakespeare's Professional Career.* 1992. Canto ed. Cambridge: Cambridge University Press, 1994.

Tottel's Miscellany (1557–1587). Edited by Hyder Edward Rollins. 2 vols. Cambridge, MA: Harvard University Press, 1929.

Trimpi, Wesley. *Ben Jonson's Poems: A Study of the Plain Style.* Stanford: Stanford University Press, 1962.

Tudor Poetry and Prose. Edited by J. William Hebel et al. New York: Appleton-Century-Crofts, 1953.

Turner, Celeste. *Anthony Mundy: An Elizabethan Man of Letters.* Berkeley: University of California Press, 1928.

Untermeyer, Louis. *Lives of the Poets.* New York: Simon and Schuster, 1959.

Updike, John. "One Cheer for Literary Biography." *New York Review of Books,* 4 February 1999, 3–5.

Vale, Marcia. *The Gentleman's Recreations.* Cambridge: D. S. Brewer, Rowman and Littlefield, 1977.

van den Berg, Sara. " 'The Paths I Meant unto Thy Praise': Jonson's Poem for Shakespeare." In *Shakespeare Studies* 11 (1978): 207–18.

Velz, John W. *Shakespeare and the Classical Tradition: A Critical Guide to Commentary, 1660–1960.* Minneapolis: University of Minnesota Press, 1968.

———. "The Collier Controversy Redivivus." *Shakespeare Quarterly* 36 (spring 1985): 106–15.

Vickers, Brian, ed. *Shakespeare: The Critical Heritage.* 6 vols. London: Routledge and Kegan Paul, 1974–81.

Vincent, C. J. "Pettie and Greene." *Modern Language Notes* 54 (February 1939): 105–11.

Wadsworth, Frank W. *The Poacher from Stratford.* Berkeley: University of California Press, 1958.

Walker, Alice. "The Life of Thomas Lodge." *Review of English Studies* 9 (October 1933): 410–32.

Walker, Ralph S., ed. *Ben Jonson's "Timber or Discoveries."* 1953. Reprint, Westport, CT: Greenwood Press, 1976.

Wallace, Charles William. "Shakespeare in London: Fresh Documents on the Poet and His Theatres, The Globe and Blackfriars." *The Times* (London), 2 October 1909, 9; and 4 October 1909, 9.

———. "Three London Theatres of Shakespeare's Time." *University Studies of the University of Nebraska* 9 (October 1909): 287–342.

———. "Shakespeare and his London Associates as Revealed in Recently Discovered Documents." *University Studies of the University of Nebraska,* 10 (October 1910): 261–360.

———. "New Light on Shakespeare: History of the Globe Theatre." *The Times* (London), 30 April 1914, 9–10; and 1 May 1914, 4.

———. "Other William Shakespeares." *The Times* (London), 8 May 1915, 6; and 15 May 1915, 11.

Watson, Thomas. *Hekatompathia or Passionate Centurie of Love.* Ca. 1581. Reprint, New York: Burt Franklin, 1967.

Weever, John. *Ancient Funerall Monuments.* 1631. Facsimile reprint, Norwood, NJ: Walter J. Johnson, 1979.

Wells, Stanley. *Shakespeare: A Life in Drama.* New York: Norton, 1995.

Wells, Stanley, and Gary Taylor with John Jowett and William Montgomery. *William Shakespeare: A Textual Companion.* 1987. Reprinted with corrections, New York: Norton, 1997.

Werstein, Paul. "Narratives About Printed Shakespearean Texts: 'Foul Papers' and 'Bad' Quartos." *Shakespeare Quarterly* 41 (spring 1990): 65–86.

Wheatley, Henry B. *Notes on the Life of John Payne Collier with a Complete List of His Works and an Account of Such Shakespeare Documents as Are Believed to Be Spurious.* London, 1884.

Whitaker, Virgil K. *Shakespeare's Use of Learning: An Inquiry into the Growth of his Mind and Art.* San Marino: Huntington Library, 1964.

Williams, Franklin B., Jr. "Commendatory Verses: The Rise of the Art of Puffing." *Studies in Bibliography* 19 (1966): 1–14.

Willobie His Avisa. Edited by G. B. Harrison. The Bodley Head. London: John Lane, 1926.

Wilson, F. P. *Marlowe and the Early Shakespeare.* 1953. Reprint, London: Oxford University Press, 1967.

Wilson, Ian. *Shakespeare: The Evidence.* New York: St. Martin's Press, 1993.

Wilson, J. Dover. *The Essential Shakespeare.* London: Cambridge University Press, 1937.

———. "Ben Jonson and *Julius Caesar.*" *Shakespeare Survey* 2 (1949): 36–43.

———. "Malone and the Upstart Crow." *Shakespeare Survey* 4 (1951): 56–68.

Wivell, Abraham. *An Inquiry into the History, Authenticity, and Characteristics of the Shakspeare Portraits.* London, 1827.

Wright, Celeste Turner. "Some Conventions Regarding the Usurer in Eliz-abethan Literature." *Studies in Philology* 31 (1934), 176–97. *See also* Celeste Turner.

Wright, Louis B., and Virginia A. LaMar, eds. *Life and Letters in Tudor and Stuart England*. The Folger Shakespeare Library. Ithaca, NY: Cornell University Press, 1962.

Wyther, George. *Abuses Stript, and Whipt or Satirical Essayes*. London: Francis Burton, 1613. Microfilm of the original in the Henry E. Huntington Library. Ann Arbor, MI: University Microfilms, 1978.

UNORTHODOX WORKS

Brooks, Alden. *Will Shakspere and the Dyer's Hand*. New York: Charles Scribner's Sons, 1943.

Chaplin, Charles. *My Autobiography*. New York: Simon and Schuster, 1964.

Downs, Gerald E. "A Reconsideration of Heywood's Allusion to Shake-speare." *Elizabethan Review* 1 (fall 1993): 18–35.

———. "Dugdale's Sketch and Shakespeare's Stratford Monument." Pre-sentation at the annual meeting of The Shakespeare Oxford Society, Carmel, CA, October 1994.

Greenwood, Sir George. *The Shakespeare Problem Restated*. The Bodley Head. London: John Lane, 1908.

———. *Is There a Shakespeare Problem?* The Bodley Head. London: John Lane, 1916.

———. *Ben Jonson and Shakespeare*. London: Cecil Palmer, 1921.

———. *The Stratford Bust and the Droeshout Engraving*. London: Cecil Palmer, 1925.

Hannas, Andrew. "From Thence, To Honor Thee . . . 'Small Latine' Tis the Key." Paper presented at the annual meeting of The Shakespeare Oxford Society, Cleveland, OH, October 1993.

Hope, Warren, and Kim Holston. *The Shakespeare Controversy: An Analysis of the Claimants to Authorship, and Their Champions and Detractors*. Jefferson, NC: McFarland, 1992.

Johnson, Morse. Untitled article, supplement to the *Shakespeare Oxford So-ciety Newsletter* 26 (summer 1990): 1–11.

Lefranc, Abel. *Under the Mask of William Shakespeare*. Translated by Cecil Cragg. Braunton, UK: Merlin Books, 1988.

Looney, J. Thomas. *"Shakespeare" Identified in Edward de Vere, Seventeenth Earl of Oxford, and The Poems of Edward de Vere*. 1920. Edited by Ruth Loyd Miller. 2 vols. 3rd ed. Port Washington, NY: Kennikat Press for Minos Publishing, 1975.

———. "Jonson v. Jonson." *Shakespeare Pictorial*. London (April 1935): 64.

Magri, Noemi. "No Errors in Shakespeare: Historical Truth and the Two Gentlemen of Verona." *De Vere Society Newsletter* 2 (May 1998): 9–22.

Michell, John. *Who Wrote Shakespeare?* London: Thames and Hudson, 1996.

Miller, Ruth Loyd: "Oxford's 'Stratford Moniment.' " Paper presented at the Pasadena Public Library, February 1990.

Moore, Peter R. "Ben Jonson's 'On Poet-Ape.' " *Shakespeare Oxford Society Newsletter* 24 (summer 1988): 7–9.

———. "Masked Adonis and Stained Purple Robes." *Shakespeare Oxford Society Newsletter* 25 (summer 1989): 9–12.

———. "Groatsworth and Shake-scene." *Shakespeare Newsletter* (winter 1991): 56.

———. "Shake-hyphen-speare." *Elizabethan Review* 1 (spring 1993): 58–60.

———. "The Date of F. B.'s Verse Letter to Ben Jonson." *Notes and Queries* (September 1995): 347–52.

———. "The Abysm of Time: The Chronology of Shakespeare's Plays." *Elizabethan Review* 5 (fall 1997): 24–60.

Ogburn, Charlton. *The Mysterious William Shakespeare.* New York: Dodd, Mead, 1984.

Parisious, Roger Nyle. "Occultist Influence on the Authorship Controversy." *Elizabethan Review* 6 (spring 1998): 9–43.

Platt, Isaac Hull. "Had Heminges and Condell Studied Law or Read Pliny's *Natural History?*" "Marginalia" column, *New Shakespeareana* 3:3, The Shakespeare Society of New York (July 1904): 103–6.

Porohovshikov, Pierre S. *Shakespeare Unmasked.* London: Arco Publishers, 1955.

Price, Diana. "What's in a Name? Shakespeare, Shake-scene and the Clayton Loan." *Elizabethan Review* 4 (spring 1996): 3–13.

———. "Shaxicon and Shakespeare's Acting Career." *Shakespeare Newsletter* (summer 1996): 27–28, 46.

———. "Shaxicon and Shakespeare's Acting Career. A Reply to Donald Foster." *Shakespeare Newsletter* (spring 1997): 11, 14.

———. "Reconsidering Shakespeare's Monument." *Review of English Studies* 48 (May 1997): 168–82.

———. "Shakespeare and Documentary Evidence: A Critical Approach to Shakespeare's Authorship." Three lectures presented at various times at Cleveland State University, 1995–98.

———. "A Tale of Two Epithets: Jonson's 'Gentle' Shakespeare and the 'Natural' Genius." Paper presented at the Shakespearean Research Symposium, Los Angeles, CA, October 1998.

Roe, Richard Paul. "The Perils of the Tempest." *The Shakespeare Newsletter* (fall–winter 1989): 36–37.

————. "Going to Italy Can be Serious Business." Paper presented at the annual meeting of The Shakespeare Oxford Society, Carmel, CA, October 1994.

————. "Two Shakespearean Trips to Italy: to Milan and to Florence." Paper presented at the Shakespearean Research Symposium, Los Angeles, October 1998.

Twain, Mark. *Is Shakespeare Dead? from My Autobiography.* New York: Harper and Brothers, 1909.

Ward, B. M. *The Seventeenth Earl of Oxford 1550–1604.* London: John Murray, 1928.

Whalen, Richard F. *Shakespeare: Who Was He? The Oxford Challenge to the Bard of Avon.* Westport, CT: Praeger, 1994.

————. "A Monumental Problem." *Shakespeare Oxford Society Newsletter* 33 (fall 1997/winter 1998): 10–11.

Whitman, Walt. *The Works of Walt Whitman.* The Deathbed Edition. 2 vols. New York: Funk and Wagnall, 1968.

Index

About the Author

DIANA PRICE is an independent scholar who has published her Shakespearean research in such journals as the *Review of English Studies* and the *Elizabethan Review*. Her three-part lecture series, "Shakespeare and Documentary Evidence," was developed for the classroom and first presented at Cleveland State University.